missions OF LOVE

Volume 9

Ema Toyama

Missions of Love
Ema Toyama

Character

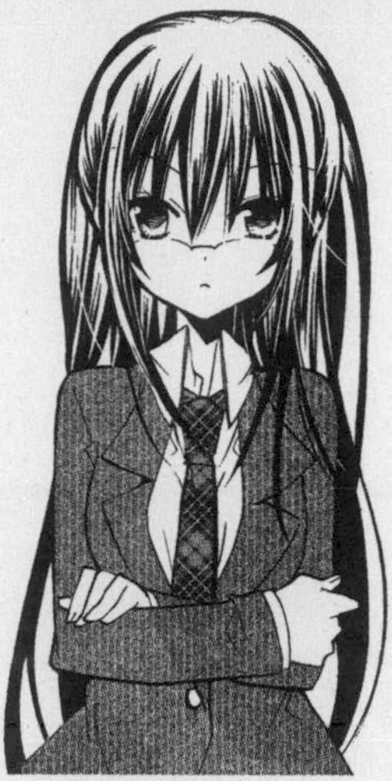

Yukina Himuro

A third-year junior high student who strikes terror in the hearts of all around her with her piercing gaze, feared as the "Absolute Zero Snow Woman." Only Akira knows that she is also the popular cell phone novelist Yupina.

Shigure Kitami

The ever-popular, yet black-hearted, student body president. He made a game of charming all the girls and making them confess their love to him, then writing it all down in his student notebook, but Yukina discovered his secret!

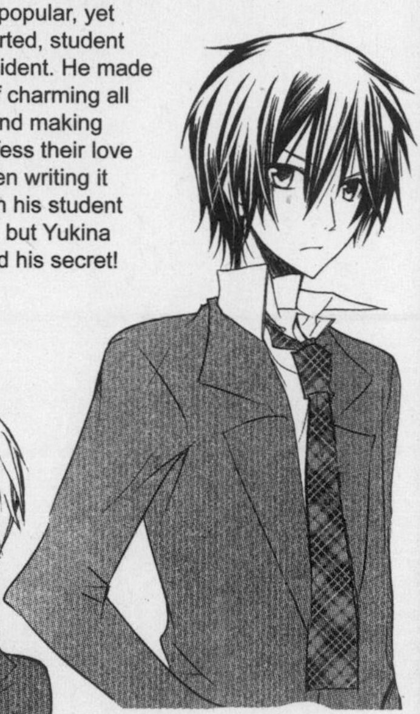

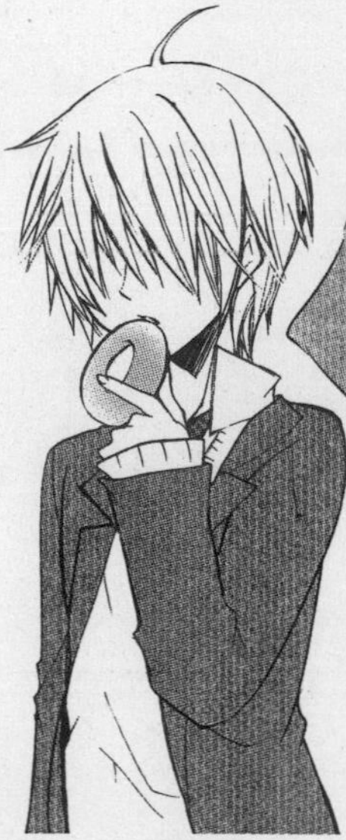

Akira Shimotsuki

Yukina's cousin and fellow student. He loves to eat. Yukina's confidant, he can always be found nearby, watching over her. He has confessed his love to Yukina. There's a good-looking face hiding behind that hair.

me!

Mami Mizuno

A childhood friend of Shigure's. A sickly girl. The teachers love her, and she's very popular with the boys. She's a beautiful young girl who always wears a smile, but deep down, her heart is black. She has told Shigure how she feels about him, but...

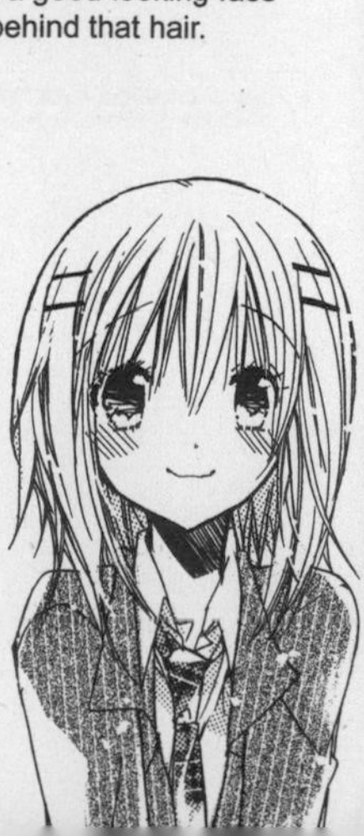

Story

Through her blackmail of Shigure, Yukina has been gaining more and more romantic experience. Yukina starts accepting "reverse missions" to fix her weakness, and gradually the distance between her and Shigure grows smaller. While all this is going on, Yukina encounters Kirishima—the cause of her weakness. She is deeply shaken by the encounter, but she also realizes that Kirishima was her first love. And it's possible that her feelings for him haven't changed!

Missions of Love

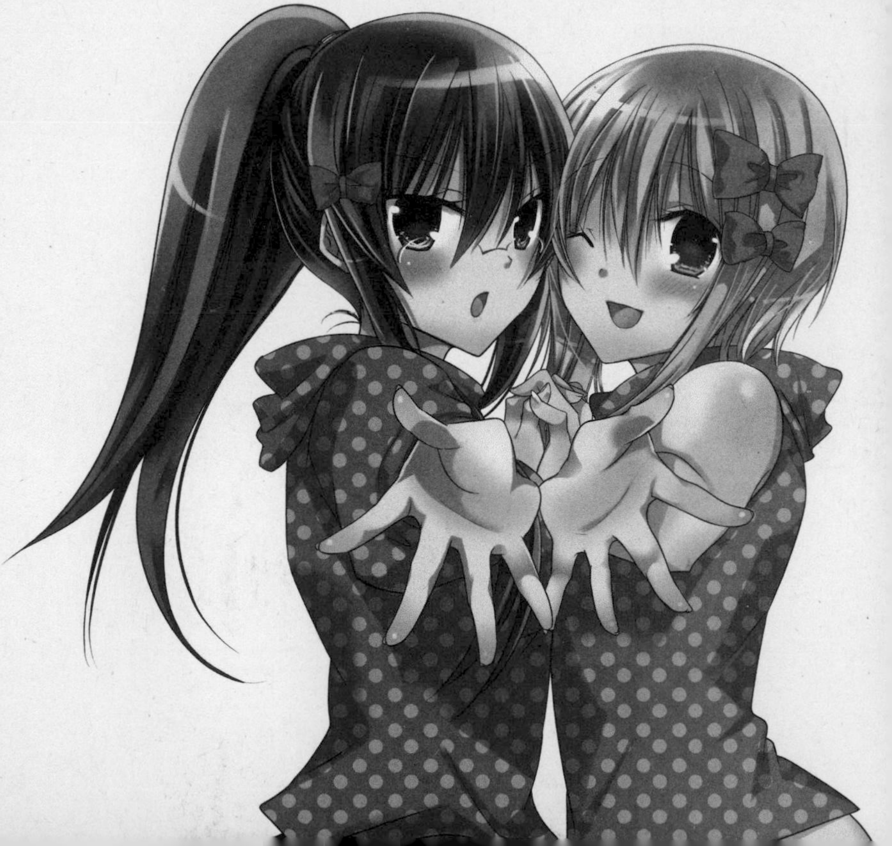

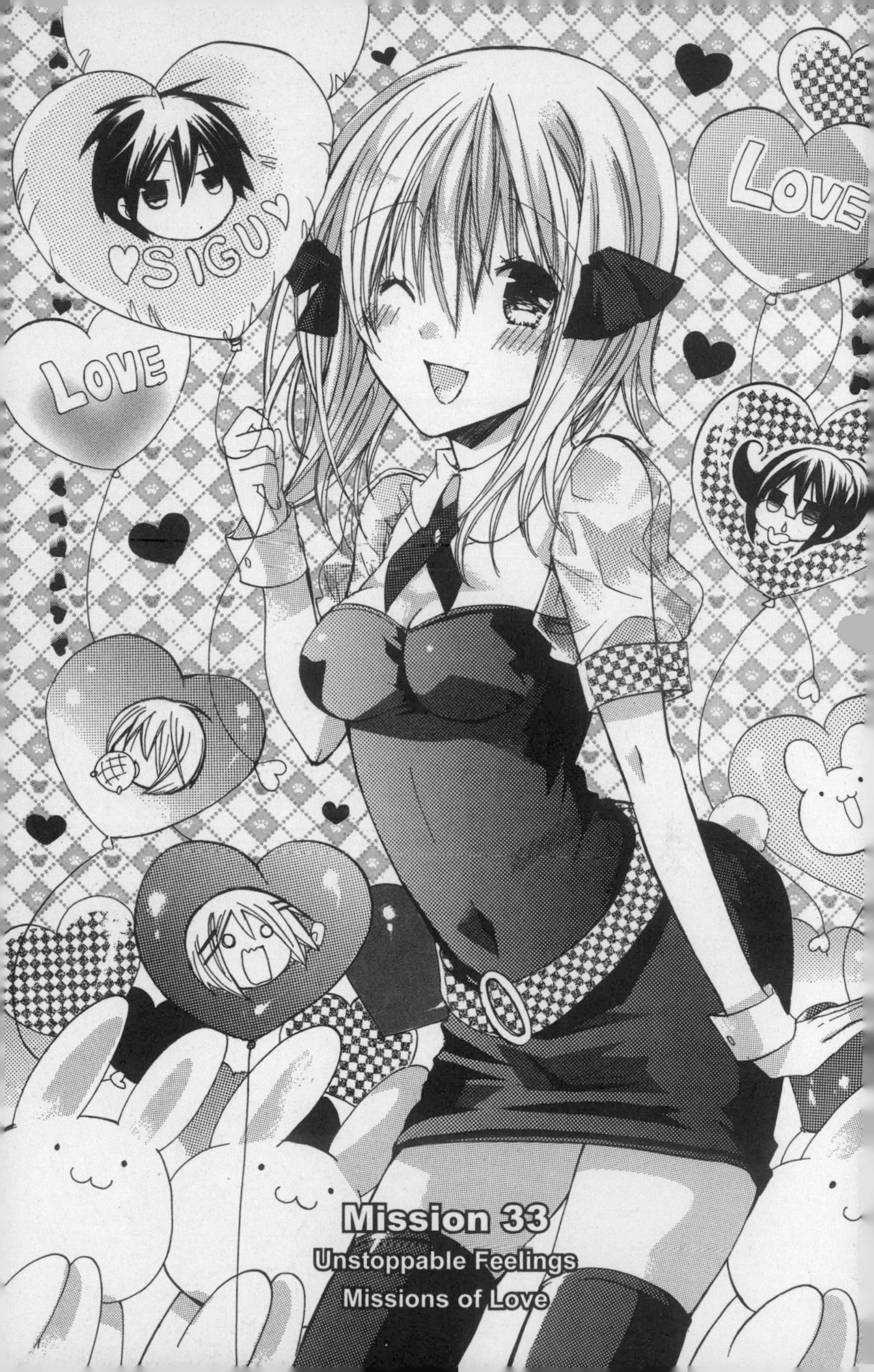
♥SIGU♥
LOVE
LOVE

Mission 33
Unstoppable Feelings
Missions of Love

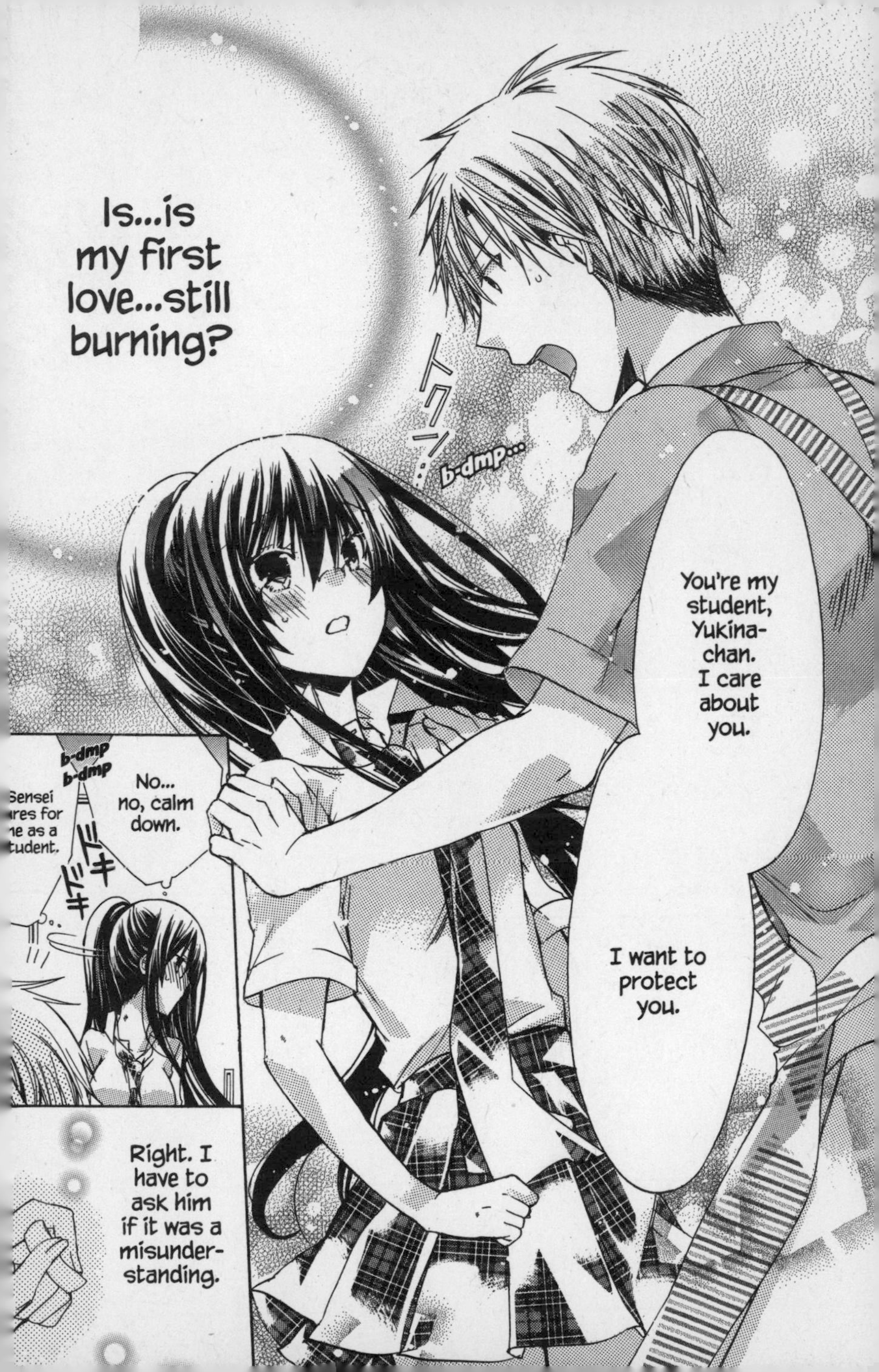
Is...is my first love...still burning?
トクン…
b-dmp...
You're my student, Yukina-chan. I care about you.
I want to protect you.
b-dmp b-dmp
ドキドキ
No... no, calm down.
Sensei ares for ne as a tudent.
Right. I have to ask him if it was a misunder-standing.

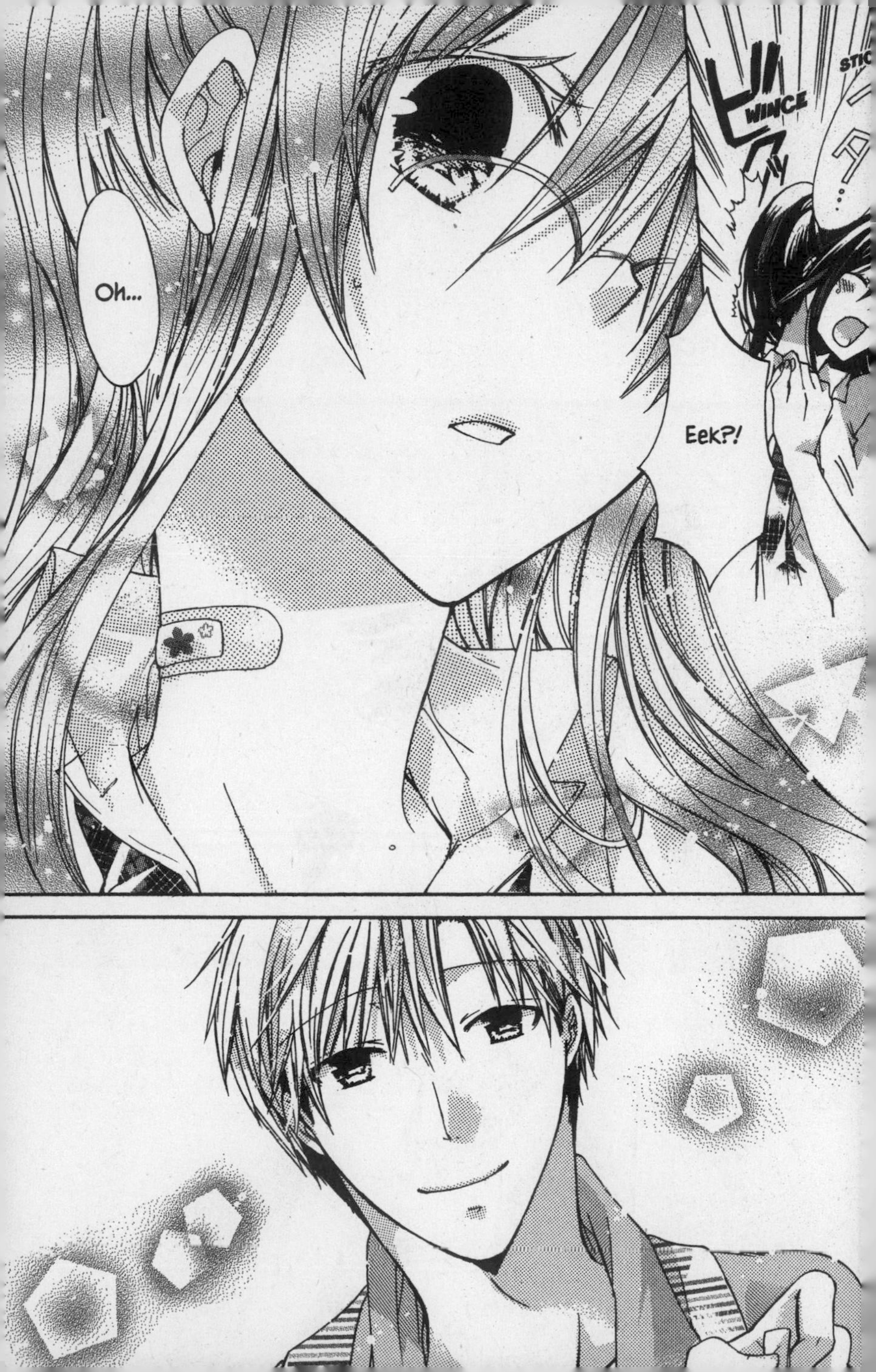
STIC
WINCE
Eek?!
Oh...

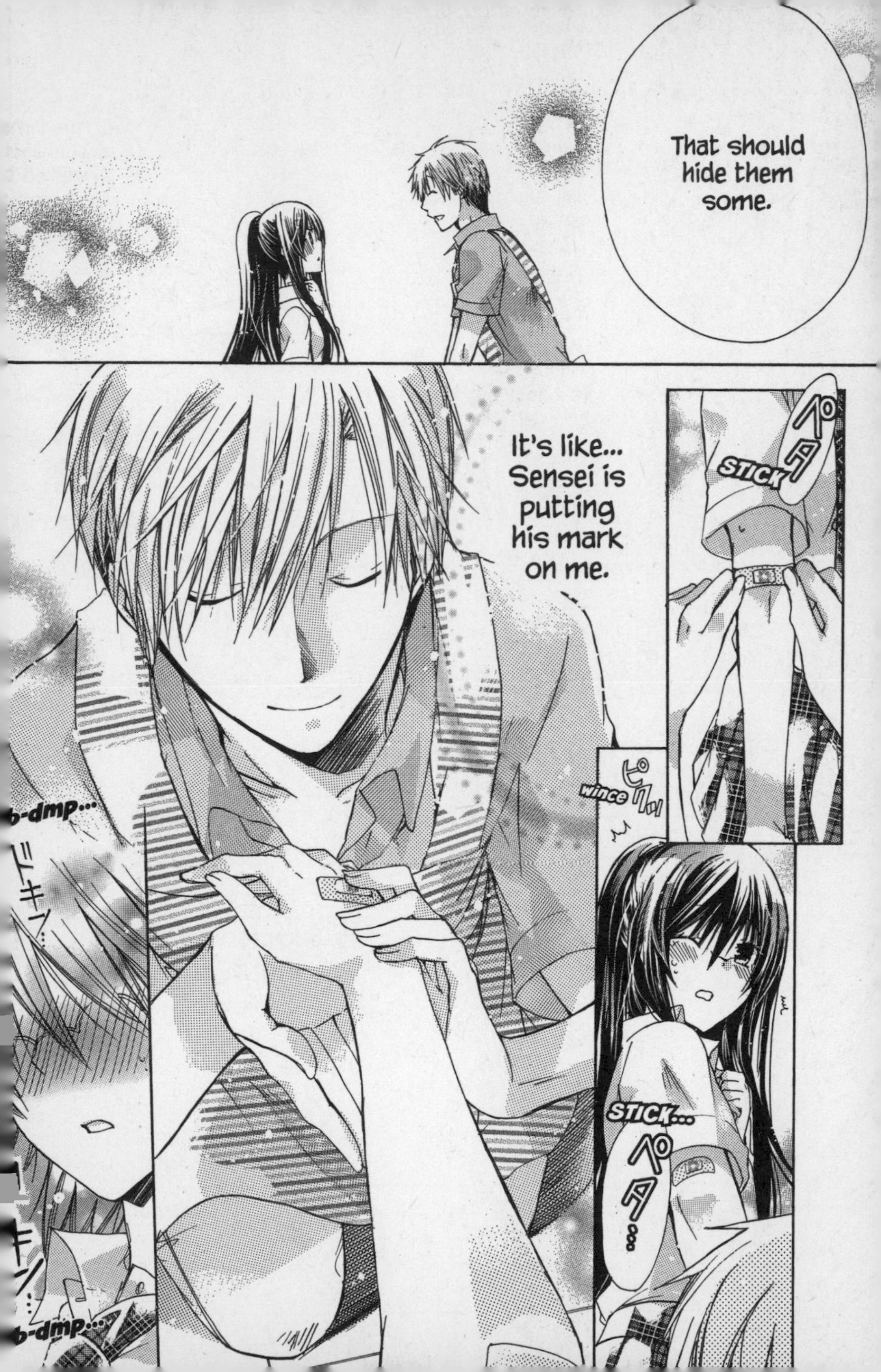
That should hide them some.
STICK
ペタ
wince
ピクッ
STICK...
ペタ…
It's like... Sensei is putting his mark on me.
b-dmp...
b-dmp...

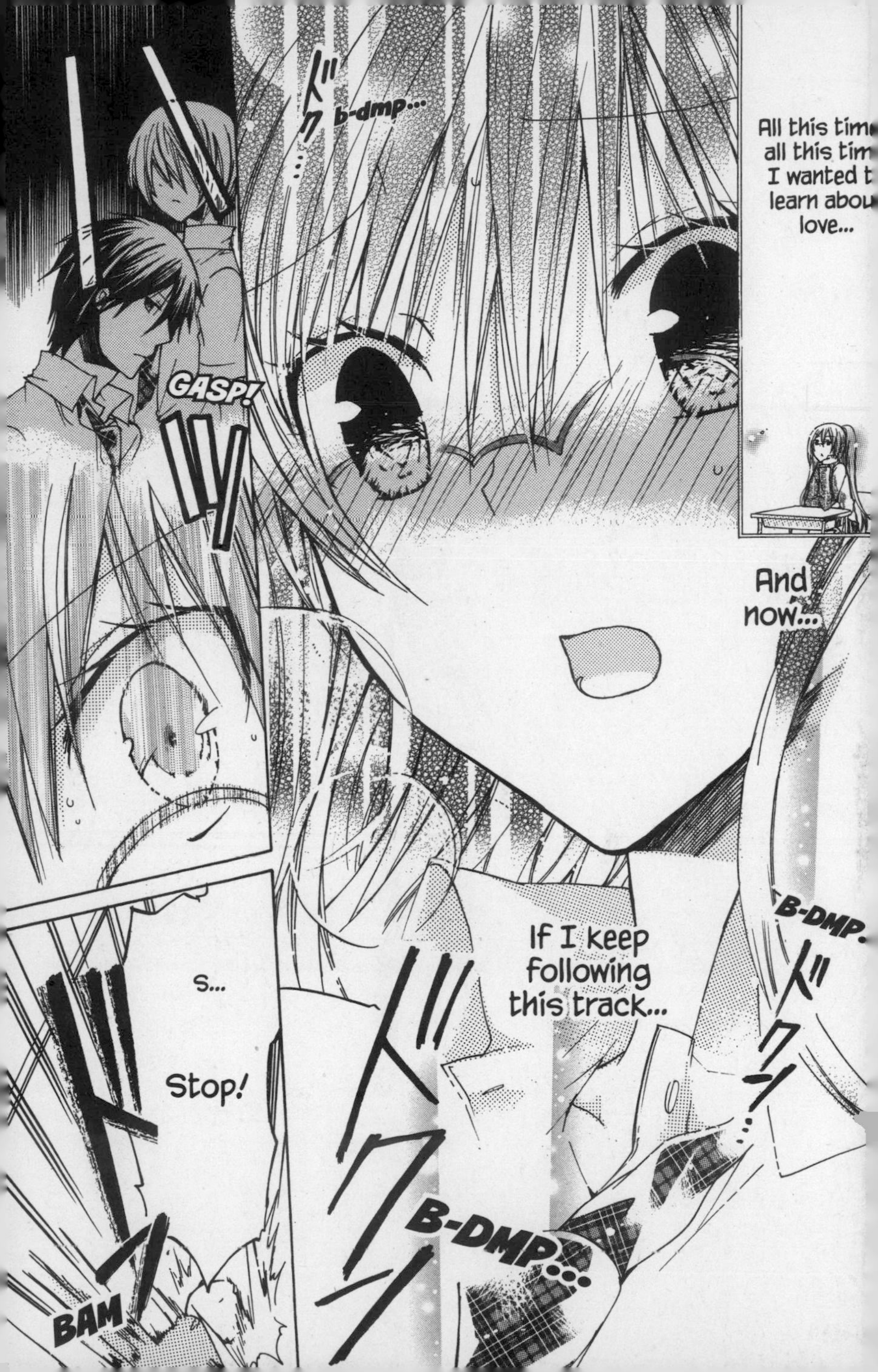
All this tim
all this tim
I wanted t
learn abou
love...
ドク...
b-dmp...
And now...
If I keep following this track...
ドクン...
B-DMP...
ドクン
B-DMP...
GASP!
S...
Stop!
ドン
BAM

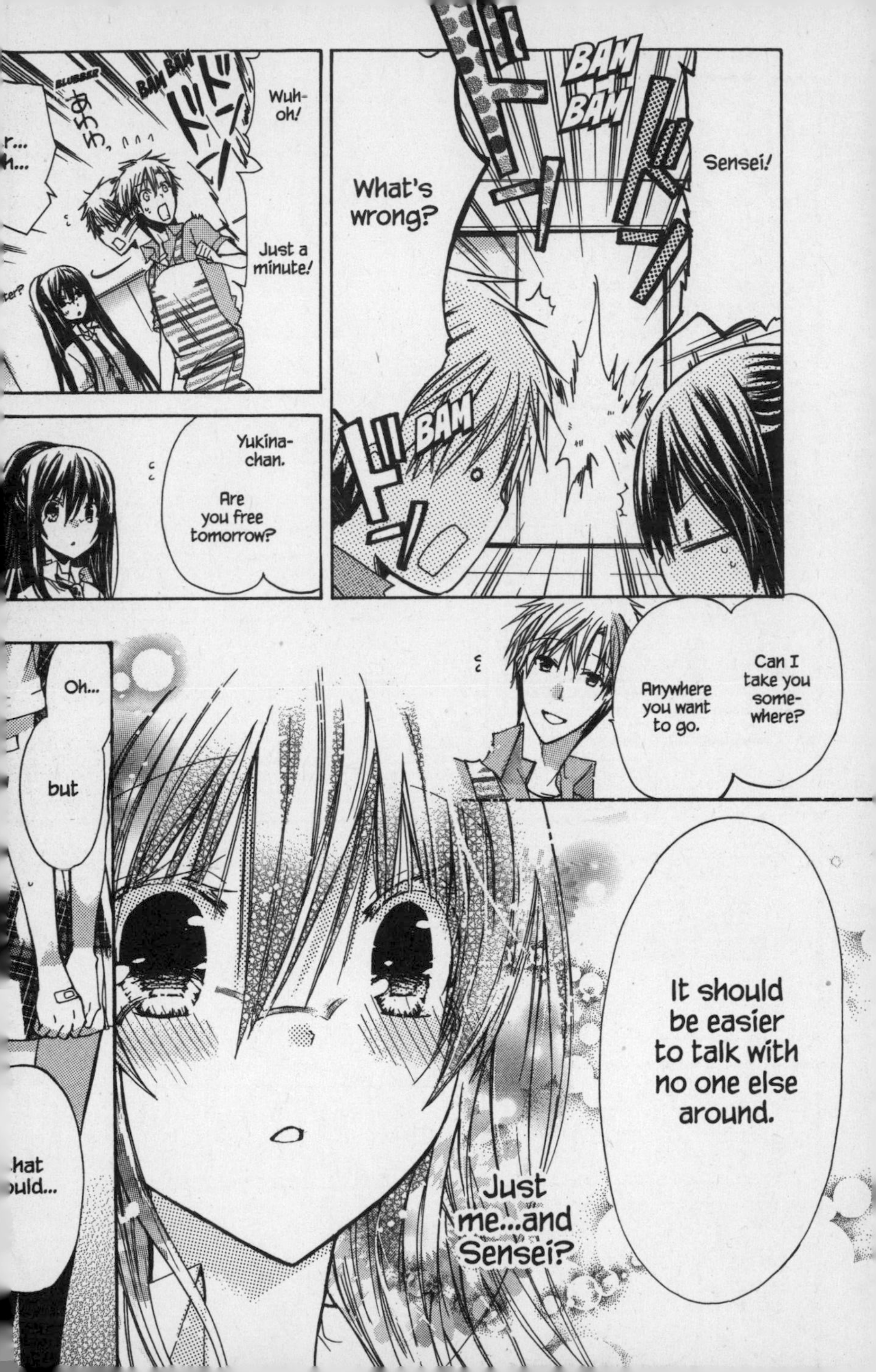
BAM BAM
Sensei!
What's wrong?
BAM
BAM BAM
BLUBBER
Wuh-oh!
Just a minute!
Yukina-chan.
Are you free tomorrow?
Can I take you somewhere?
Anywhere you want to go.
It should be easier to talk with no one else around.
Just me...and Sensei?
Oh...
but

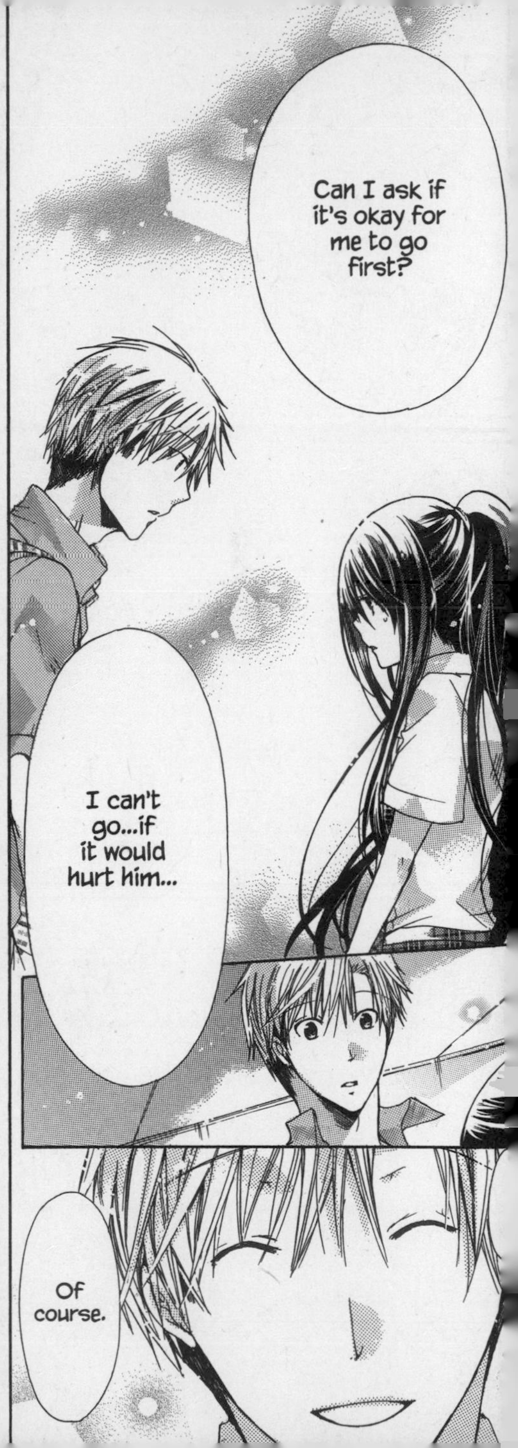
Can I ask if it's okay for me to go first?
I can't go...if it would hurt him...
Of course.

The Freezing Bed 1

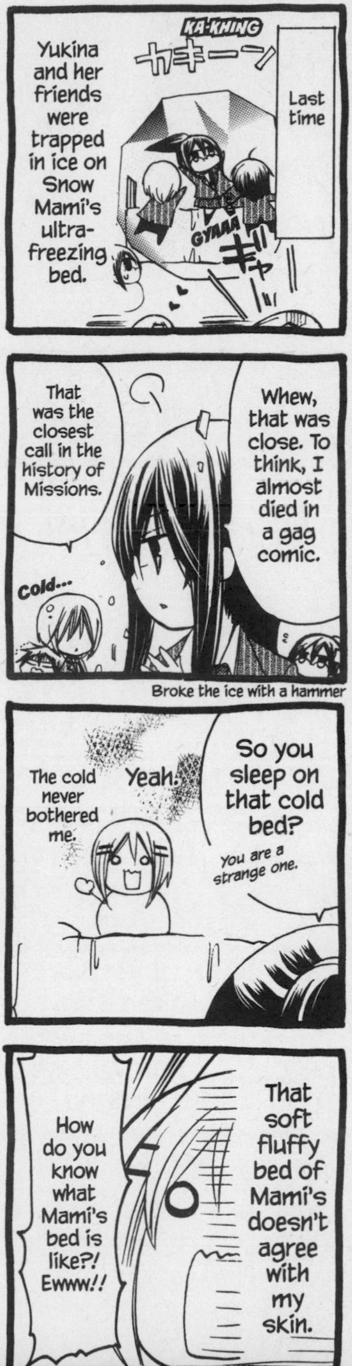
Last time
KA-KHING
カキーン
Yukina and her friends were trapped in ice on Snow Mami's ultra-freezing bed.
GYAAA
ギャ
Whew, that was close. To think, I almost died in a gag comic.
That was the closest call in the history of Missions.
Cold...
Broke the ice with a hammer
So you sleep on that cold bed?
You are a strange one.
Yeah.
The cold never bothered me.
That soft fluffy bed of Mami's doesn't agree with my skin.
How do you know what Mami's bed is like?! Ewww!!

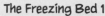

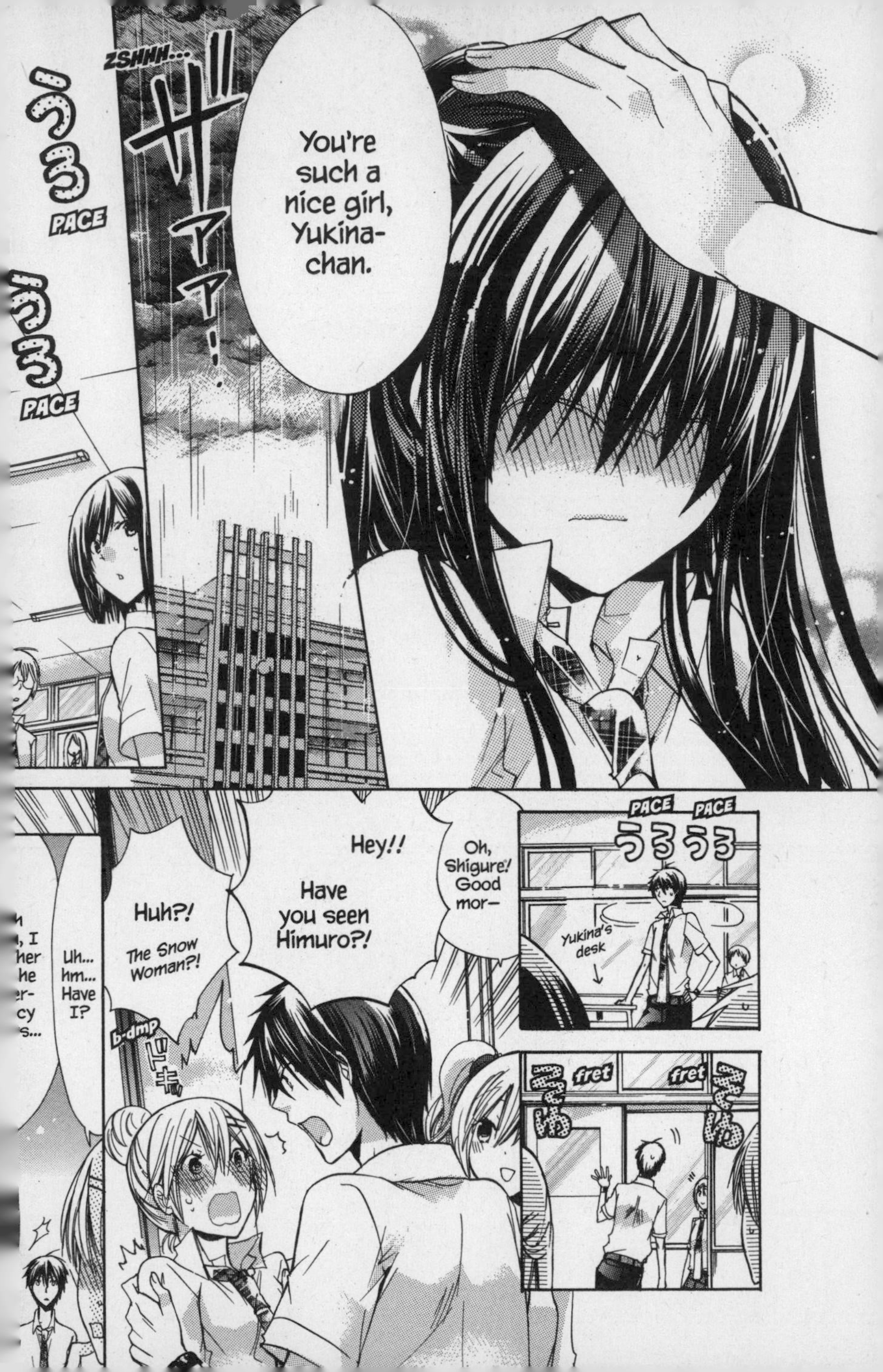
ZSHHH...
You're such a nice girl, Yukina-chan.
PACE
PACE
PACE PACE
Yukina's desk
fret fret
Oh, Shigure! Good mor—
Hey!!
Have you seen Himuro?!
Huh?!
The Snow Woman?!
b-dmp
Uh... hm... Have I?

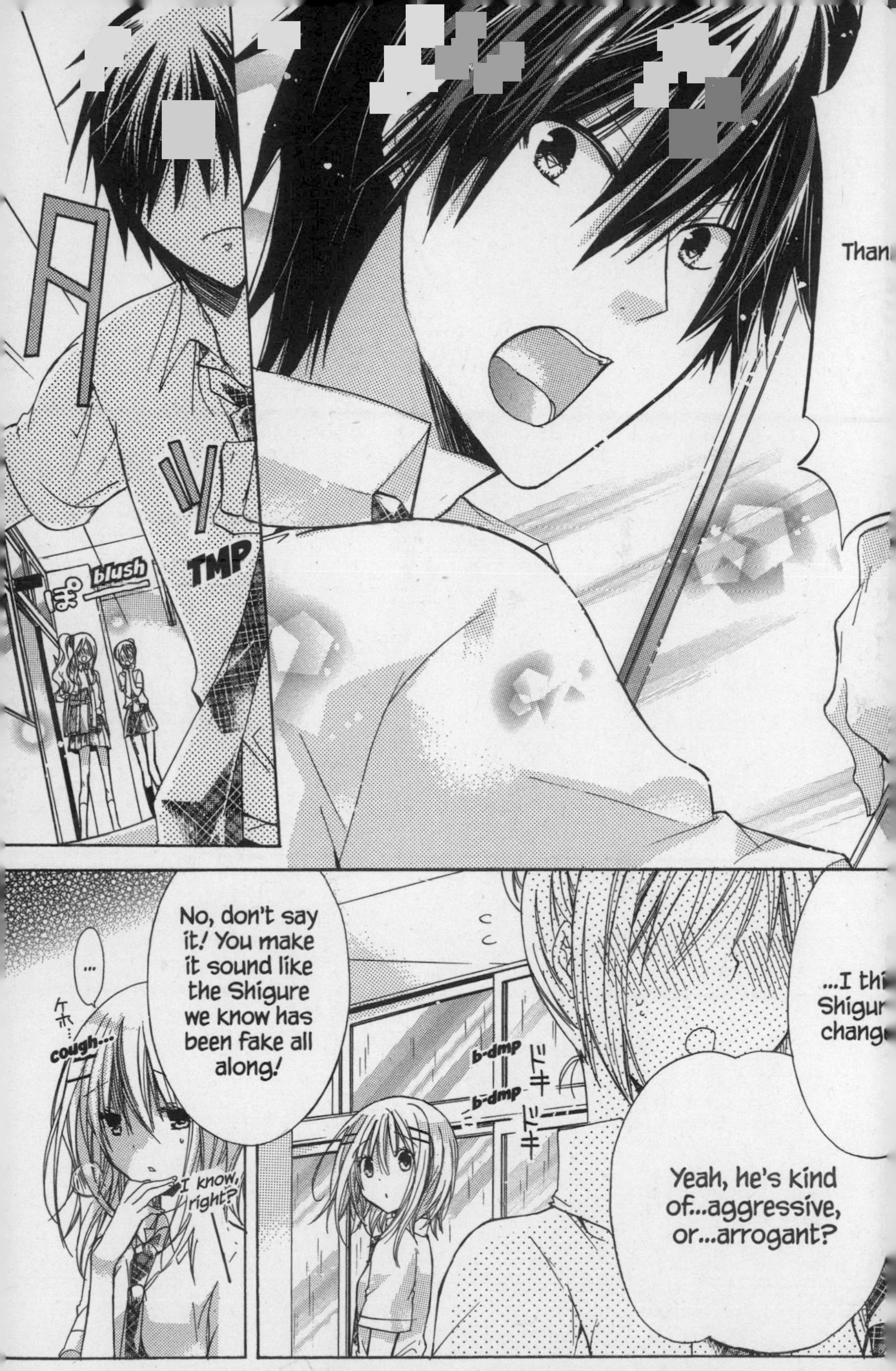
Than
TMP
blush
ぽ
...I thi
Shigur
chang
Yeah, he's kind of...aggressive, or...arrogant?
b-dmp ドキ
b-dmp ドキ
No, don't say it! You make it sound like the Shigure we know has been fake all along!
...
ケホ
cough...
I know, right?

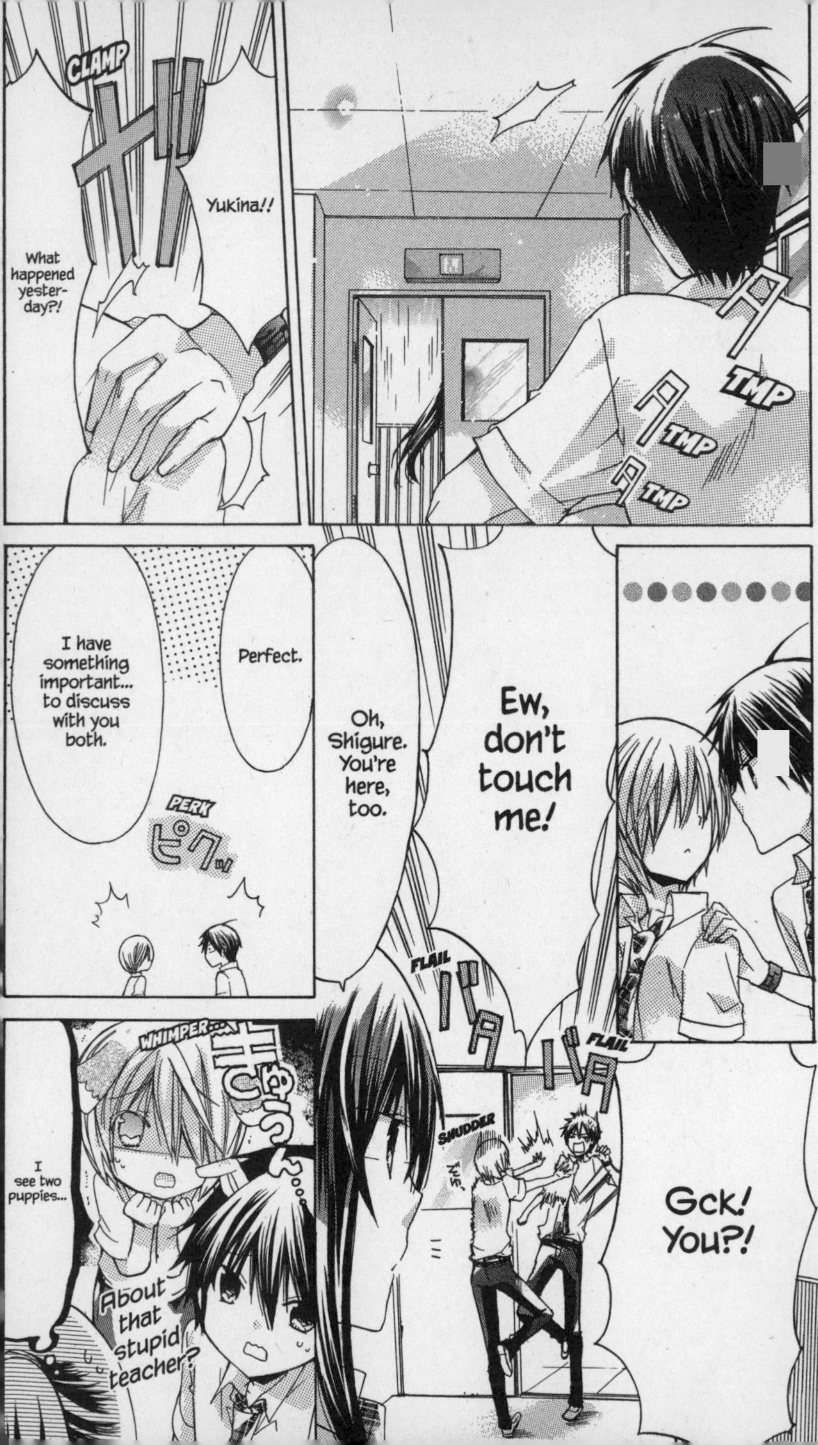
TMP
TMP
TMP
CLAMP
Yukina!!
What happened yester-day?!
Ew, don't touch me!
Oh, Shigure. You're here, too.
Perfect.
I have something important... to discuss with you both.
PERK
FLAIL
FLAIL
SHUDDER
Gck! You?!
WHIMPER...
I see two puppies...
About that stupid teacher?

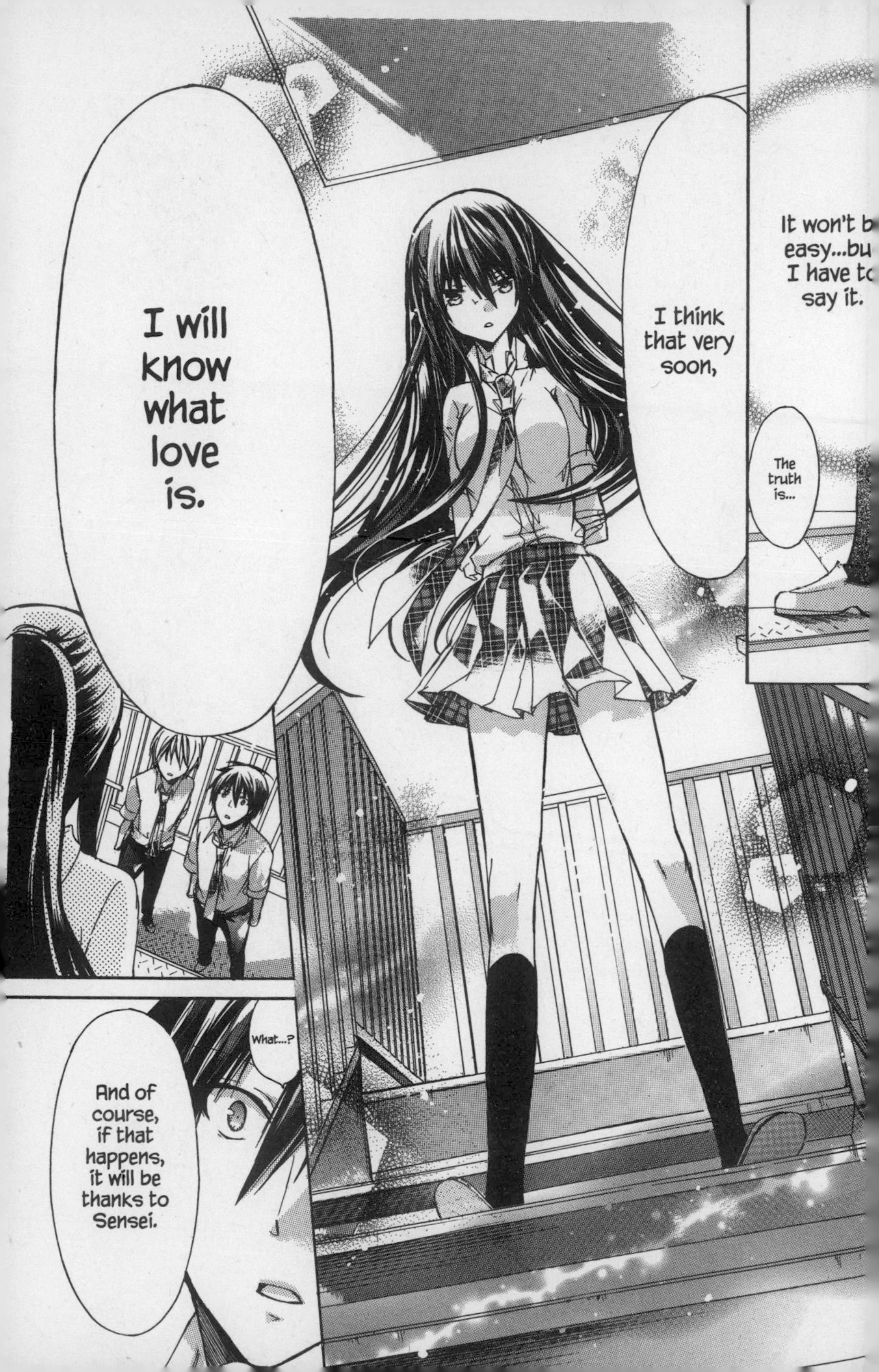
It won't b
easy...bu
I have t
say it.
The truth is...
I think that very soon,
I will know what love is.
What...?
And of course, if that happens, it will be thanks to Sensei.

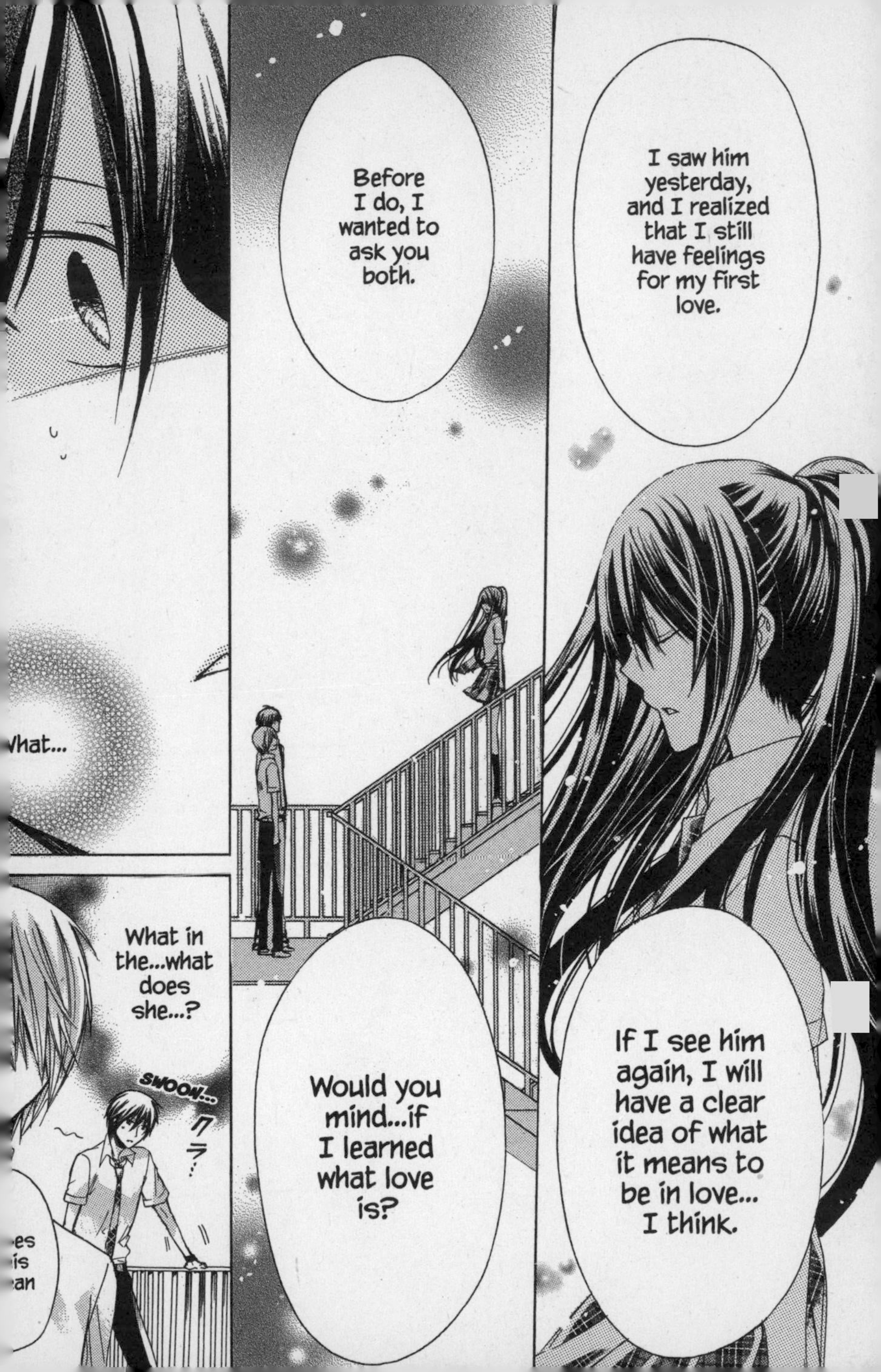

I saw him yesterday, and I realized that I still have feelings for my first love.
If I see him again, I will have a clear idea of what it means to be in love... I think.
Before I do, I wanted to ask you both.
Would you mind...if I learned what love is?
What in the...what does she...?
SWOON...
クラ...

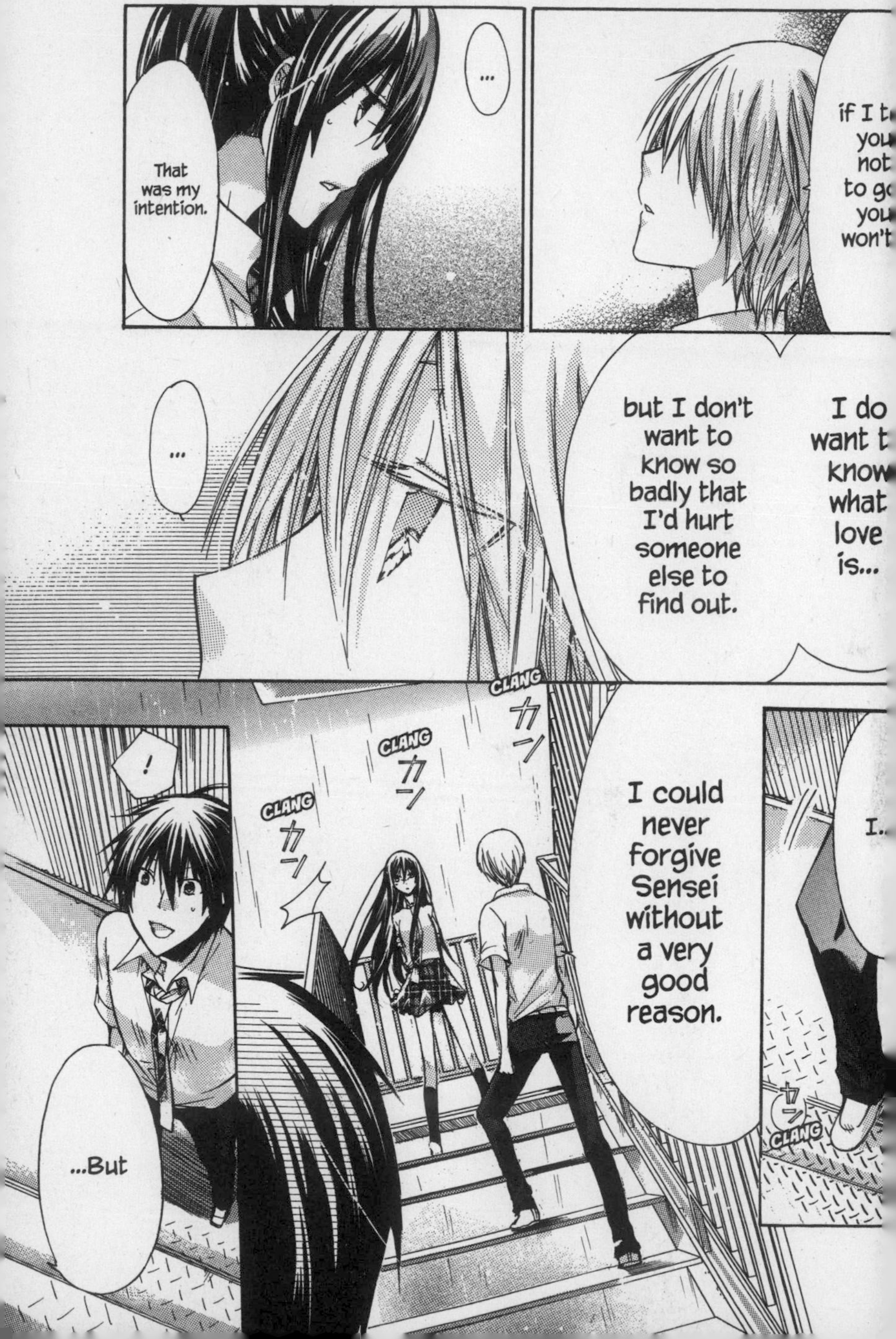

if I t
you
not
to g
you
won't
...
That was my intention.
I do
want t
know
what
love
is...
but I don't want to know so badly that I'd hurt someone else to find out.
...
I...
CLANG
I could never forgive Sensei without a very good reason.
CLANG
CLANG
CLANG
!
...But

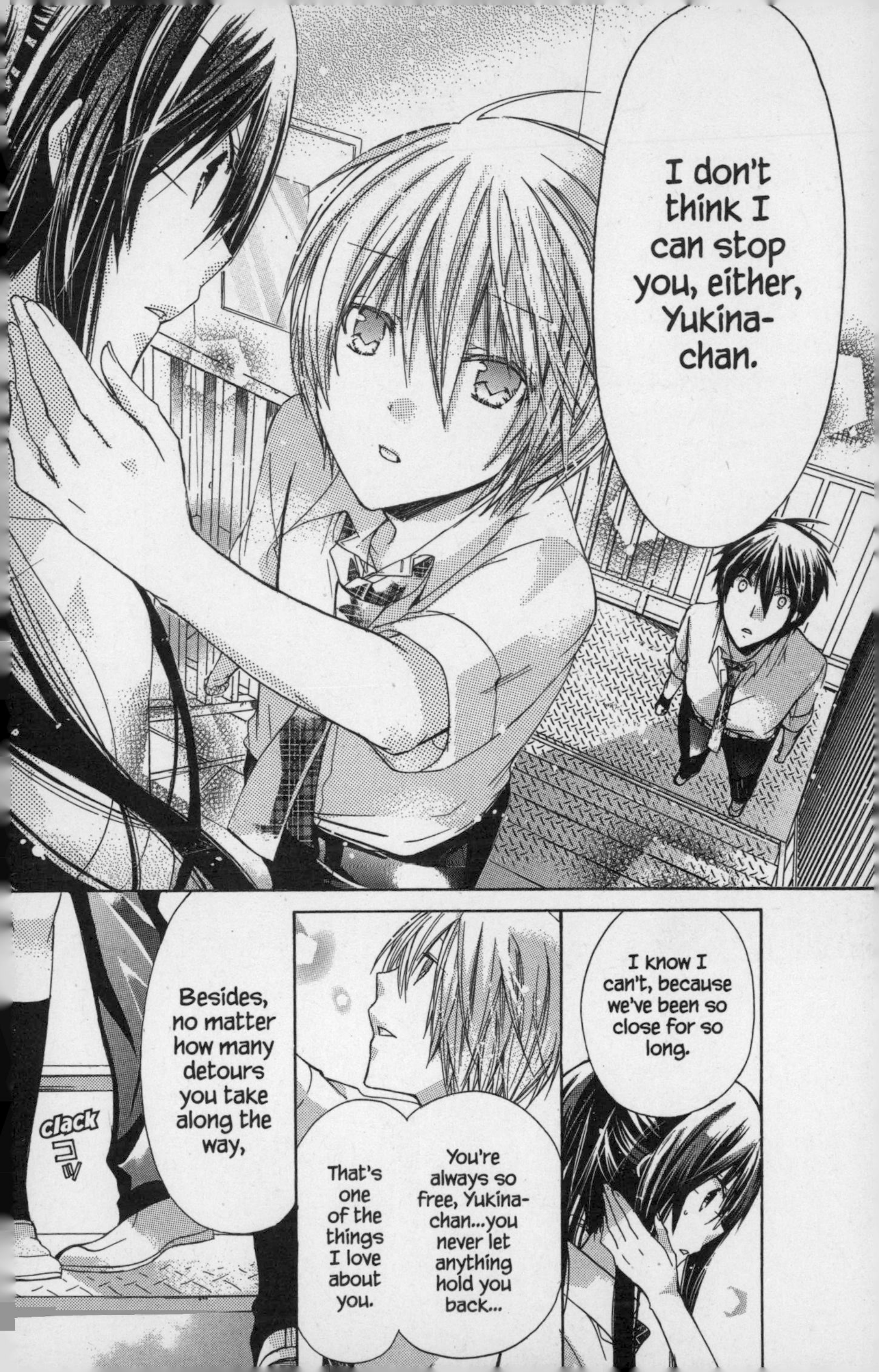
I don't think I can stop you, either, Yukina-chan.
I know I can't, because we've been so close for so long.
You're always so free, Yukina-chan...you never let anything hold you back...
That's one of the things I love about you.
Besides, no matter how many detours you take along the way,
clack

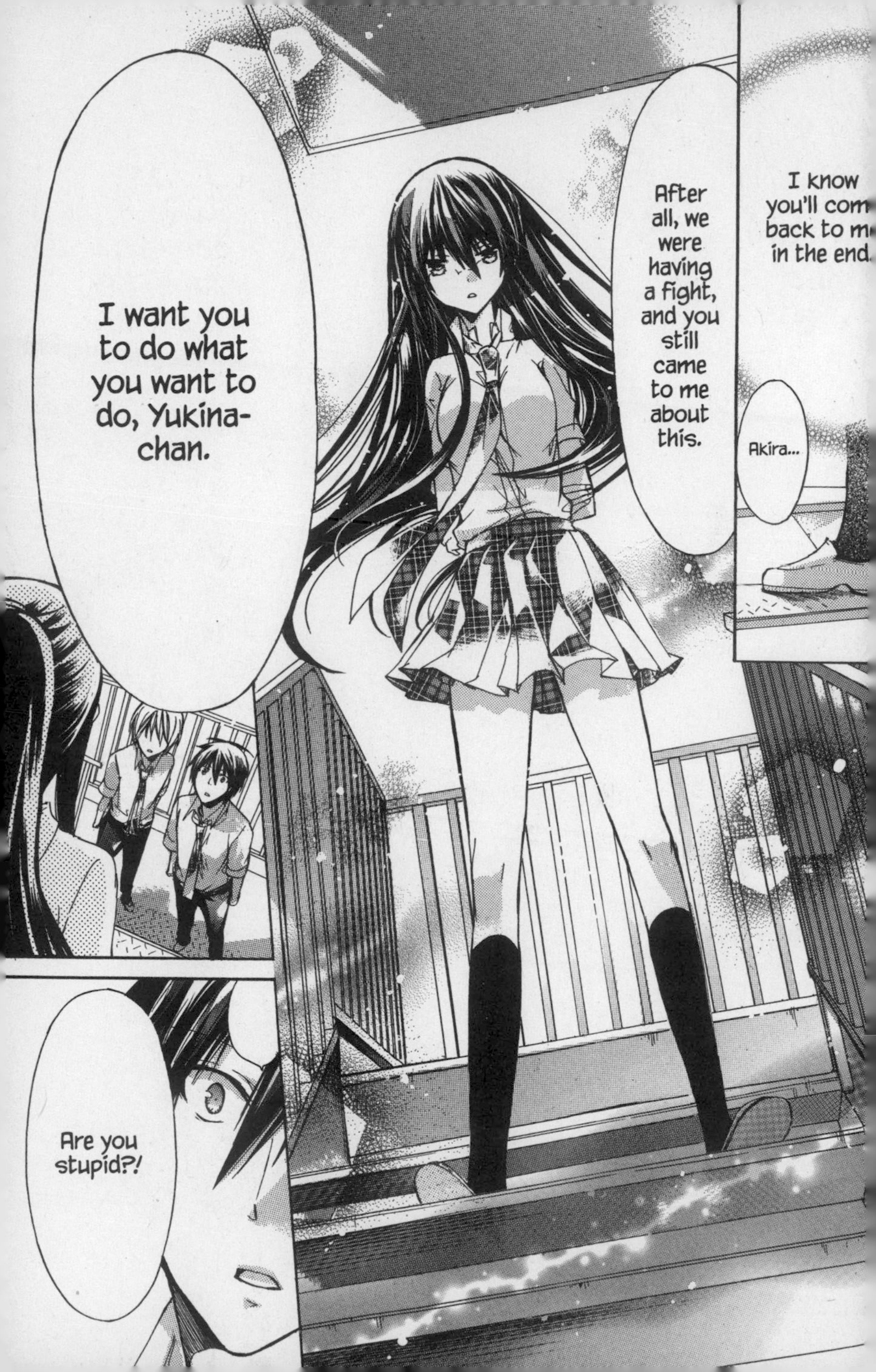
I know you'll com back to m in the end.
Akira...
After all, we were having a fight, and you still came to me about this.
I want you to do what you want to do, Yukina-chan.
Are you stupid?!

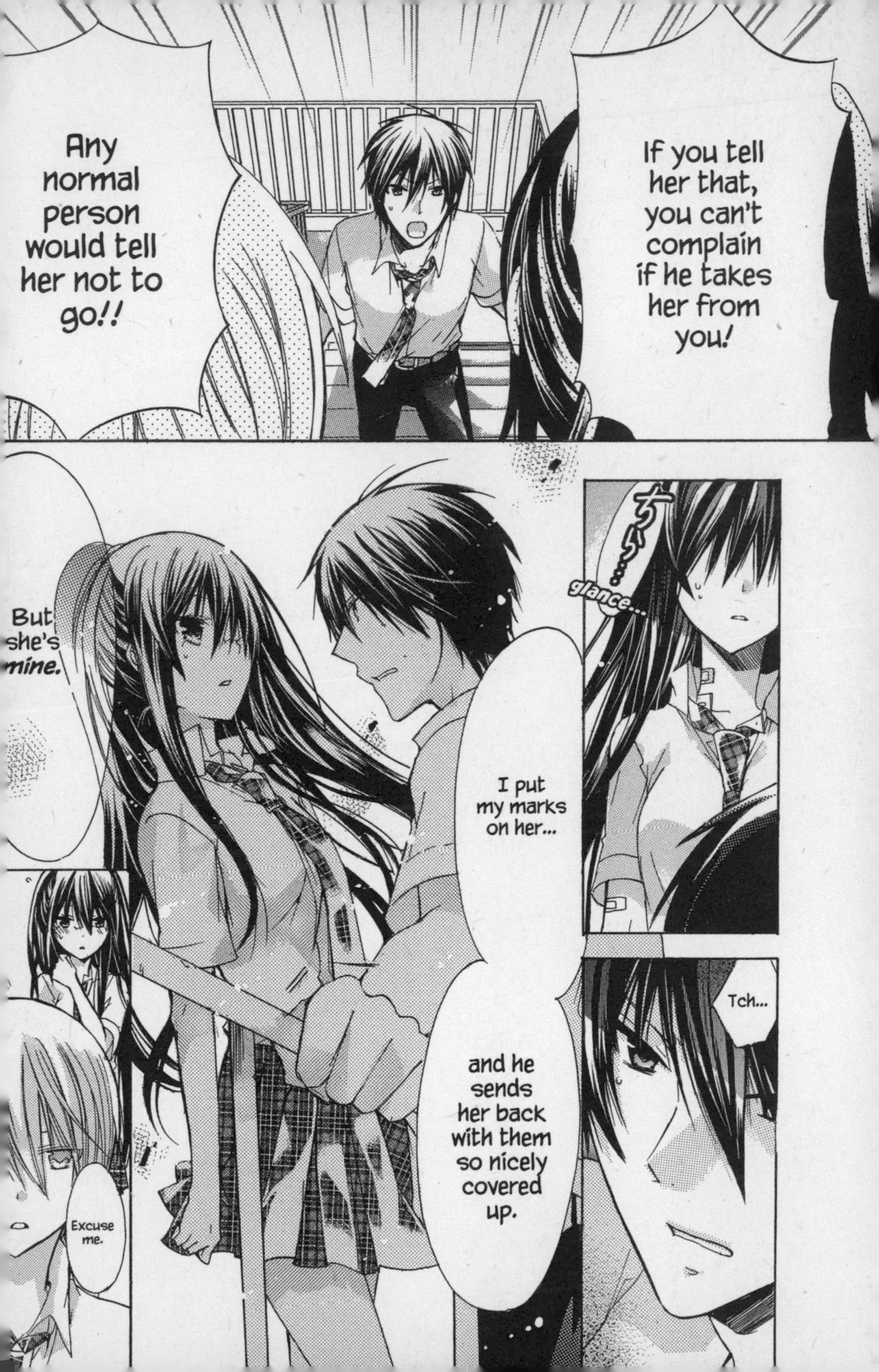
If you tell her that, you can't complain if he takes her from you!
Any normal person would tell her not to go!!
ちら…
glance...
Tch...
I put my marks on her...
and he sends her back with them so nicely covered up.
But she's mine.
Excuse me.

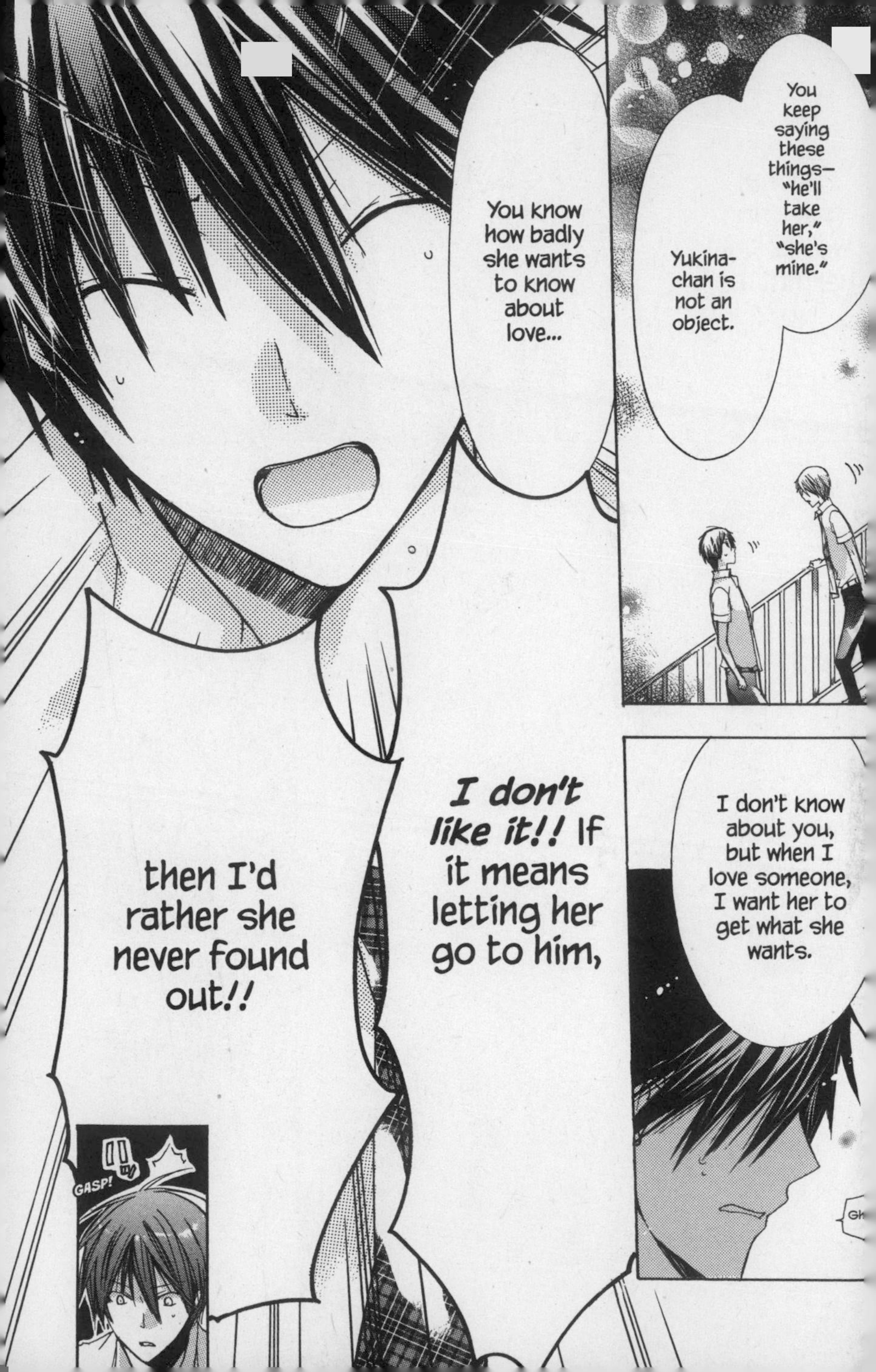
You keep saying these things— "he'll take her," "she's mine."
Yukina-chan is not an object.
I don't know about you, but when I love someone, I want her to get what she wants.
Gk
You know how badly she wants to know about love...
I don't like it!! If it means letting her go to him,
then I'd rather she never found out!!
GASP!

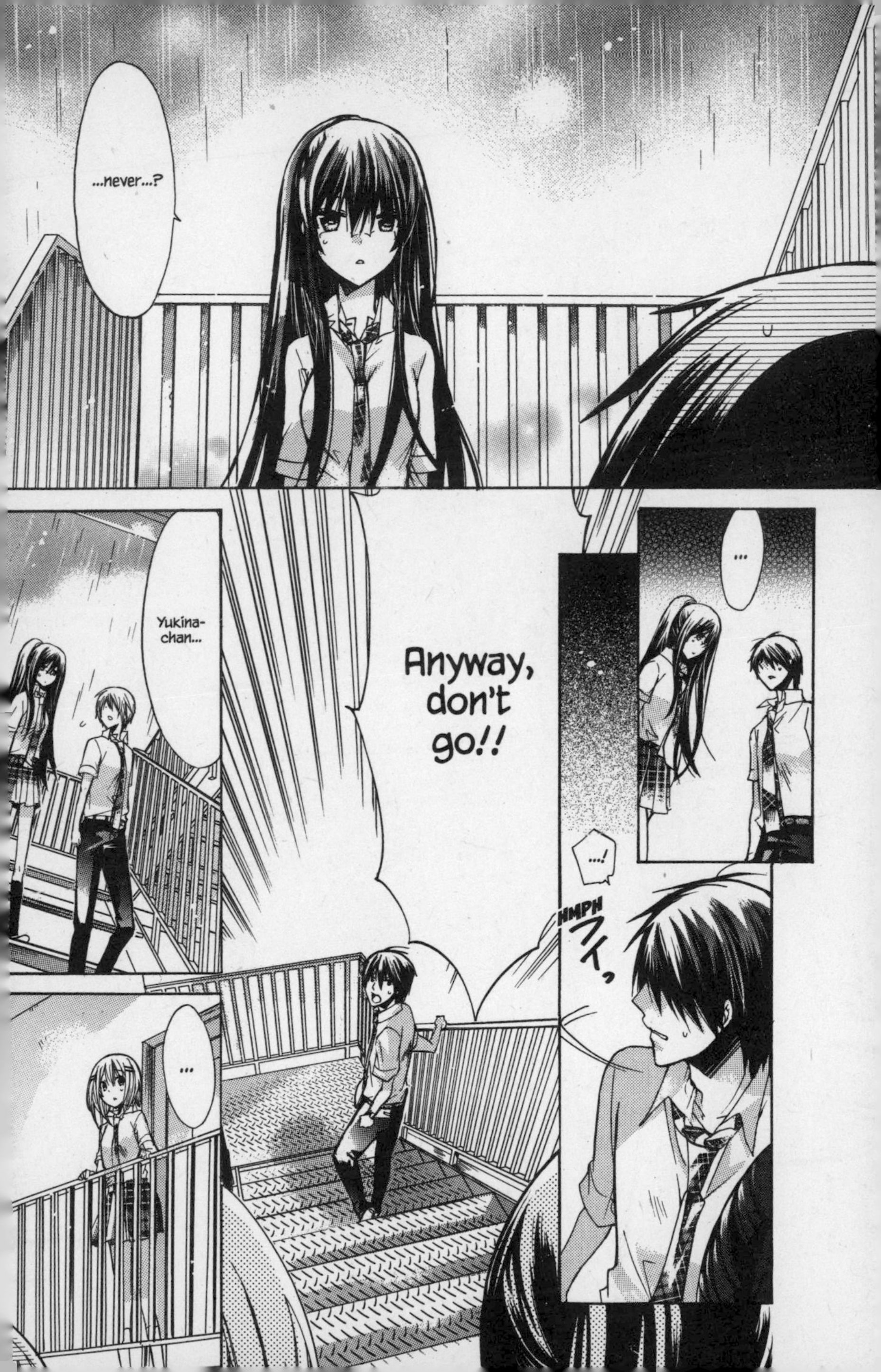
...never...?
...
...!
HMPH
フイっ
Anyway, don't go!!
Yukina-chan...
...

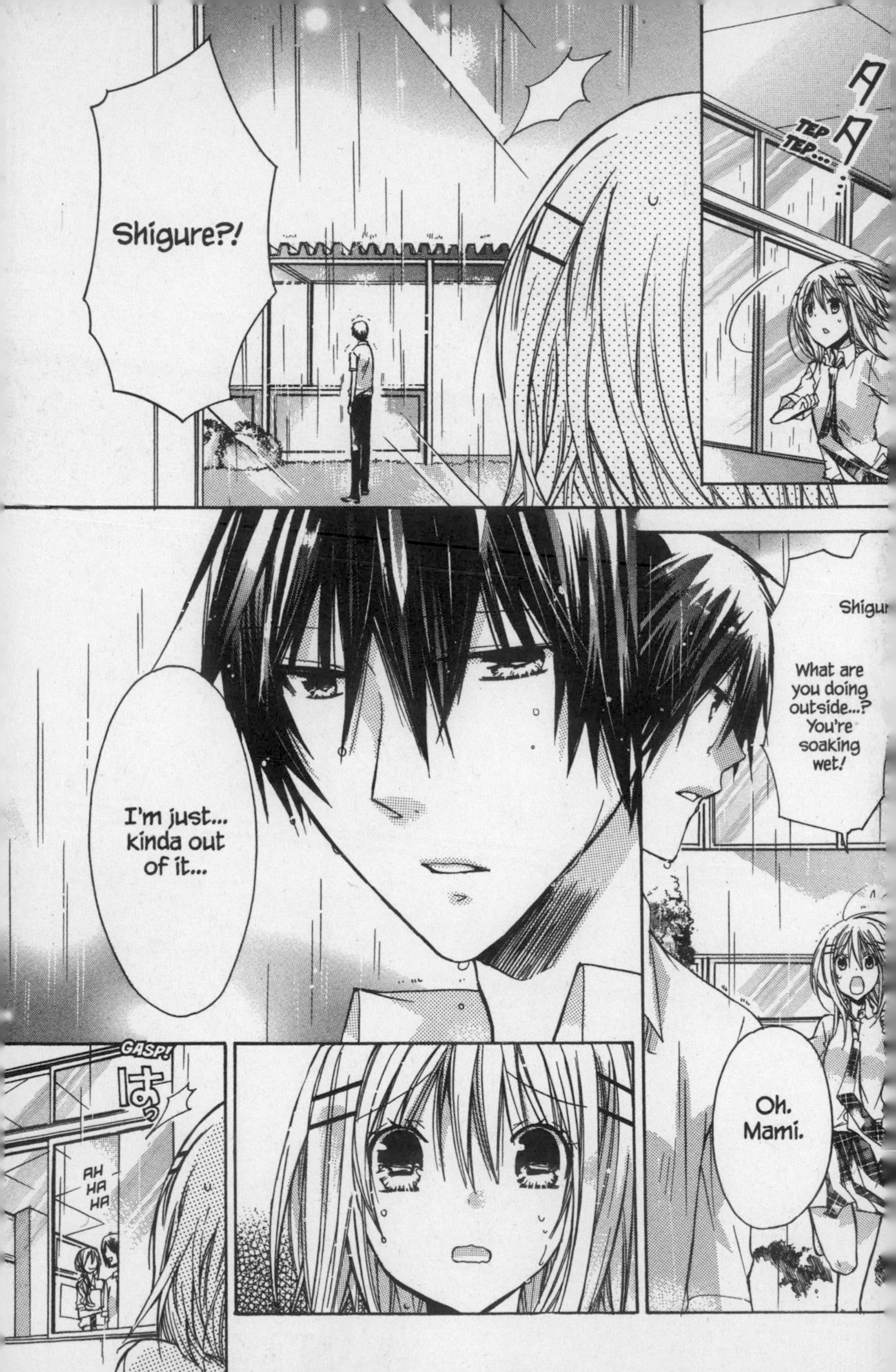
タタ
TEP TEP...
Shigure?!
Shigur
What are you doing outside...? You're soaking wet!
Oh. Mami.
I'm just... kinda out of it...
GASP!
はっ
AH HA HA

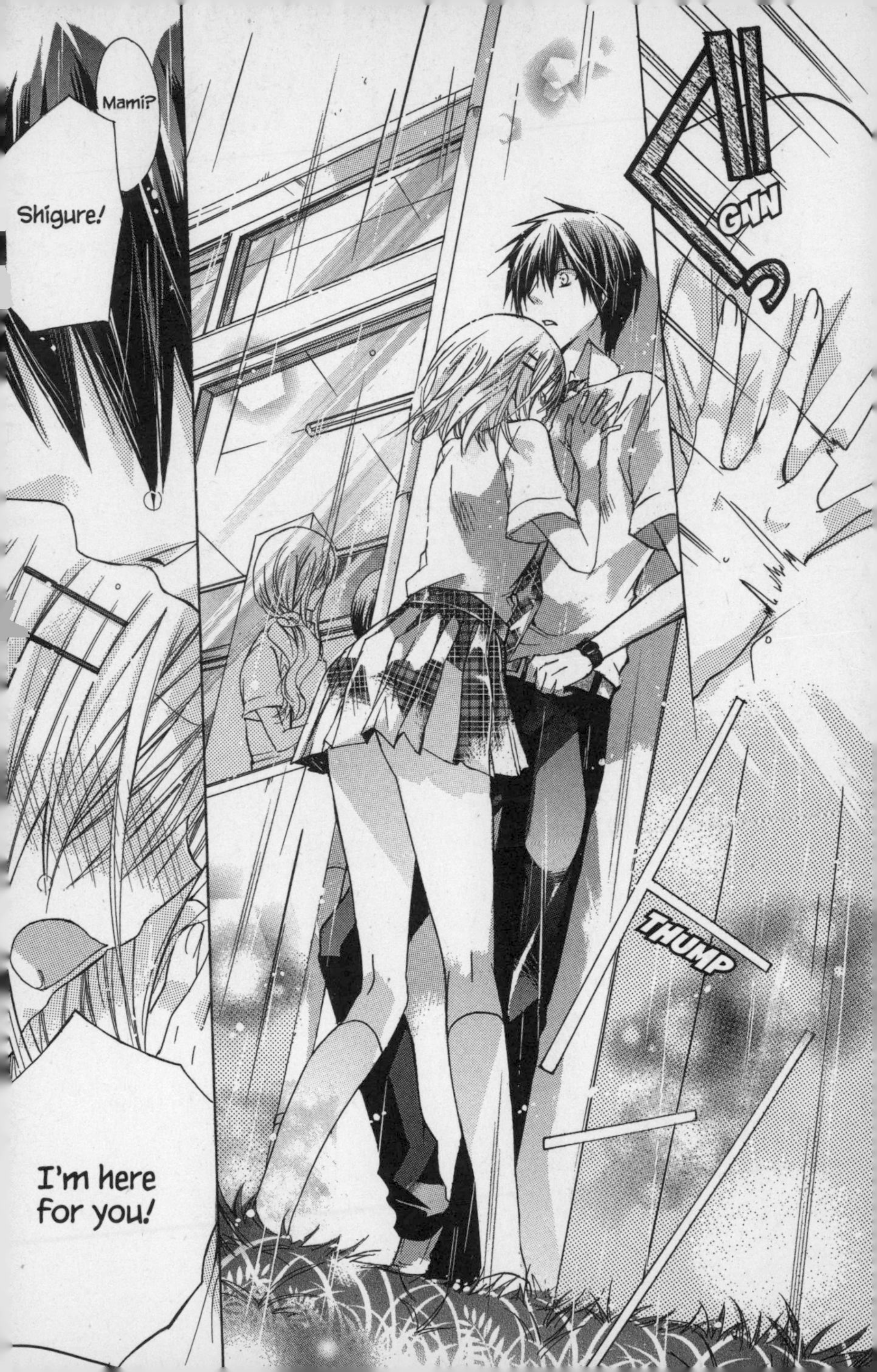
GNN
THUMP
Mami?
Shigure!
I'm here for you!

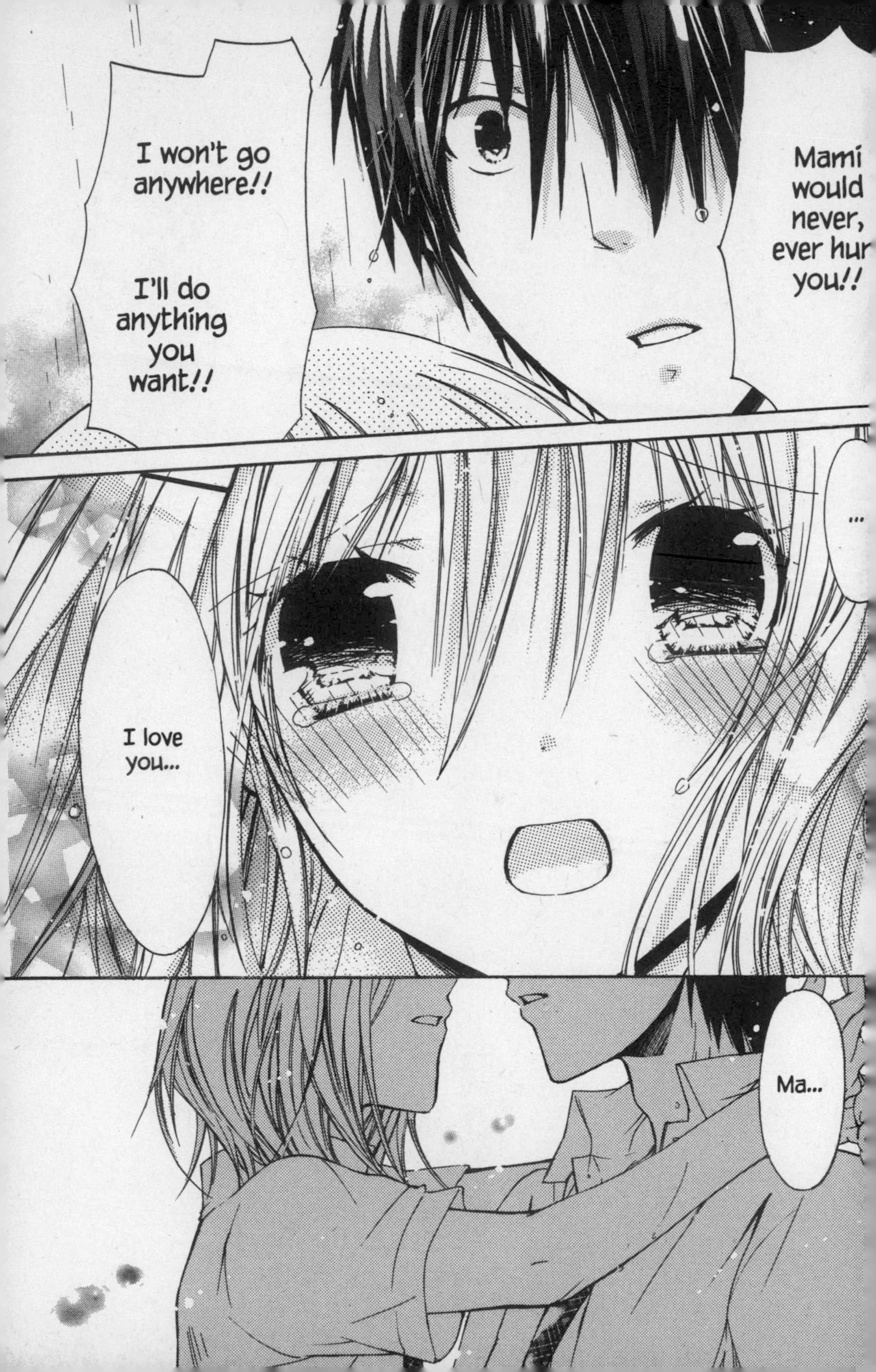
Mami would never, ever hur you!!
I won't go anywhere!!
I'll do anything you want!!
...
I love you...
Ma...

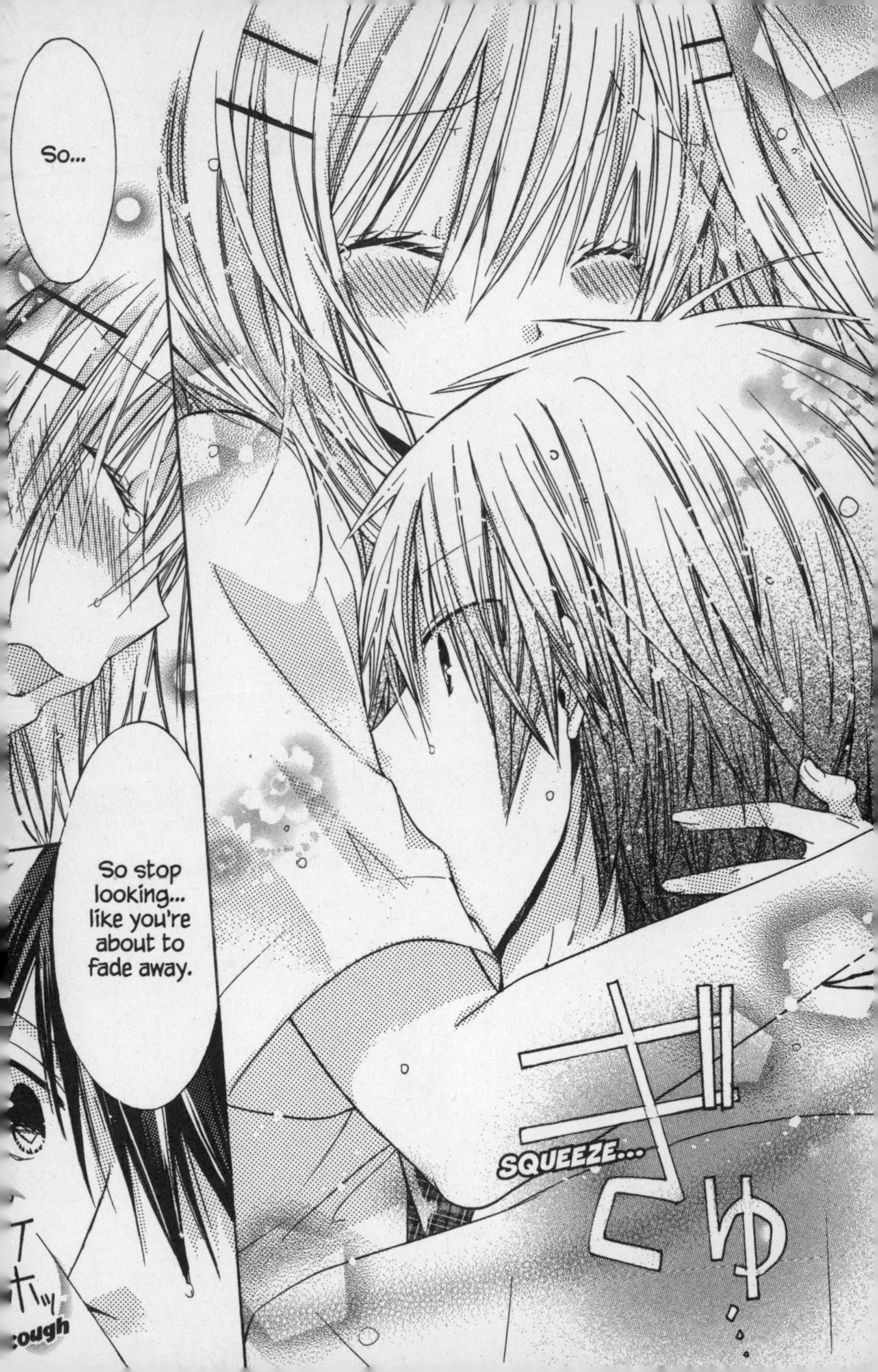
So...
So stop looking... like you're about to fade away.
ぎゅ...
SQUEEZE...
cough

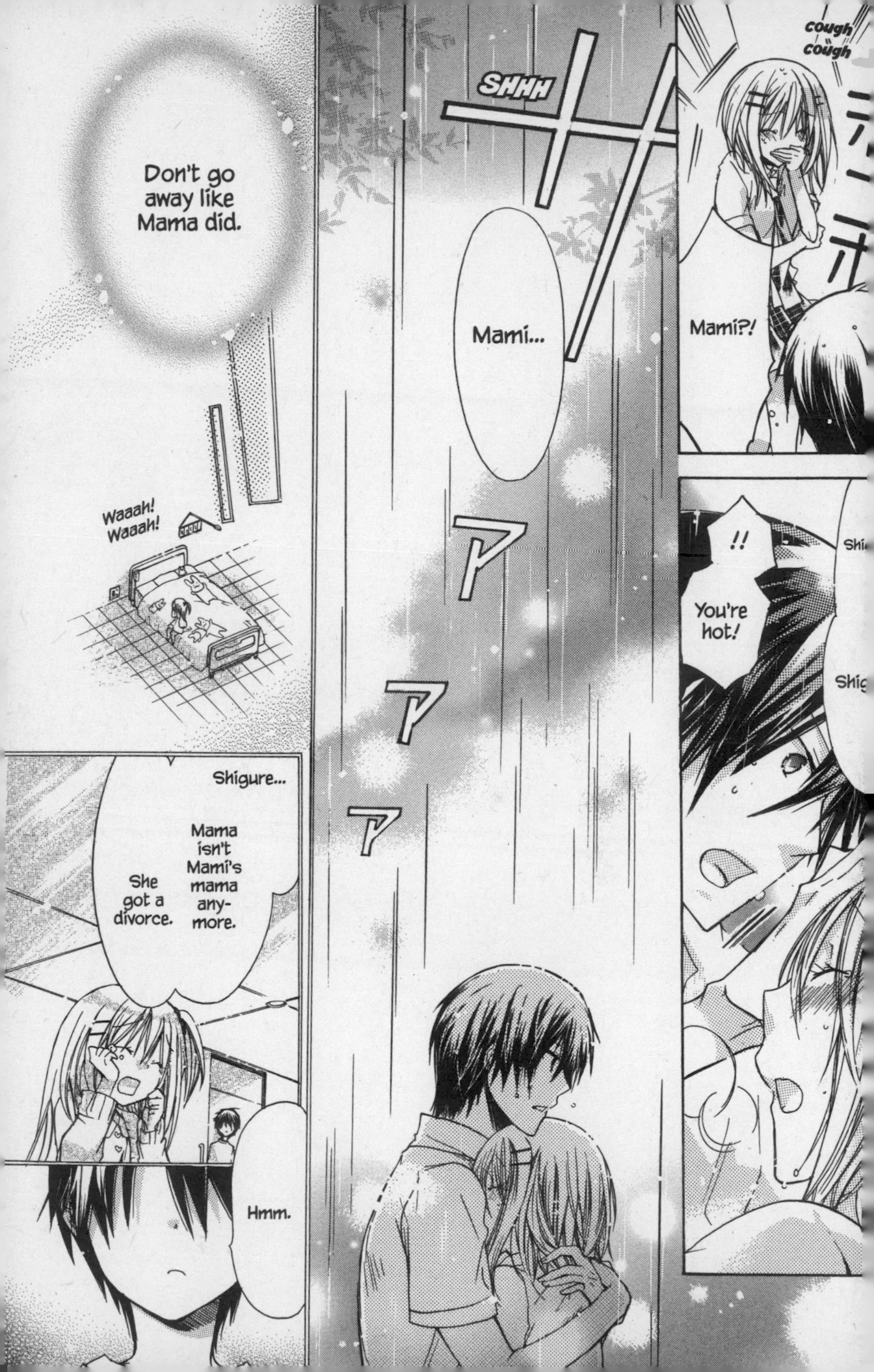
cough cough
Mami?!
!!
You're hot!
SHHH
Mami...
Don't go away like Mama did.
Waaah! Waaah!
Shigure...
Mama isn't Mami's mama anymore.
She got a divorce.
Hmm.

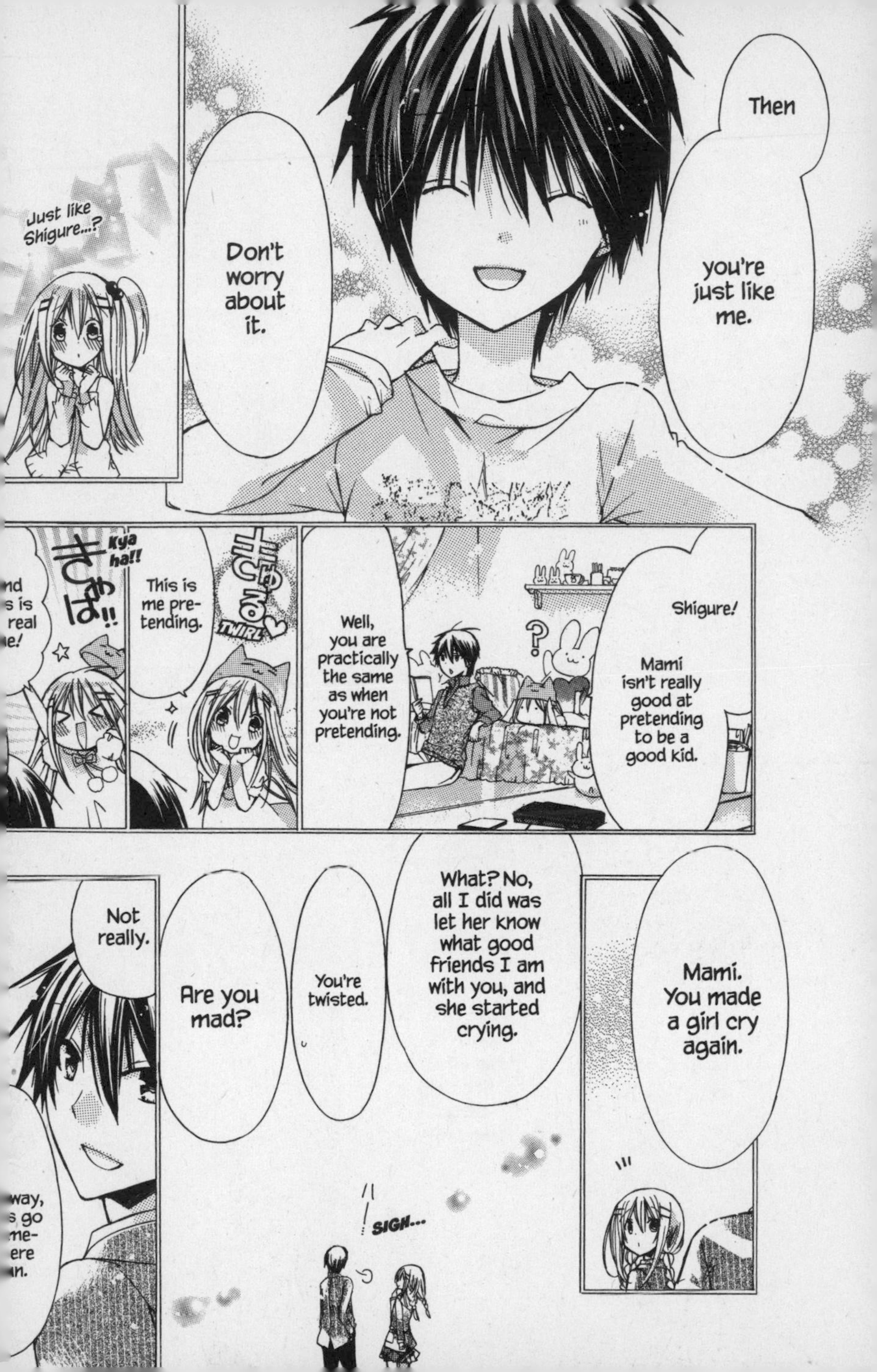
Then
you're just like me.
Don't worry about it.
Just like Shigure...?
Shigure!
Mami isn't really good at pretending to be a good kid.
Well, you are practically the same as when you're not pretending.
きゅる
TWIRL
This is me pre-tending.
Kya ha!!
きゃは!!
Mami. You made a girl cry again.
What? No, all I did was let her know what good friends I am with you, and she started crying.
You're twisted.
Are you mad?
Not really.
SIGH...

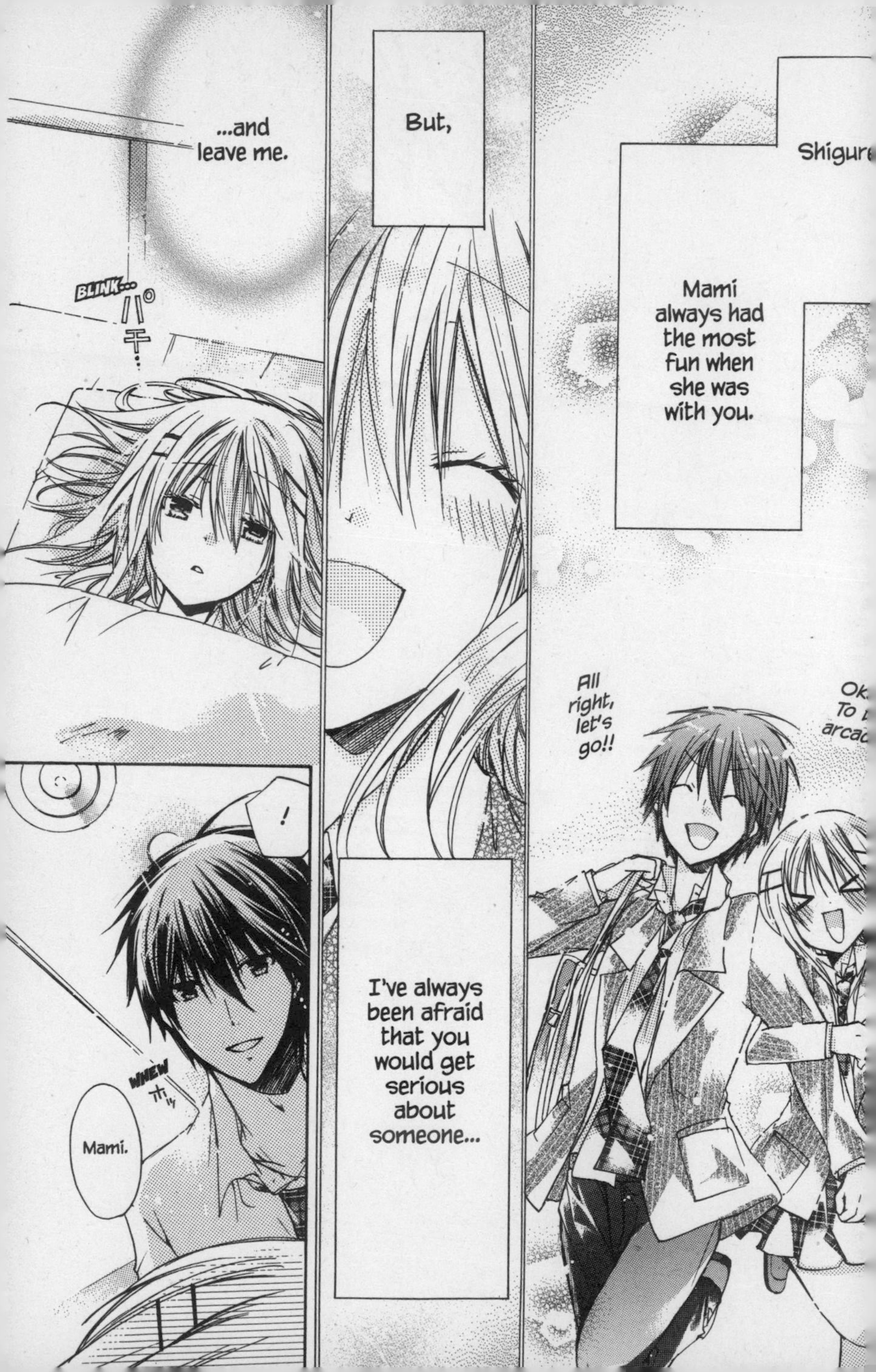
Shigure
Mami always had the most fun when she was with you.
All right, let's go!!
But,
I've always been afraid that you would get serious about someone...
...and leave me.
BLINK... パチ
!
WHEW ホッ
Mami.

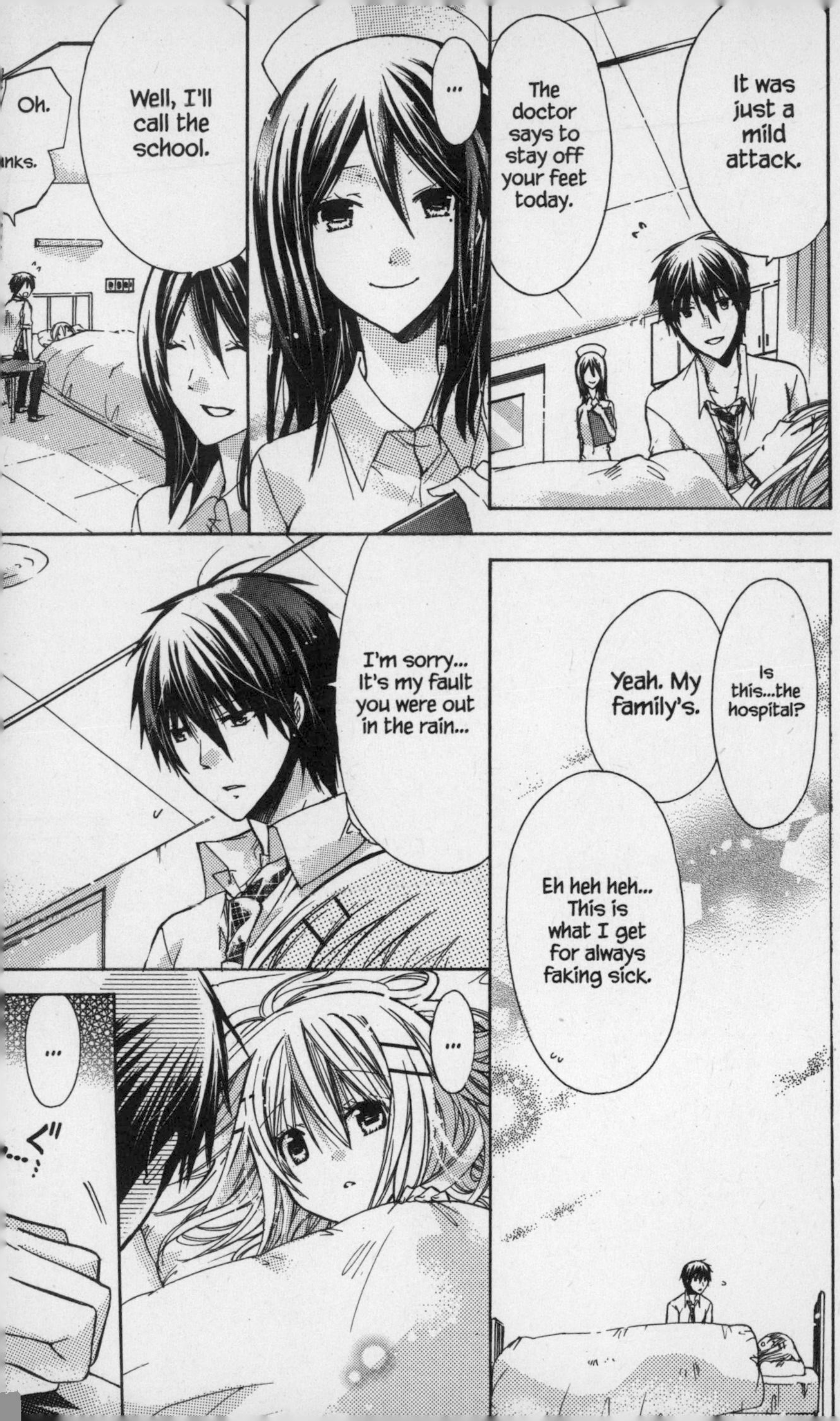
It was just a mild attack.
The doctor says to stay off your feet today.
...
Well, I'll call the school.
Oh.
nks.
Is this...the hospital?
Yeah. My family's.
Eh heh heh... This is what I get for always faking sick.
I'm sorry... It's my fault you were out in the rain...
...
...

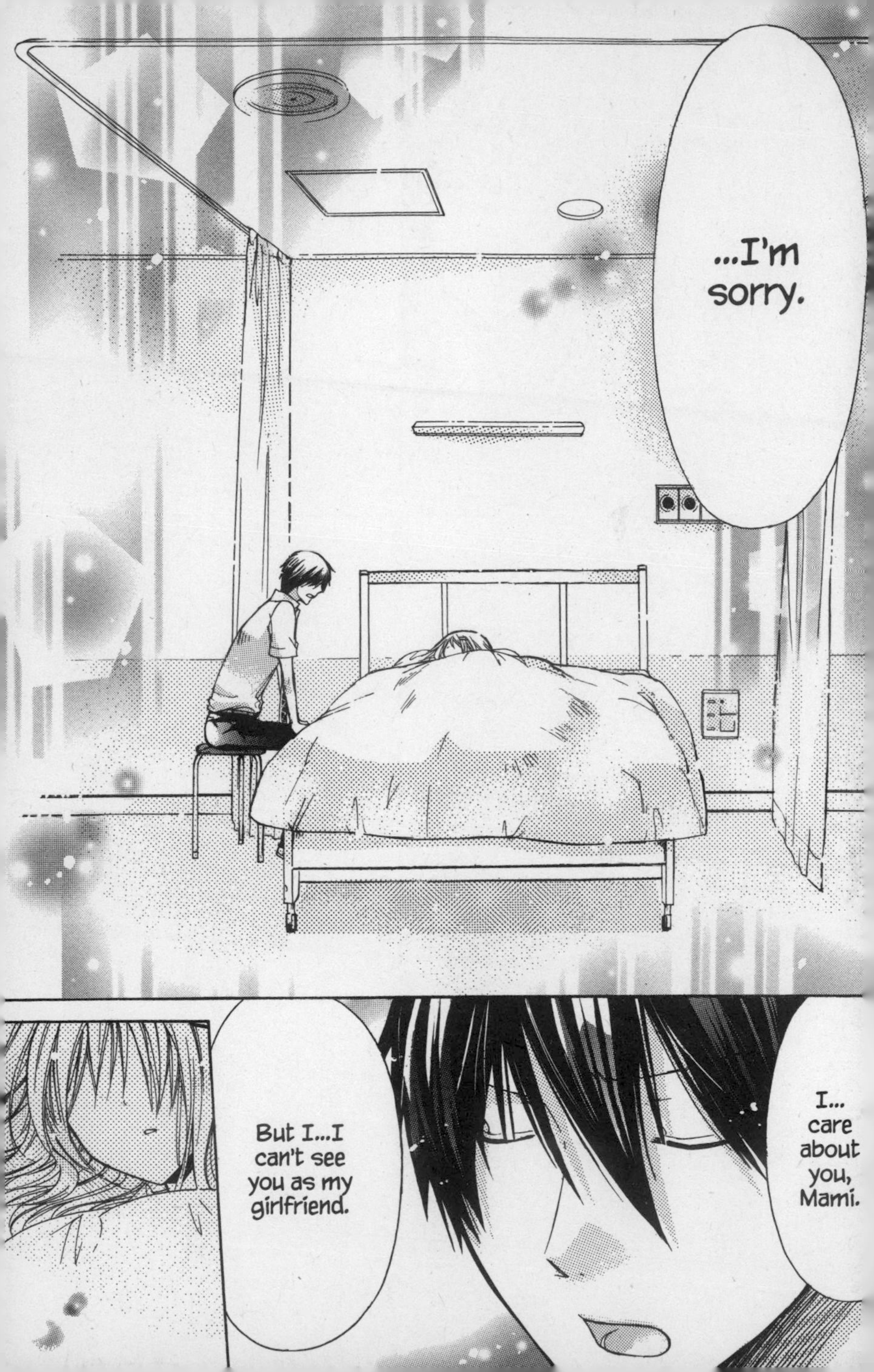
...I'm sorry.
I... care about you, Mami.
But I...I can't see you as my girlfriend.

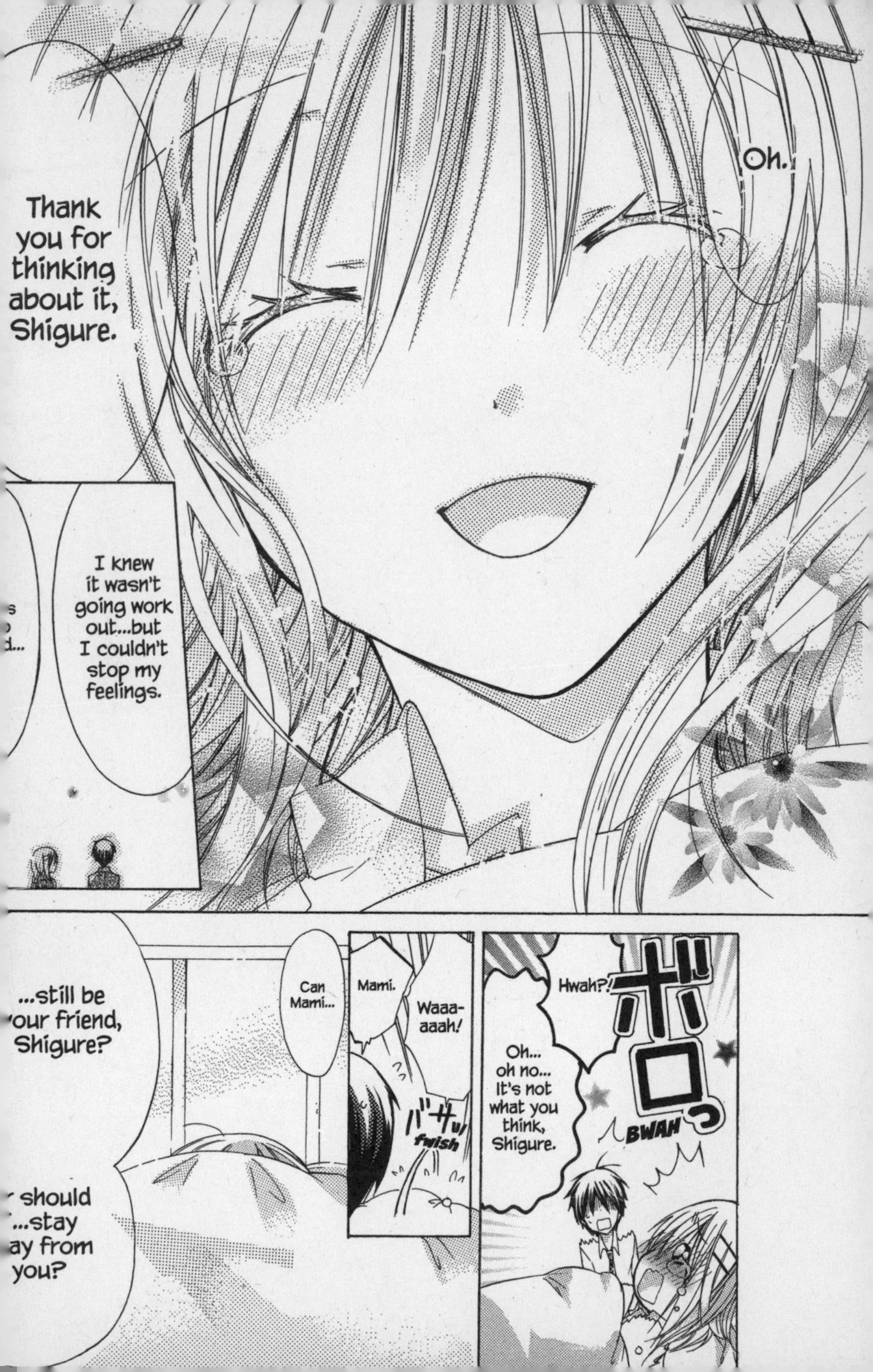
Oh.
Thank you for thinking about it, Shigure.
I knew it wasn't going work out...but I couldn't stop my feelings.
Hwah?!
ボロっ
BWAH
Oh... oh no... It's not what you think, Shigure.
Mami.
Waaa-aaah!
バサッ
fwish
Can Mami...
...still be your friend, Shigure?
should ...stay ay from you?

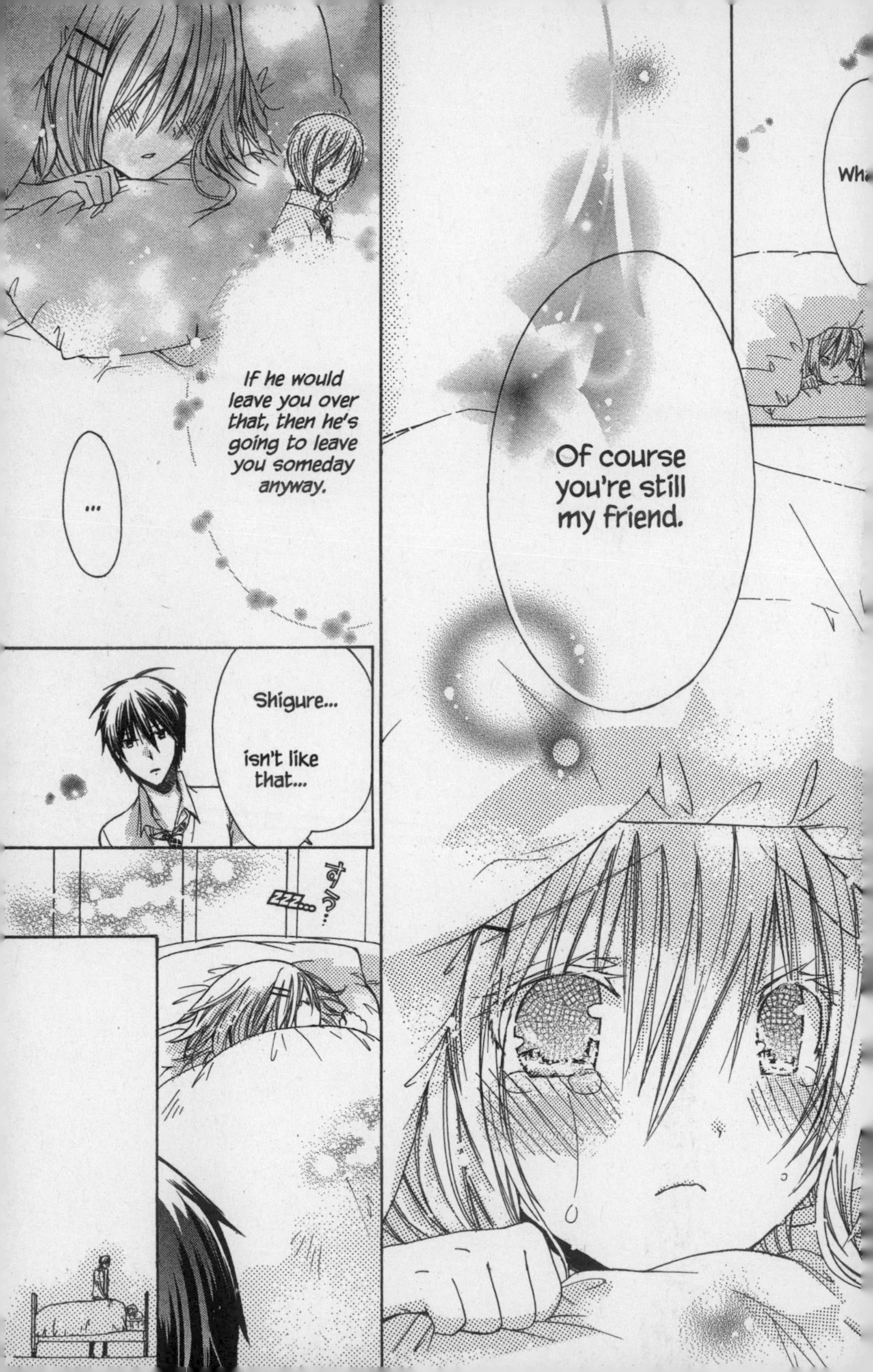
Wha
Of course you're still my friend.
If he would leave you over that, then he's going to leave you someday anyway.
...
Shigure...
isn't like that...
すう...
zzz...

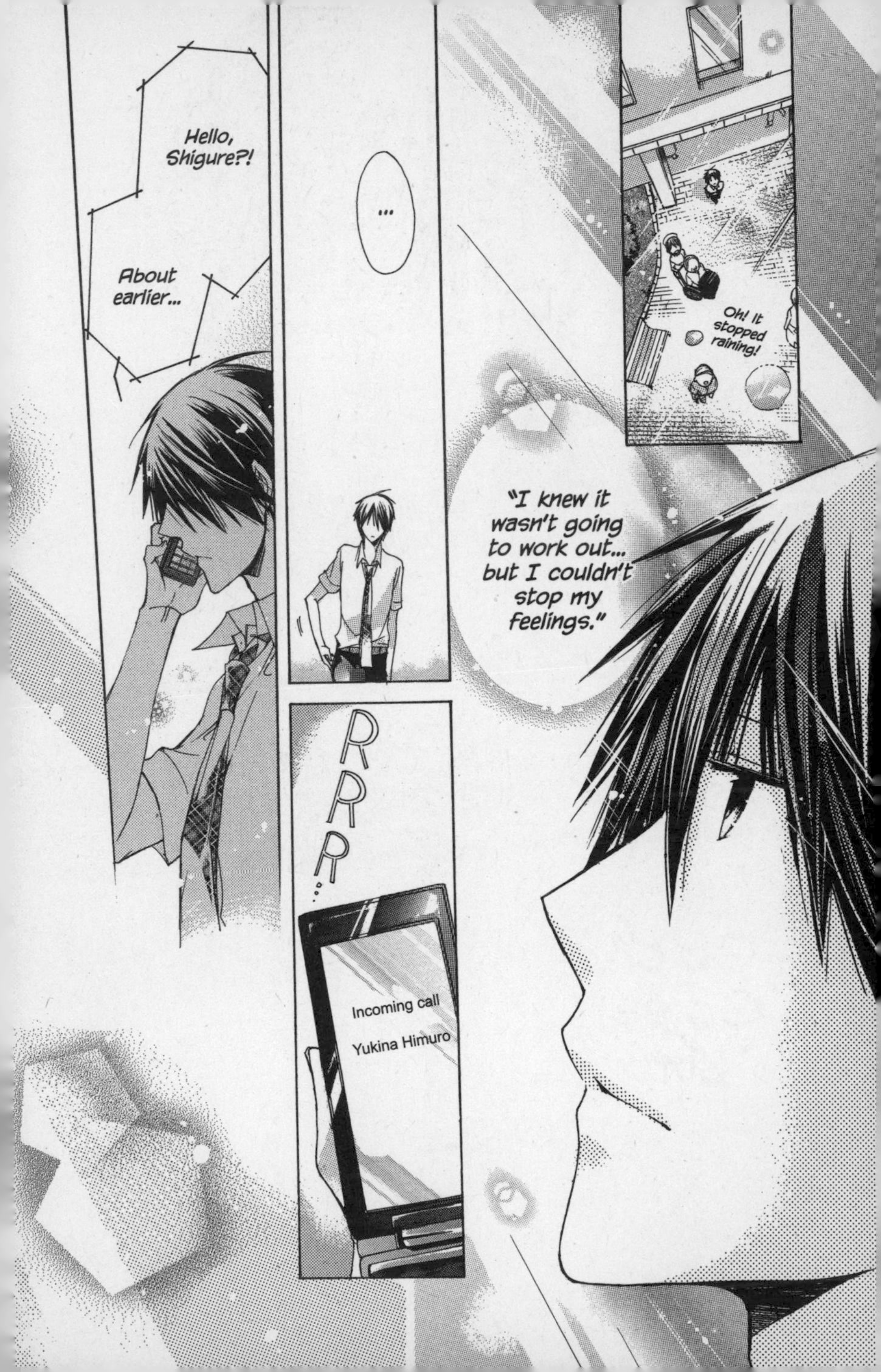
Oh! It stopped raining!
"I knew it wasn't going to work out... but I couldn't stop my feelings."
...
RRR
Incoming call
Yukina Himuro
Hello, Shigure?!
About earlier...

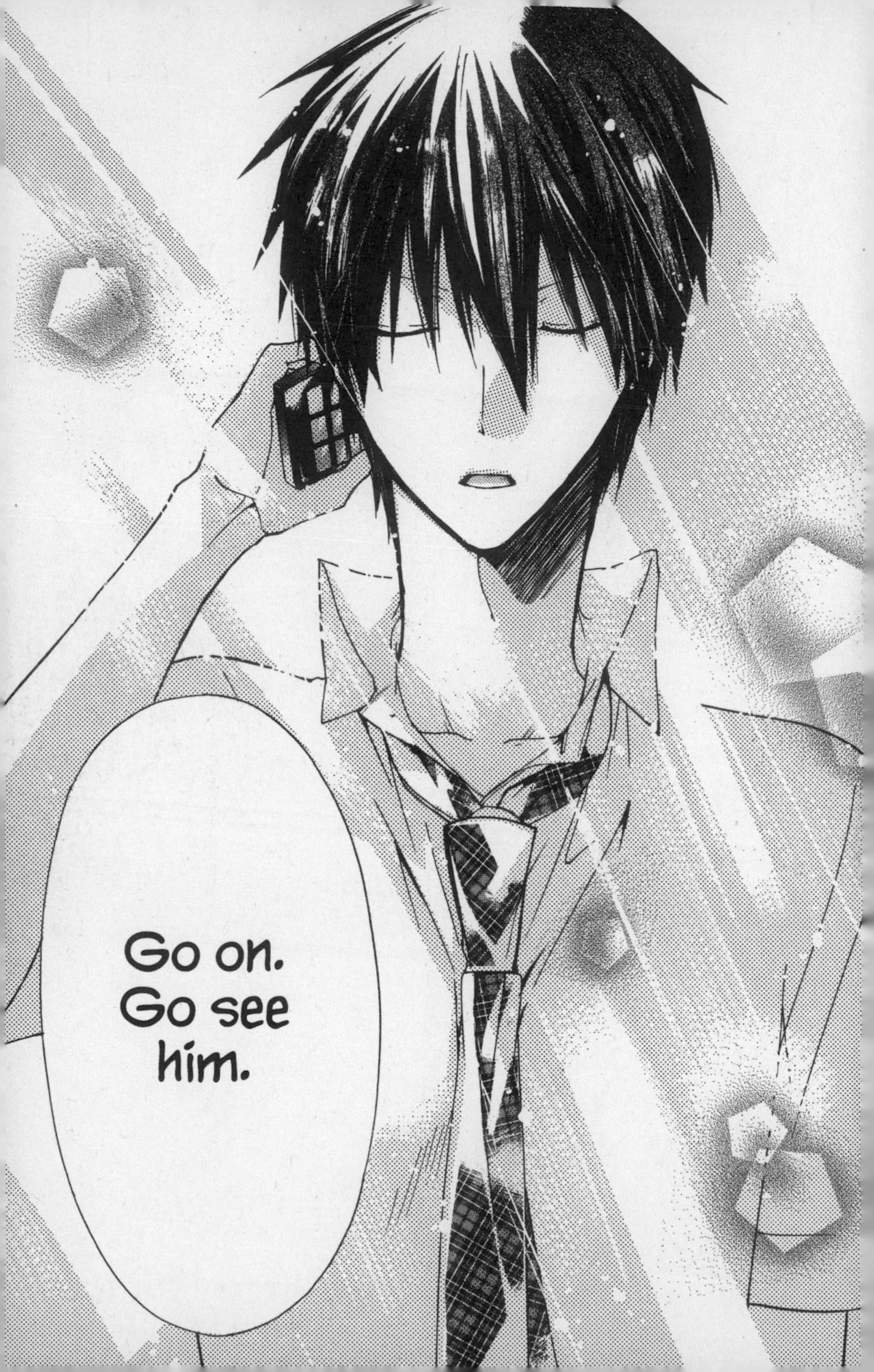
Go on. Go see him.

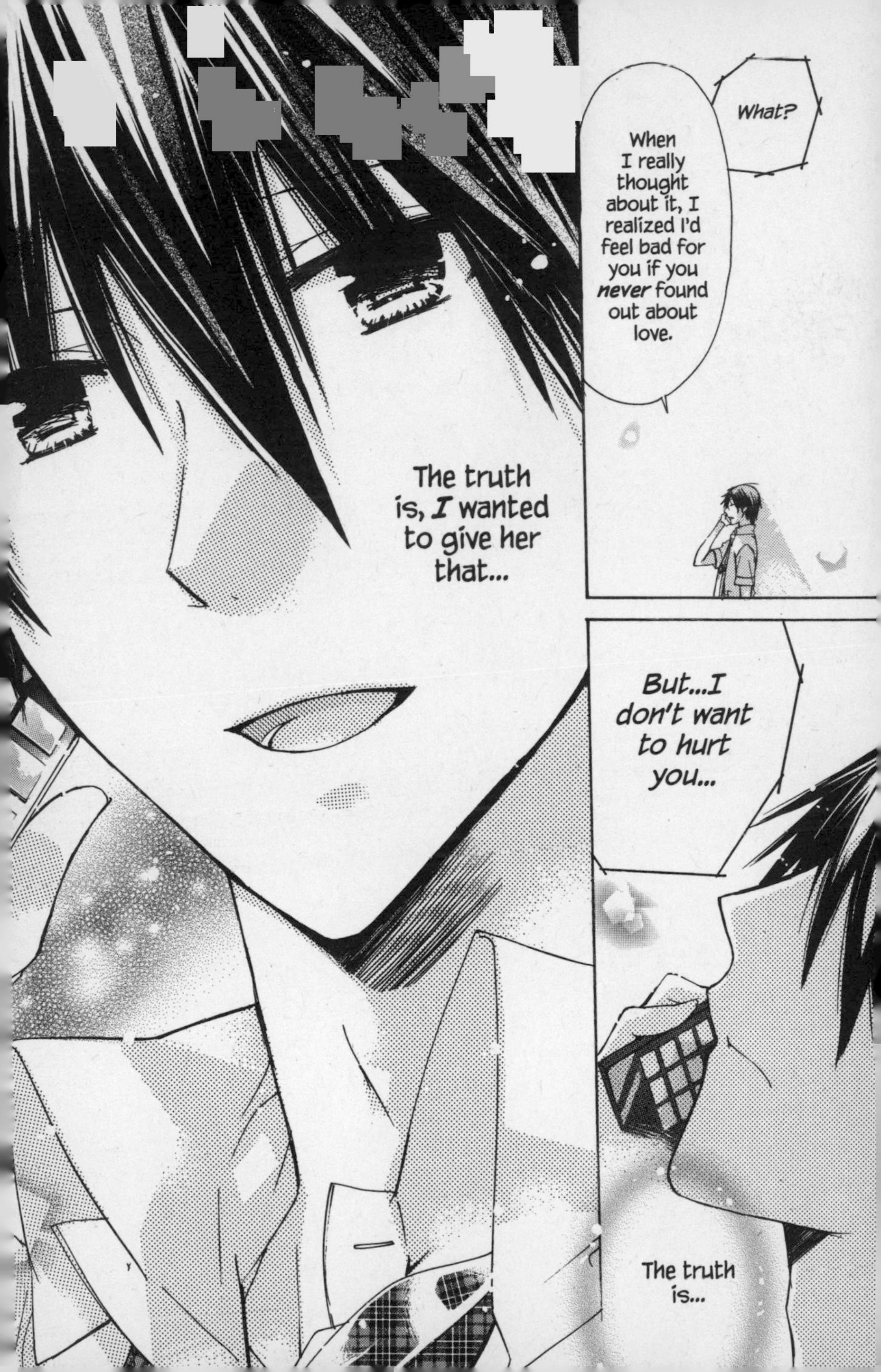
What?
When I really thought about it, I realized I'd feel bad for you if you *never* found out about love.
But...I don't want to hurt you...
The truth is...
The truth is, *I* wanted to give her that...

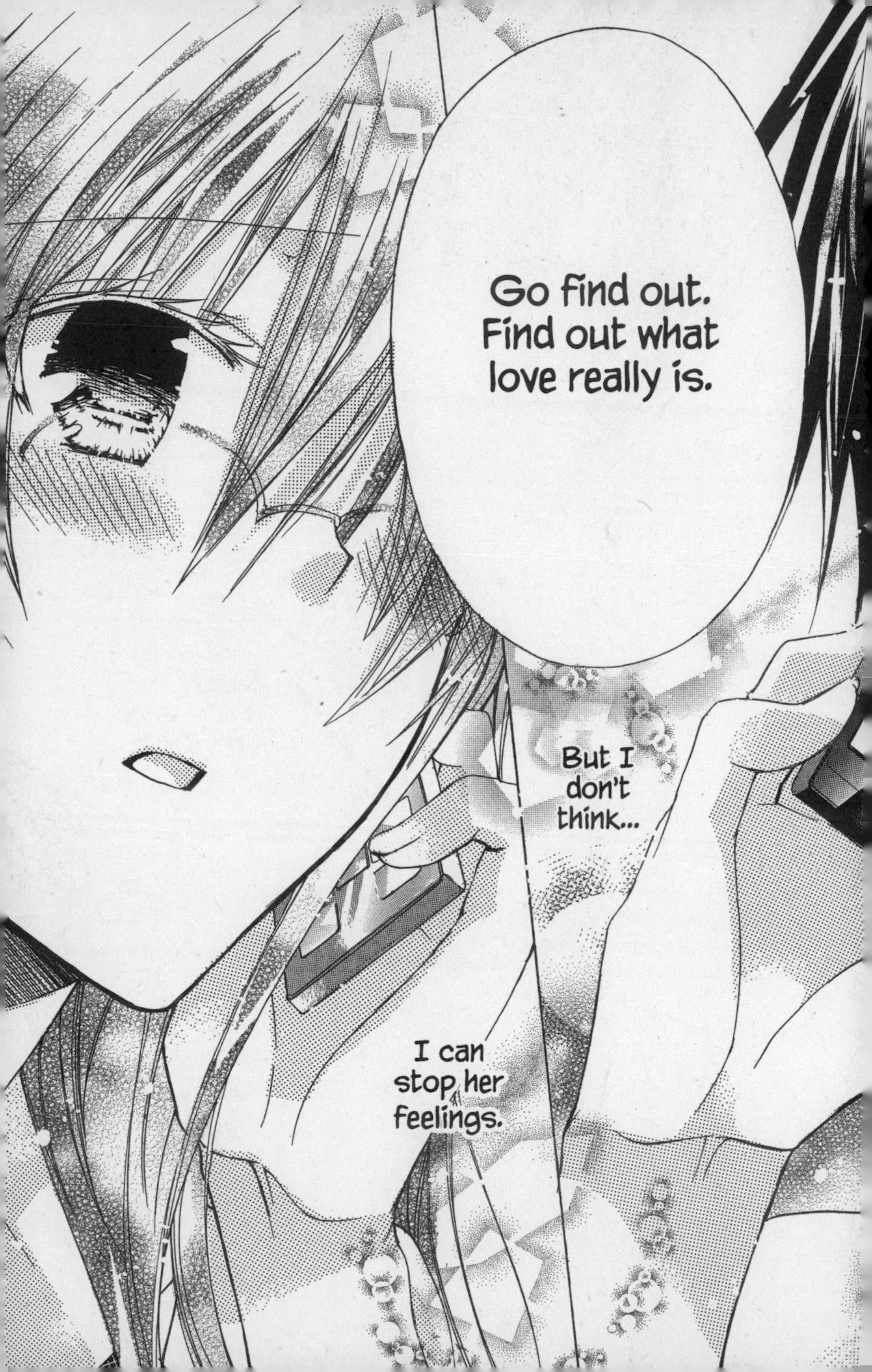
Go find out. Find out what love really is.
But I don't think...
I can stop her feelings.

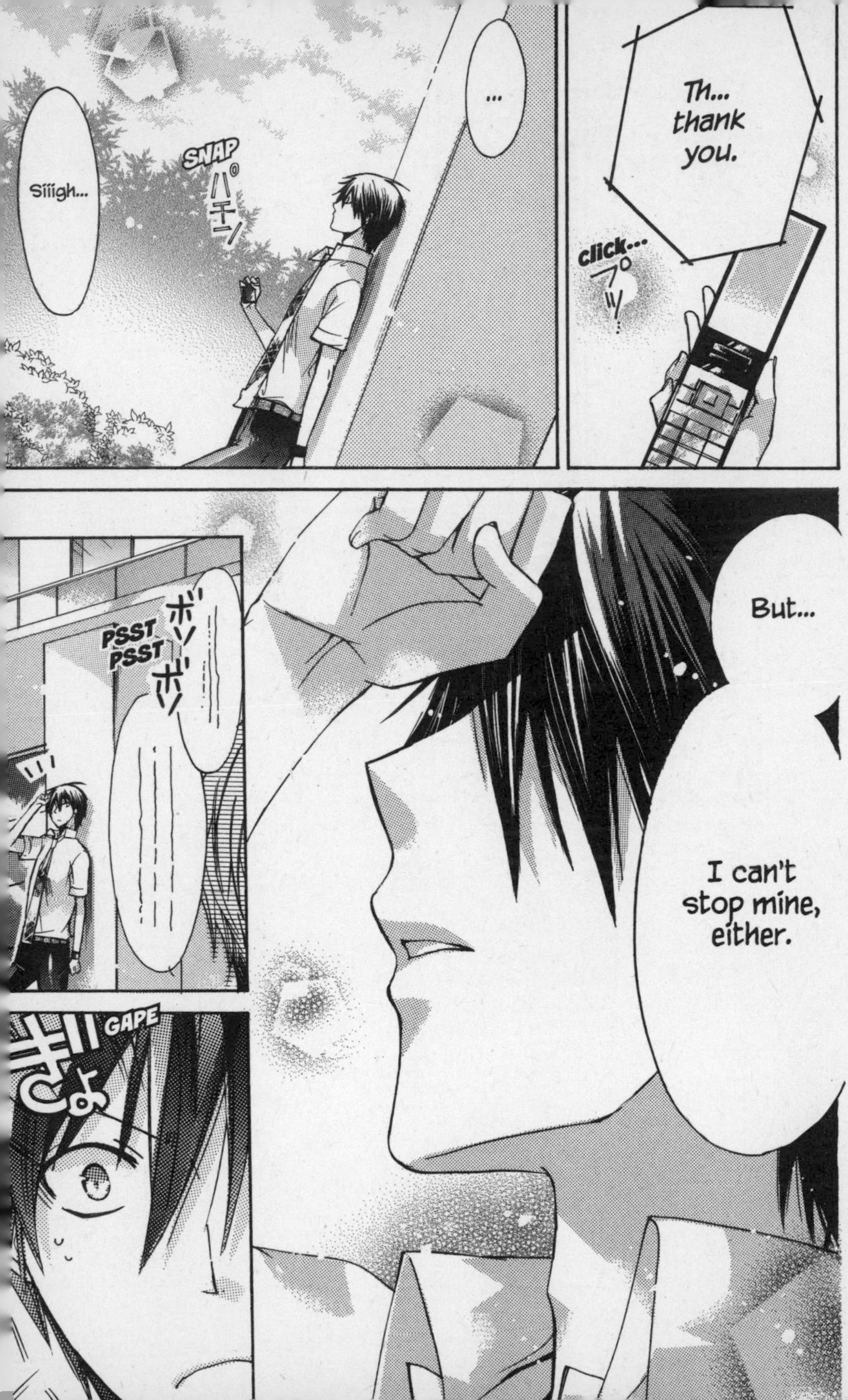
Th... thank you.
click...
プッ
...
SNAP
パチーン
Siiigh...
But...
I can't stop mine, either.
PSST PSST
ボソボソ
GAPE
ぎょ

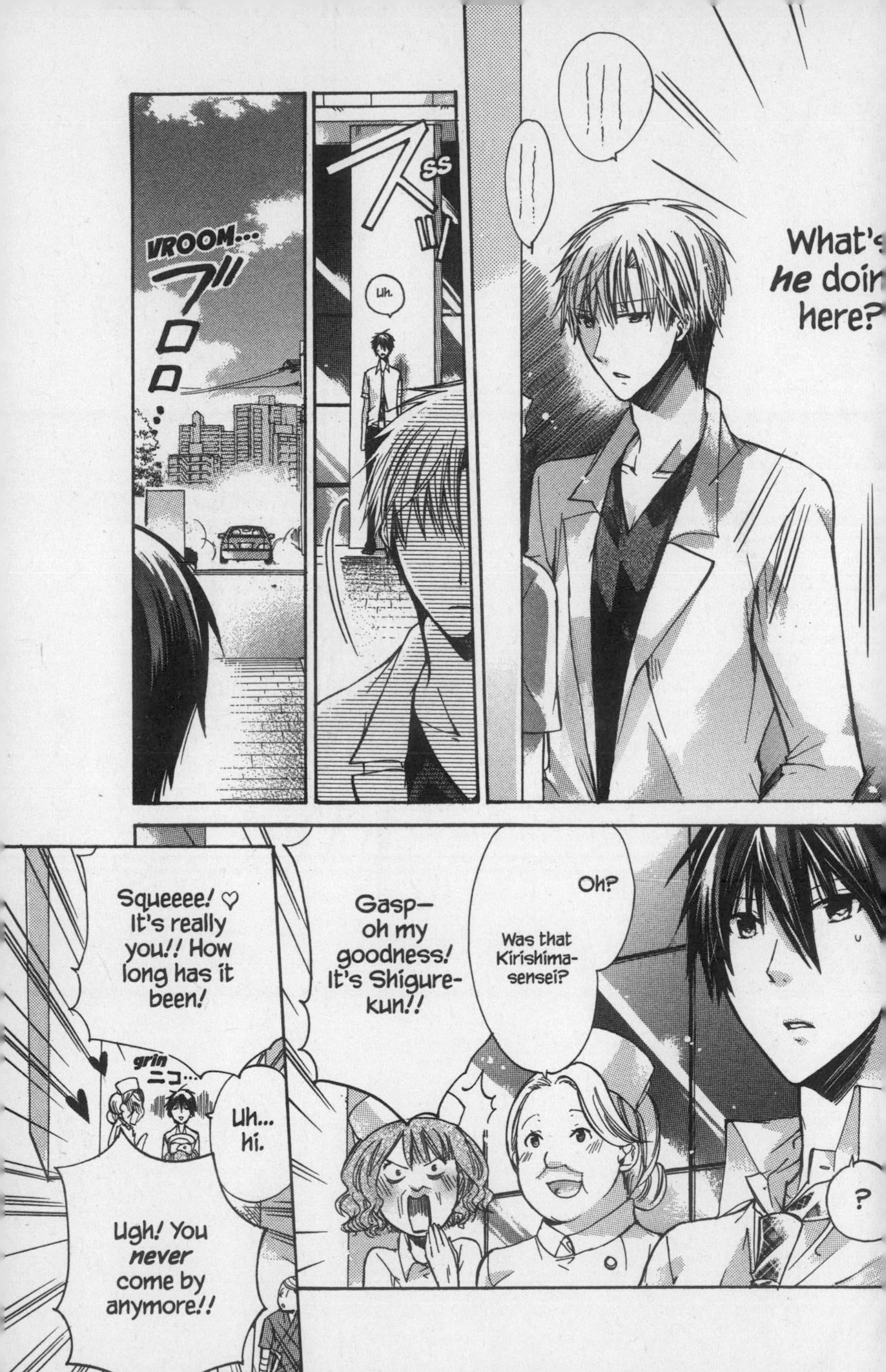
What's he doin here?
SS
スッ
Uh.
VROOM...
ブロロロ...
Oh?
Was that Kirishima-sensei?
?
Gasp—oh my goodness! It's Shigure-kun!!
Squeeee! ♡ It's really you!! How long has it been!
grin
ニコ...
Uh... hi.
Ugh! You never come by anymore!!

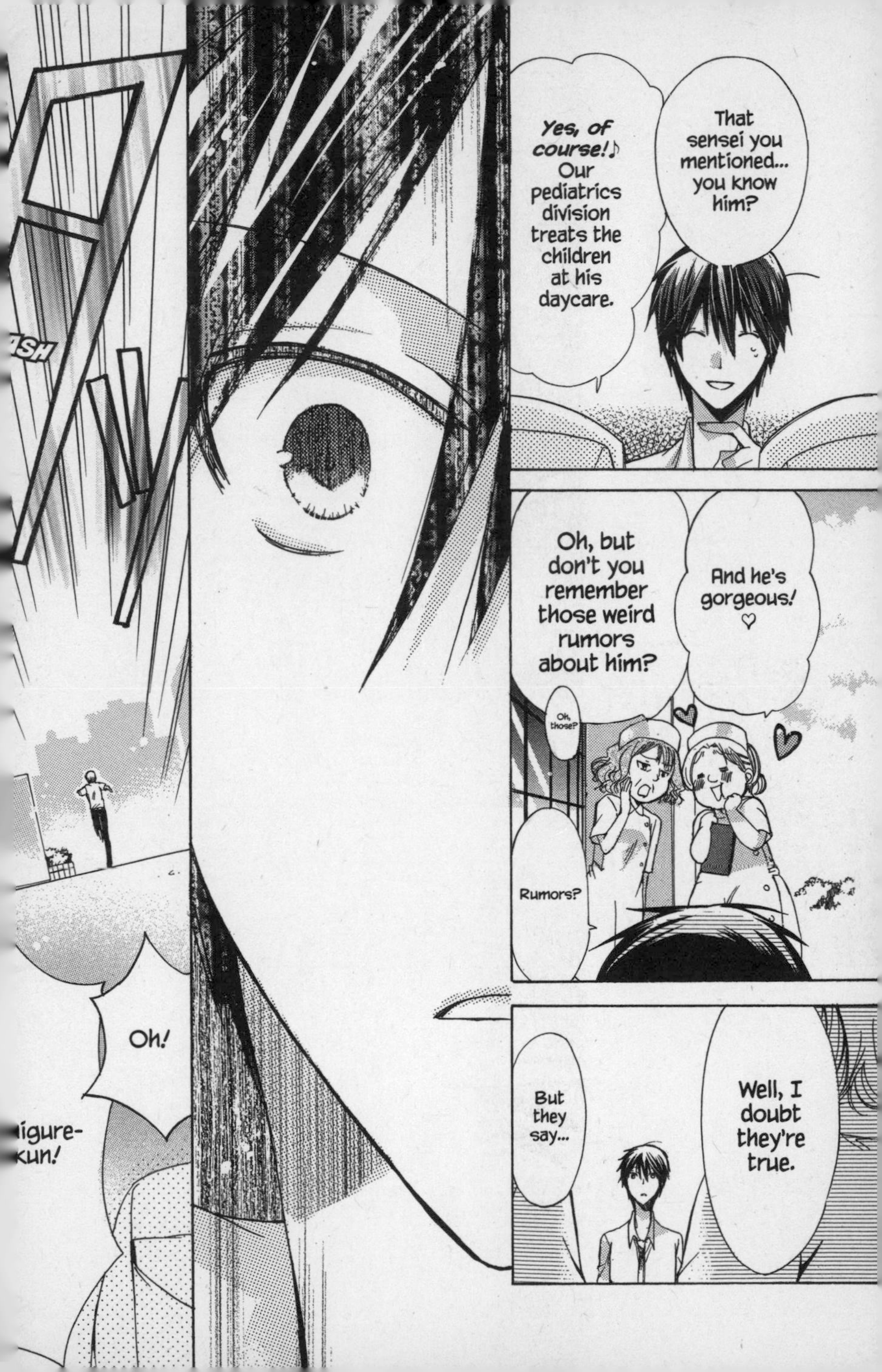
That sensei you mentioned... you know him?
Yes, of course!♪ Our pediatrics division treats the children at his daycare.
And he's gorgeous! ♡
Oh, but don't you remember those weird rumors about him?
Oh, those?
Rumors?
Well, I doubt they're true.
But they say...
Oh!
igure-kun!

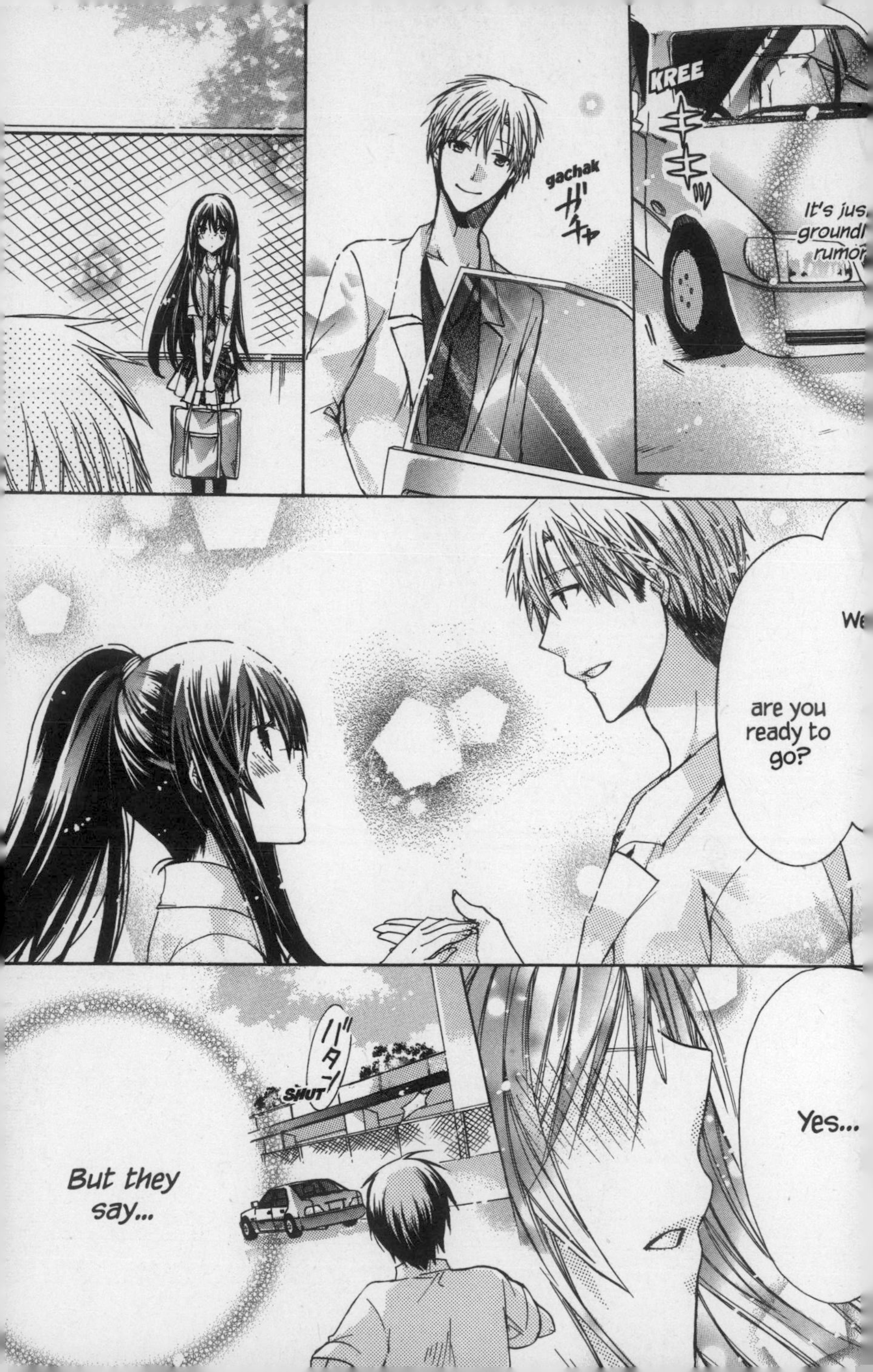
KREE
キキッ
It's jus
groundl
rumor
gachak
ガチャ
We
are you ready to go?
Yes...
バタン
SHUT
But they say...

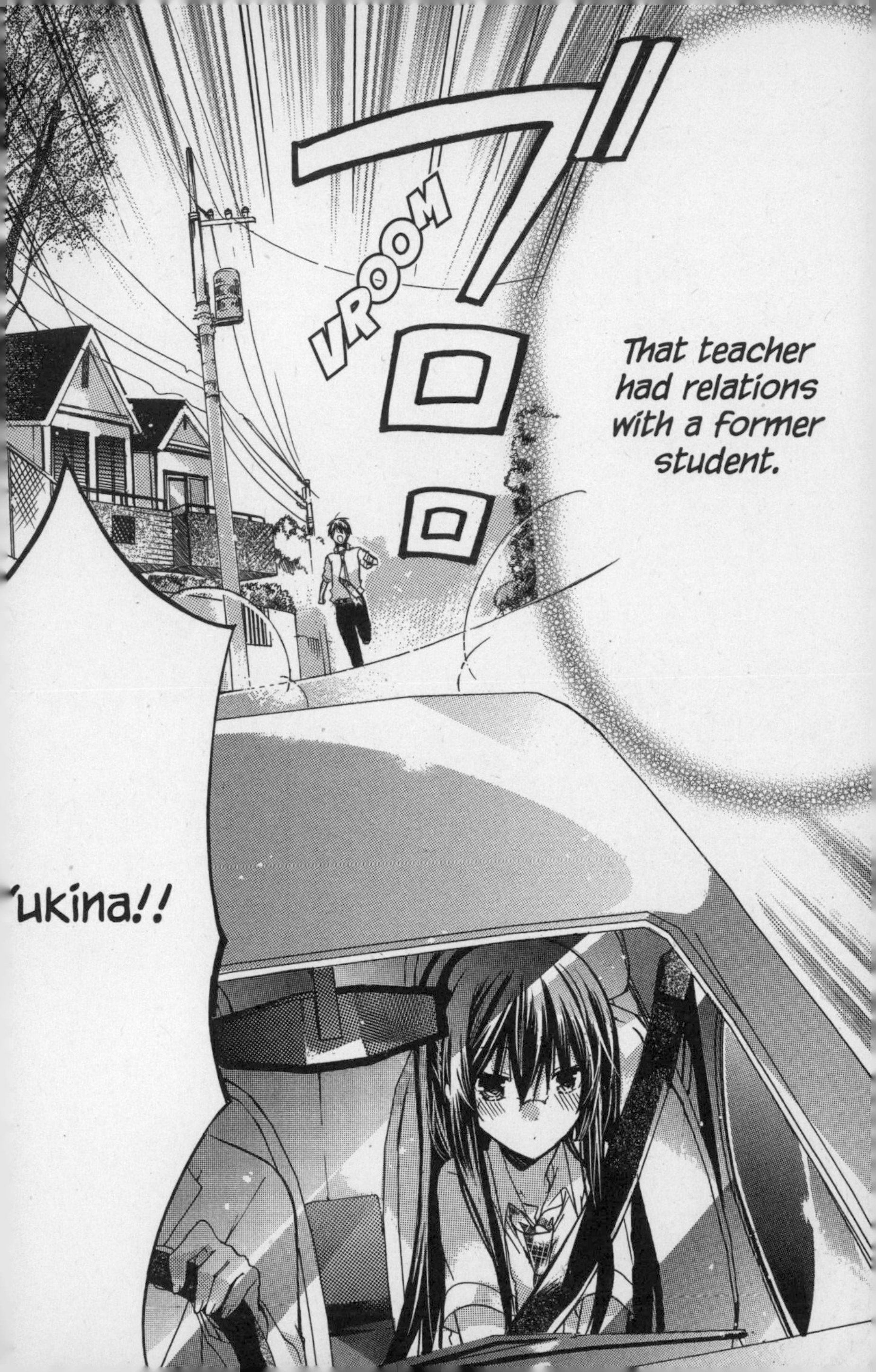
VROOM
That teacher had relations with a former student.
'ukina!!

Missions of Love

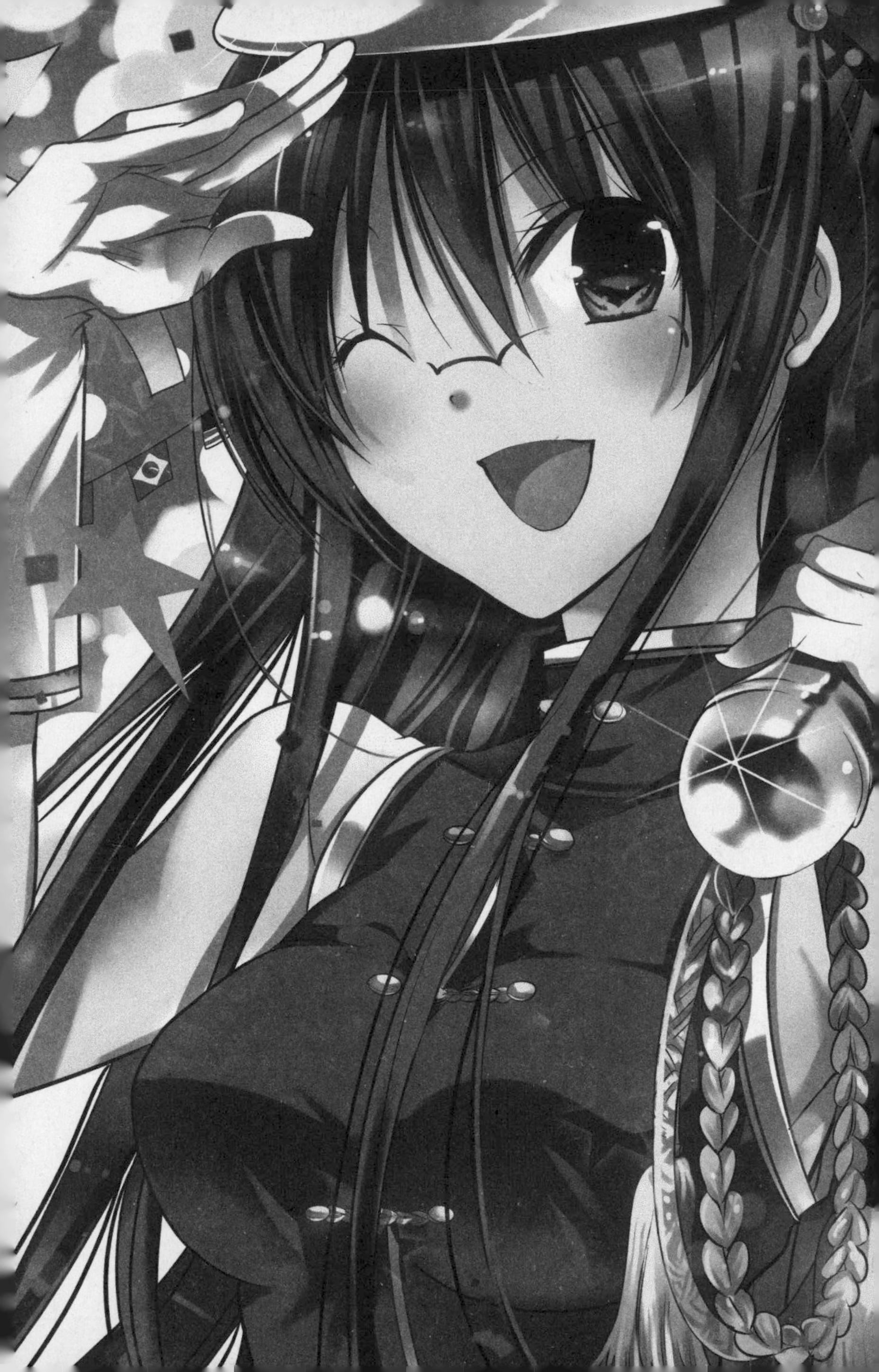

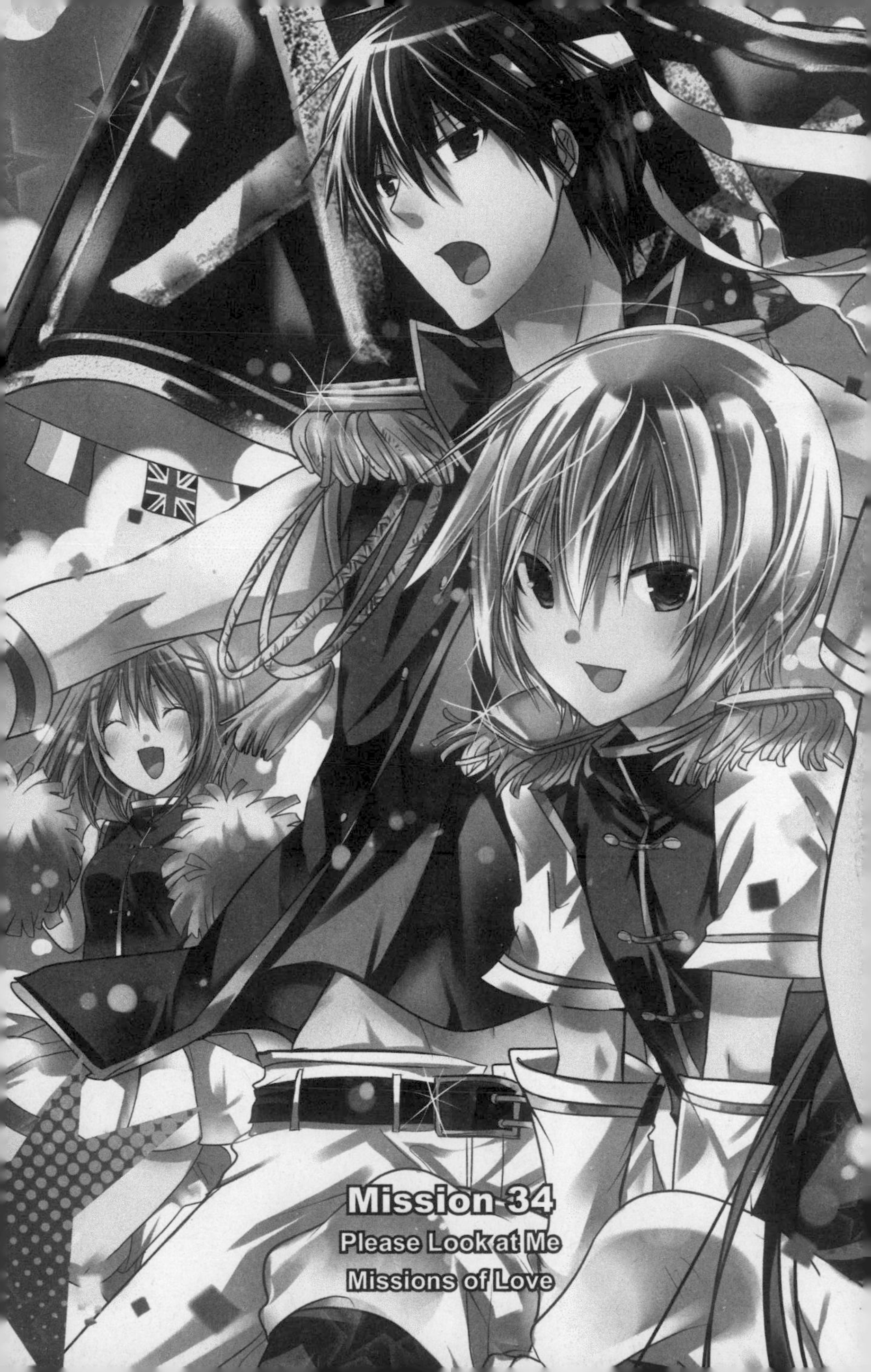
Mission 34
Please Look at Me
Missions of Love

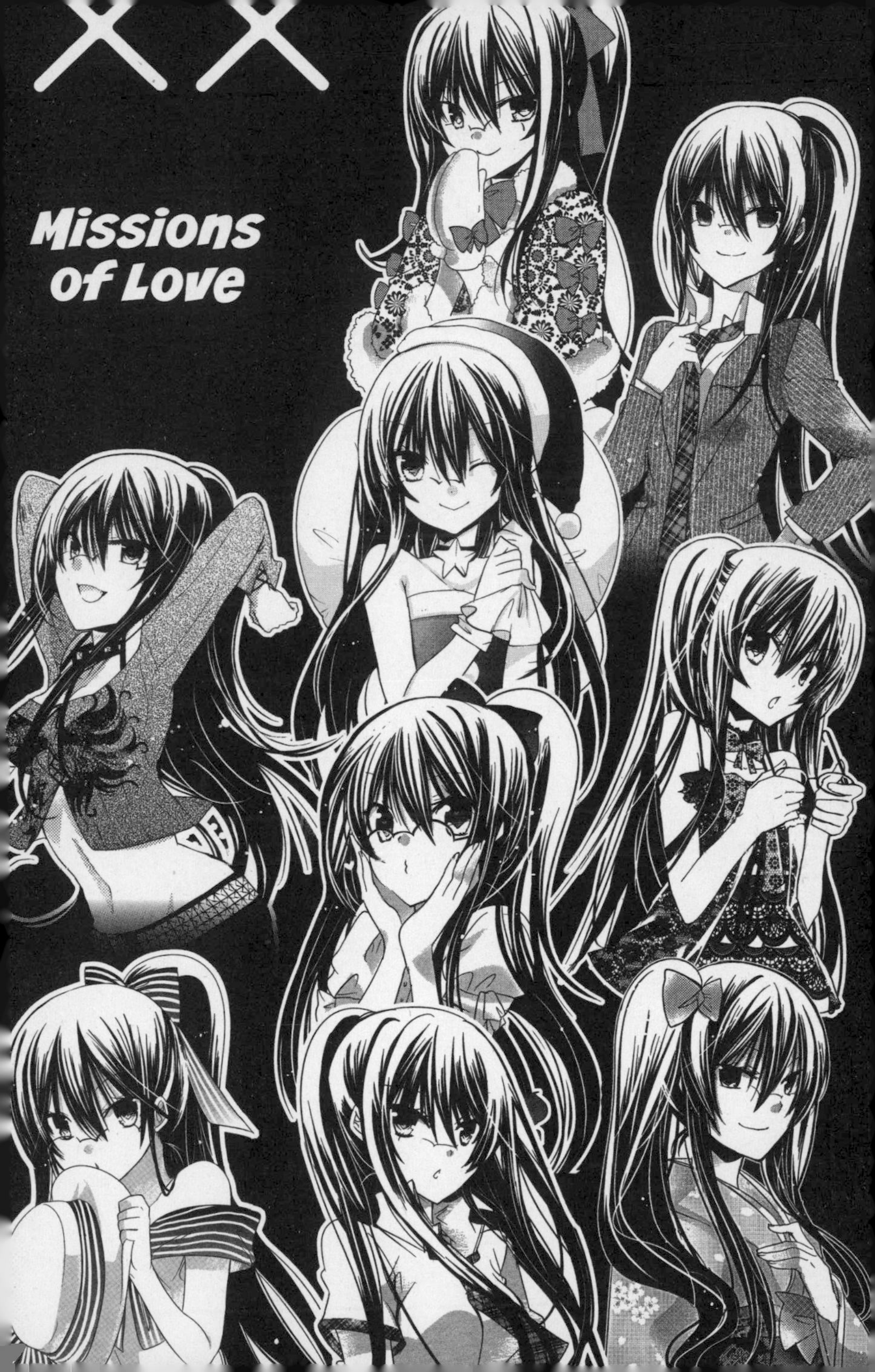
XX
Missions of Love

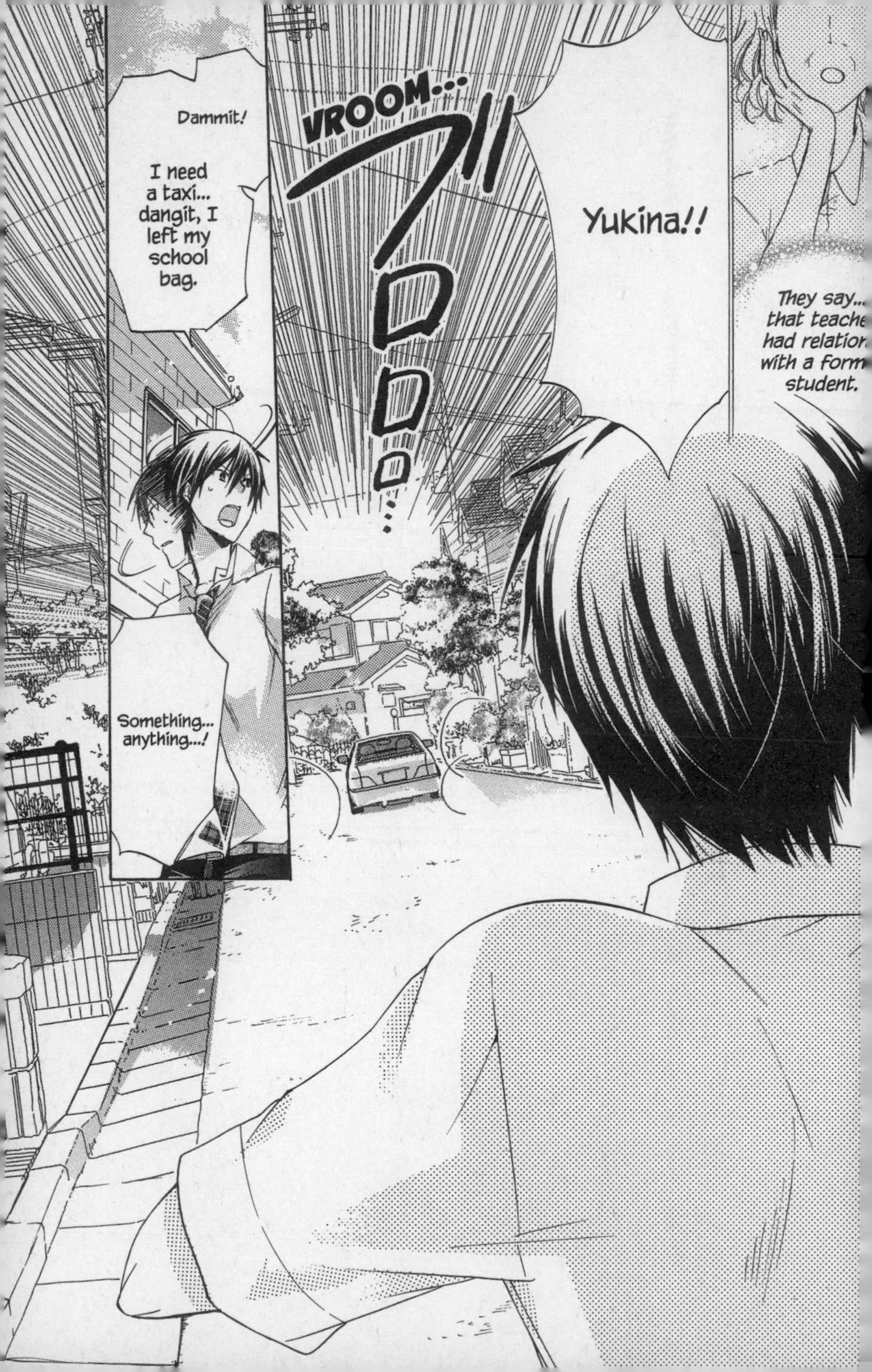
They say... that teache had relation with a form student.
Yukina!!
VROOM...
Dammit!
I need a taxi... dangit, I left my school bag.
Something... anything...!

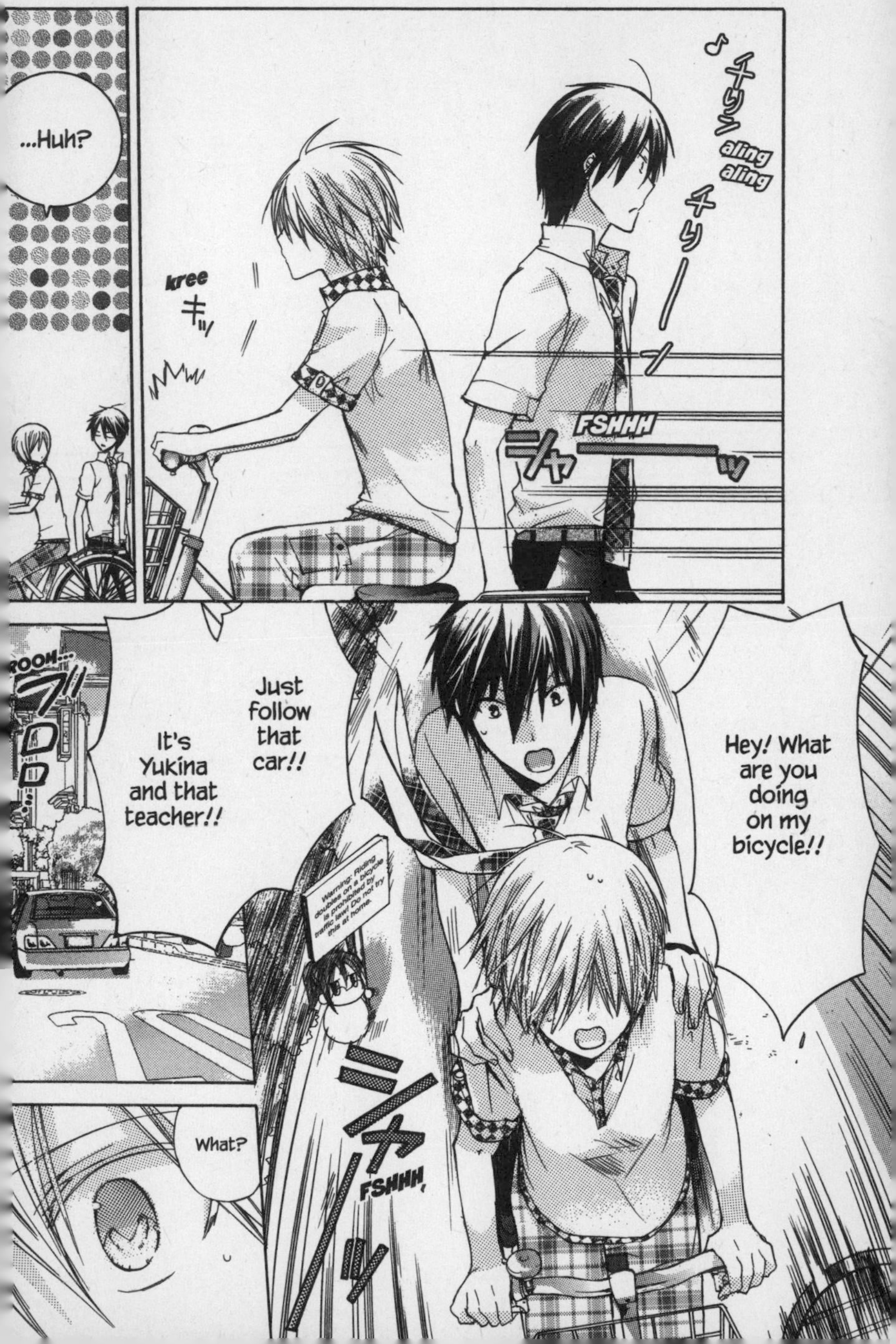
aling aling
kree
FSHHH
...Huh?
Hey! What are you doing on my bicycle!!
Just follow that car!!
It's Yukina and that teacher!!
VROOM...
Warning: Riding doubles on a bicycle is prohibited by traffic law! Do not try this at home.
FSHHH
What?

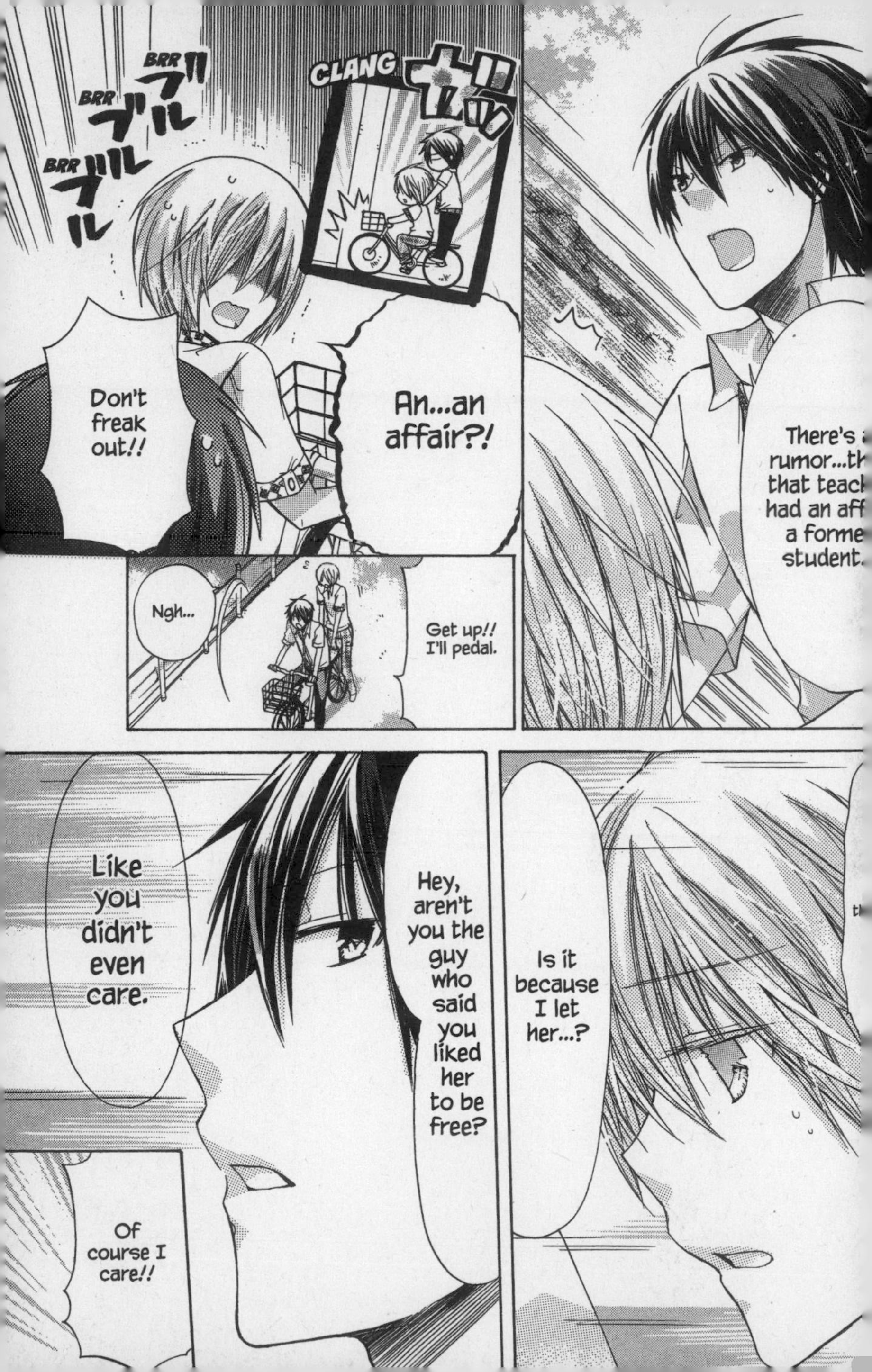
There's a
rumor...th
that teach
had an aff
a forme
student.
CLANG
BRR BRR BRR
An...an affair?!
Don't freak out!!
Get up!! I'll pedal.
Ngh...
th
Is it because I let her...?
Hey, aren't you the guy who said you liked her to be free?
Like you didn't even care.
Of course I care!!

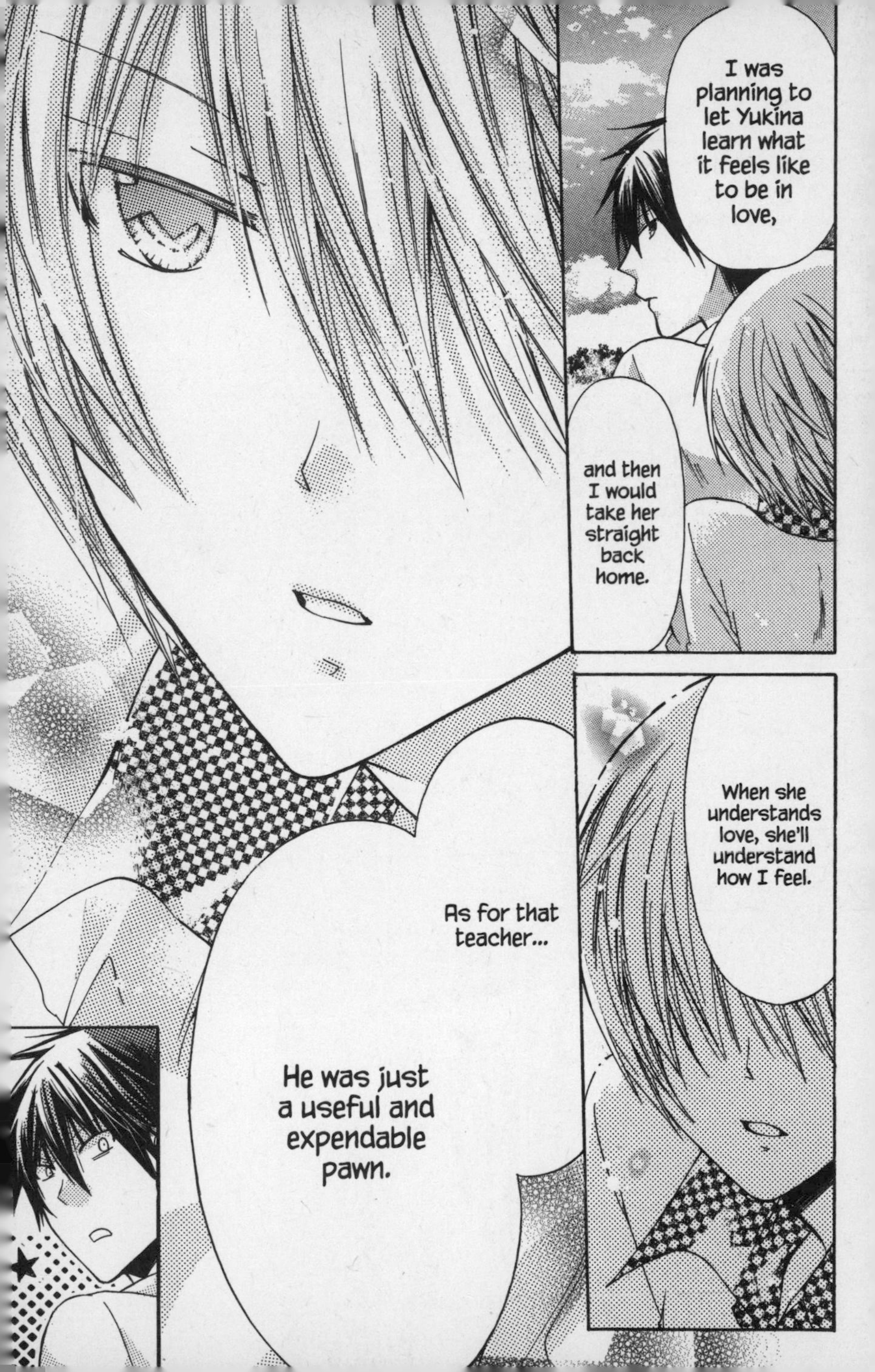
I was planning to let Yukina learn what it feels like to be in love,
and then I would take her straight back home.
When she understands love, she'll understand how I feel.
As for that teacher...
He was just a useful and expendable pawn.

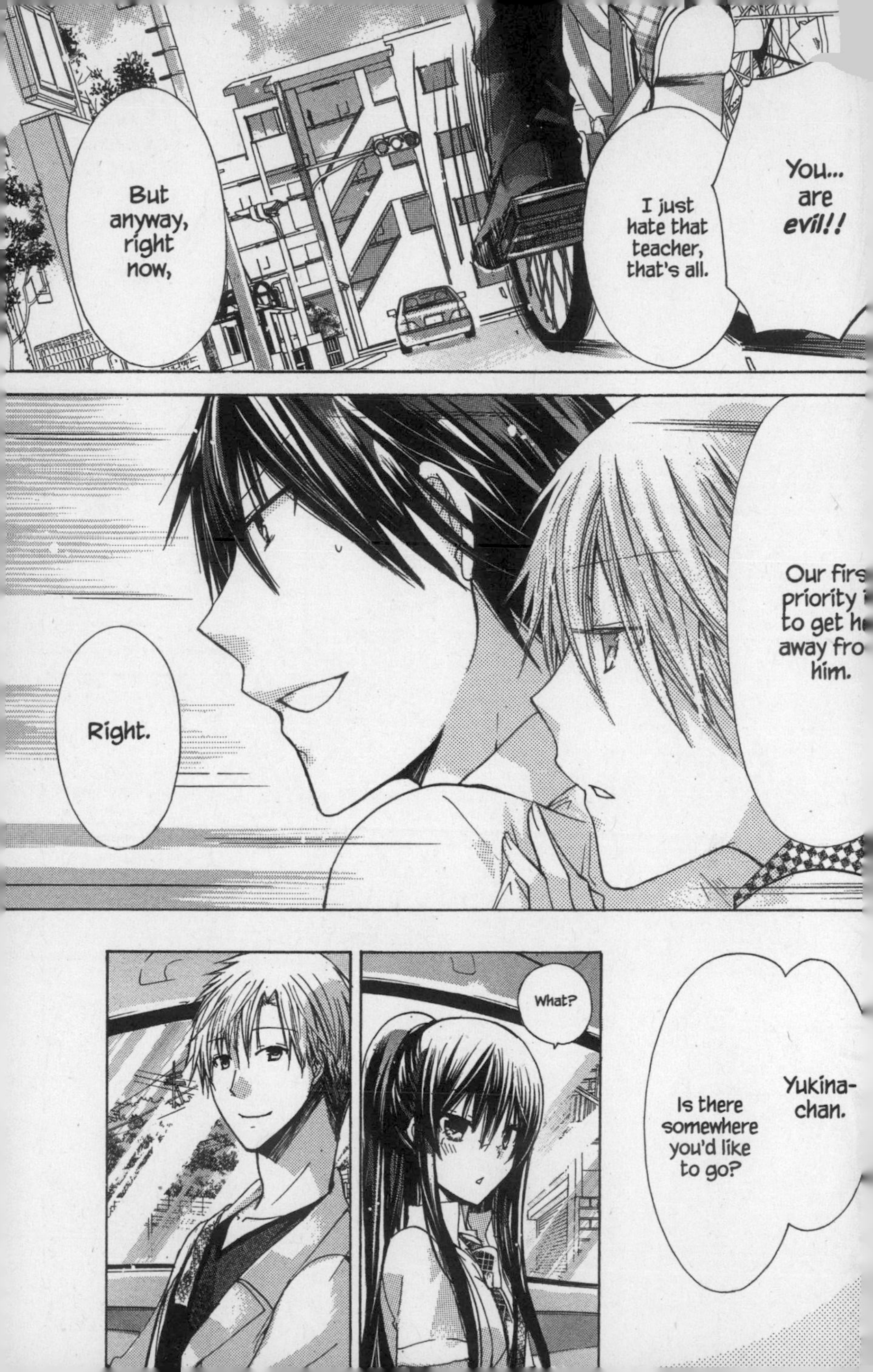
You... are evil!!
I just hate that teacher, that's all.
But anyway, right now,
Our firs priority i to get h away fro him.
Right.
Yukina-chan.
Is there somewhere you'd like to go?
What?

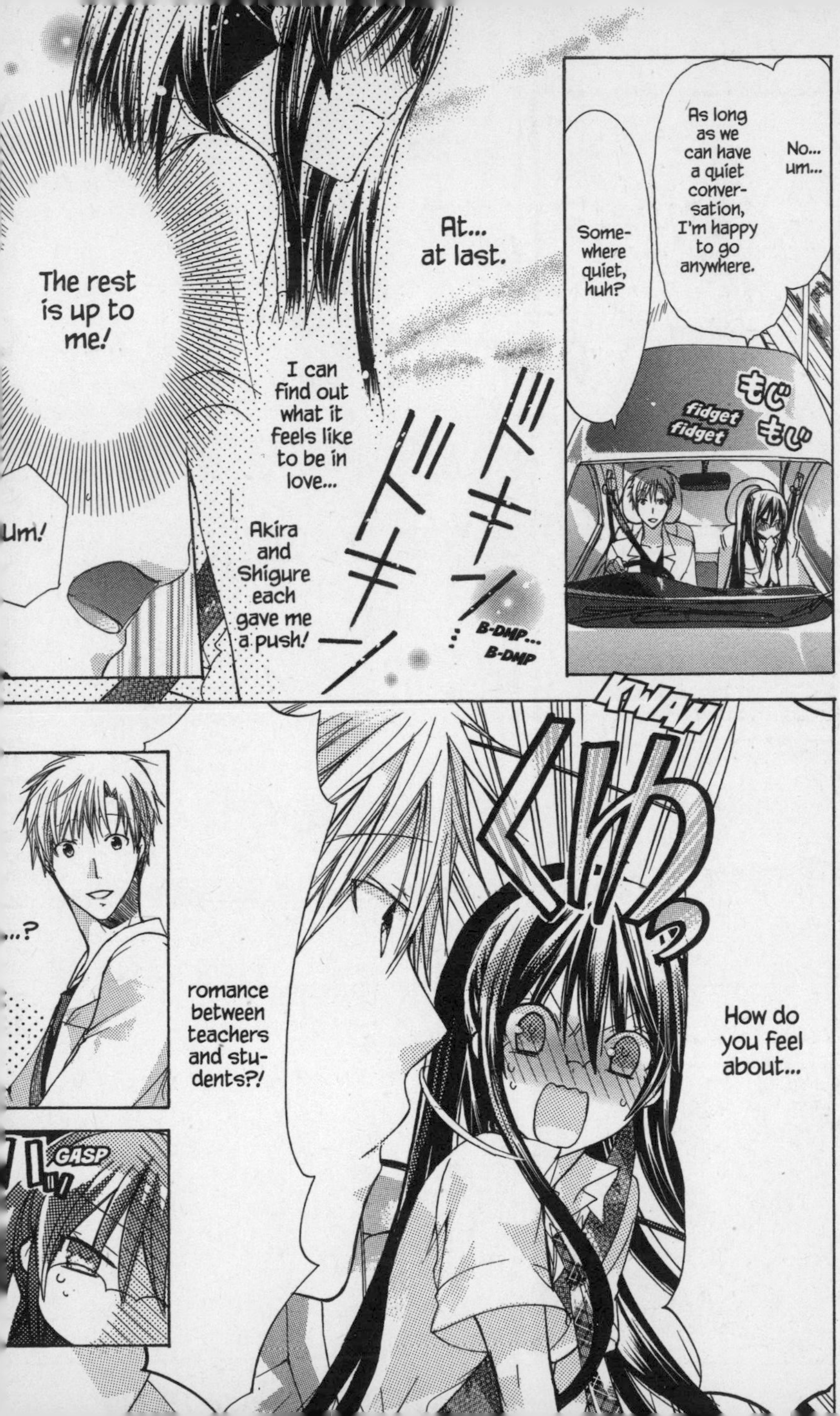
No... um...
As long as we can have a quiet conversation, I'm happy to go anywhere.
Some-where quiet, huh?
もじもじ
fidget fidget
At... at last.
ドキンドキン
B-DMP... B-DMP
I can find out what it feels like to be in love...
Akira and Shigure each gave me a push!
The rest is up to me!
Um!
KWAH
くわっ
How do you feel about...
romance between teachers and students?!
...?
GASP

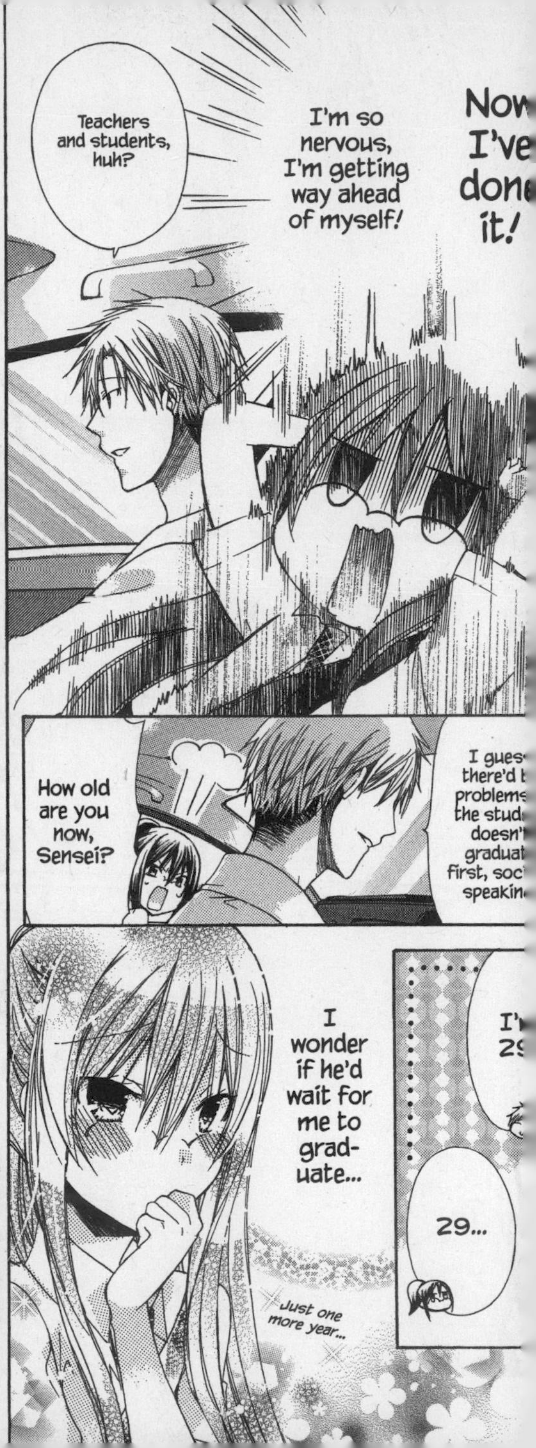
Now I've done it!
I'm so nervous, I'm getting way ahead of myself!
Teachers and students, huh?
I gues there'd b problems the stud doesn't graduat first, soci speakin
How old are you now, Sensei?
I' 29
29...
I wonder if he'd wait for me to grad-uate...
Just one more year...

The Freezing Bed 2

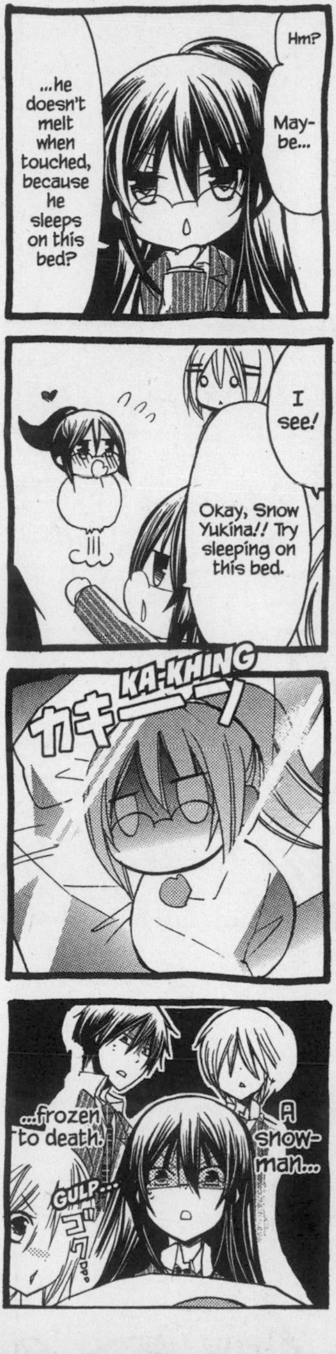
Hm?
May-be...
...he doesn't melt when touched, because he sleeps on this bed?
I see!
Okay, Snow Yukina!! Try sleeping on this bed.
カキーーーン
KA-KHING
A snow-man...
...frozen to death.
GULP...
ゴク

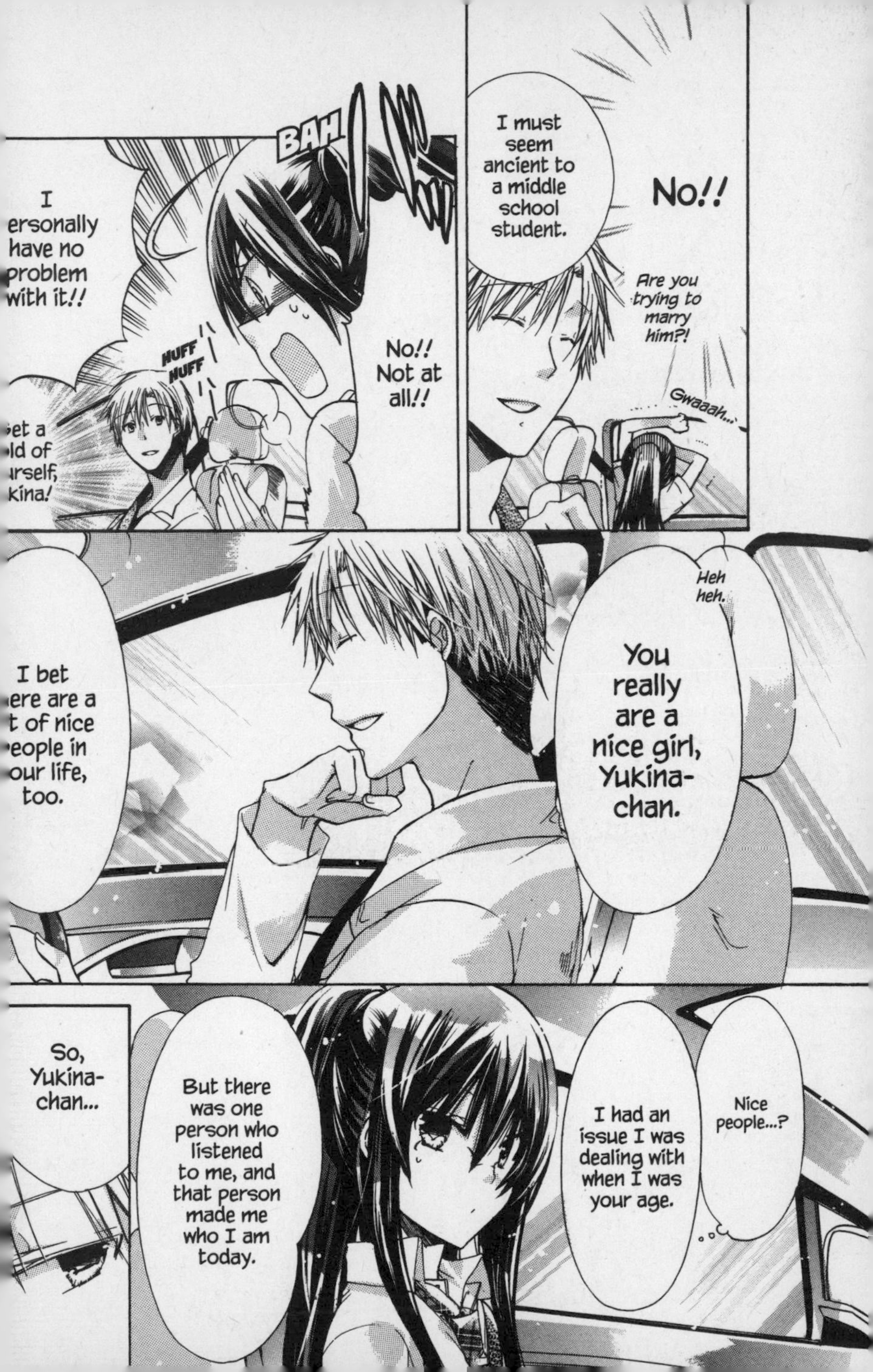
I must seem ancient to a middle school student.
No!!
Are you trying to marry him?!
Gwaaah...
BAH
No!! Not at all!!
HUFF HUFF
I ersonally have no problem with it!!
et a ld of urself, kina!
Heh heh.
You really are a nice girl, Yukina-chan.
I bet ere are a t of nice eople in our life, too.
Nice people...?
I had an issue I was dealing with when I was your age.
But there was one person who listened to me, and that person made me who I am today.
So, Yukina-chan...

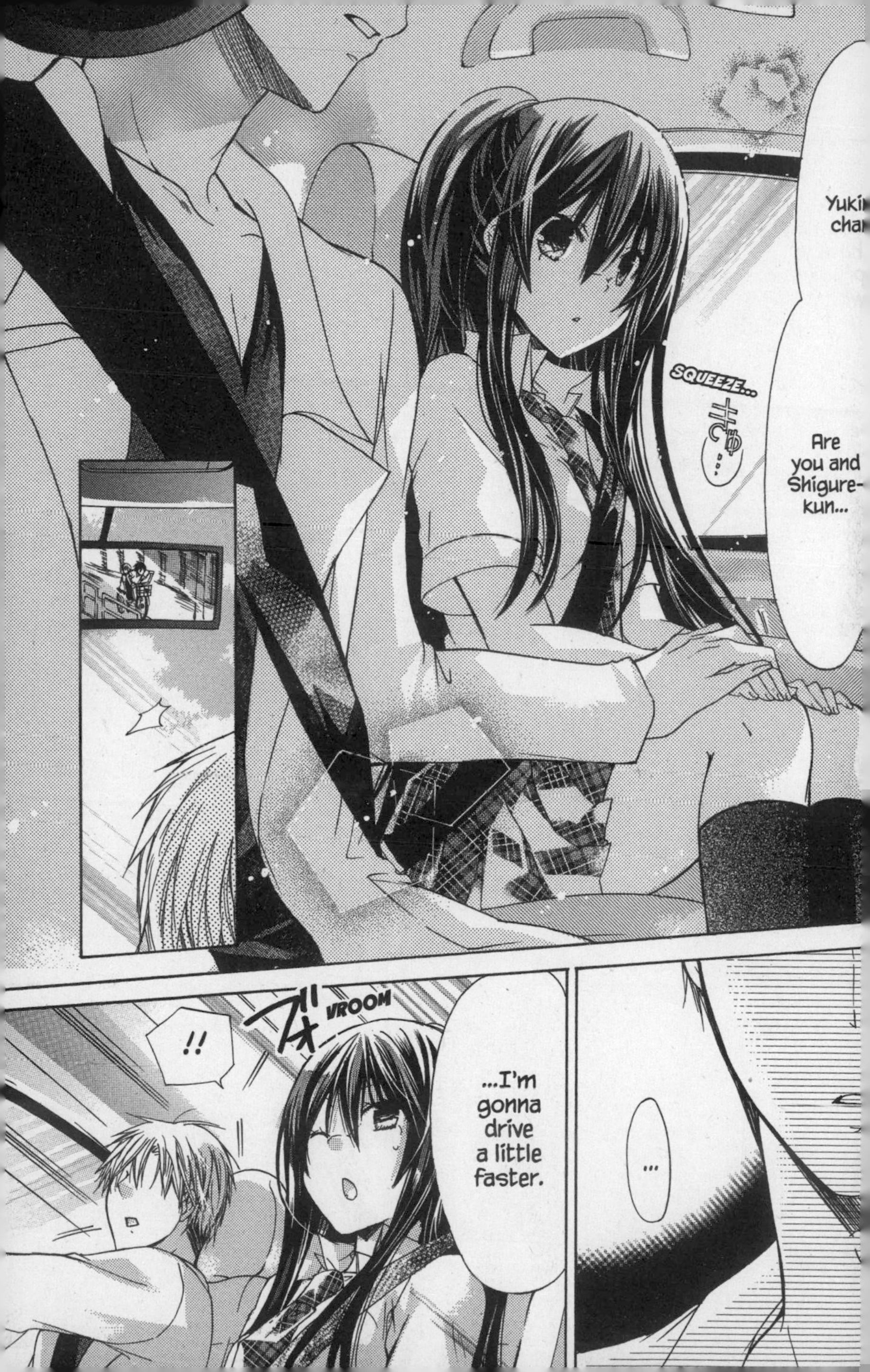

Yuki cha
Are you and Shigure-kun...
SQUEEZE...
きゅ...
...
...I'm gonna drive a little faster.
VROOM
!!

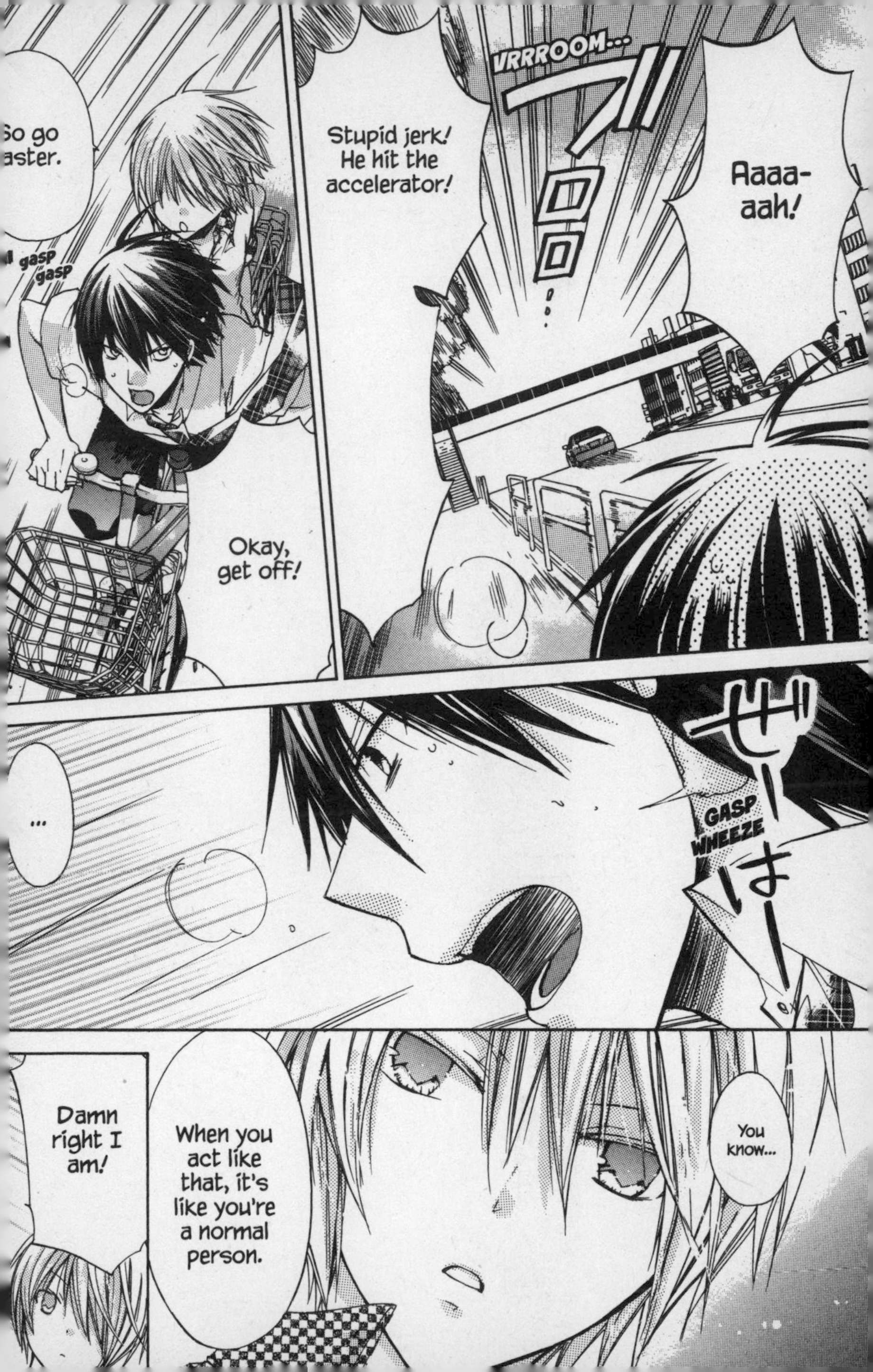
VRRROOM...
Aaaa-aah!
Stupid jerk! He hit the accelerator!
So go aster.
gasp gasp
Okay, get off!
GASP WHEEZE
...
You know...
When you act like that, it's like you're a normal person.
Damn right I am!

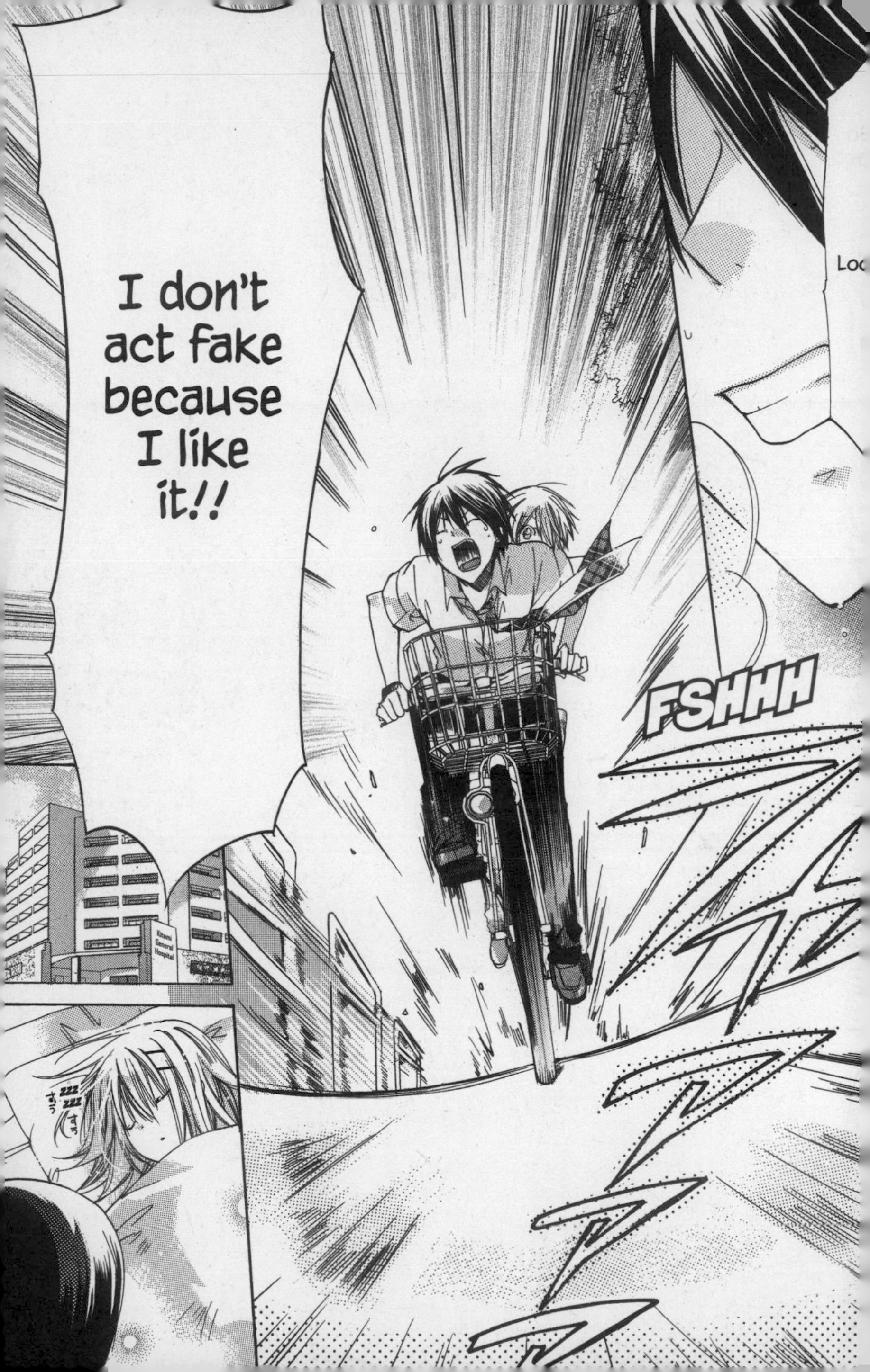
I don't act fake because I like it!!
FSHHH
Kitami General Hospital
zzz zzz
すぅ すぅ

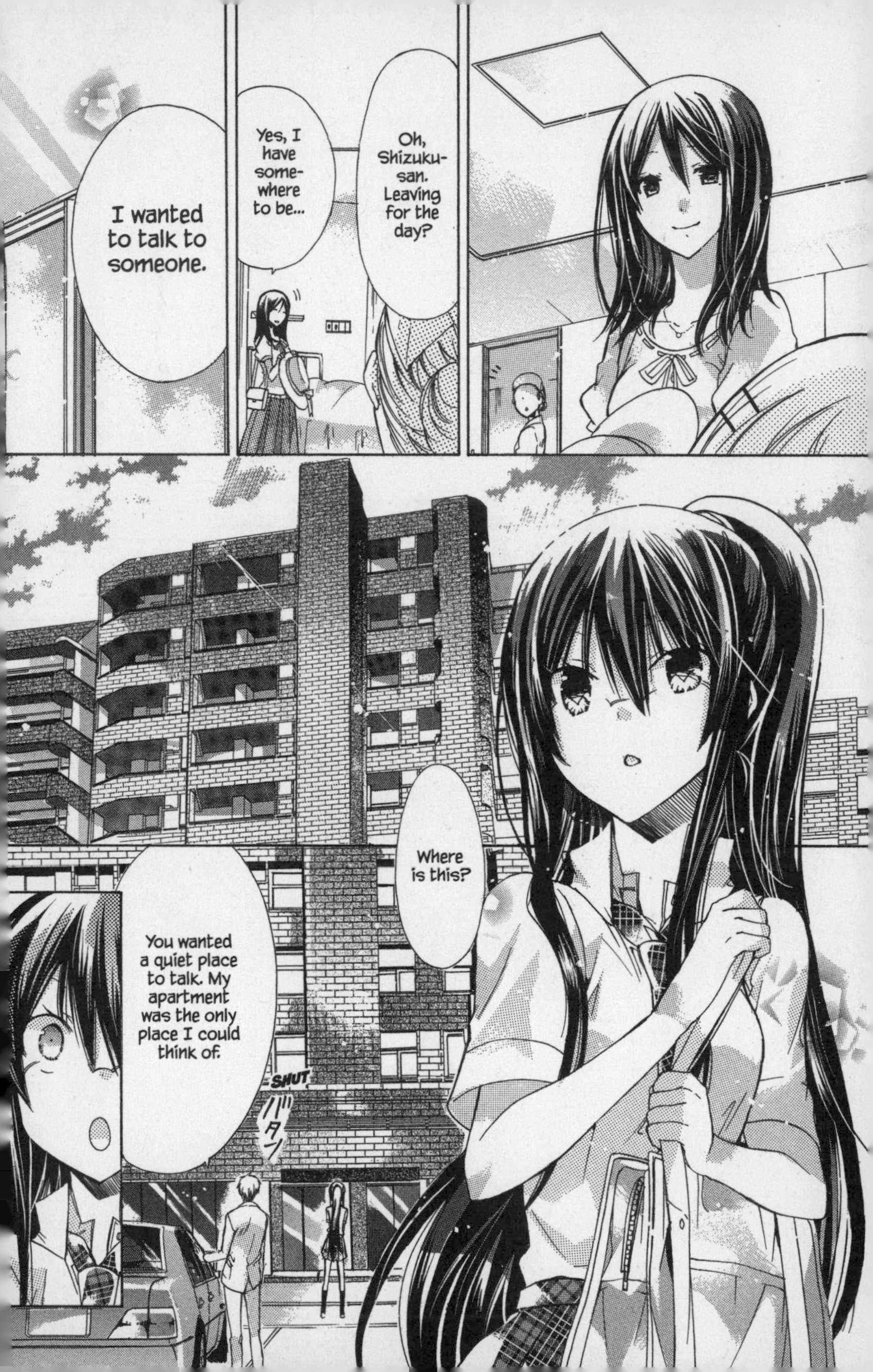
Oh, Shizuku-san. Leaving for the day?
Yes, I have some-where to be...
I wanted to talk to someone.
Where is this?
You wanted a quiet place to talk. My apartment was the only place I could think of.
SHUT
バタン

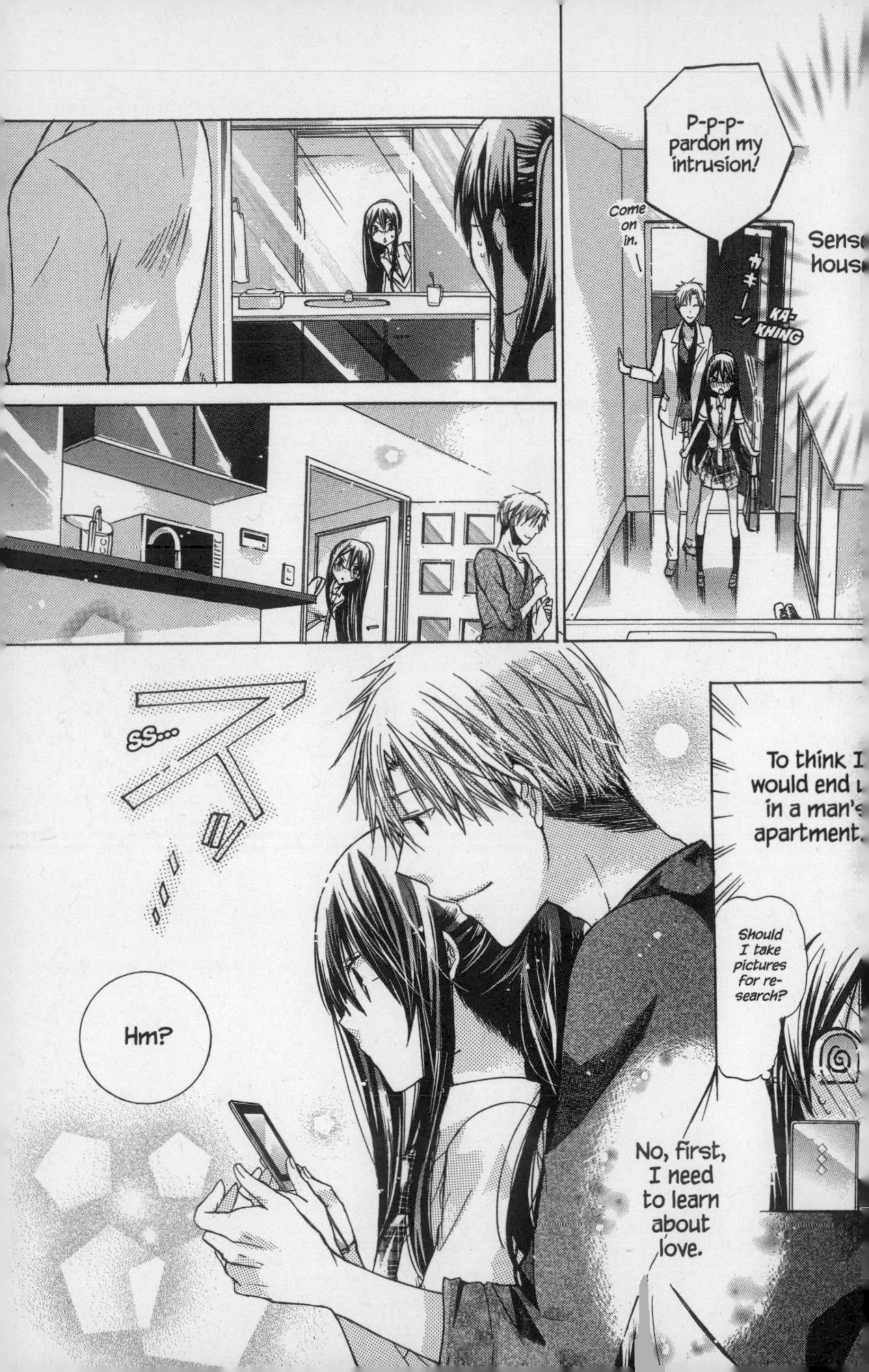

Sense hous
P-p-p-pardon my intrusion!
Come on in.
カキーン
KA-KHING
To think I would end u in a man's apartment.
Should I take pictures for re-search?
No, first, I need to learn about love.
SS...
Hm?

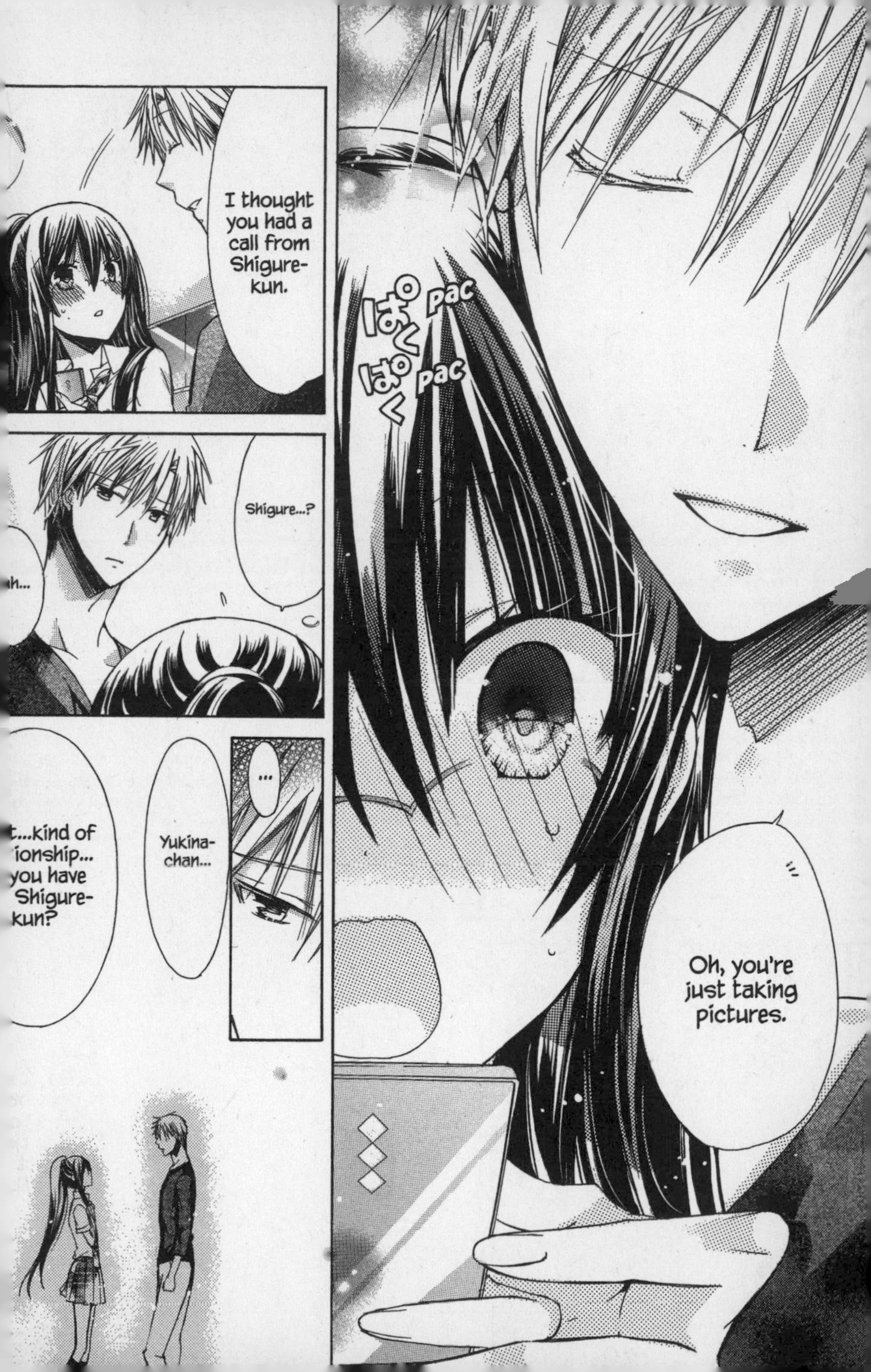
ぱく pac
ぱく pac
Oh, you're just taking pictures.
I thought you had a call from Shigure-kun.
Shigure...?
h...
...
Yukina-chan...
t...kind of ionship... you have Shigure-kun?

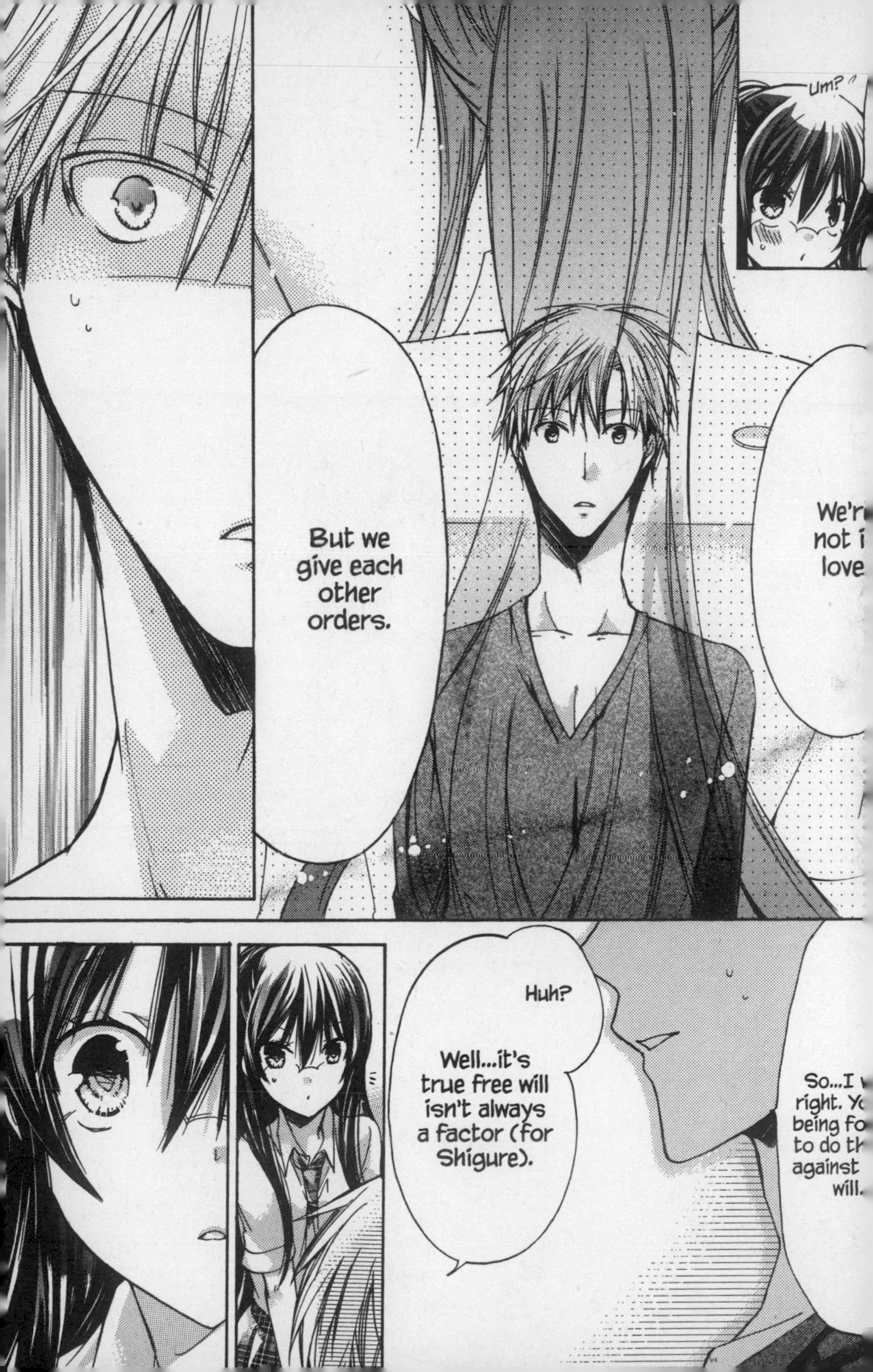
Um?
We'r
not i
love
But we give each other orders.
So...I w
right. Yo
being fo
to do th
against
will.
Huh?
Well...it's true free will isn't always a factor (for Shigure).

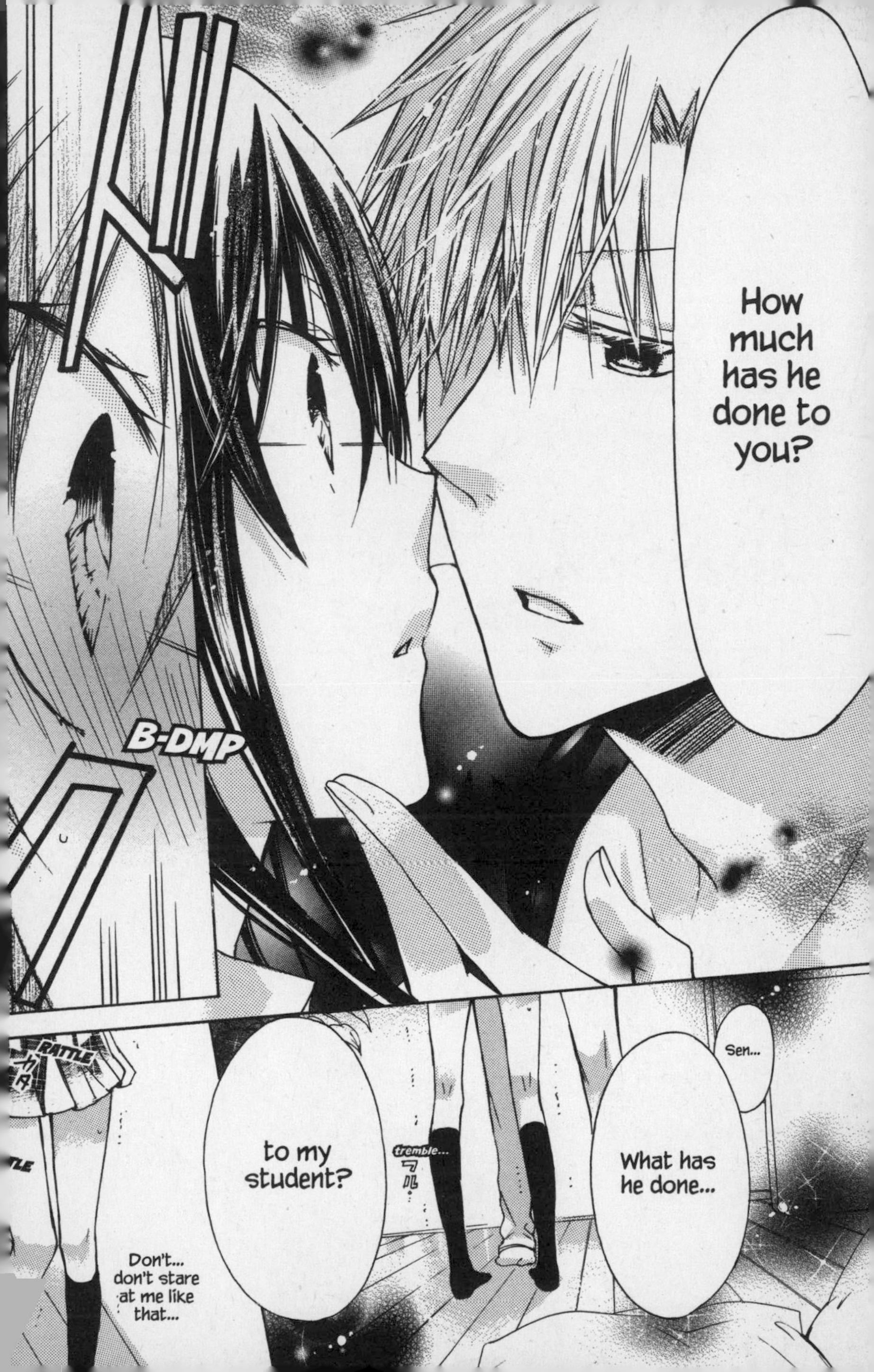
How much has he done to you?
B-DMP
Sen...
What has he done...
tremble...
to my student?
RATTLE
Don't... don't stare at me like that...

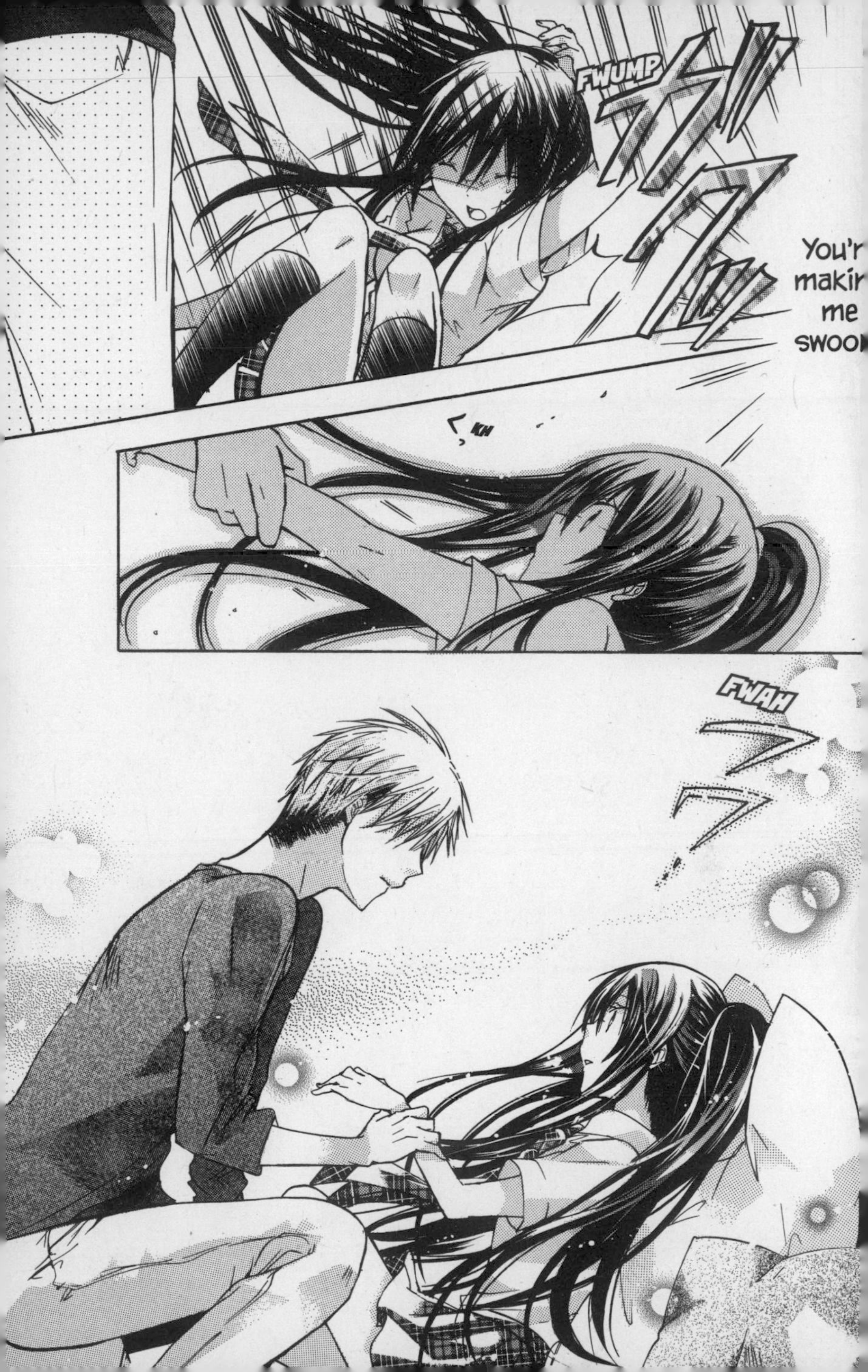
You'r maki me swoo
FWUMP
KH
FWAH

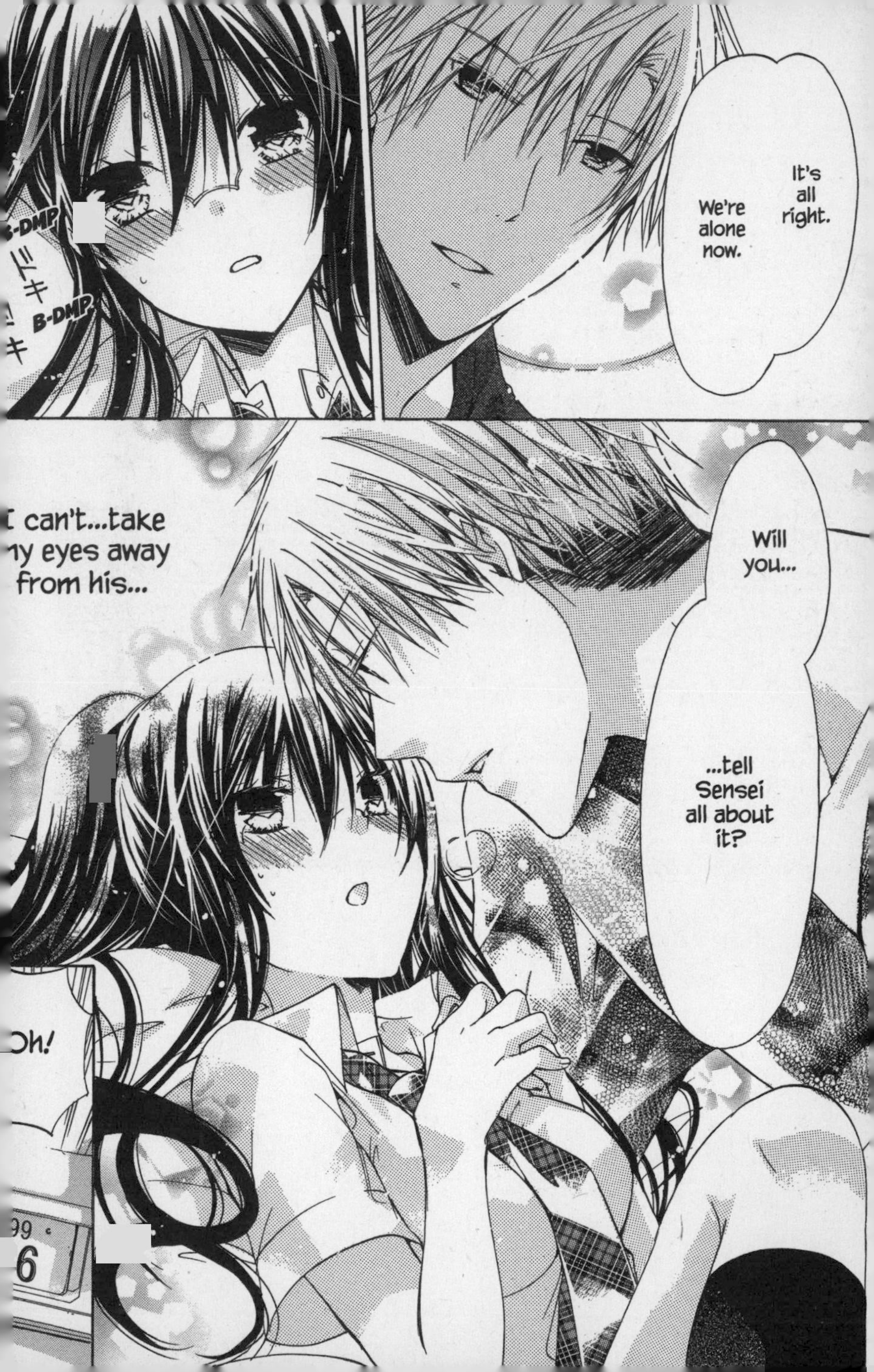
It's all right.
We're alone now.
B-DMP
ドキ
B-DMP
キ
Will you...
...tell Sensei all about it?
can't...take
y eyes away
from his...
Oh!

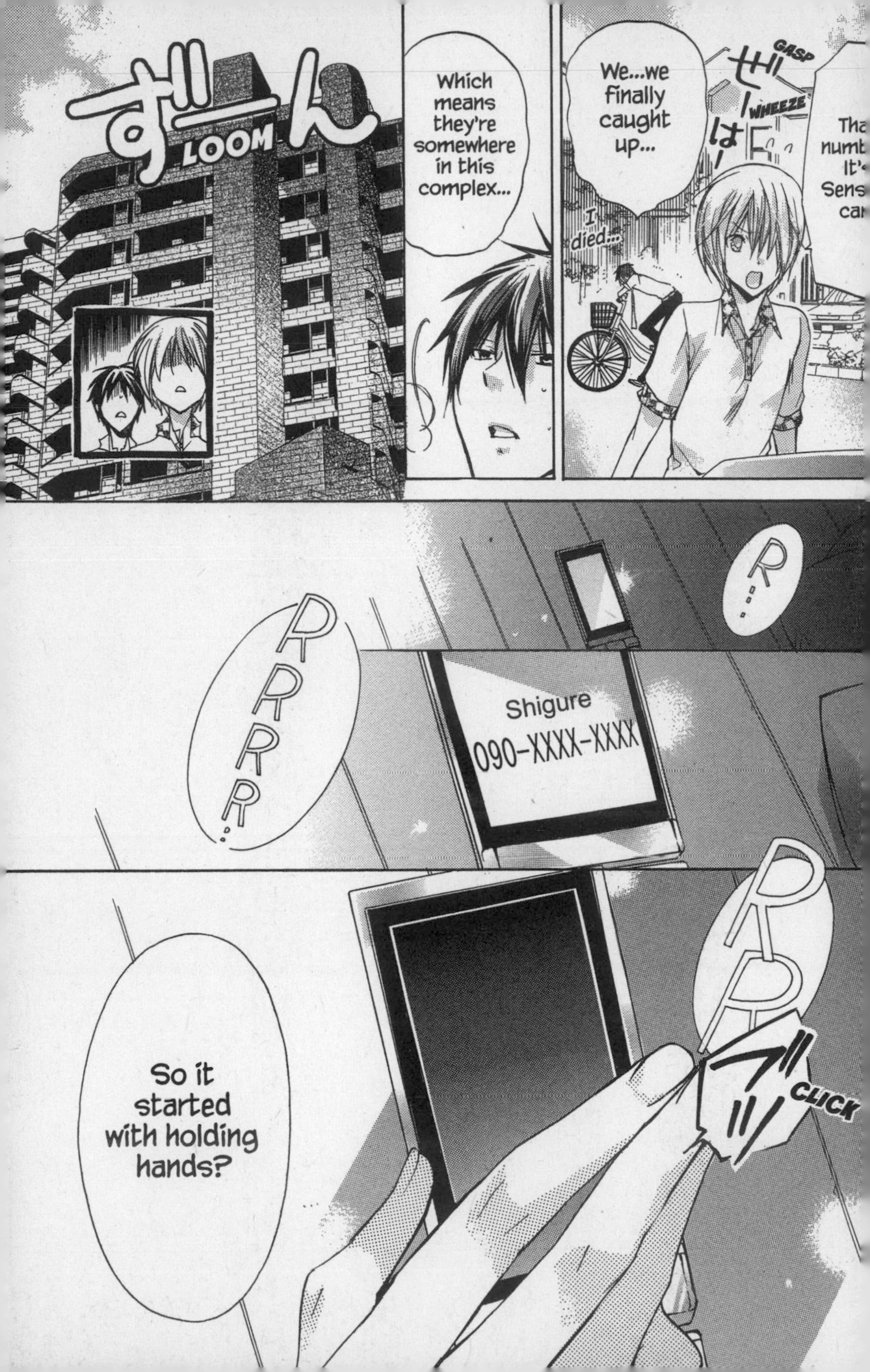

GASP
WHEEZE
We...we finally caught up...
I died...
Which means they're somewhere in this complex...
LOOM
R...
RRRR..
Shigure
090-XXXX-XXXX
RR
CLICK
So it started with holding hands?

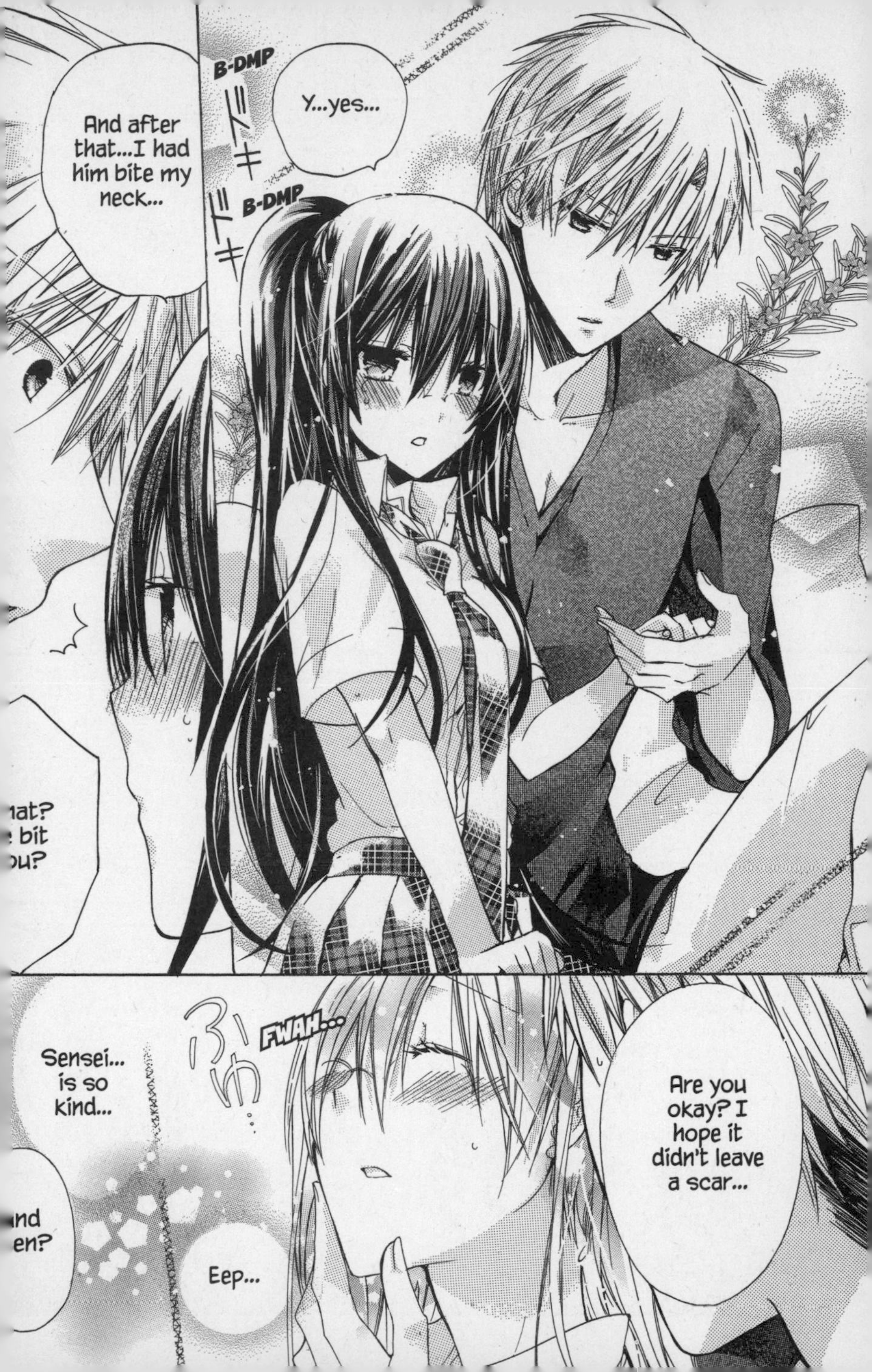
B-DMP
Y...yes...
B-DMP
And after that...I had him bite my neck...
Are you okay? I hope it didn't leave a scar...
FWAH...
Sensei... is so kind...
Eep...

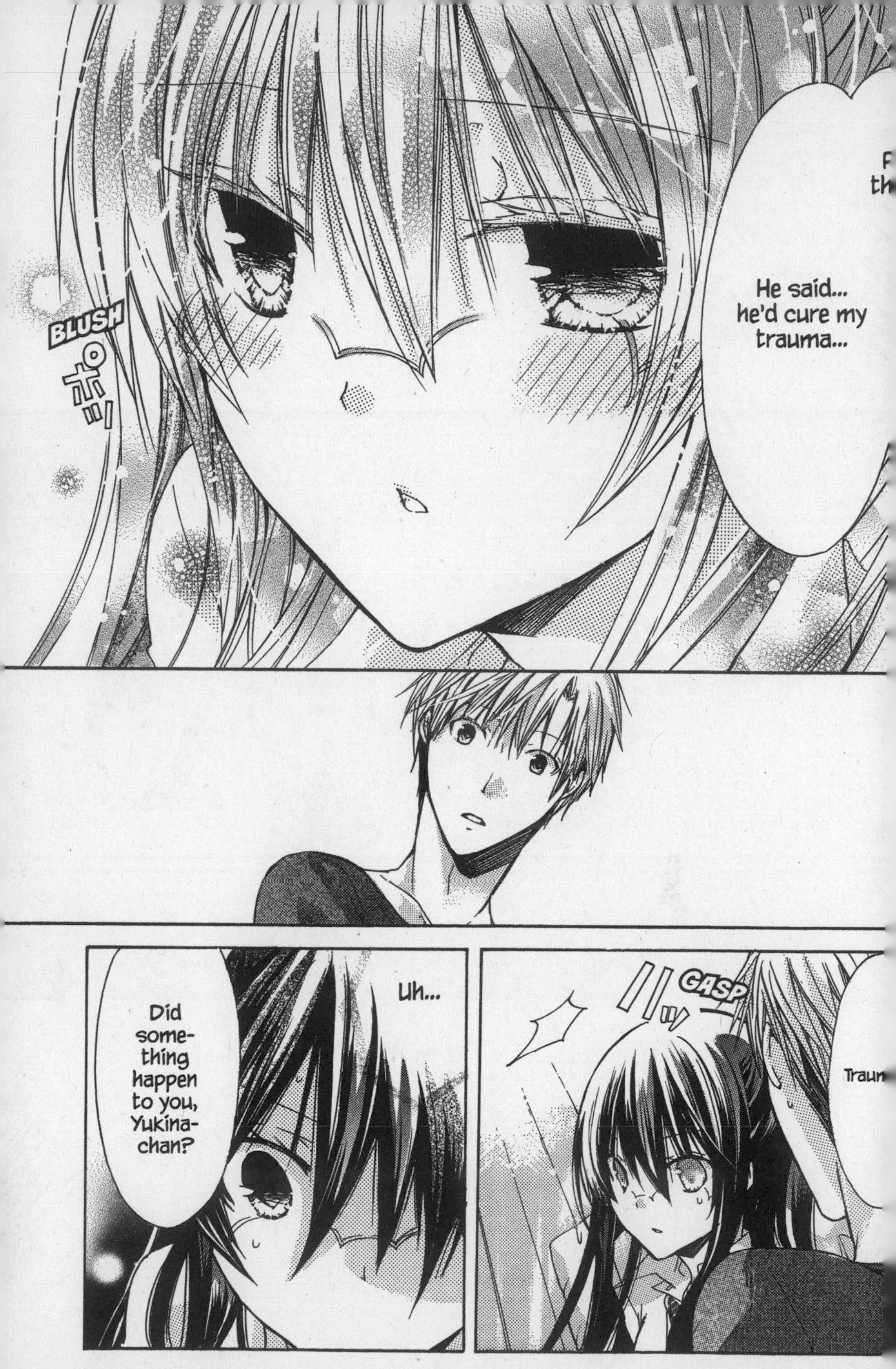
He said... he'd cure my trauma...
BLUSH
GASP
Uh...
Did something-thing happen to you, Yukina-chan?

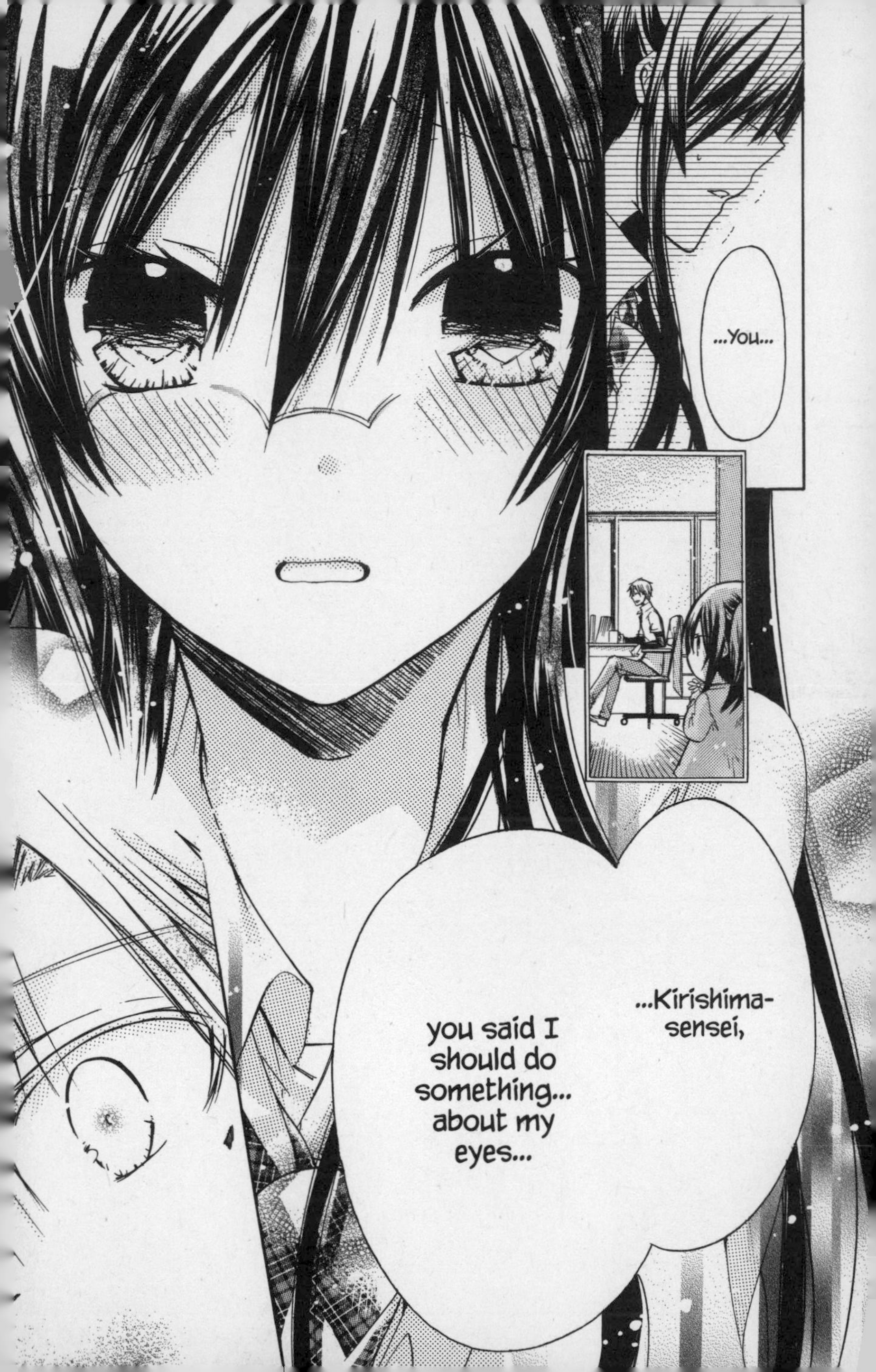
...You...
...Kirishima-sensei,
you said I should do something... about my eyes...

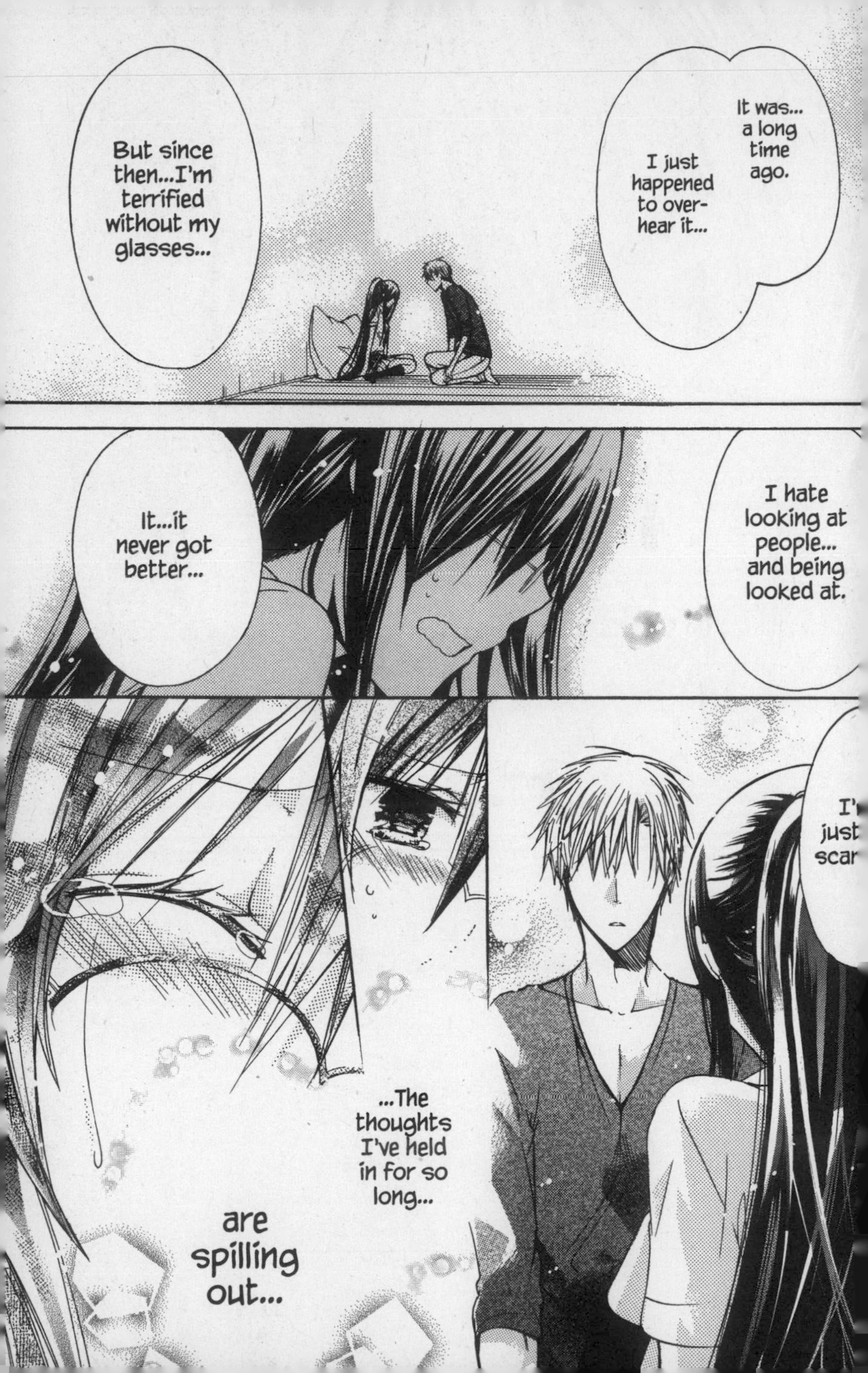
It was... a long time ago.
I just happened to over-hear it...
But since then...I'm terrified without my glasses...
I hate looking at people... and being looked at.
It...it never got better...
I' just scar
...The thoughts I've held in for so long...
are spilling out...

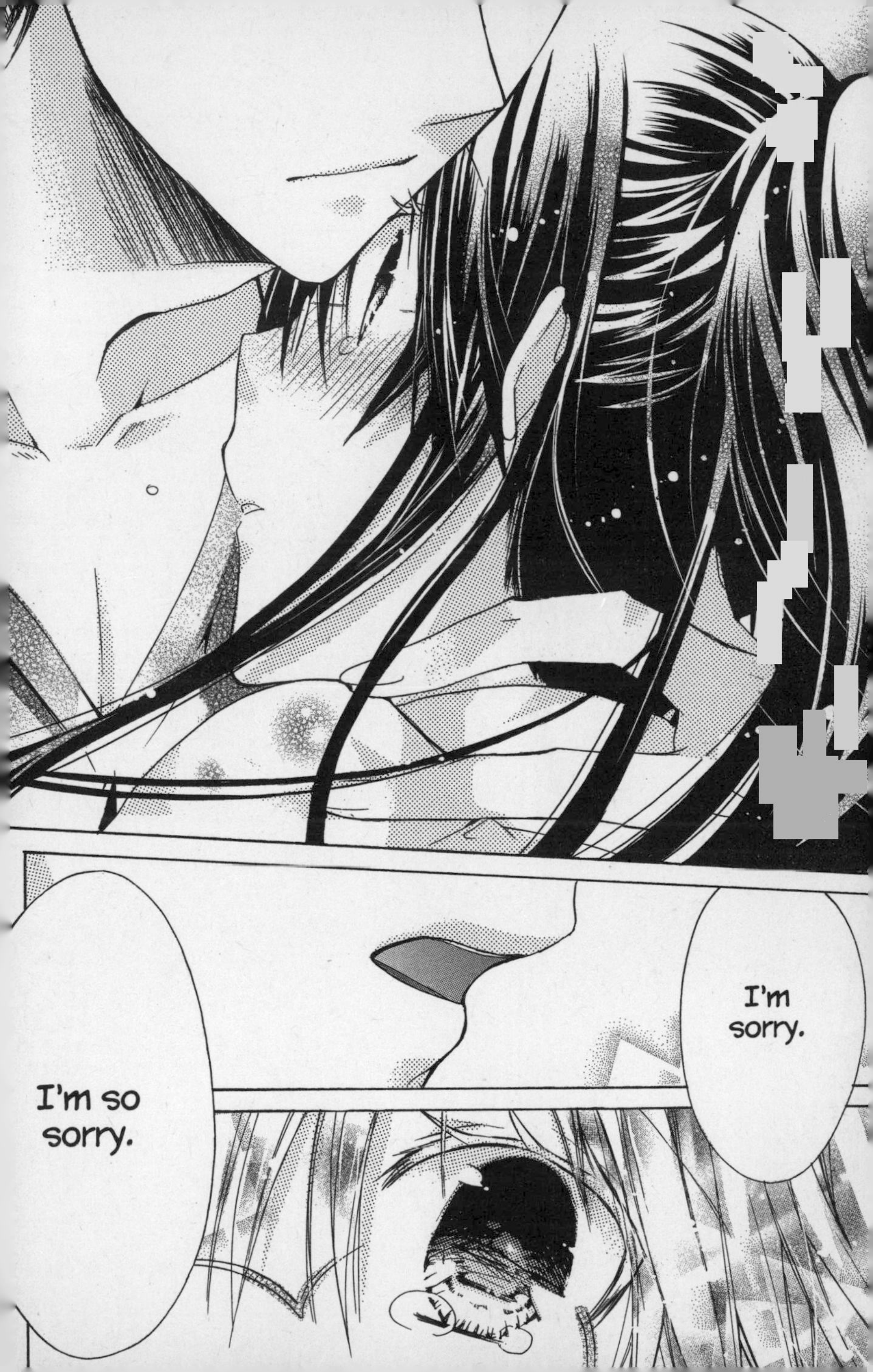
I'm sorry.
I'm so sorry.

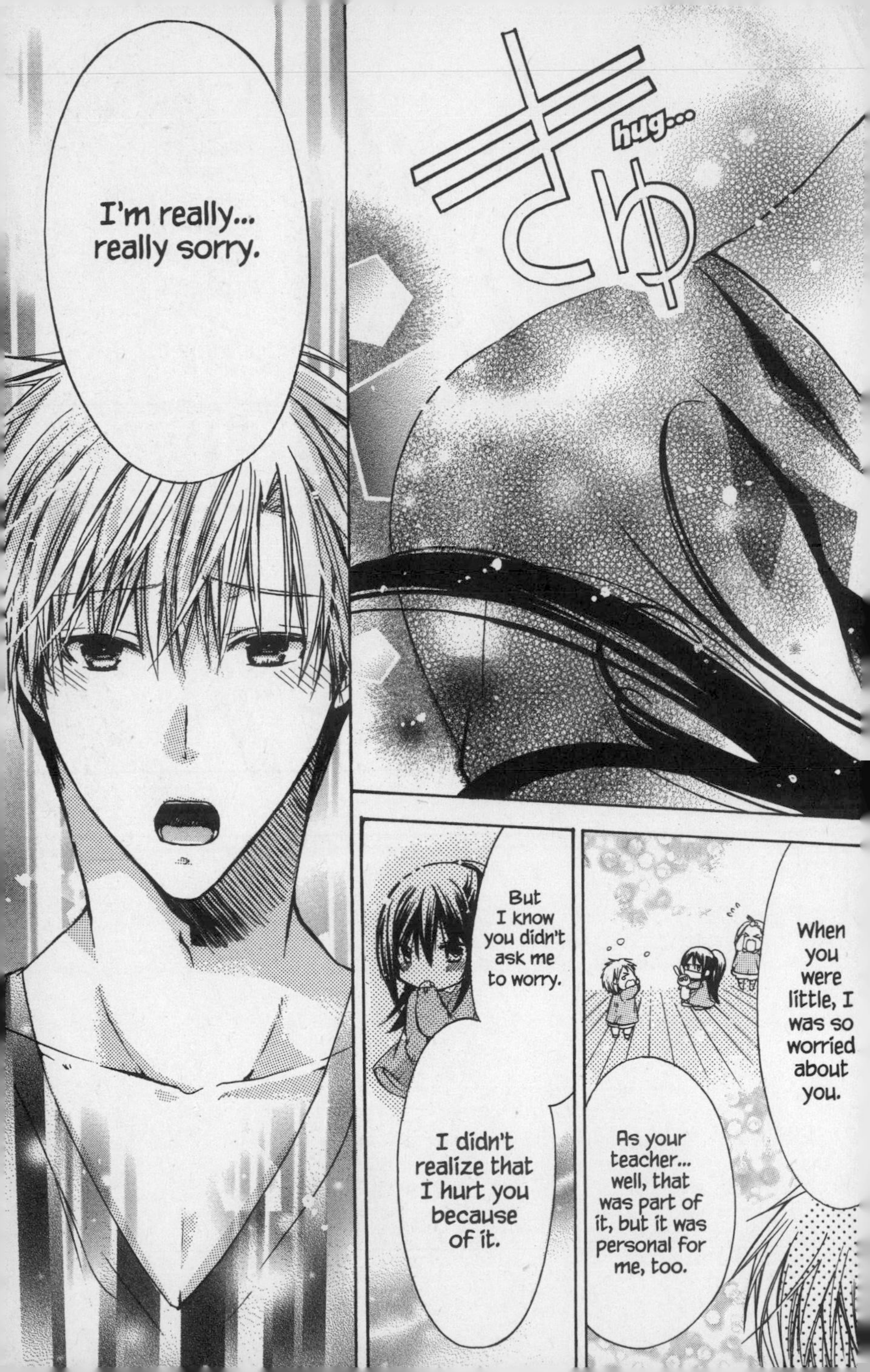
ぎゅ
hug...
When you were little, I was so worried about you.
As your teacher... well, that was part of it, but it was personal for me, too.
But I know you didn't ask me to worry.
I didn't realize that I hurt you because of it.
I'm really... really sorry.

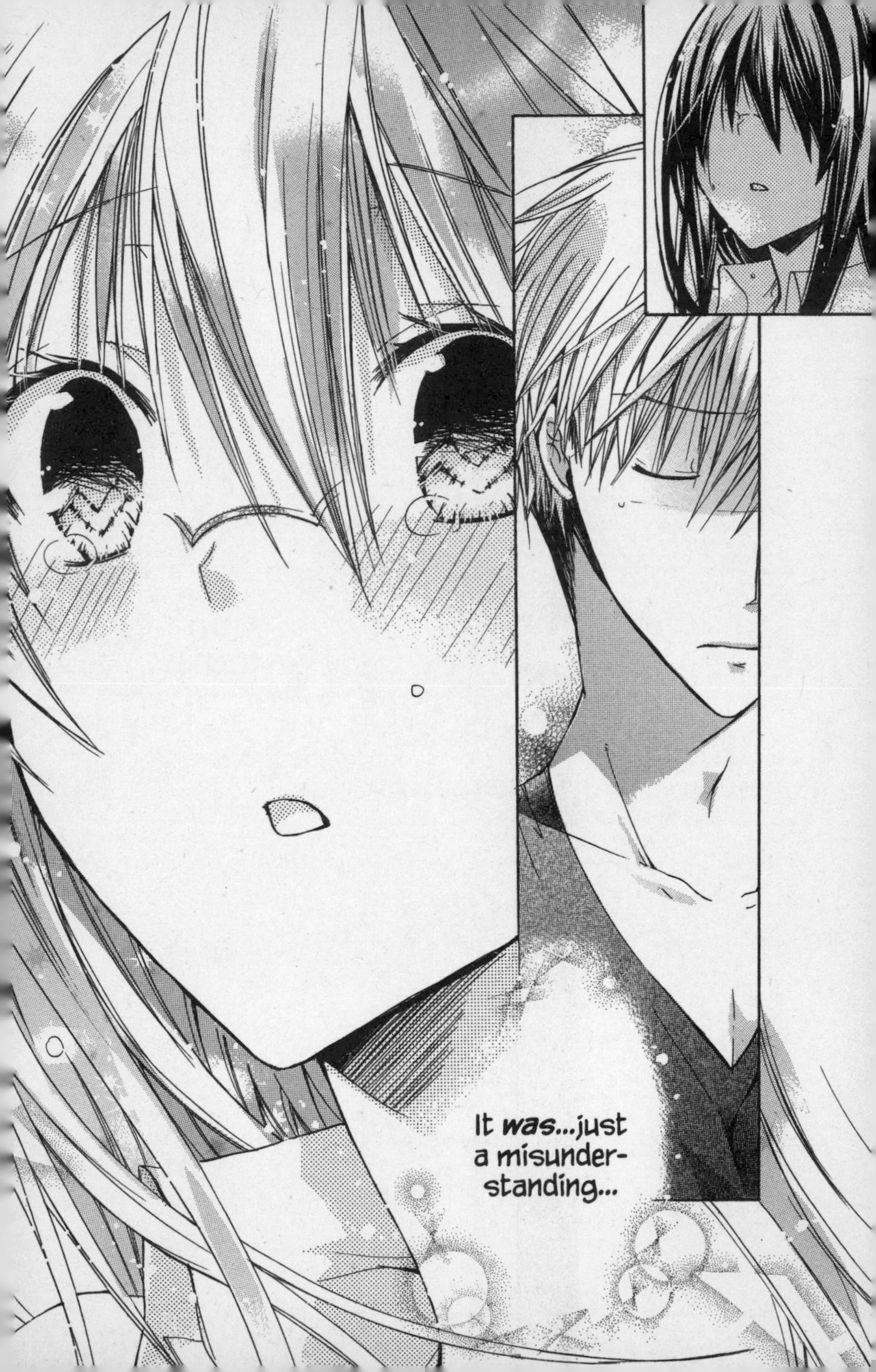
It was...just a misunder-standing...

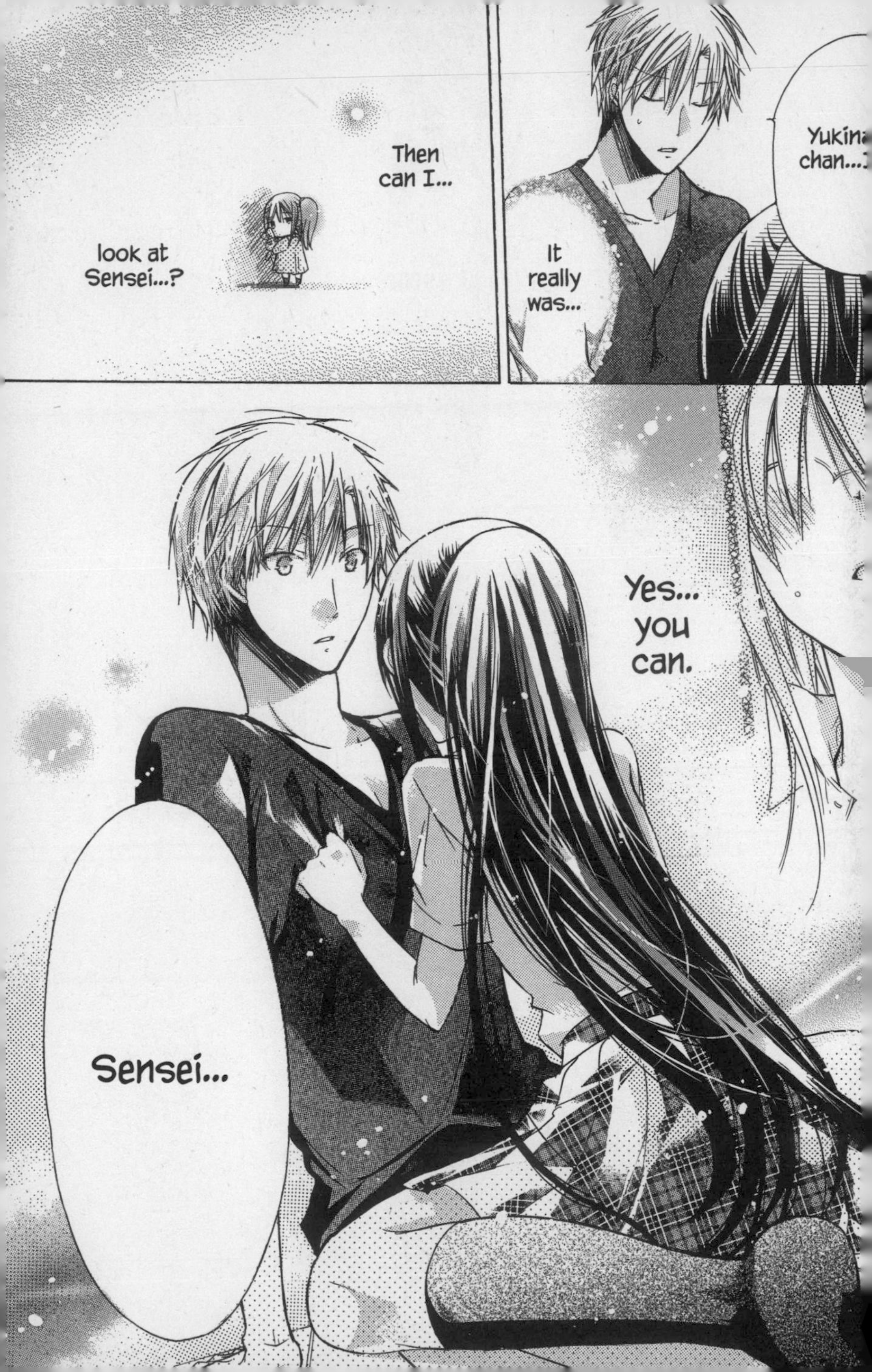
Yukina chan...
It really was...
Then can I...
look at Sensei...?
Yes... you can.
Sensei...

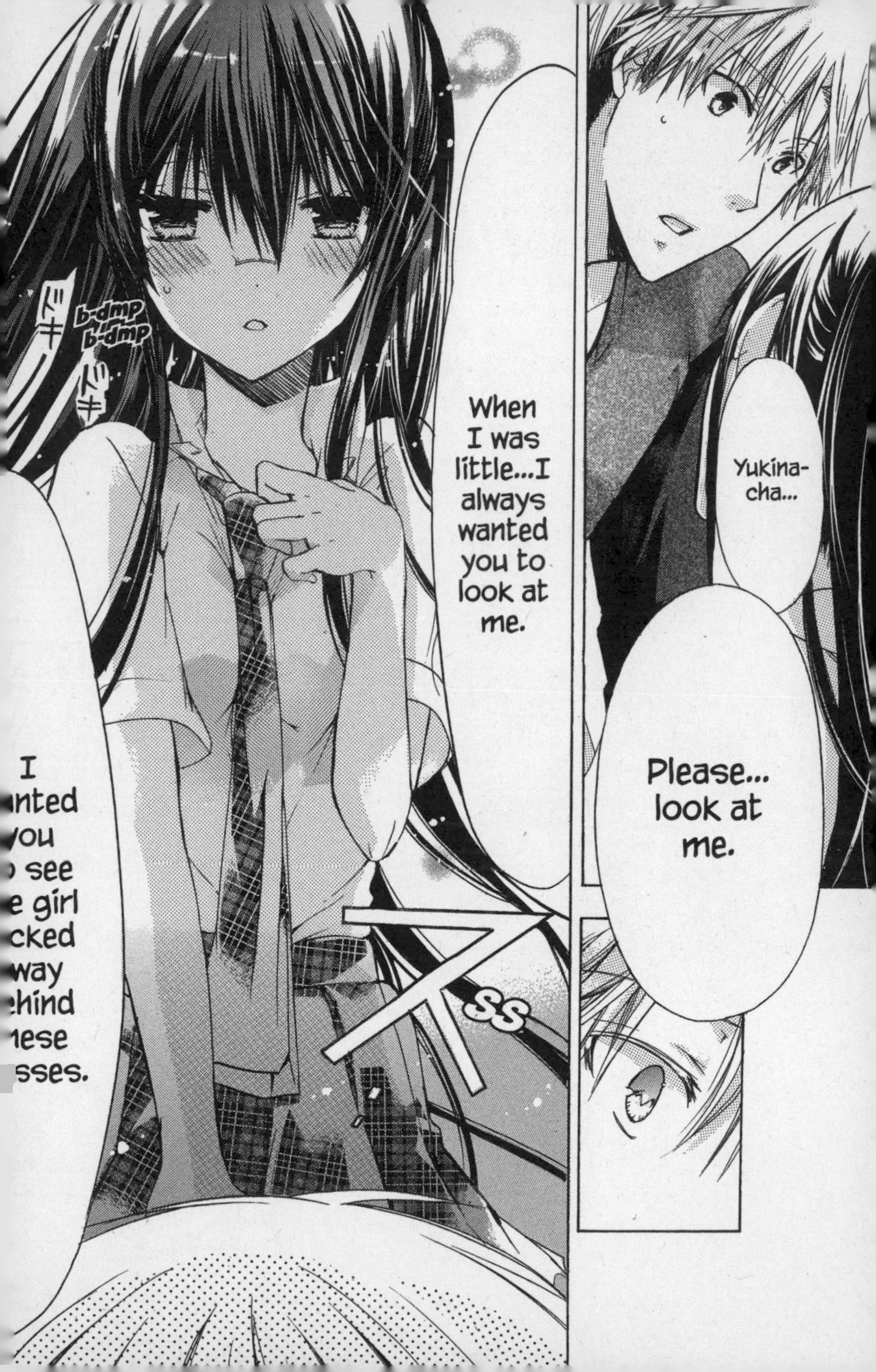
Yukina-cha...
Please... look at me.
When I was little...I always wanted you to look at me.
b-dmp b-dmp
I
nted
you
see
e girl
cked
way
hind
ese
sses.
ss

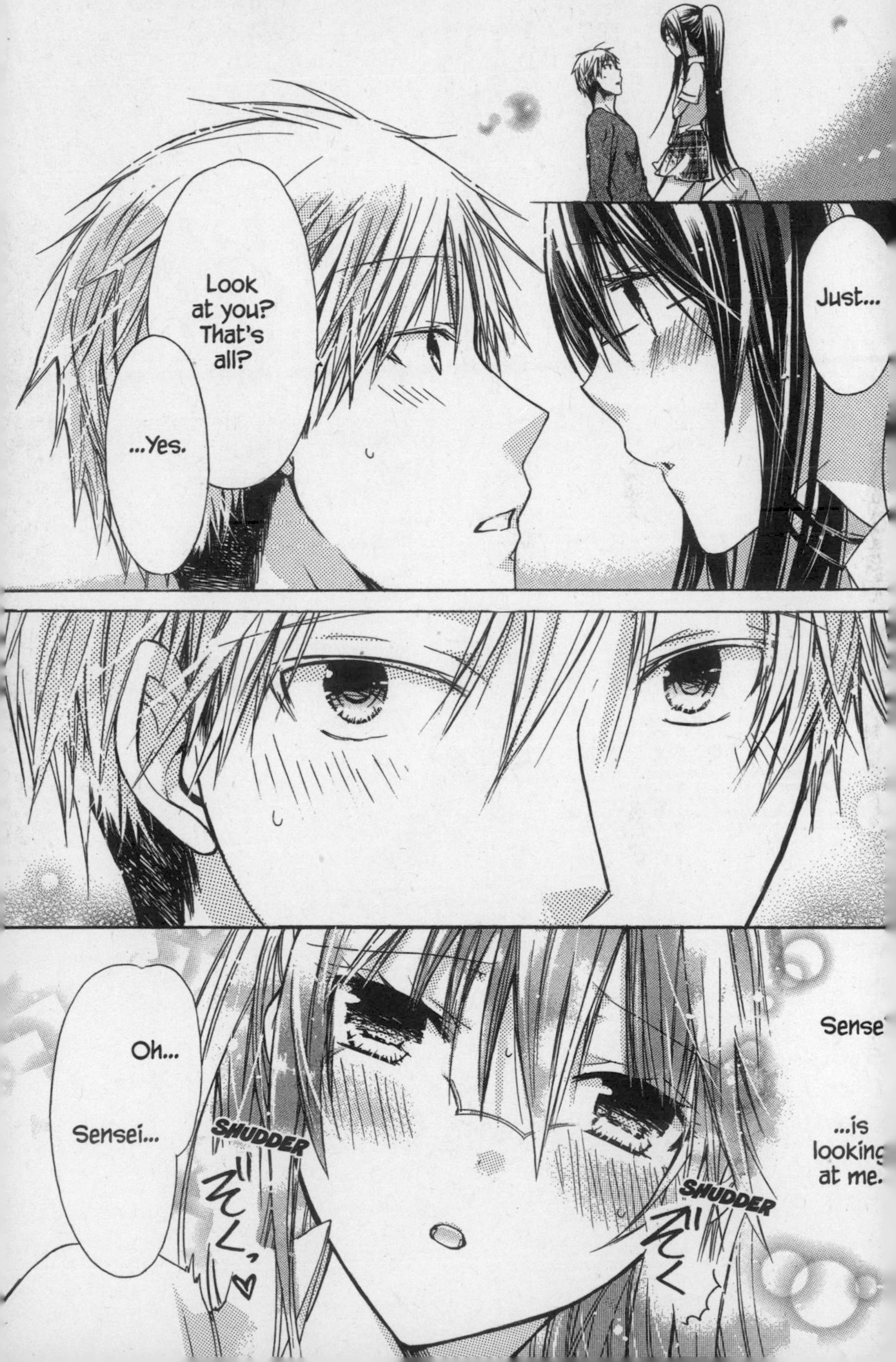
Just...
Look at you? That's all?
...Yes.
Sense
...is looking at me.
SHUDDER
Oh... Sensei...
SHUDDER

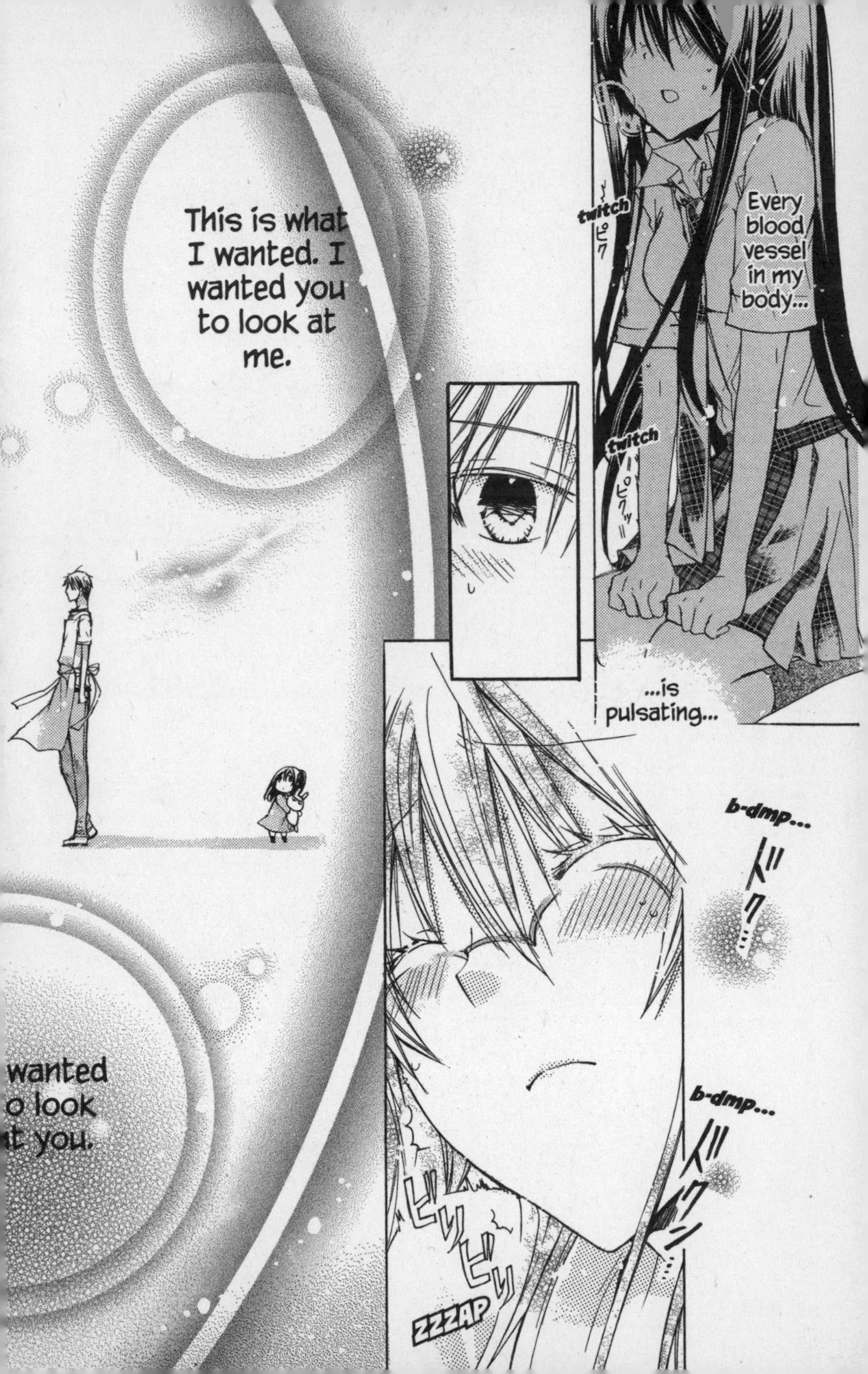
twitch
Every blood vessel in my body...
twitch
...is pulsating...
b-dmp...
b-dmp...
ZZZAP
This is what I wanted. I wanted you to look at me.
wanted
o look
t you.

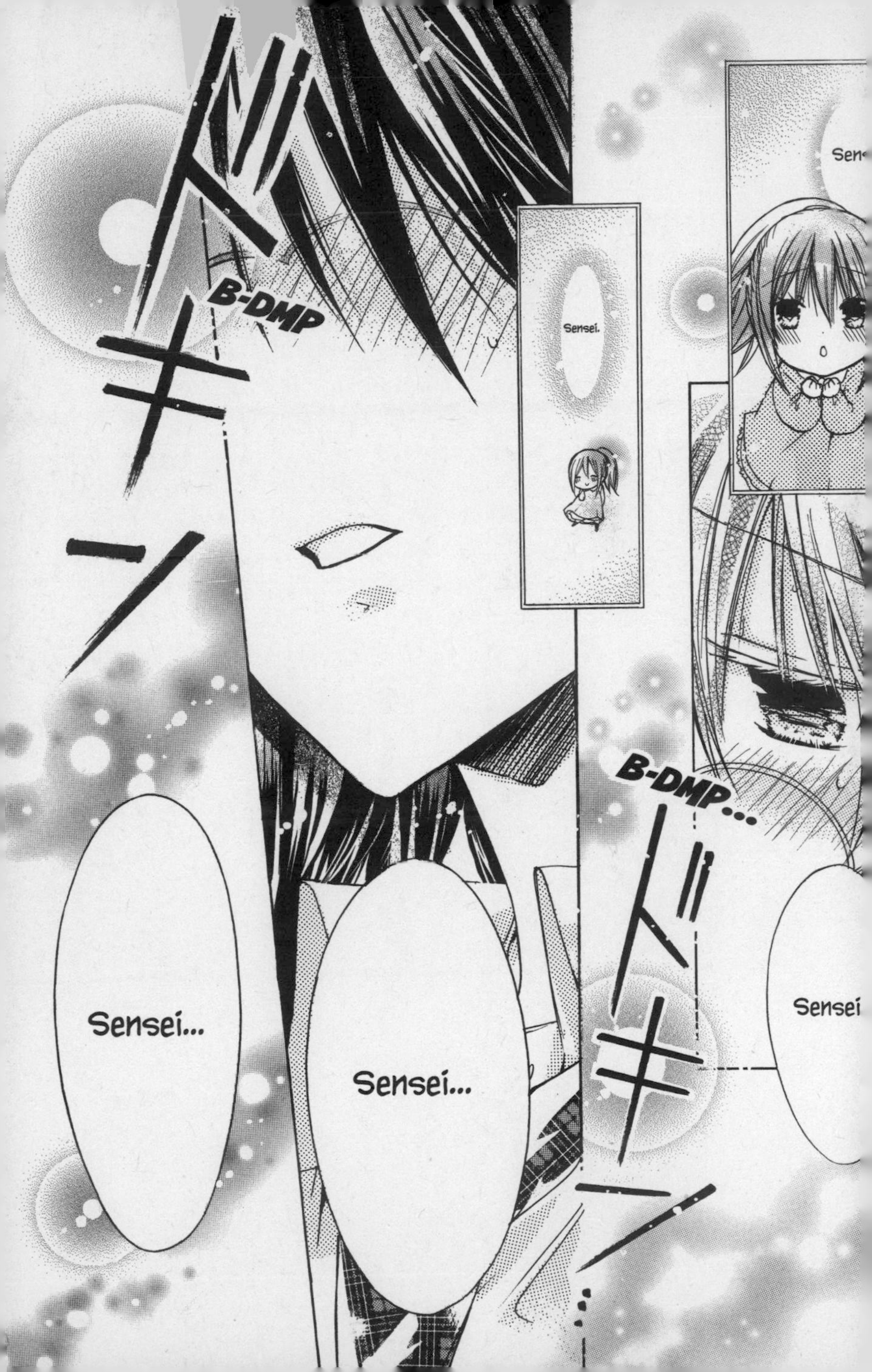
Sen
B-DMP...
Sensei
Sensei.
B-DMP
Sensei...
Sensei...

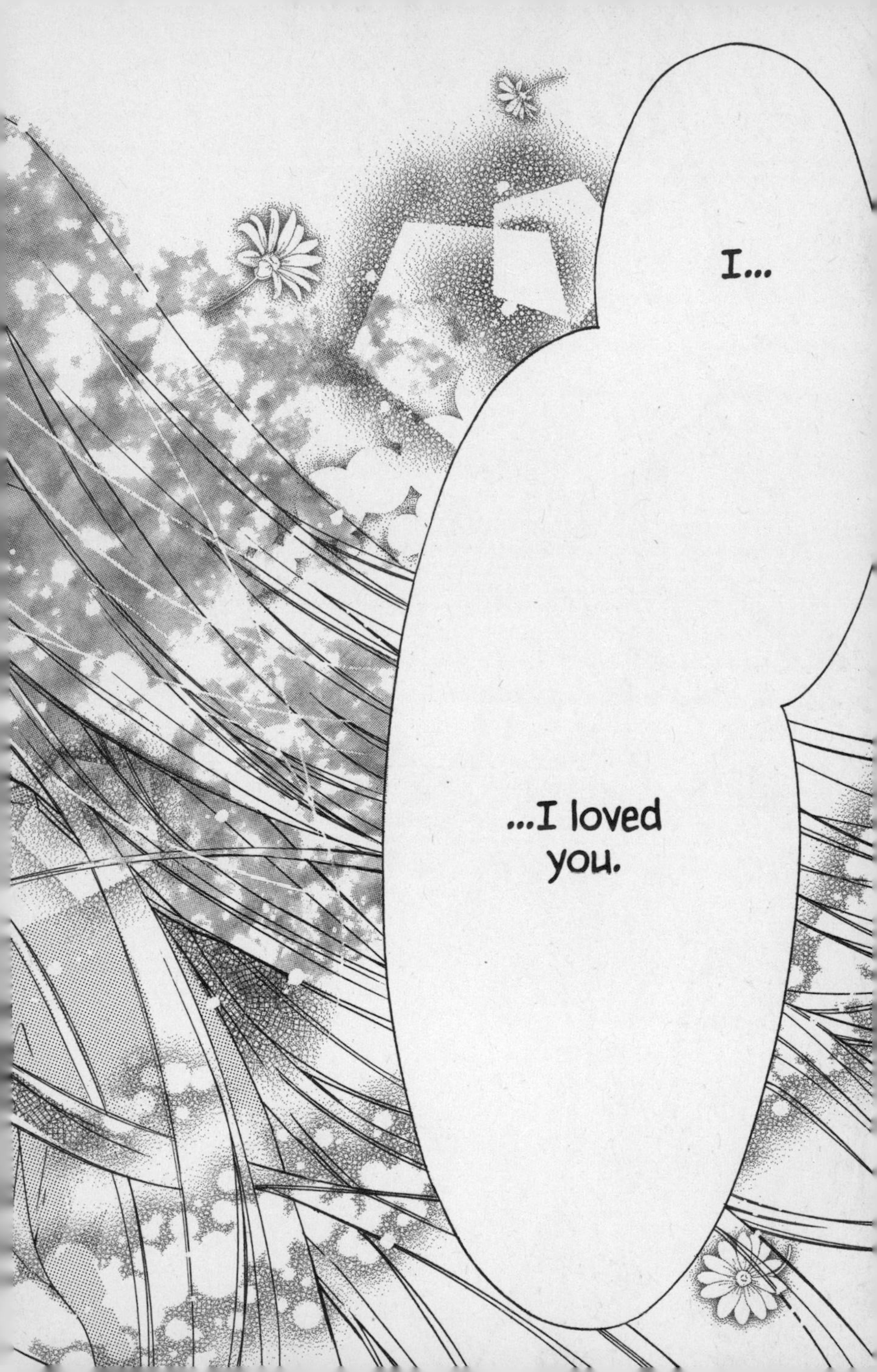
I...
...I loved you.

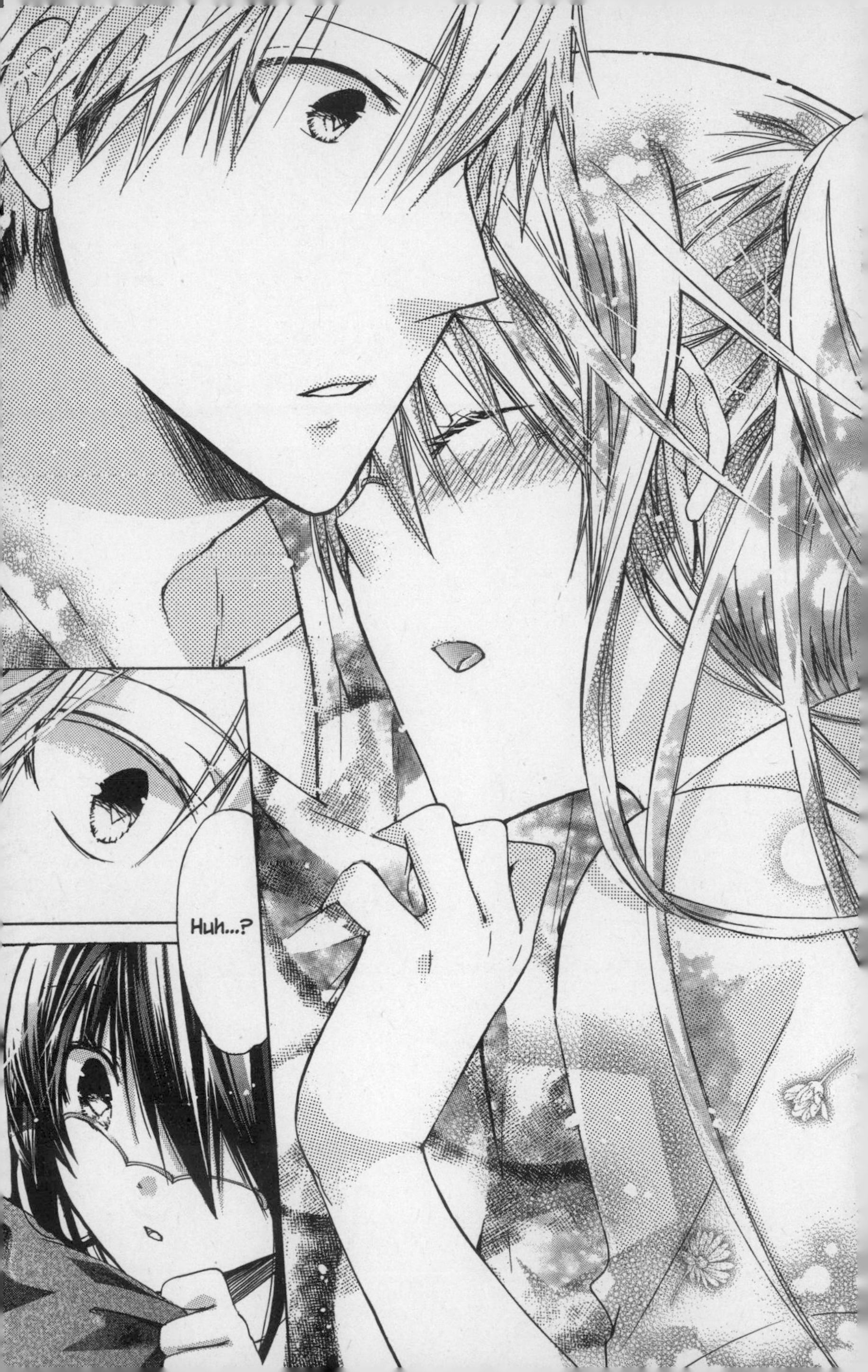
Huh...?

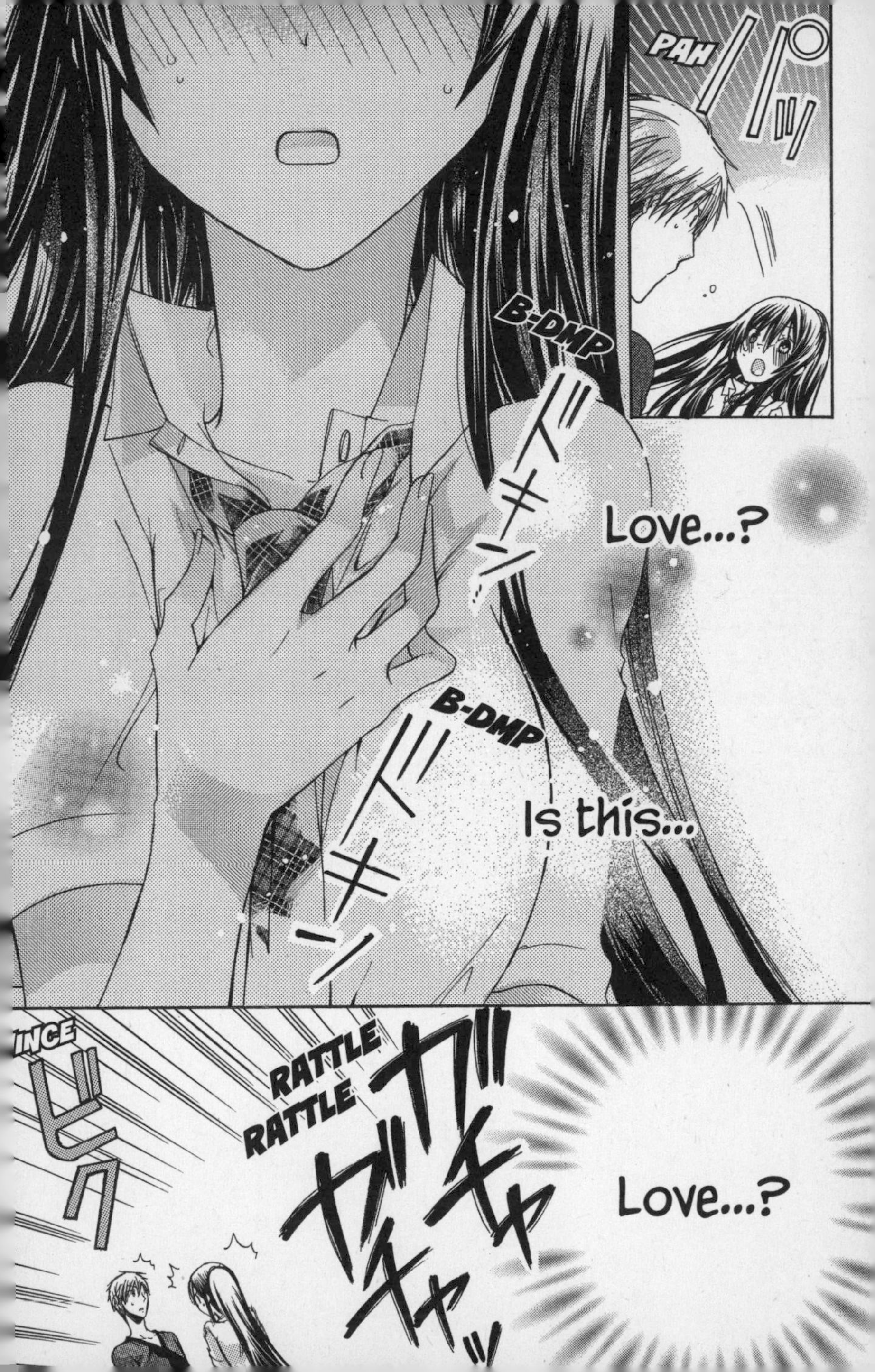

PAH
B-DMP
Love...?
B-DMP
Is this...
Love...?
RATTLE
RATTLE
INCE

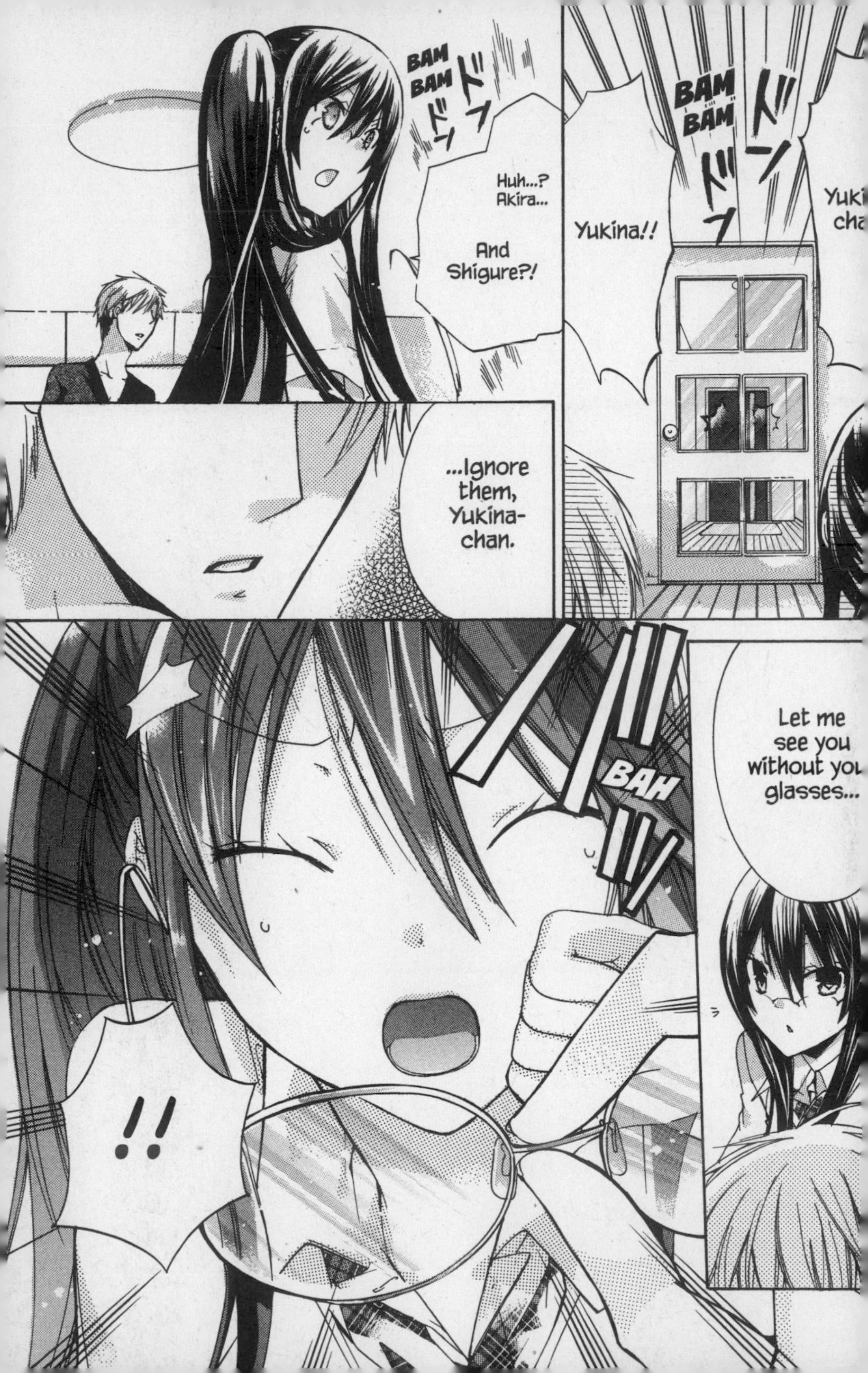
BAM BAM ドンドン
Yukina!!
Yuki cha
BAM BAM ドンドン
Huh...? Akira...
And Shigure?!
...Ignore them, Yukina-chan.
Let me see you without you glasses...
BAH
!!

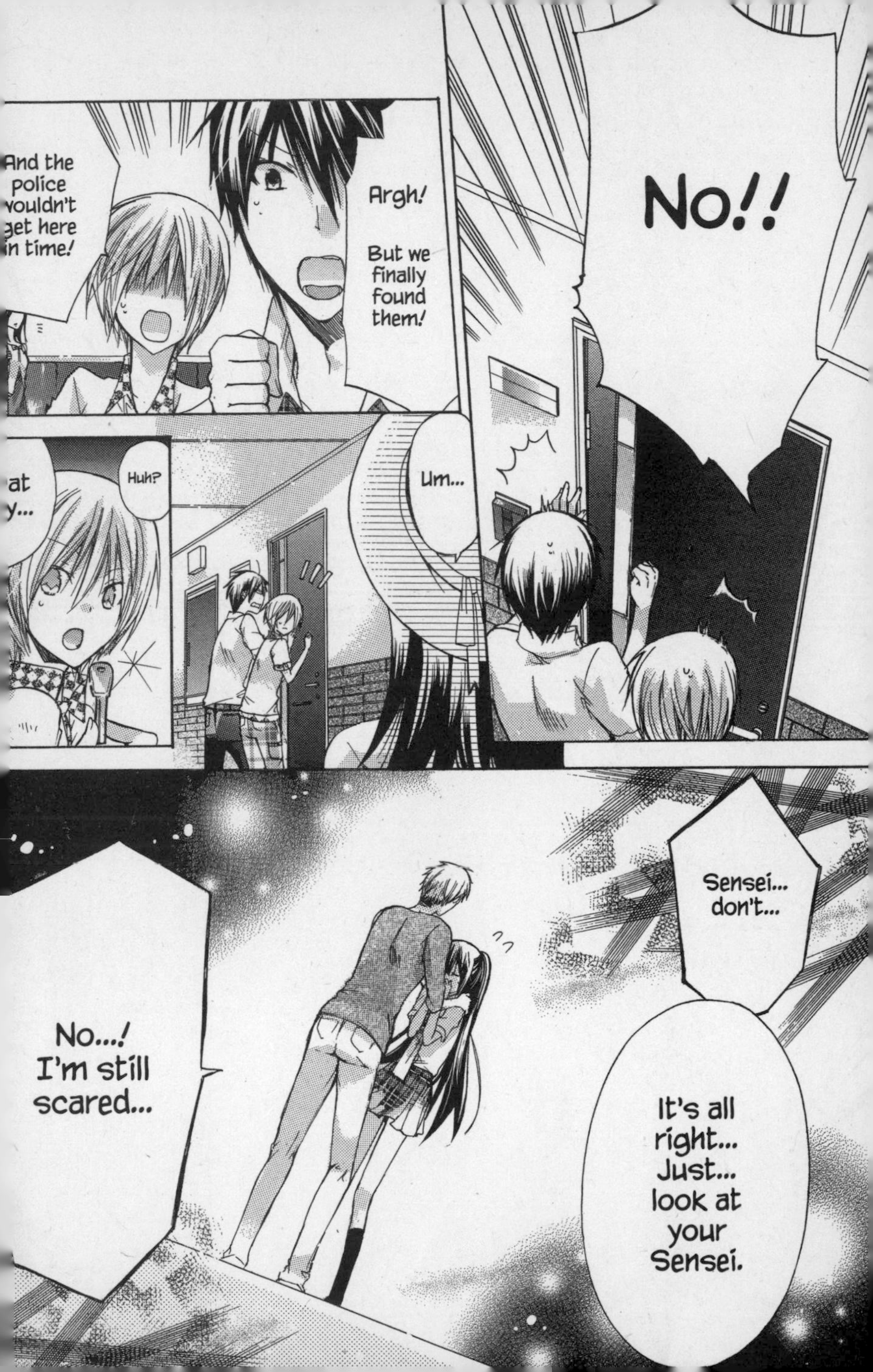
No!!
Argh!
But we finally found them!
And the police wouldn't get here in time!
Um...
Huh?
Sensei... don't...
It's all right... Just... look at your Sensei.
No...! I'm still scared...

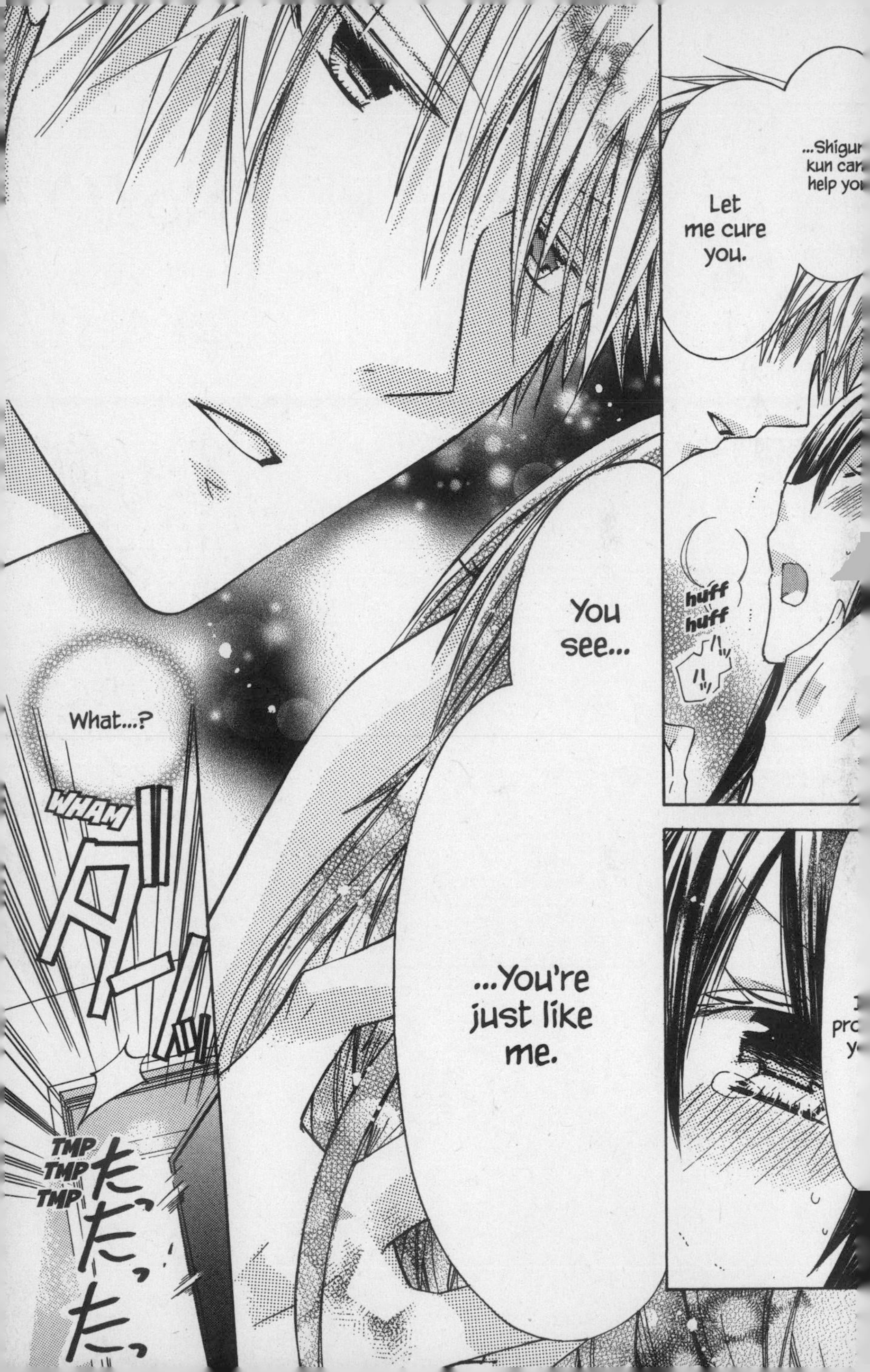
...Shigur
kun can
help yo
Let me cure you.
huff huff
You see...
...You're just like me.
What...?
WHAM
TMP TMP TMP

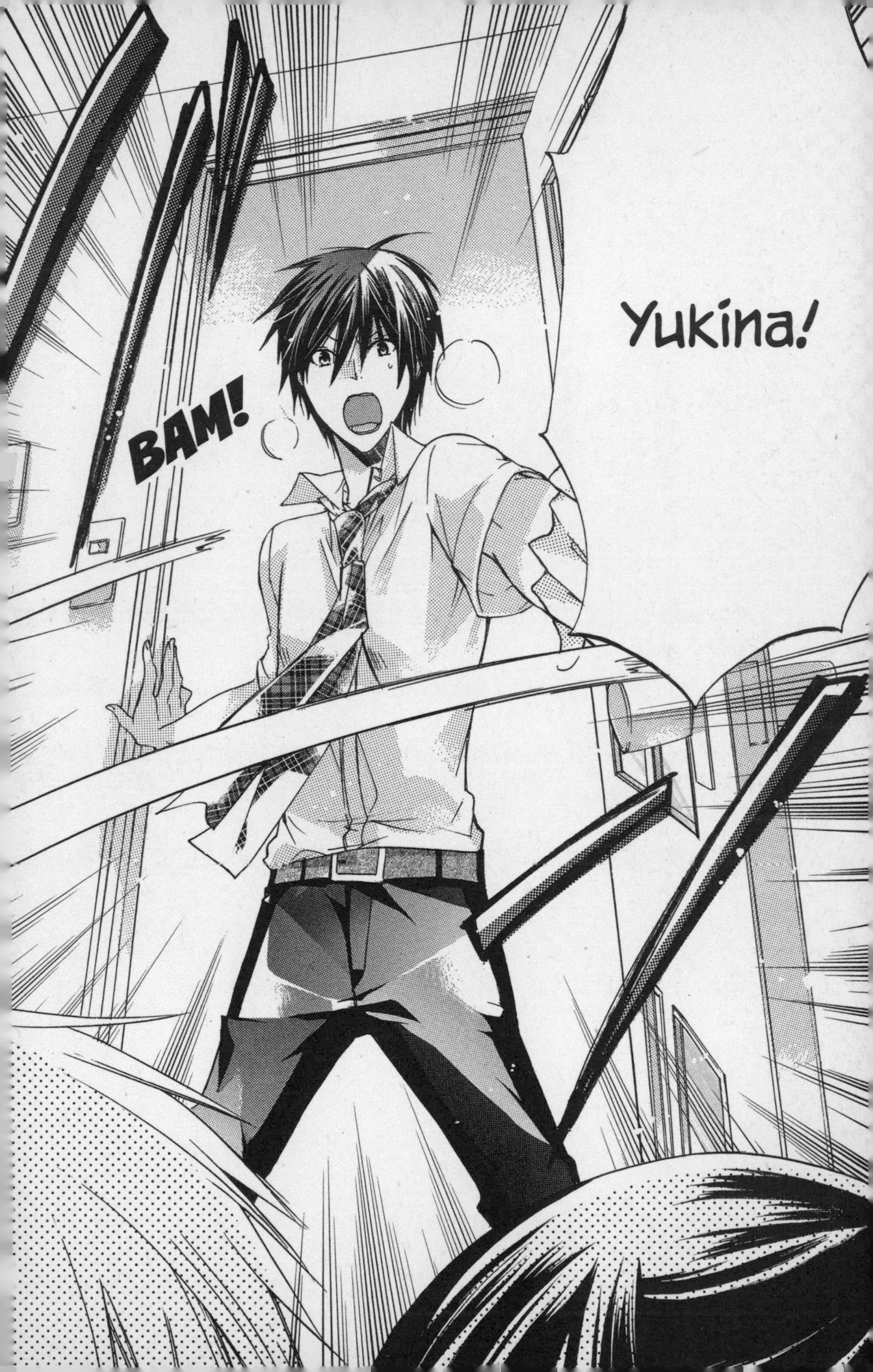
Yukina!
BAM!

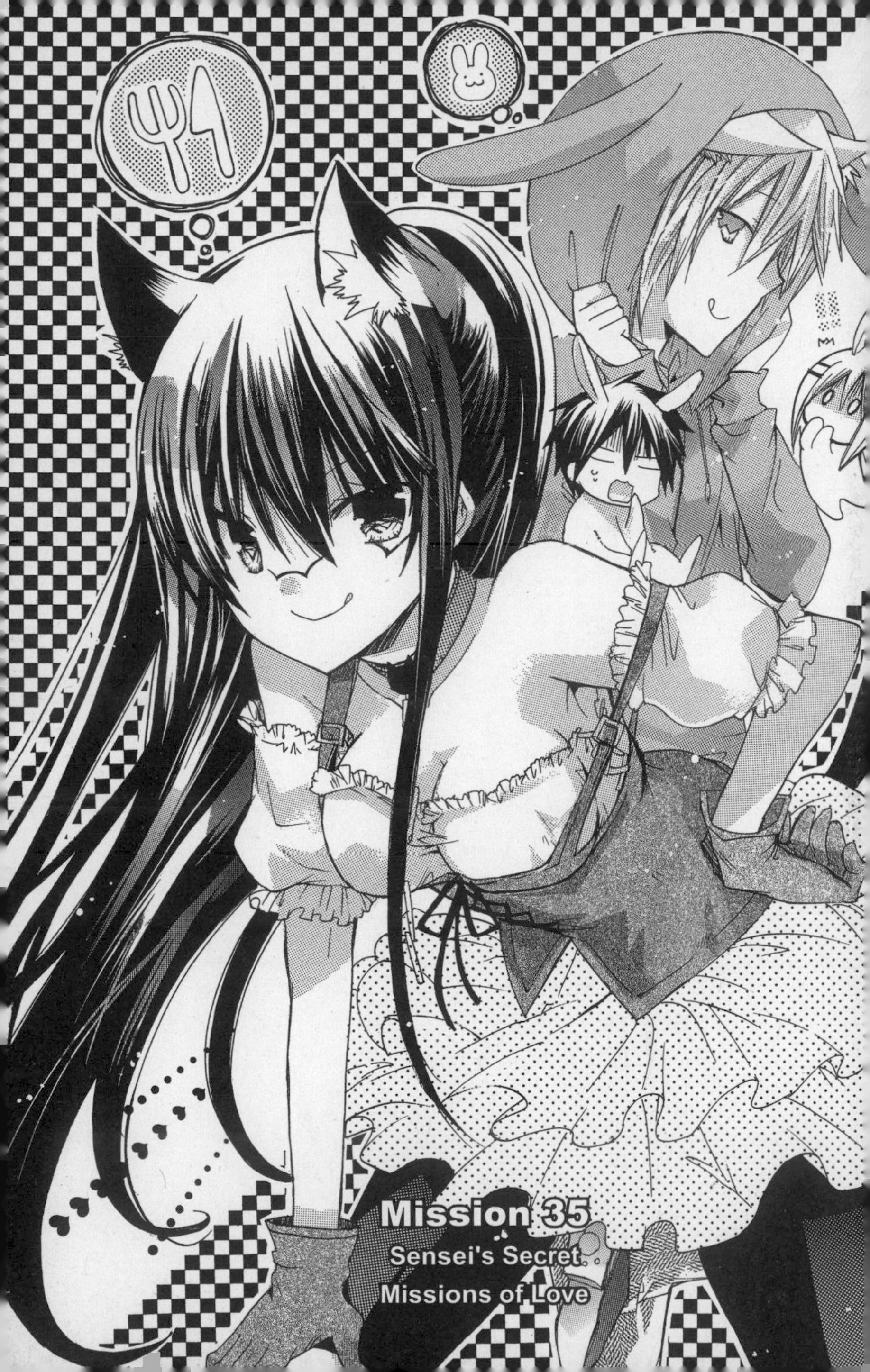
Mission 35
Sensei's Secret
Missions of Love

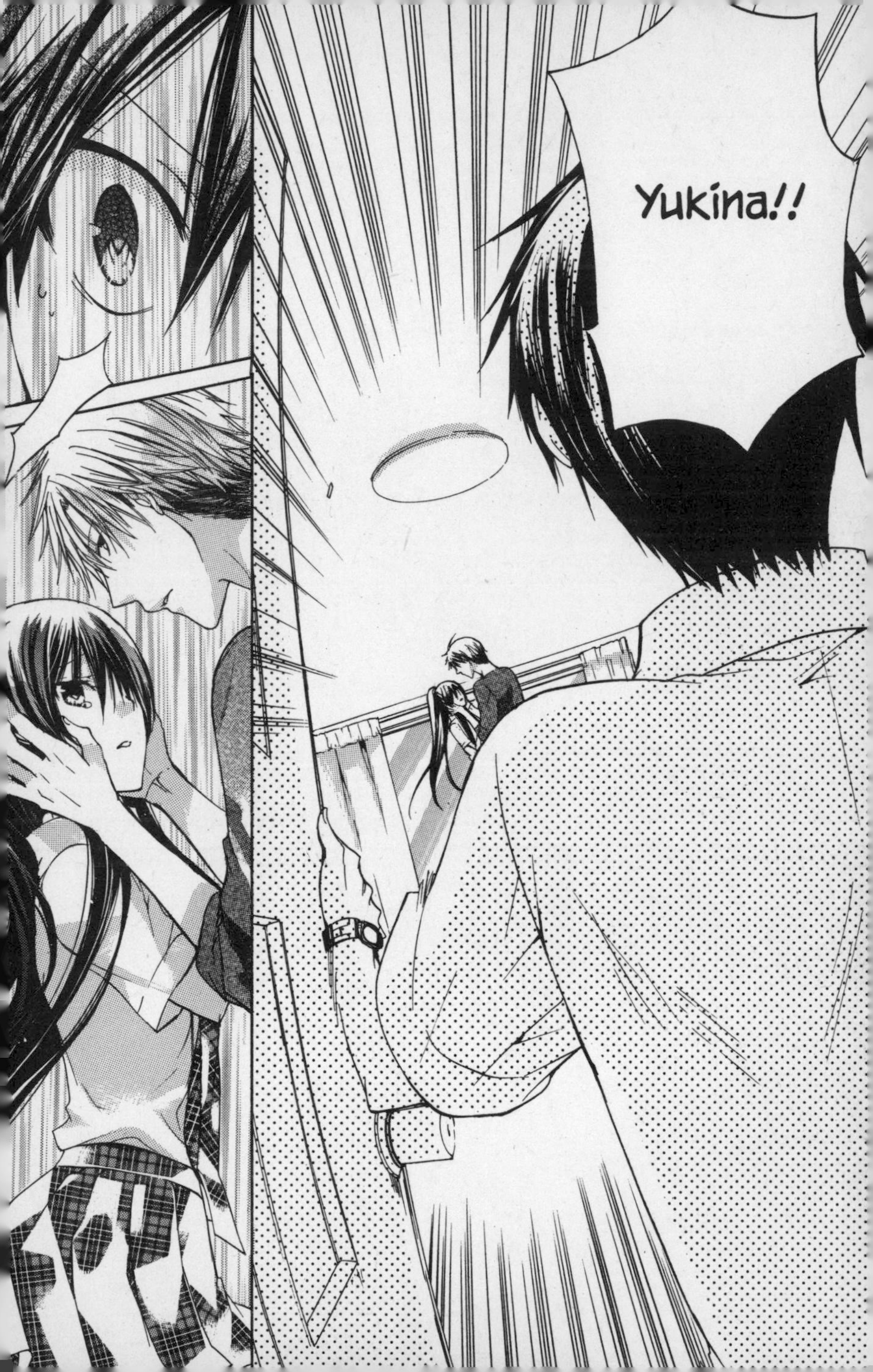
Yukina!!

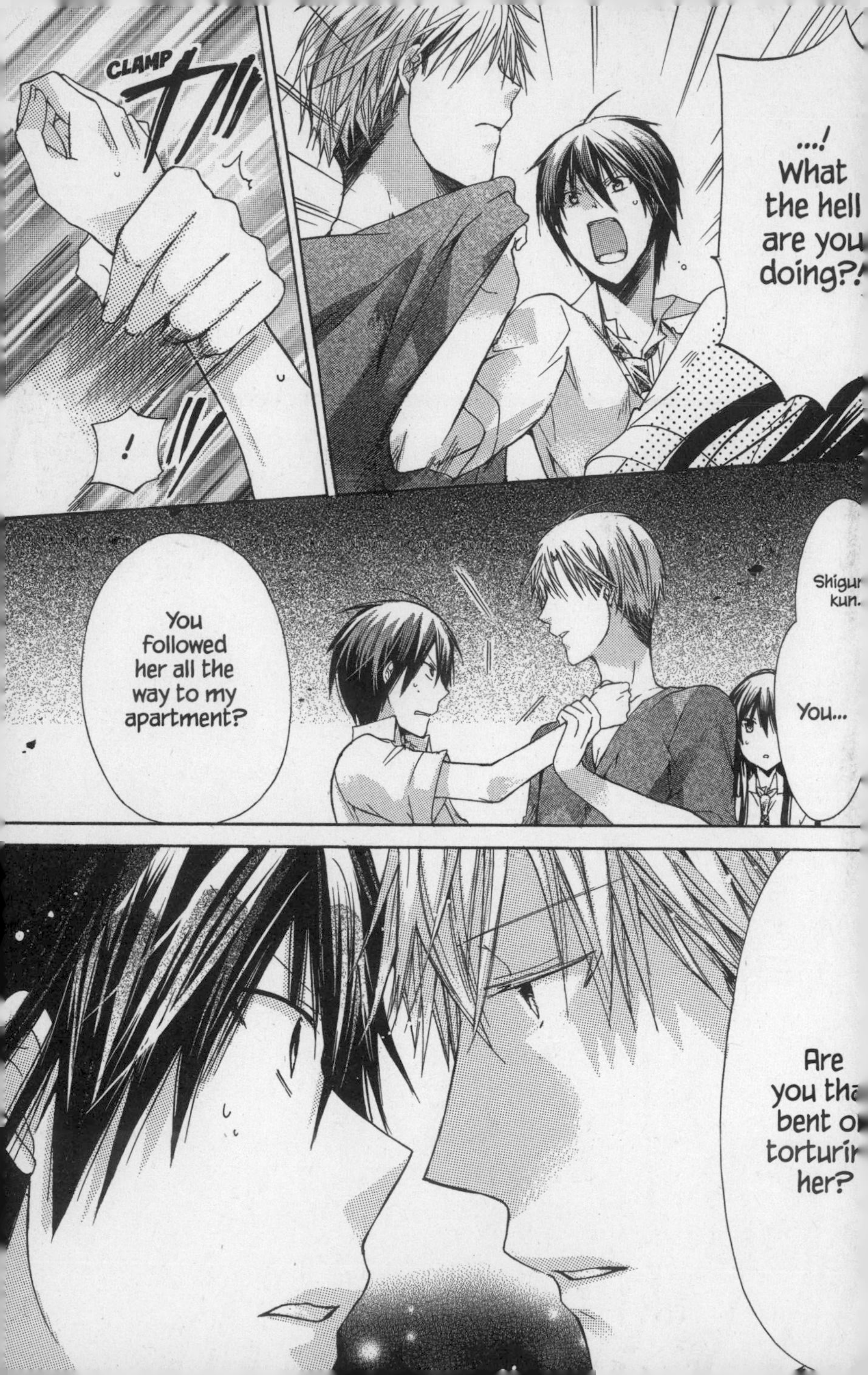
...! What the hell are you doing?!
CLAMP
!
Shigur kun.
You...
You followed her all the way to my apartment?
Are you tha bent o torturi her?

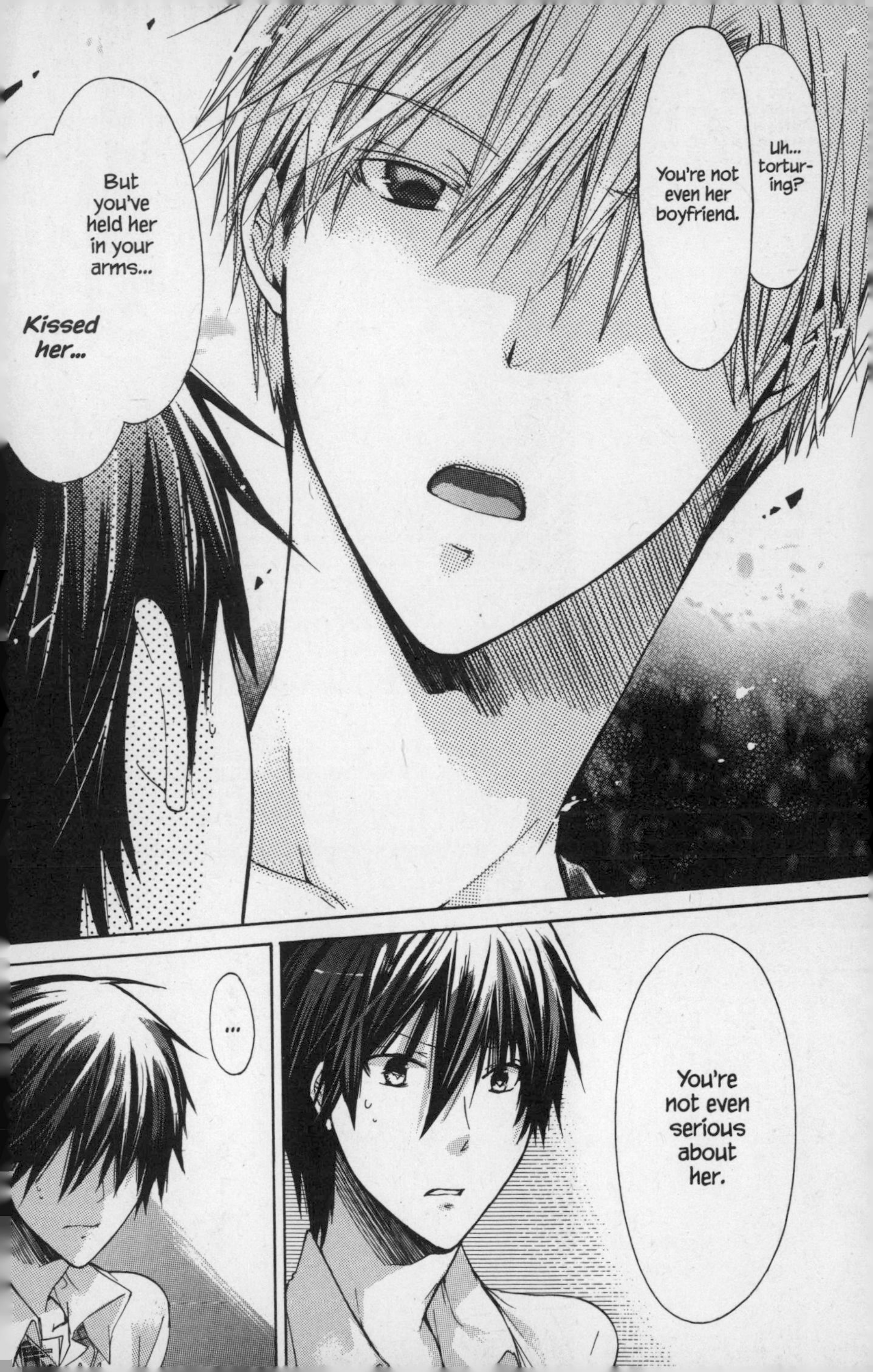
Uh... tortur-ing?
You're not even her boyfriend.
But you've held her in your arms...
Kissed her...
You're not even serious about her.
...

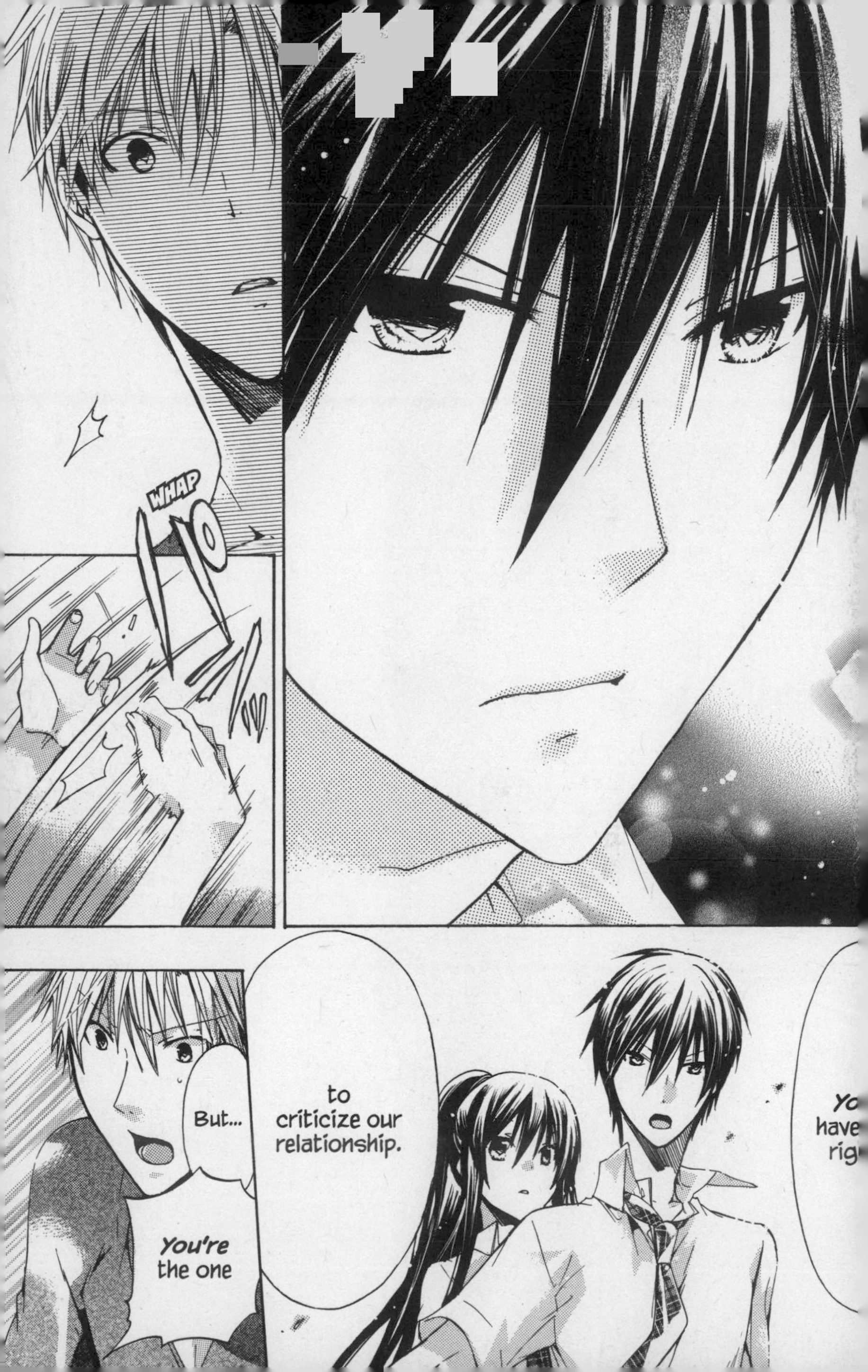
WHAP
Yo have rig
to criticize our relationship.
But...
You're the one

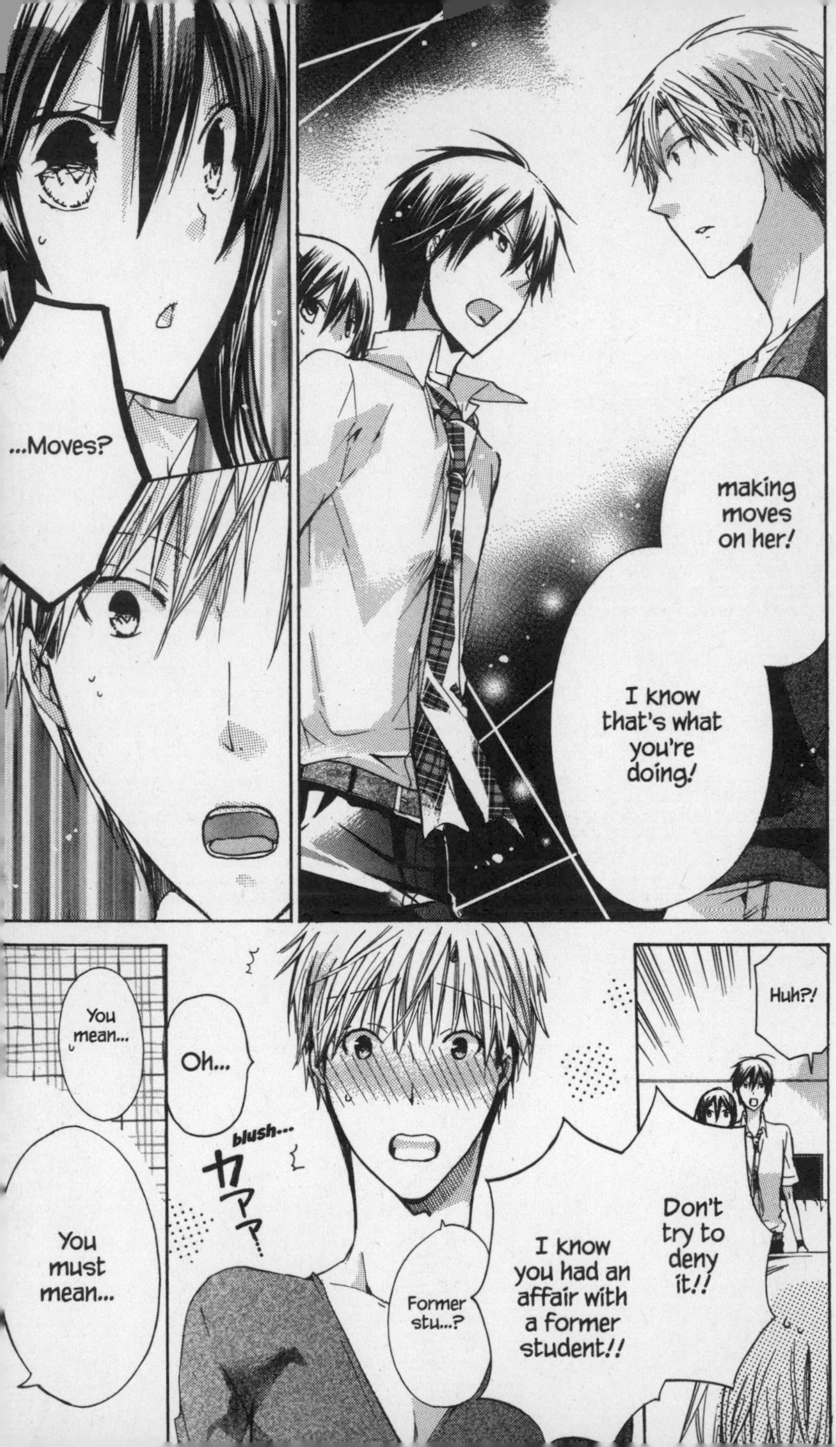
I know that's what you're doing!
making moves on her!
...Moves?
Huh?!
Don't try to deny it!!
I know you had an affair with a former student!!
Former stu...?
blush...
カァァ...
Oh...
You mean...
You must mean...

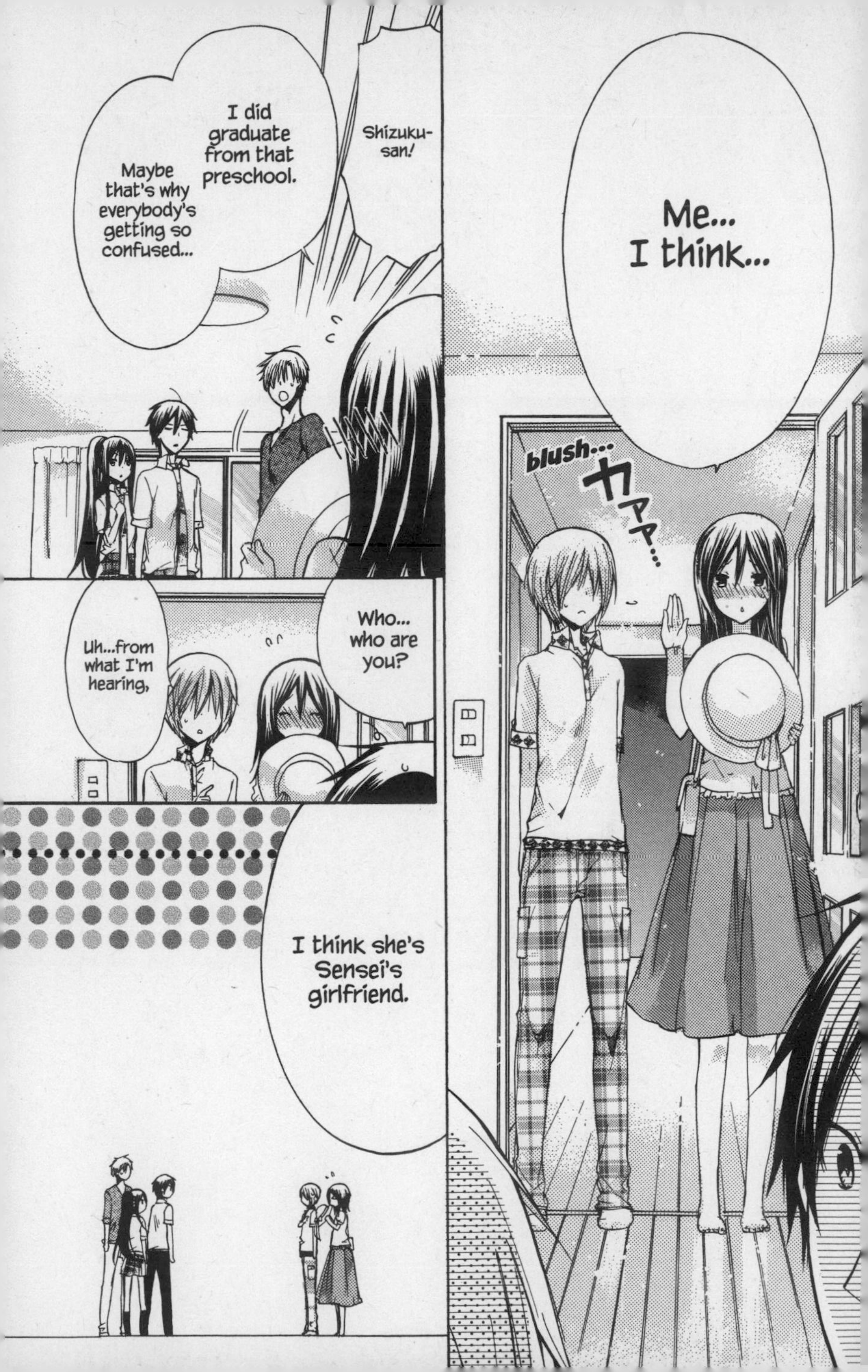
Me... I think...
blush...
ヤァァ...
Shizuku-san!
I did graduate from that preschool.
Maybe that's why everybody's getting so confused...
Who... who are you?
Uh...from what I'm hearing,
I think she's Sensei's girlfriend.

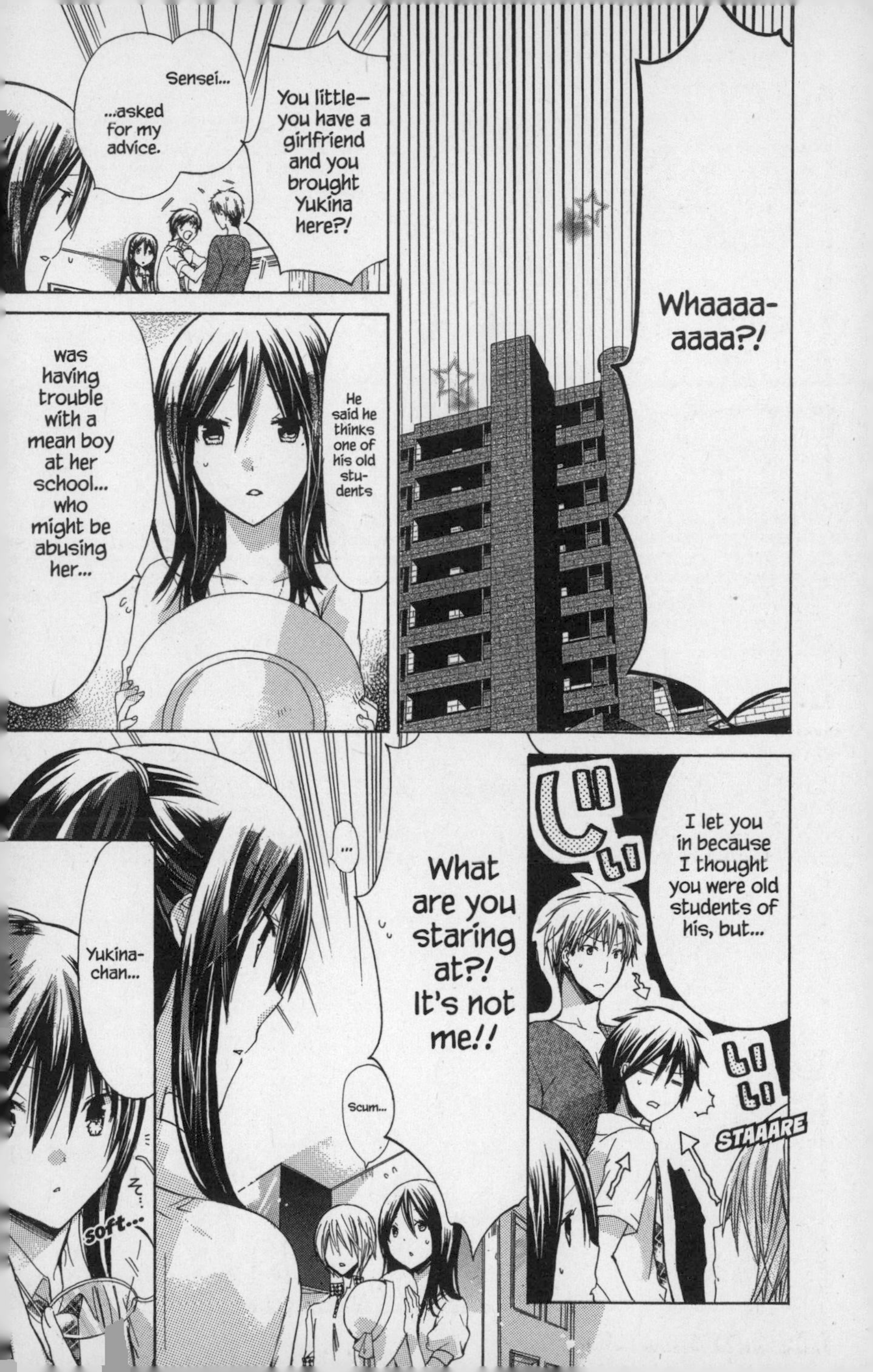
Whaaaa-aaaa?!
You little— you have a girlfriend and you brought Yukina here?!
Sensei...
...asked for my advice.
He said he thinks one of his old students
was having trouble with a mean boy at her school... who might be abusing her...
I let you in because I thought you were old students of his, but...
What are you staring at?! It's not me!!
STAAARE
...
Yukina-chan...
Scum...
soft...

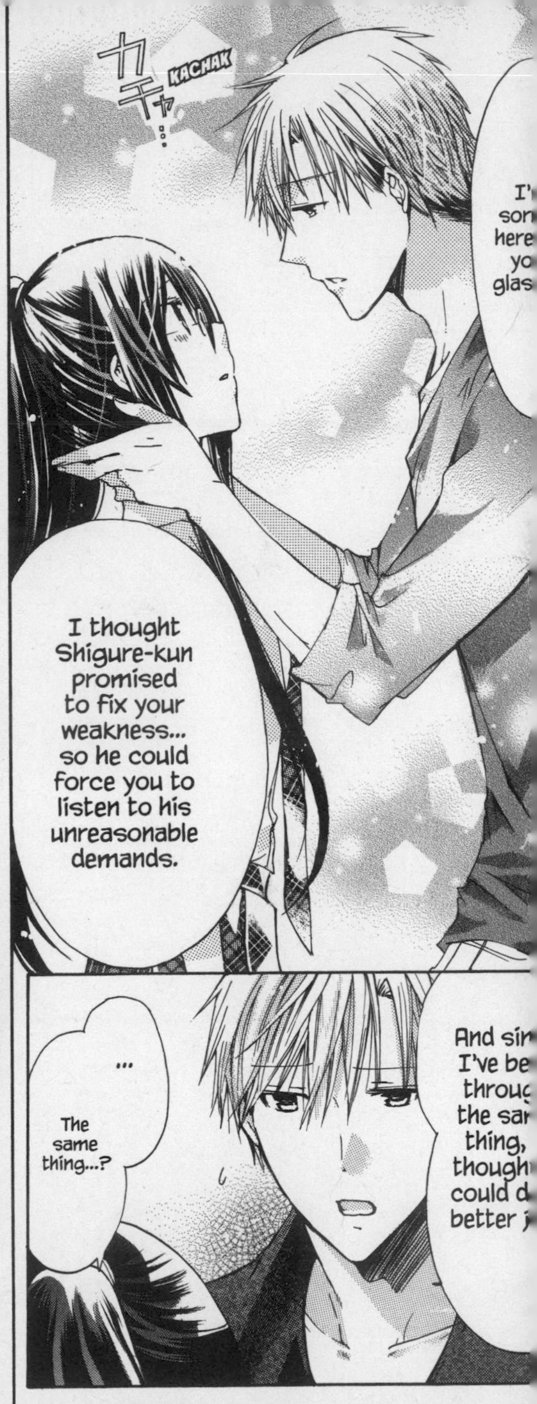
I'
son
here
yo
glas
KACHAK
カチャ…
I thought Shigure-kun promised to fix your weakness... so he could force you to listen to his unreasonable demands.
And sin
I've be
throug
the sa
thing,
though
could d
better j
...
The same thing...?

The Freezing Bed 3

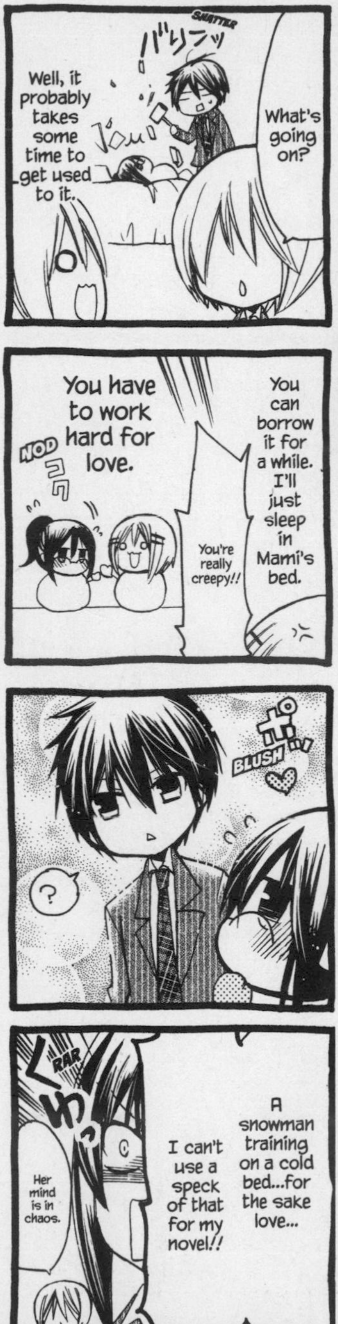
What's going on?
SHATTER
バリッ
Well, it probably takes some time to get used to it.
You can borrow it for a while. I'll just sleep in Mami's bed.
You're really creepy!!
You have to work hard for love.
NOD
コク
ポッ
BLUSH
?
A snowman training on a cold bed...for the sake love...
I can't use a speck of that for my novel!!
RAR
くわっ
Her mind is in chaos.

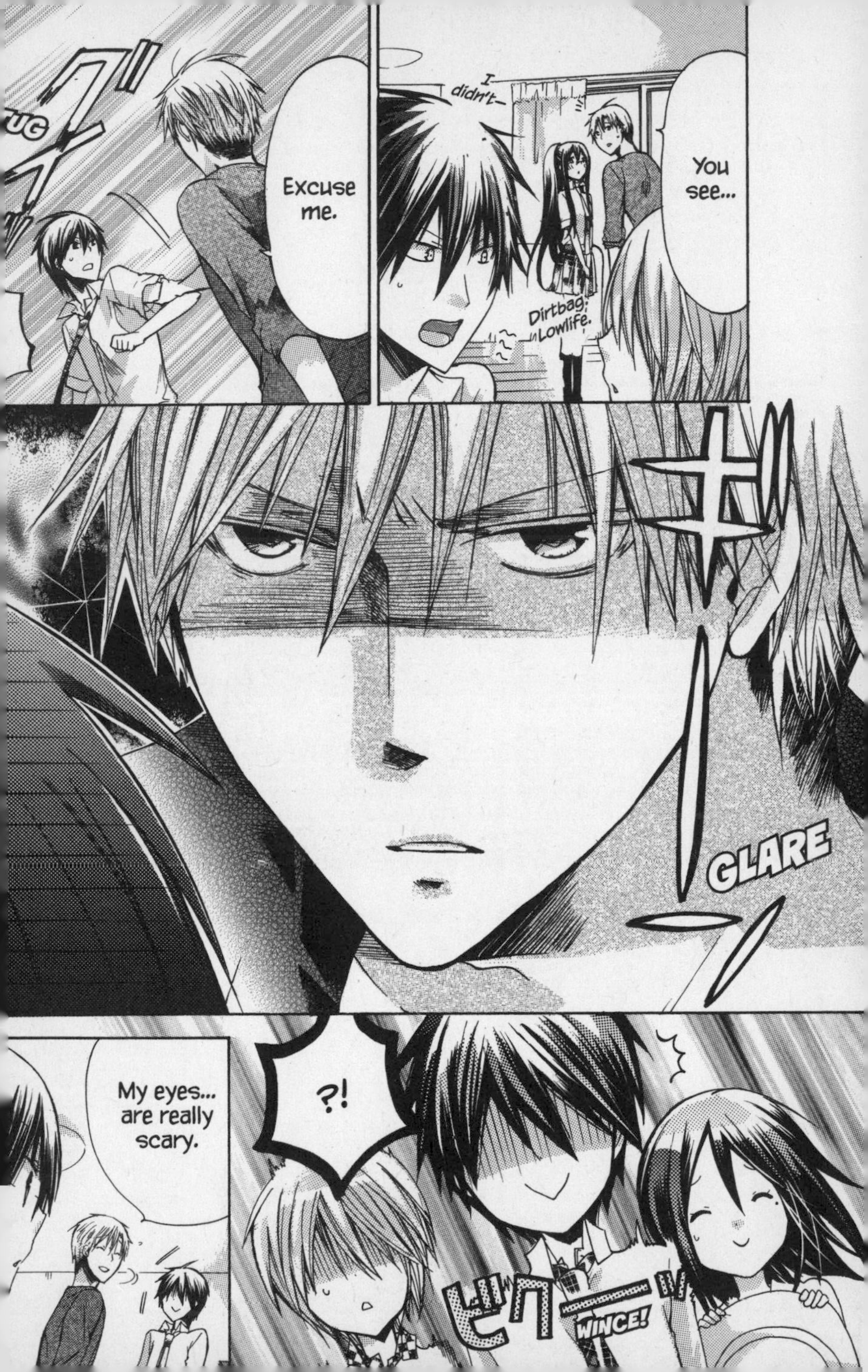
You see...
I— didn't—
Dirtbag. Lowlife.
TUG
Excuse me.
GLARE
?!
WINCE!
My eyes... are really scary.

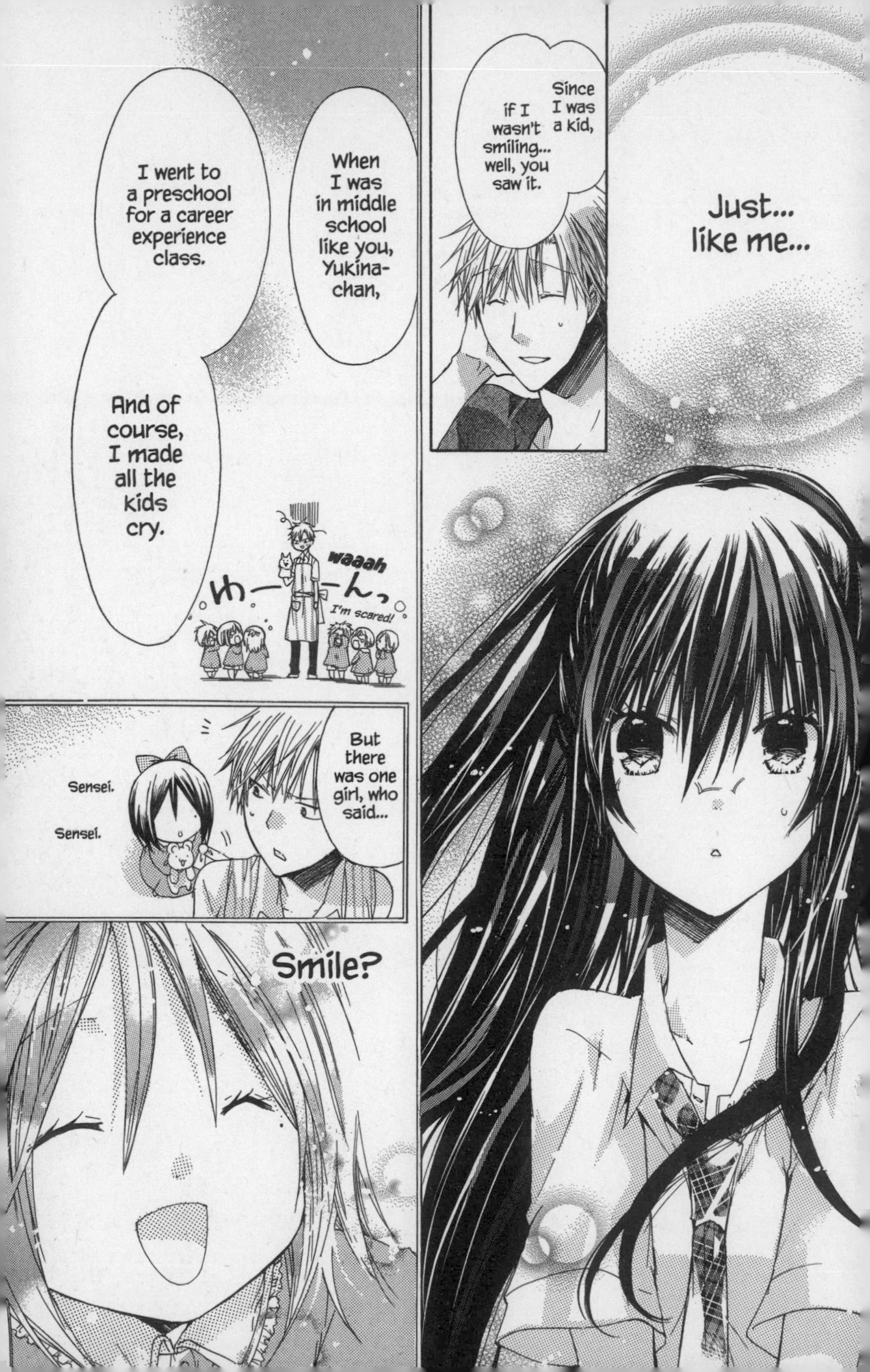
Since I was a kid, if I wasn't smiling... well, you saw it.
Just... like me...
When I was in middle school like you, Yukina-chan,
I went to a preschool for a career experience class.
And of course, I made all the kids cry.
わーーん
waaah
I'm scared!
But there was one girl, who said...
Sensei.
Sensei.
Smile?

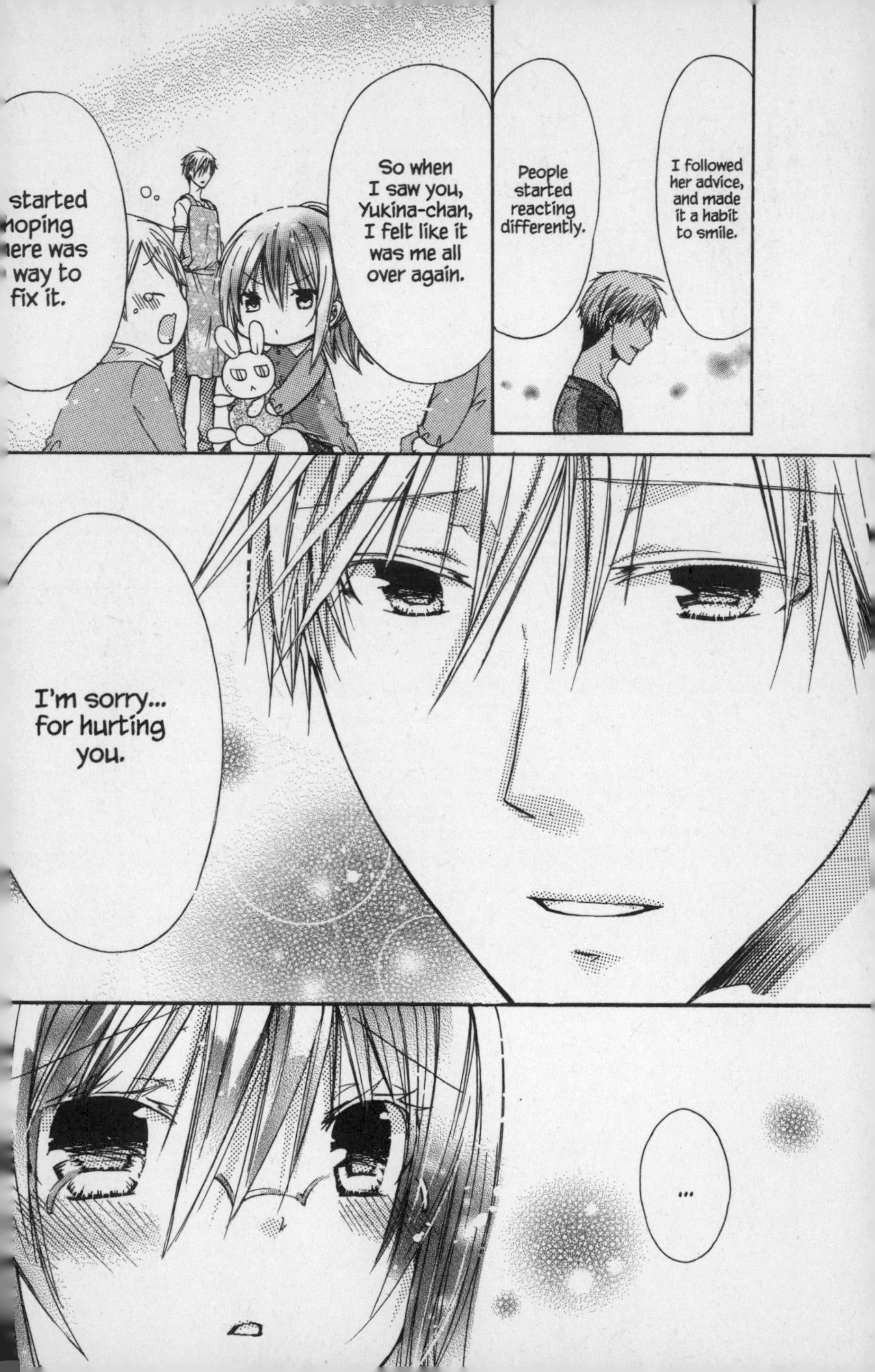
I followed her advice, and made it a habit to smile.
People started reacting differently.
So when I saw you, Yukina-chan, I felt like it was me all over again.
started hoping ere was way to fix it.
I'm sorry... for hurting you.
...

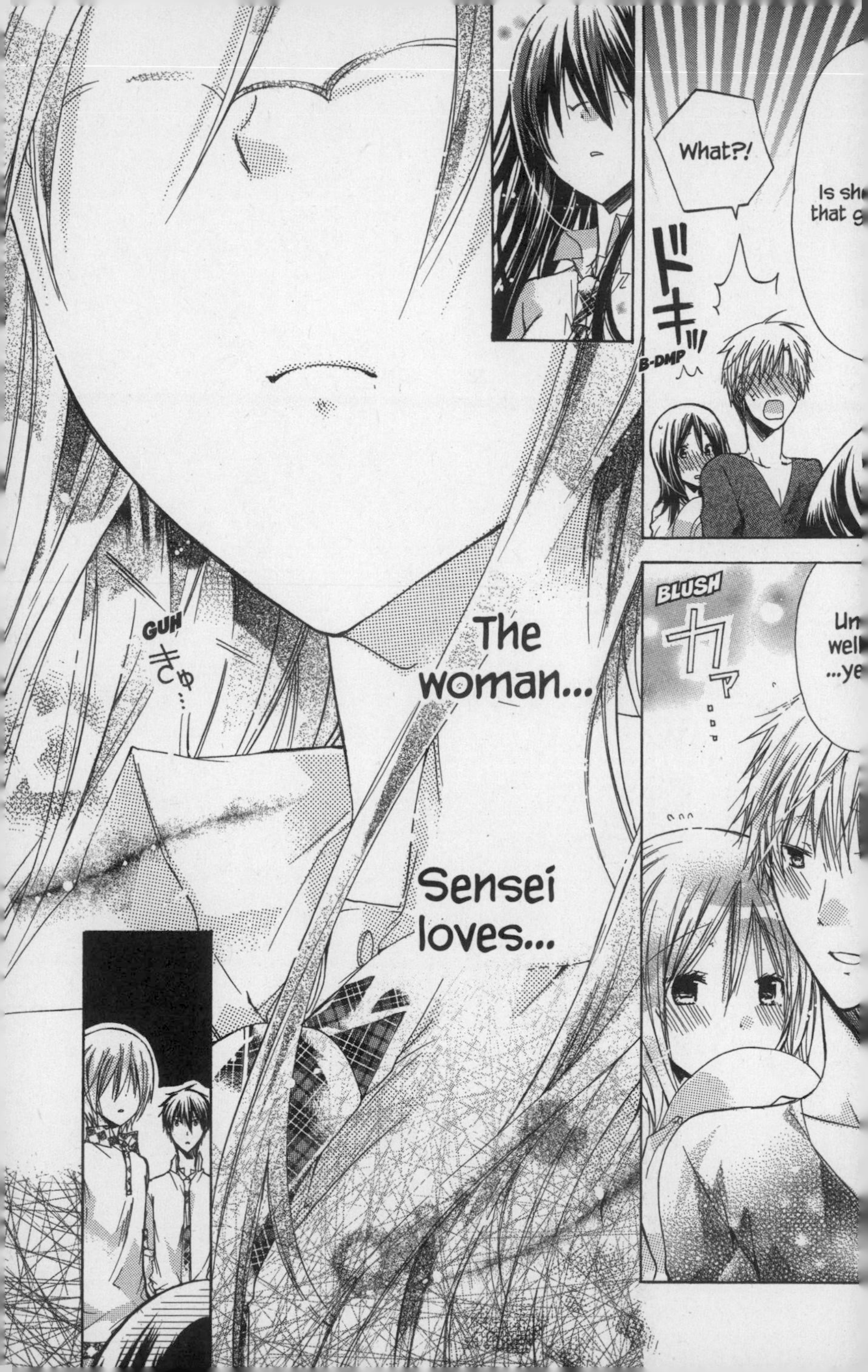

Is sh
that g
What?!
ドキッ
B-DMP
Um
well
...ye
BLUSH
カァ
...
The woman...
Sensei loves...
GUH
きゅ...

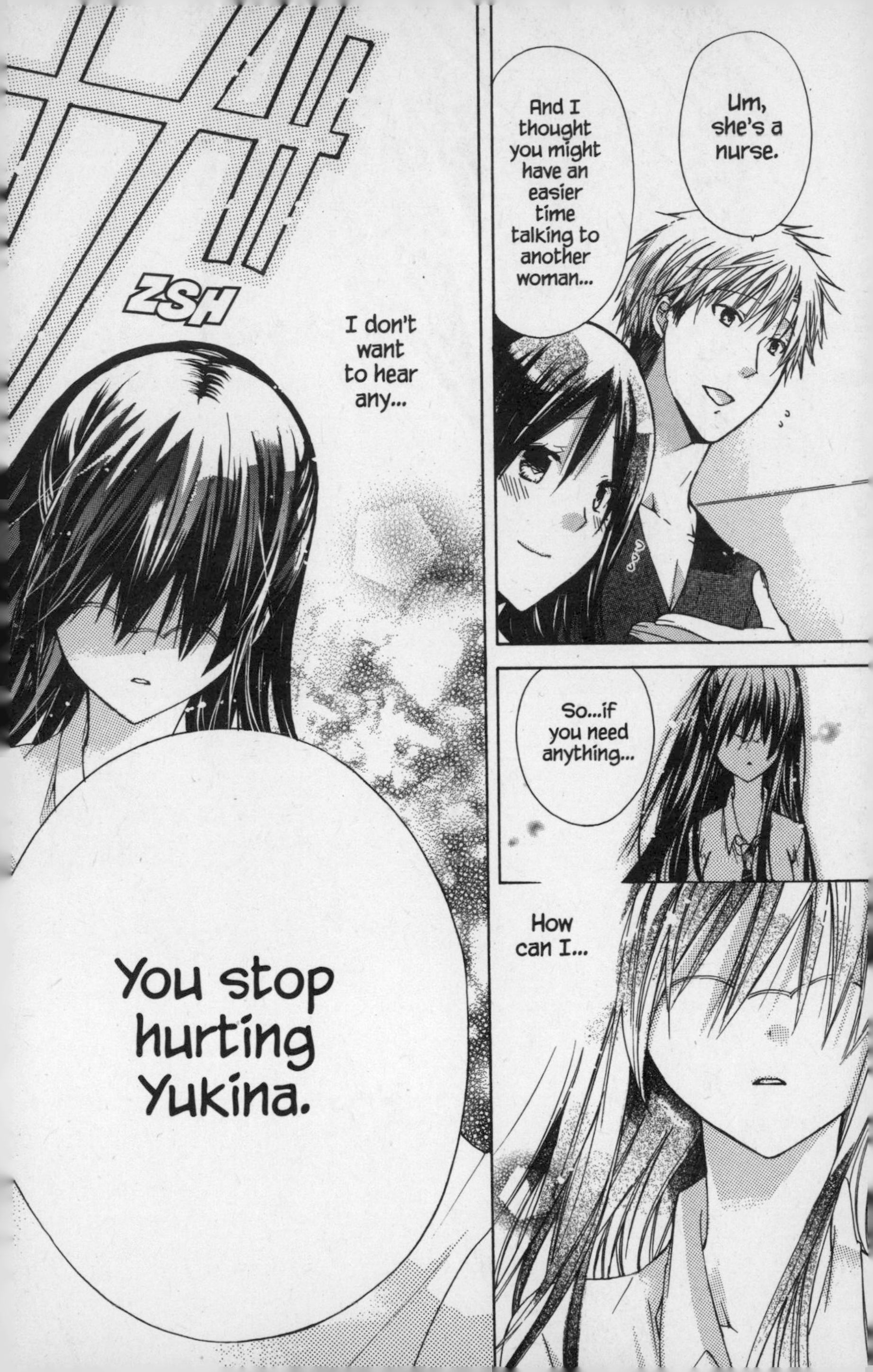
Um, she's a nurse.
And I thought you might have an easier time talking to another woman...
So...if you need anything...
How can I...
ZSH
I don't want to hear any...
You stop hurting Yukina.

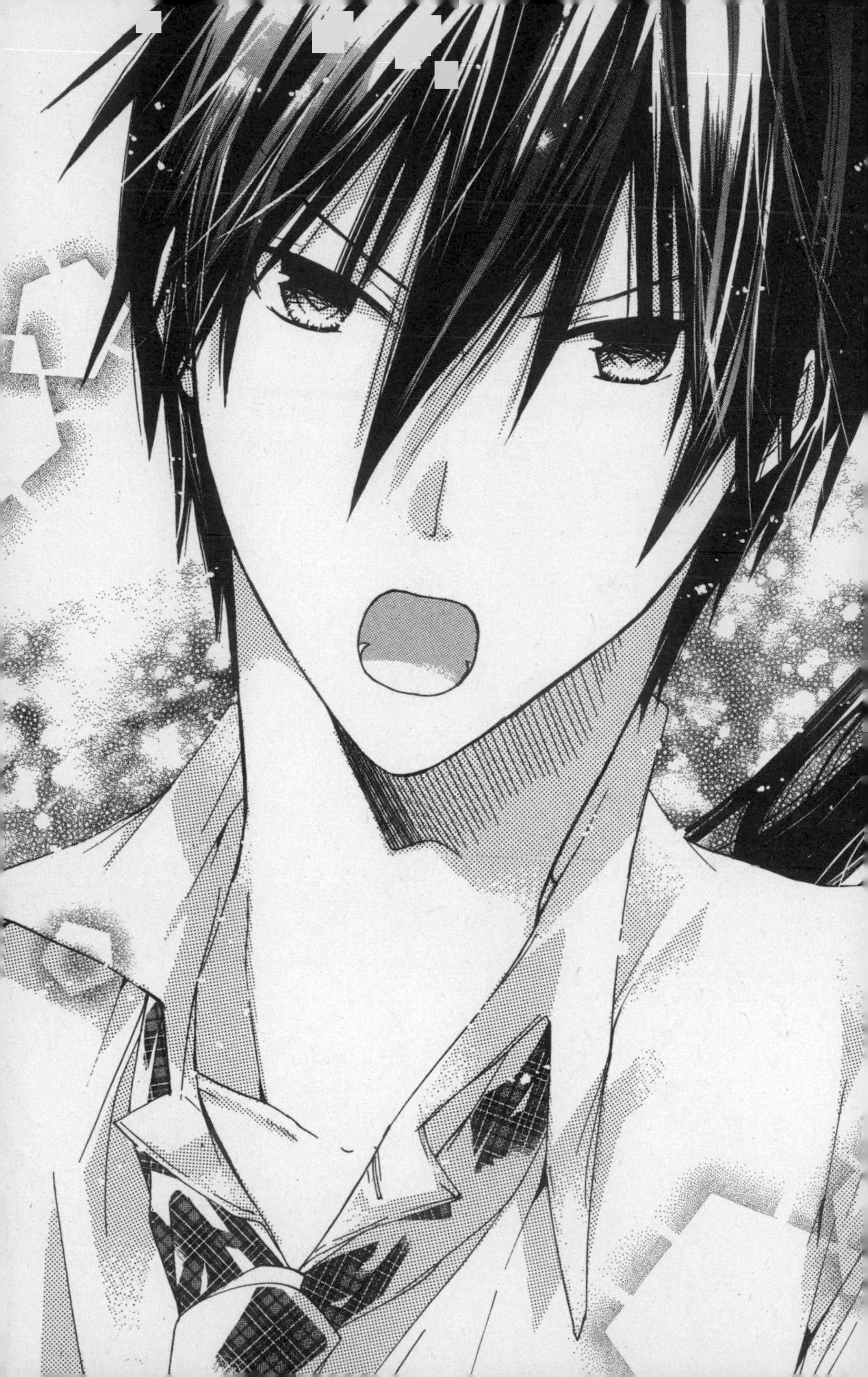

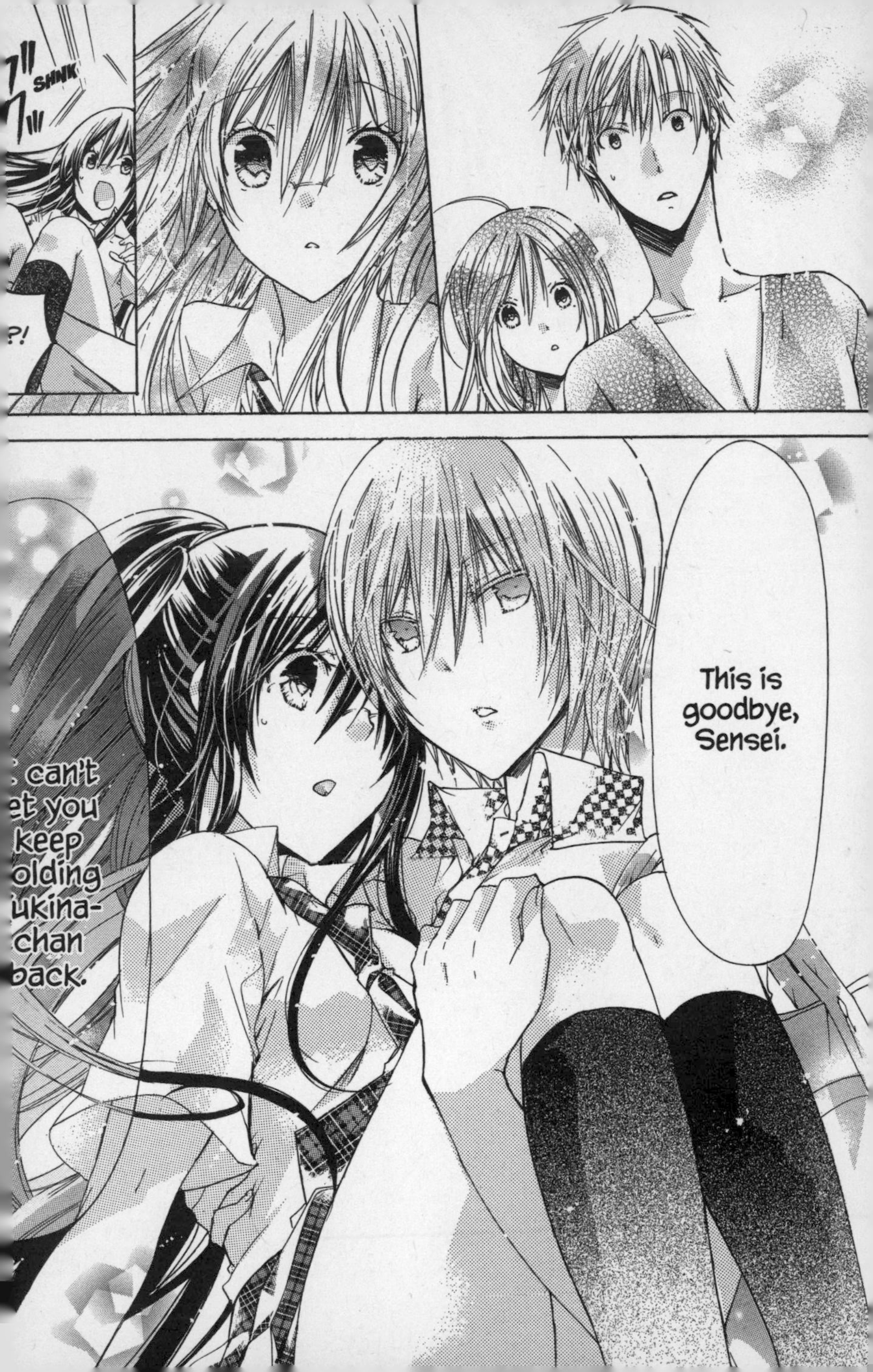

SHNK
?!
This is goodbye, Sensei.
can't
et you
keep
olding
ukina-
chan
back.

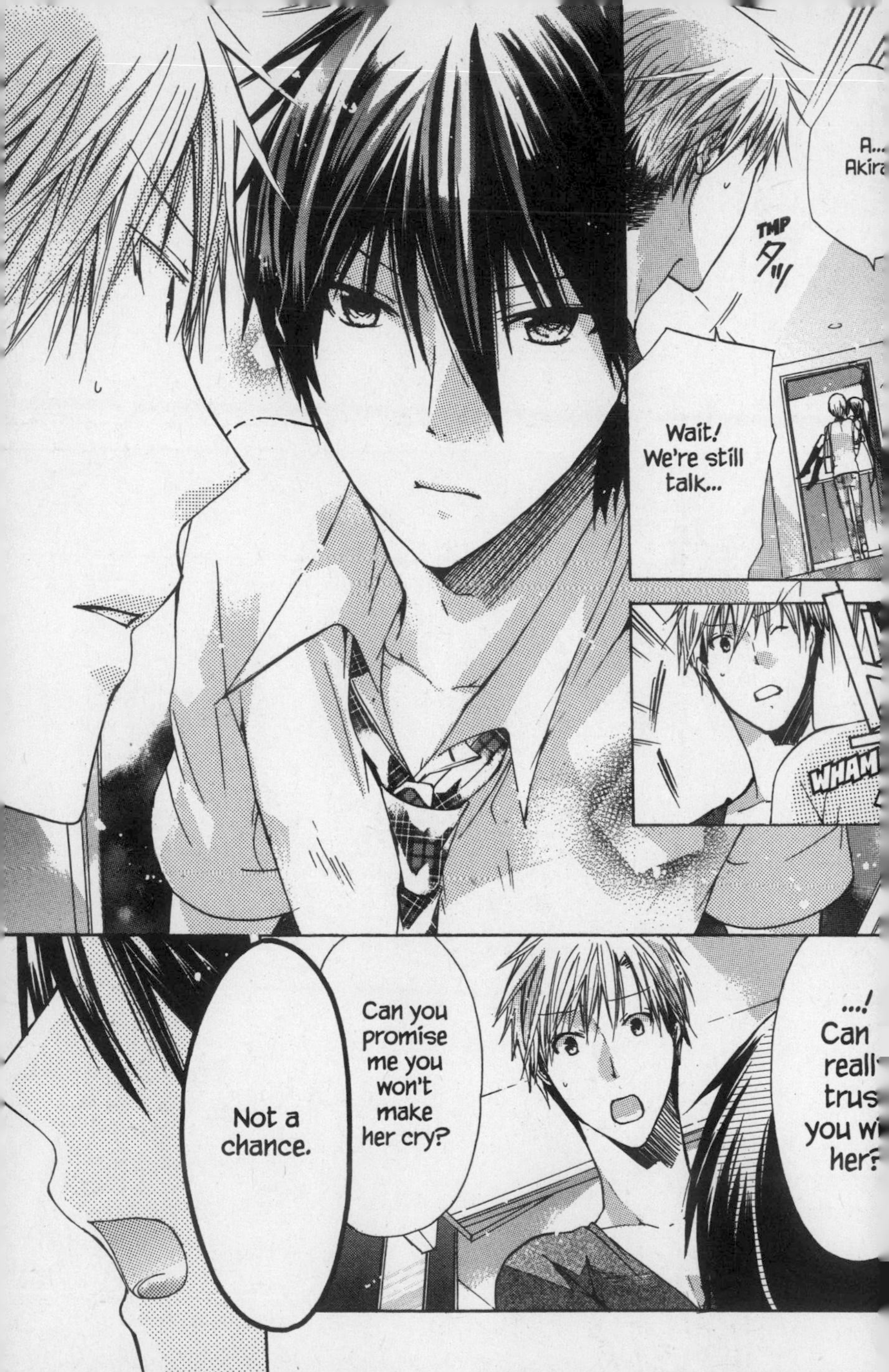
A... Akira
TMP タッ
Wait! We're still talk...
WHAM
...! Can reall trus you wi her?
Can you promise me you won't make her cry?
Not a chance.

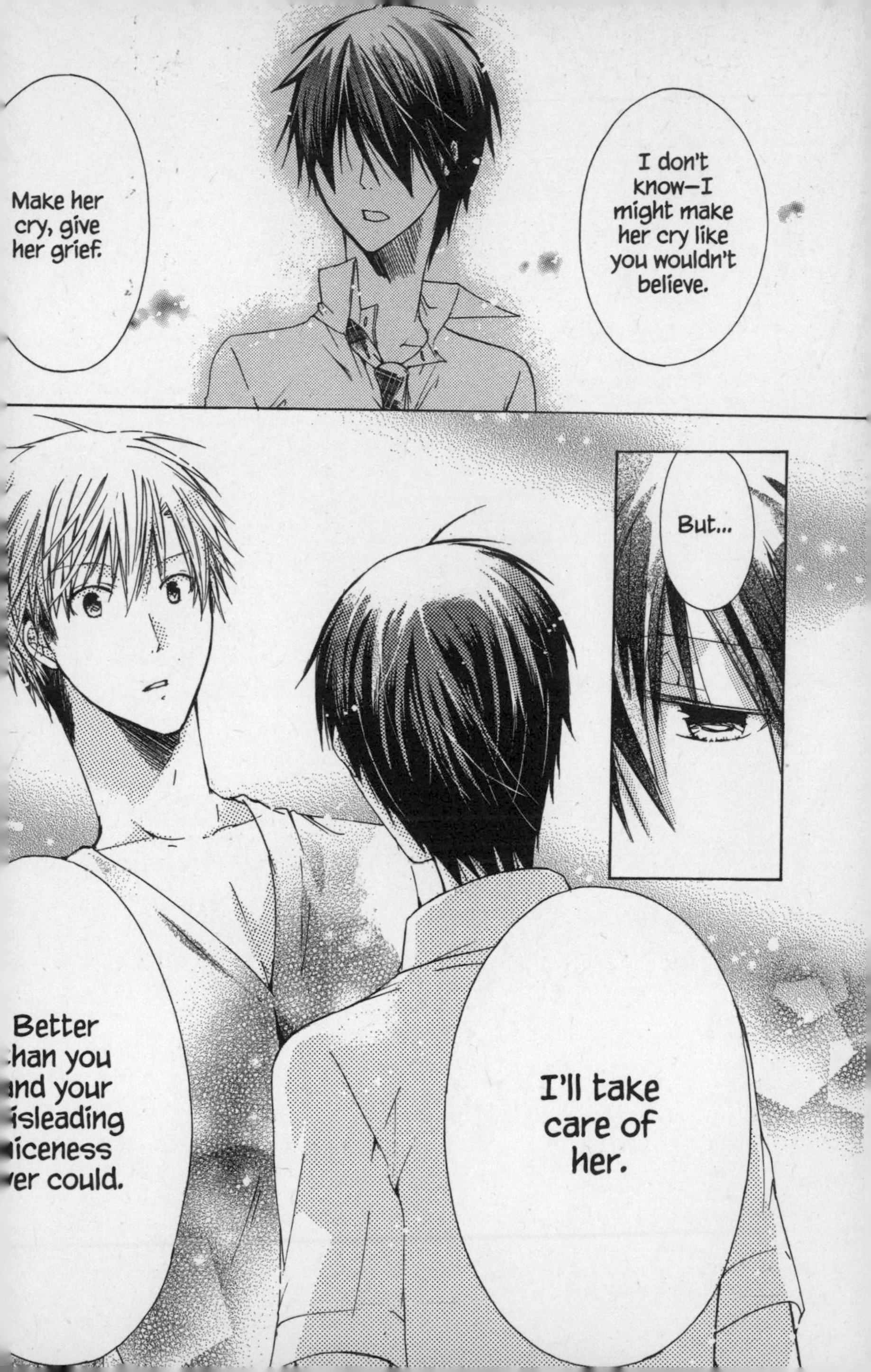
I don't know—I might make her cry like you wouldn't believe.
Make her cry, give her grief.
But...
I'll take care of her.
Better han you nd your isleading iceness ver could.

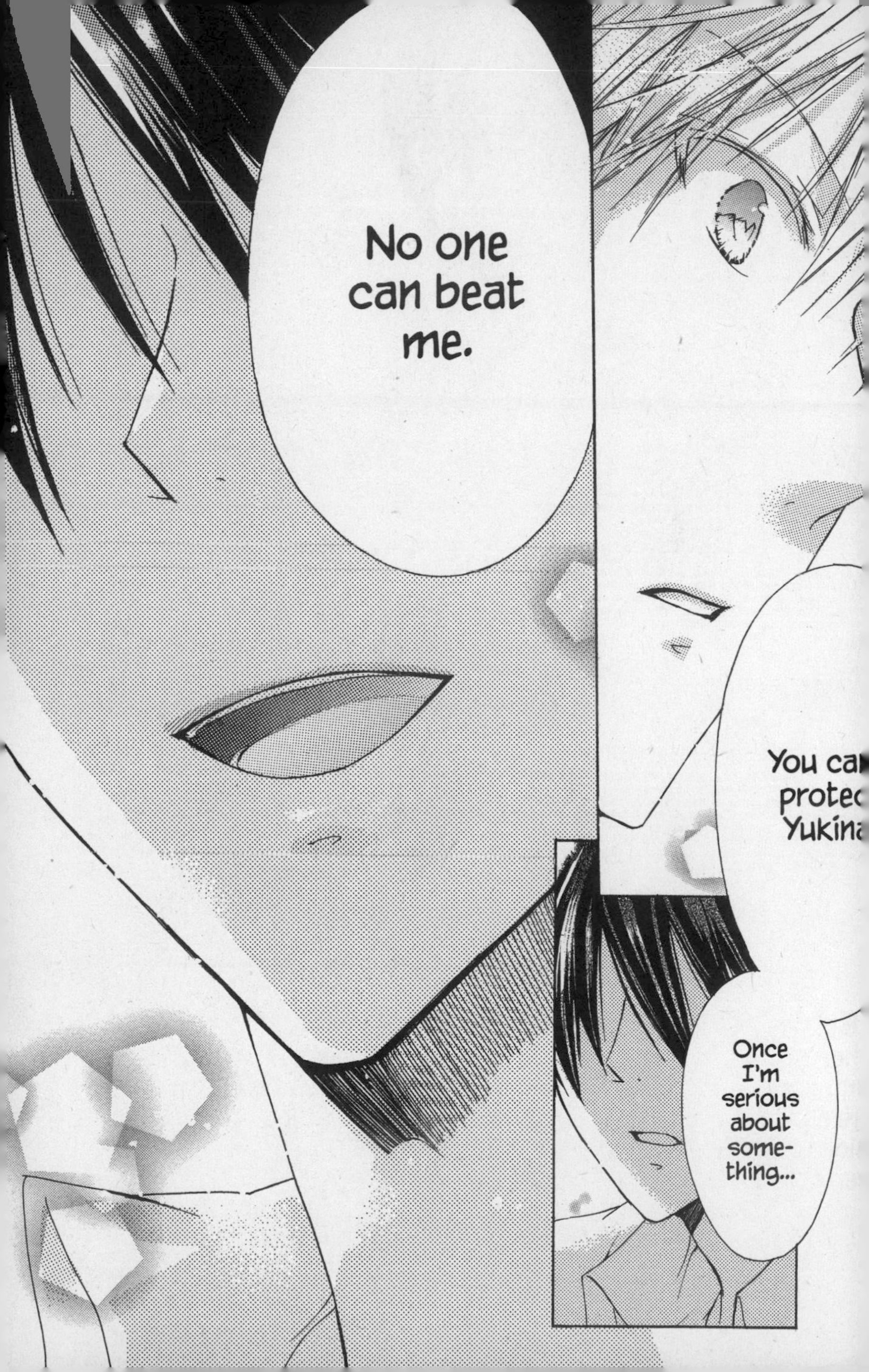
You ca protec Yukina
Once I'm serious about some-thing...
No one can beat me.

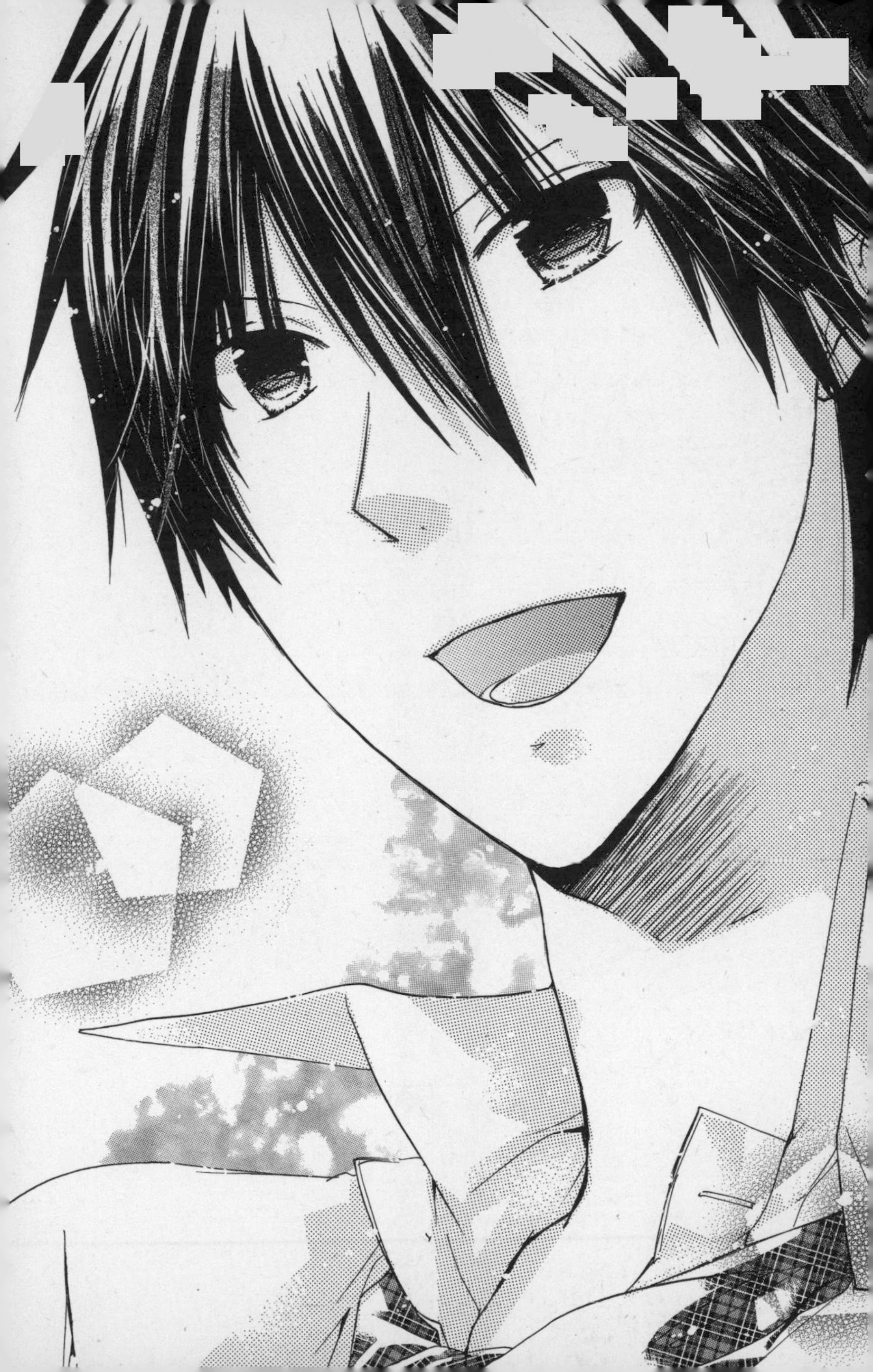

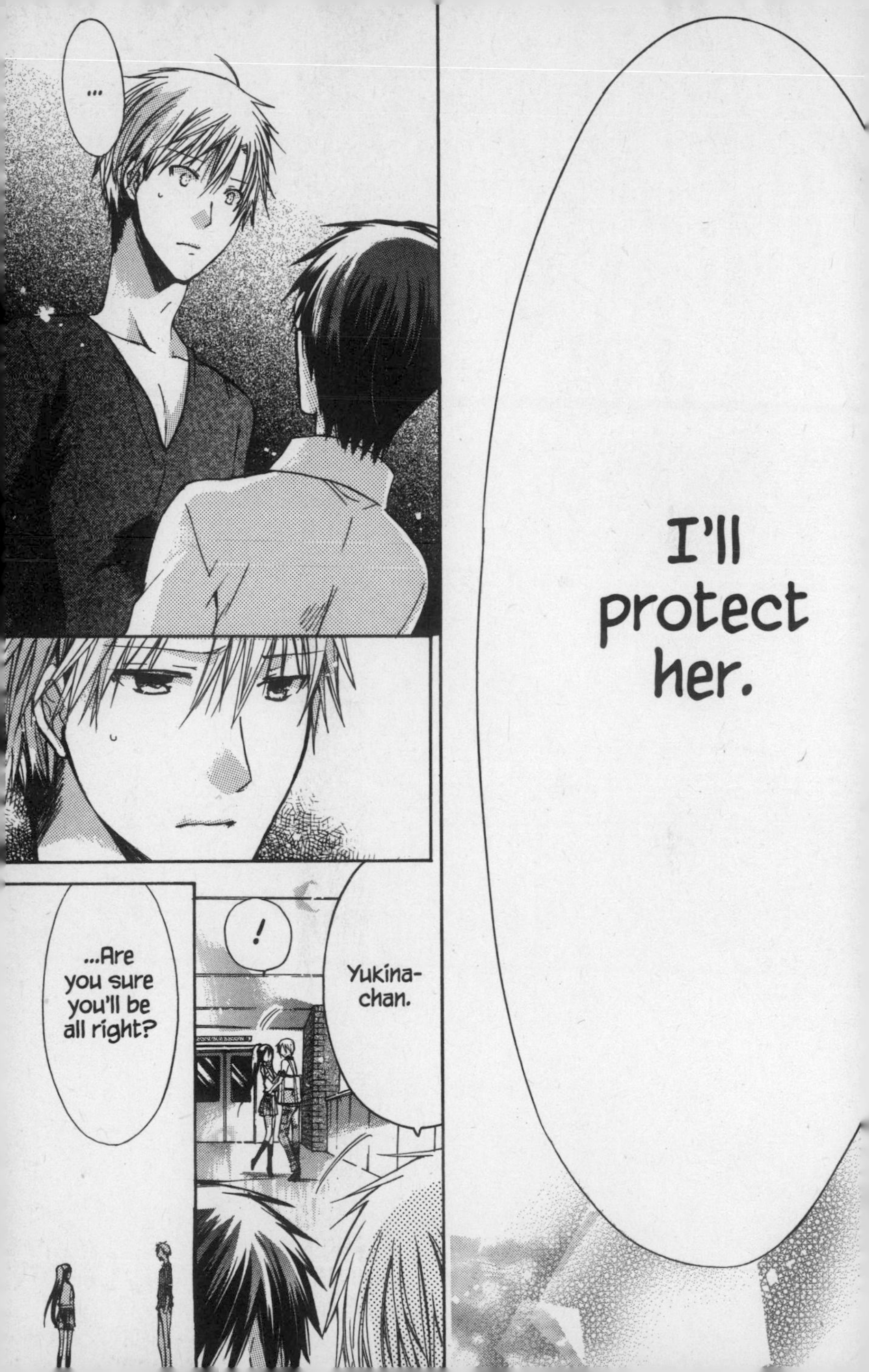
I'll protect her.
...
Yukina-chan.
!
...Are you sure you'll be all right?

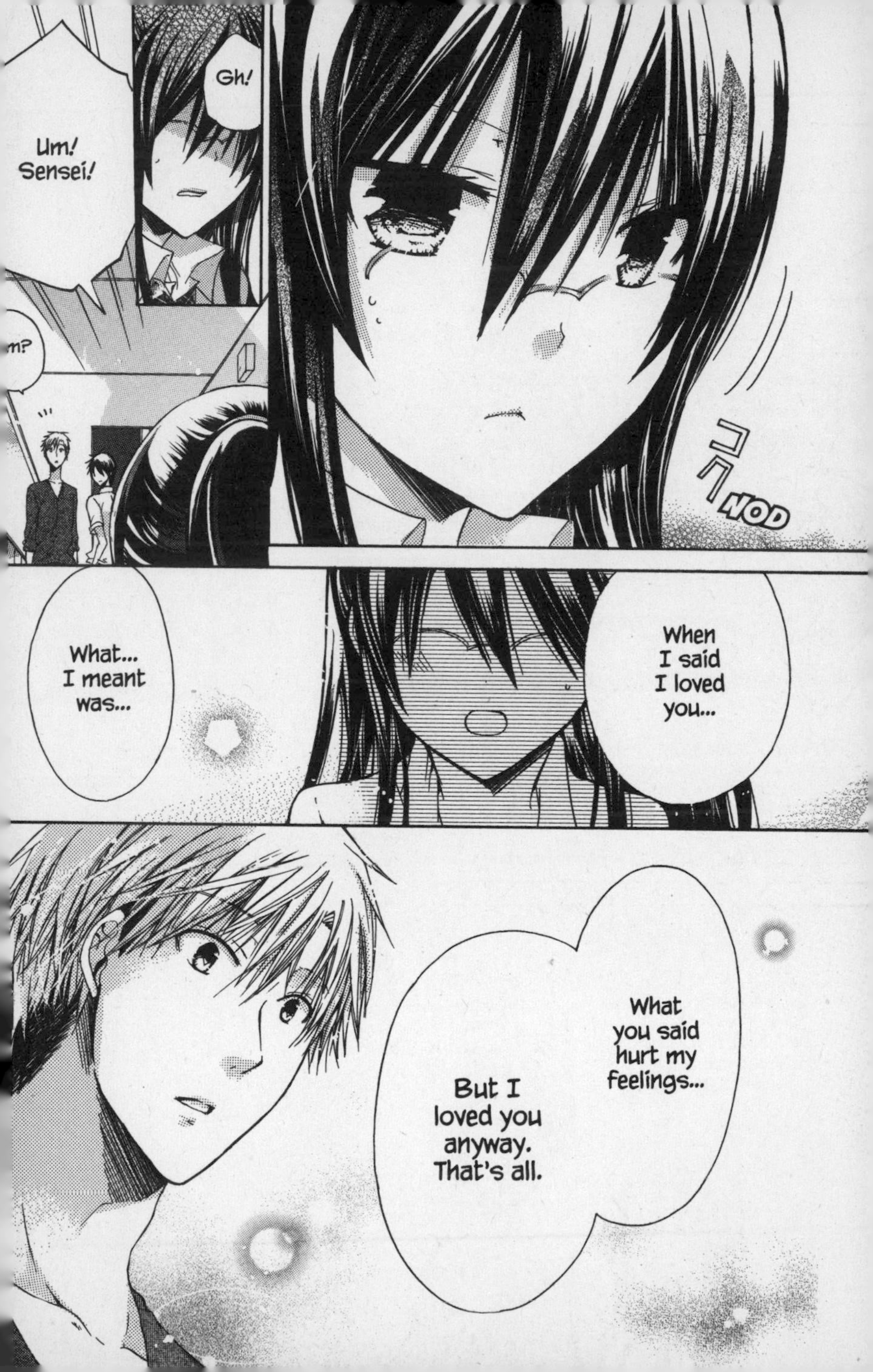
コク
NOD
Gh!
Um! Sensei!
m?
When I said I loved you...
What... I meant was...
What you said hurt my feelings...
But I loved you anyway. That's all.

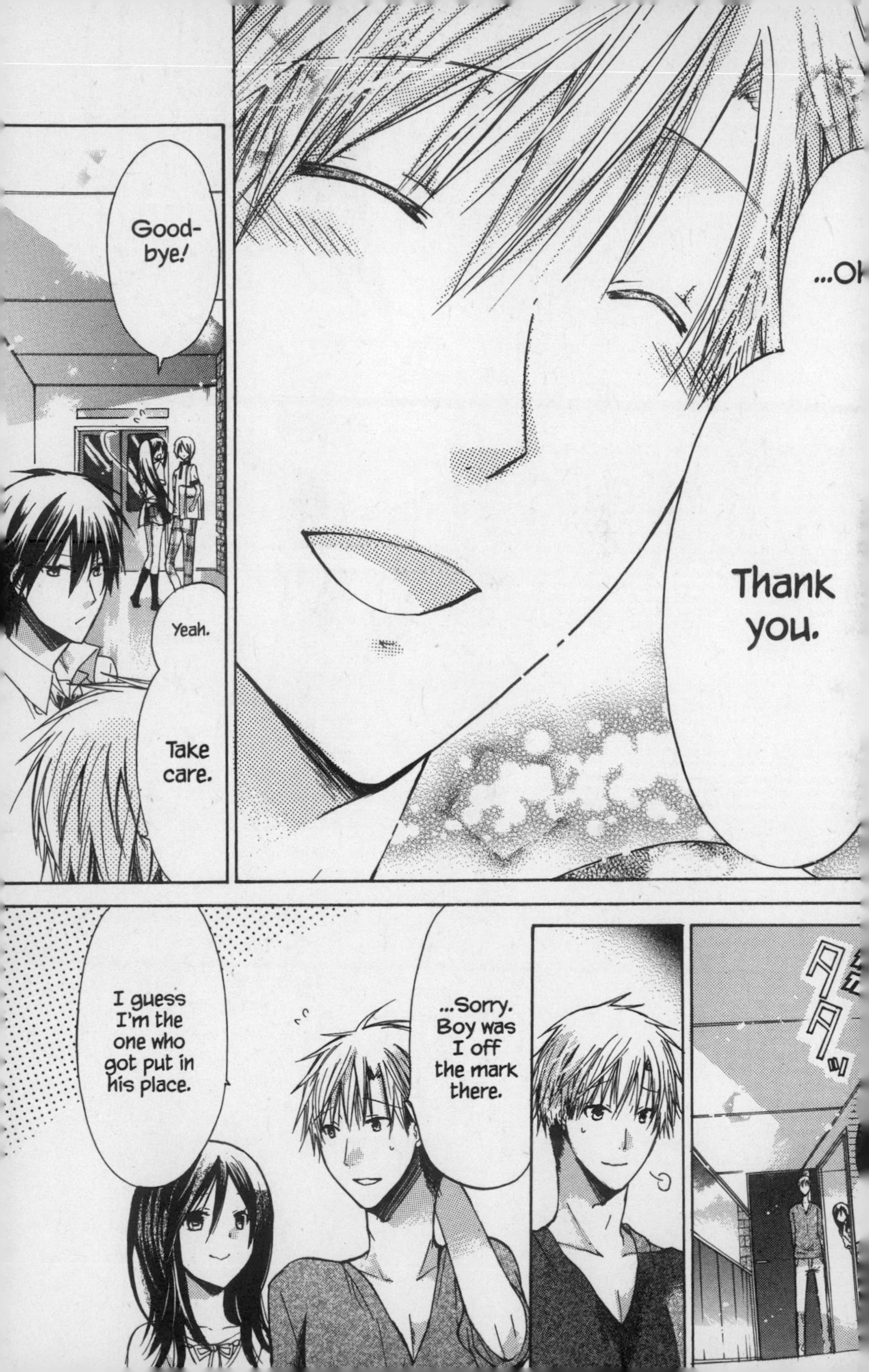

...Oh
Thank you.
Good-bye!
Yeah.
Take care.
...Sorry. Boy was I off the mark there.
I guess I'm the one who got put in his place.

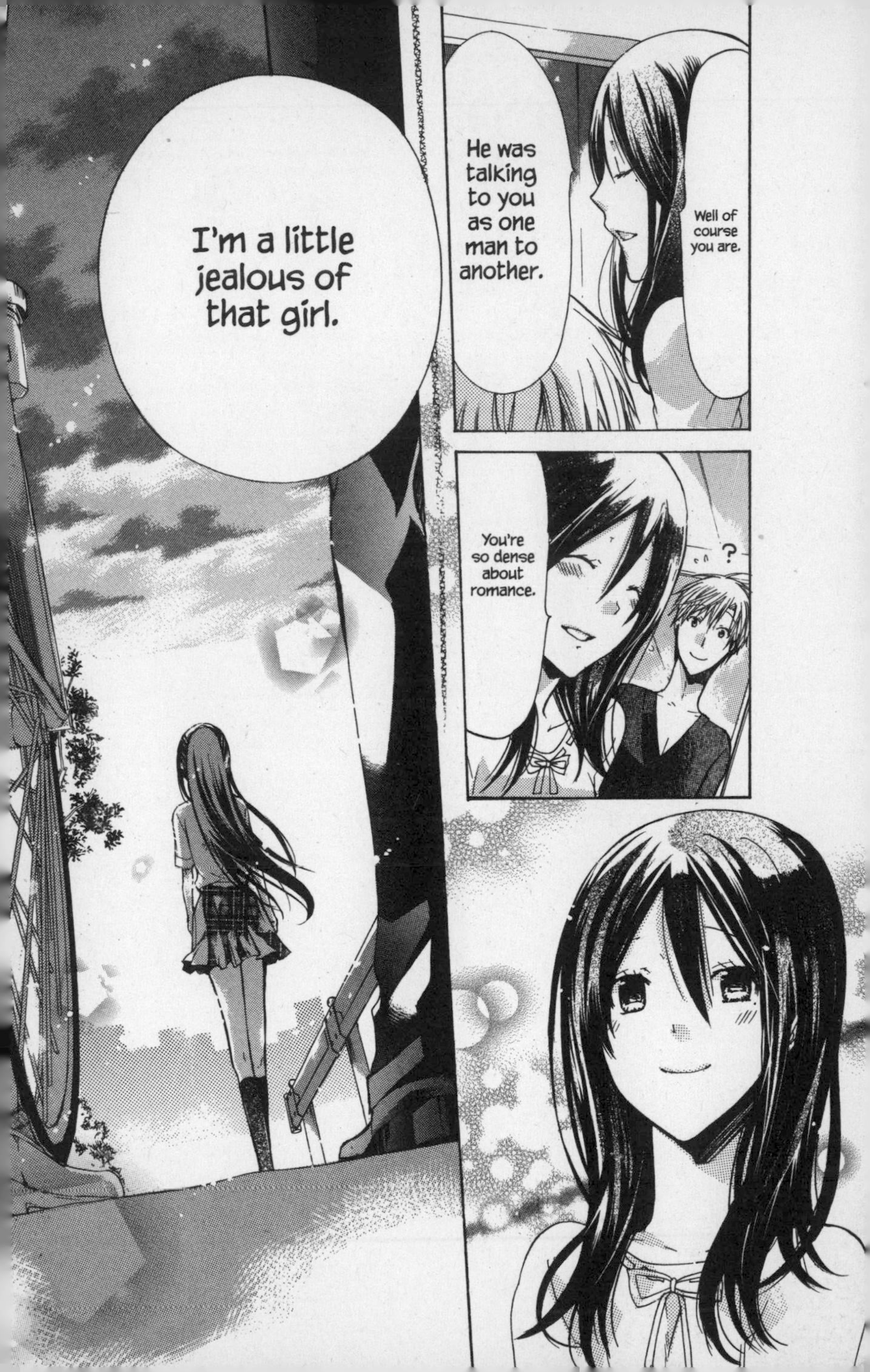
Well of course you are.
He was talking to you as one man to another.
You're so dense about romance.
?
I'm a little jealous of that girl.

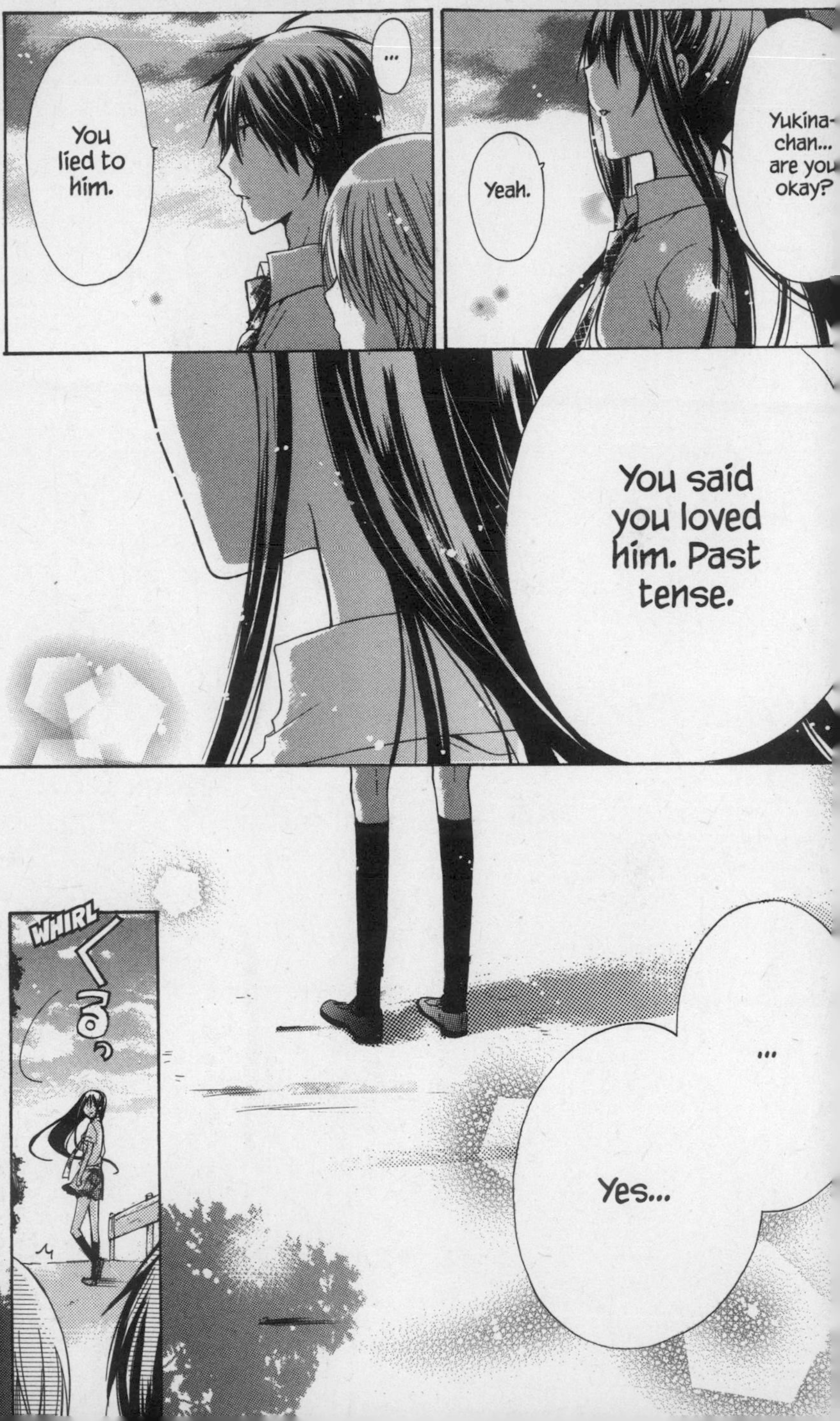
Yukina-chan... are you okay?
Yeah.
...
You lied to him.
You said you loved him. Past tense.
...
Yes...
WHIRL
くるっ

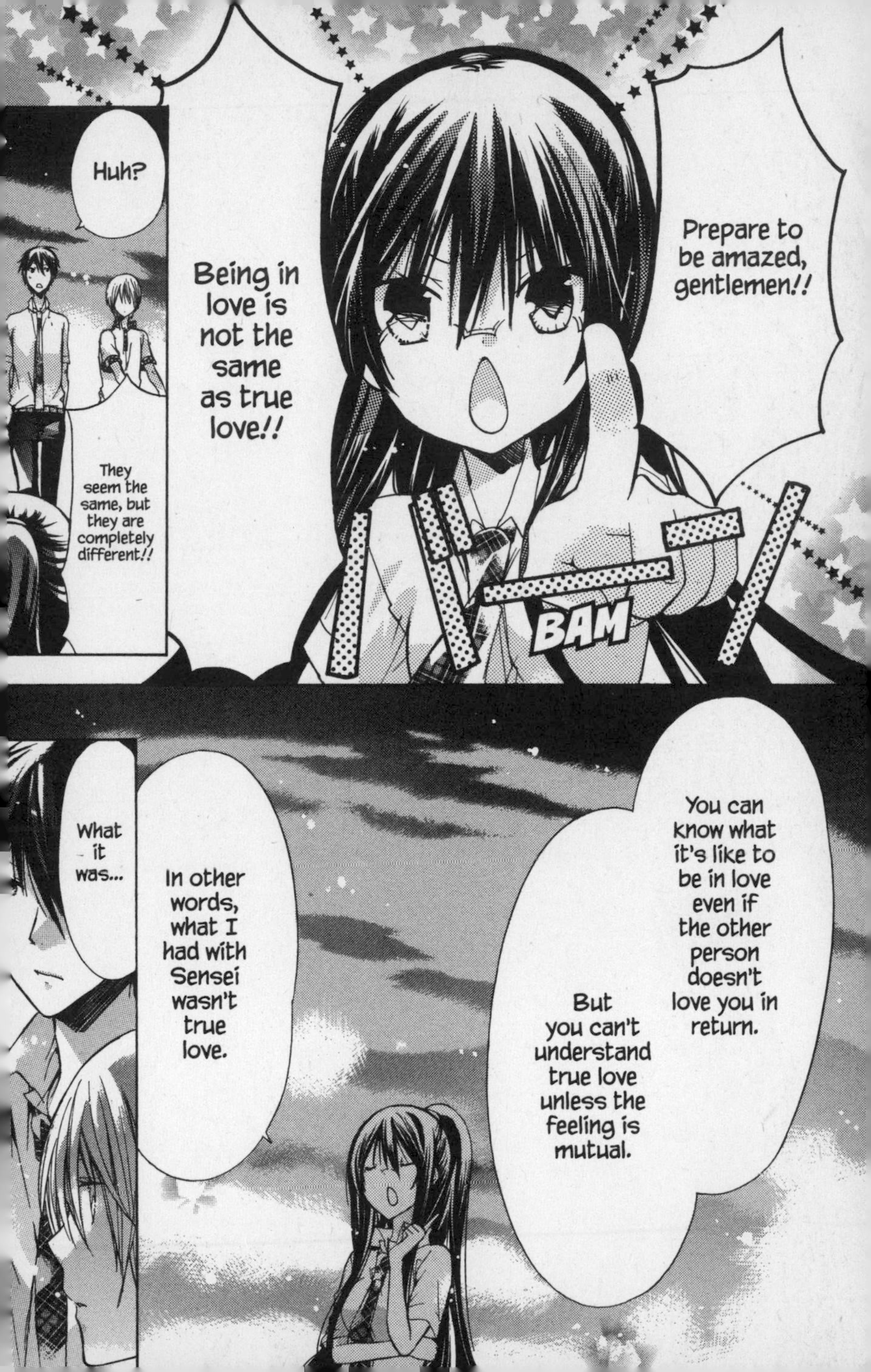
Prepare to be amazed, gentlemen!!
Being in love is not the same as true love!!
BAM
Huh?
They seem the same, but they are completely different!!
You can know what it's like to be in love even if the other person doesn't love you in return.
But you can't understand true love unless the feeling is mutual.
In other words, what I had with Sensei wasn't true love.
What it was...

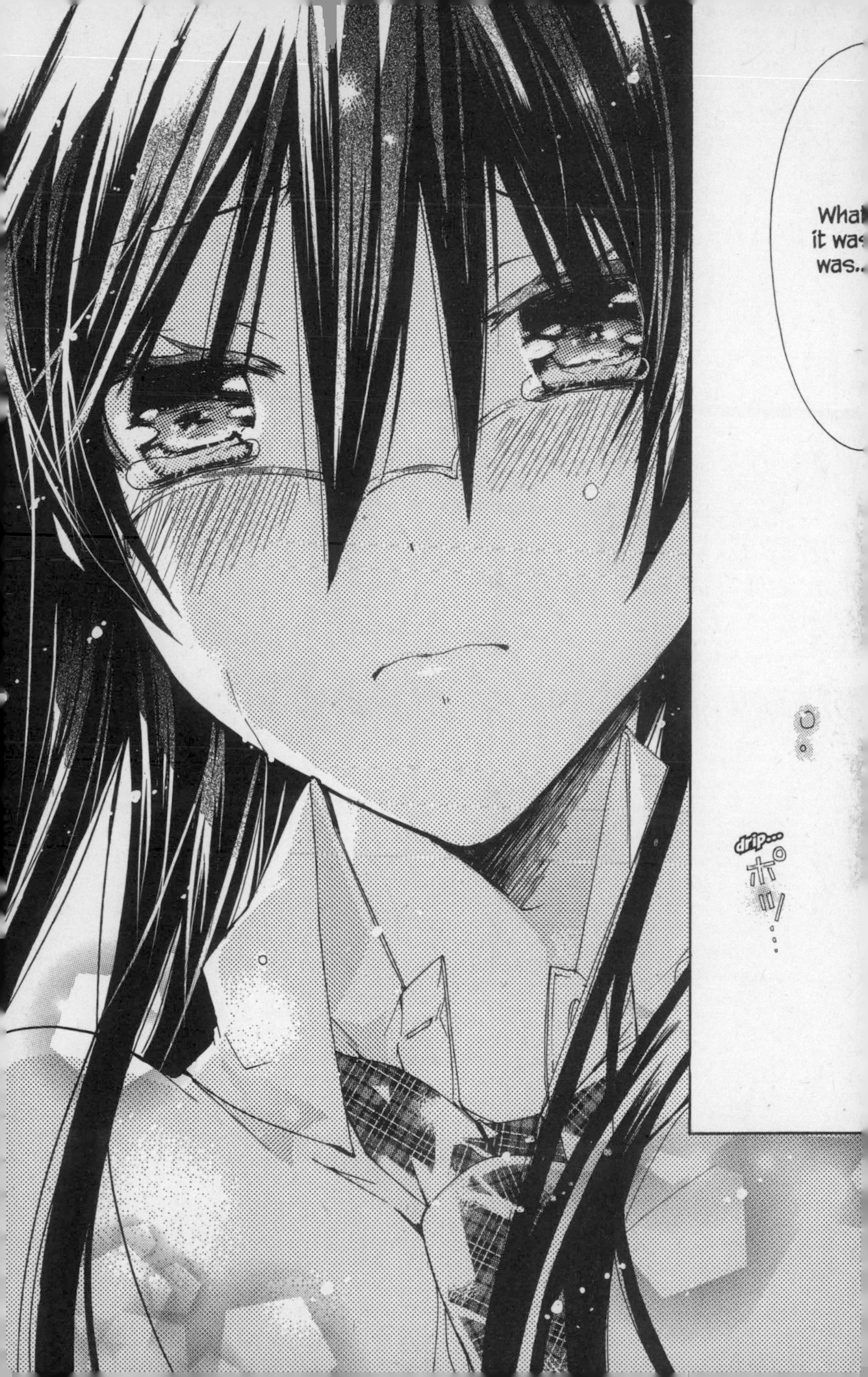
What
it was
was..
drip...
ポツ...

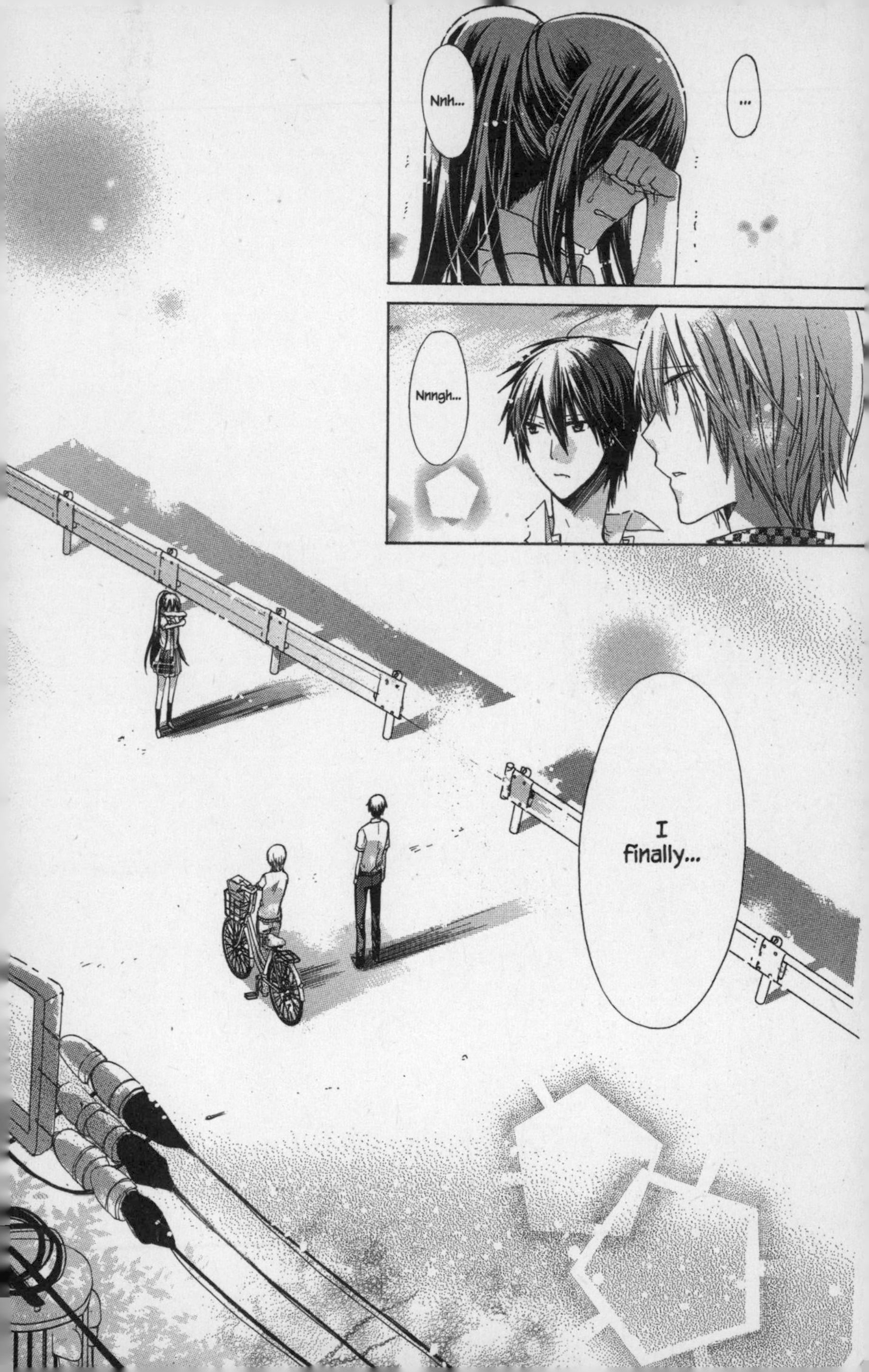
...
Nnh...
Nnngh...
I finally...

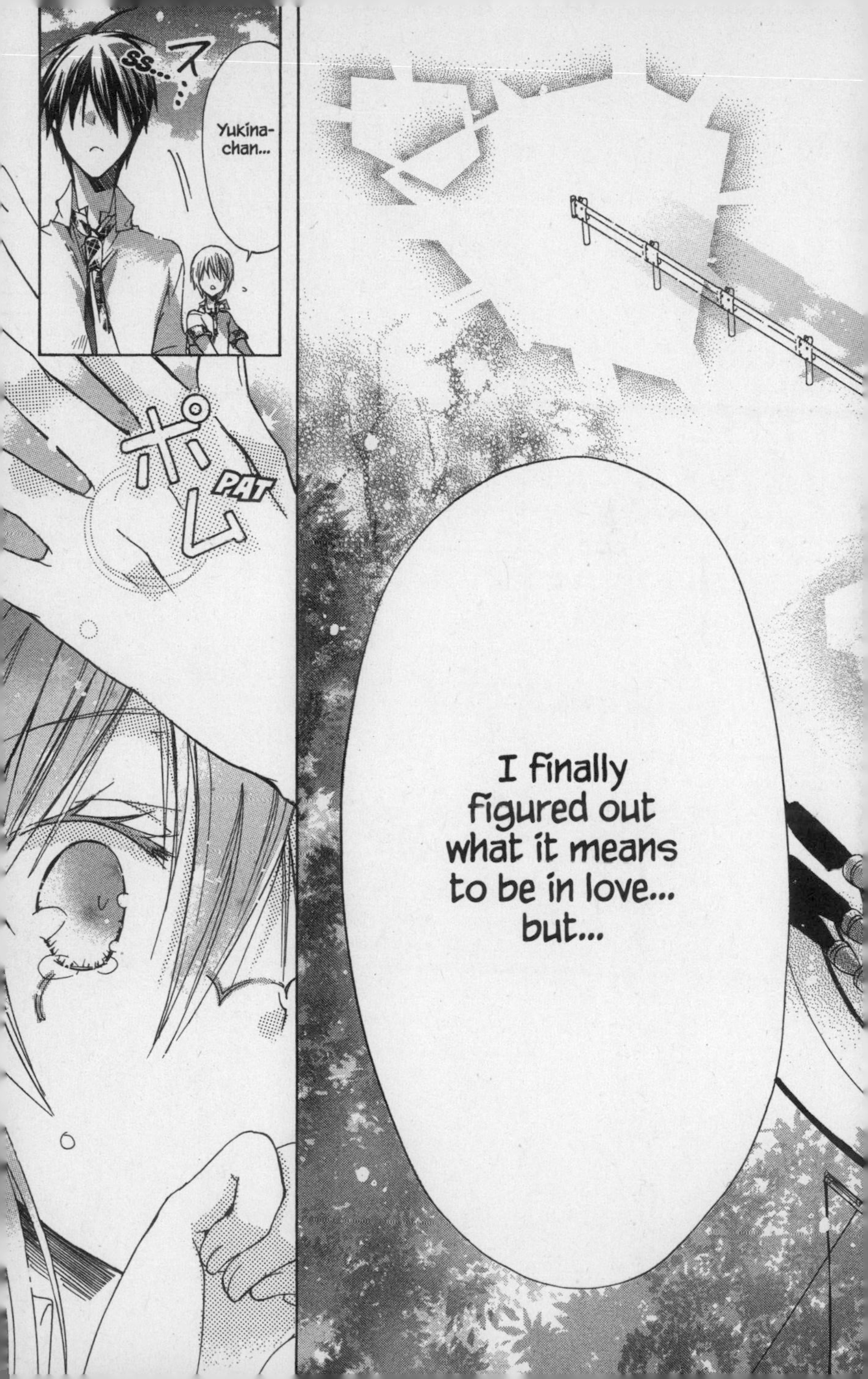
I finally figured out what it means to be in love... but...
SS...
Yukina-chan...
PAT

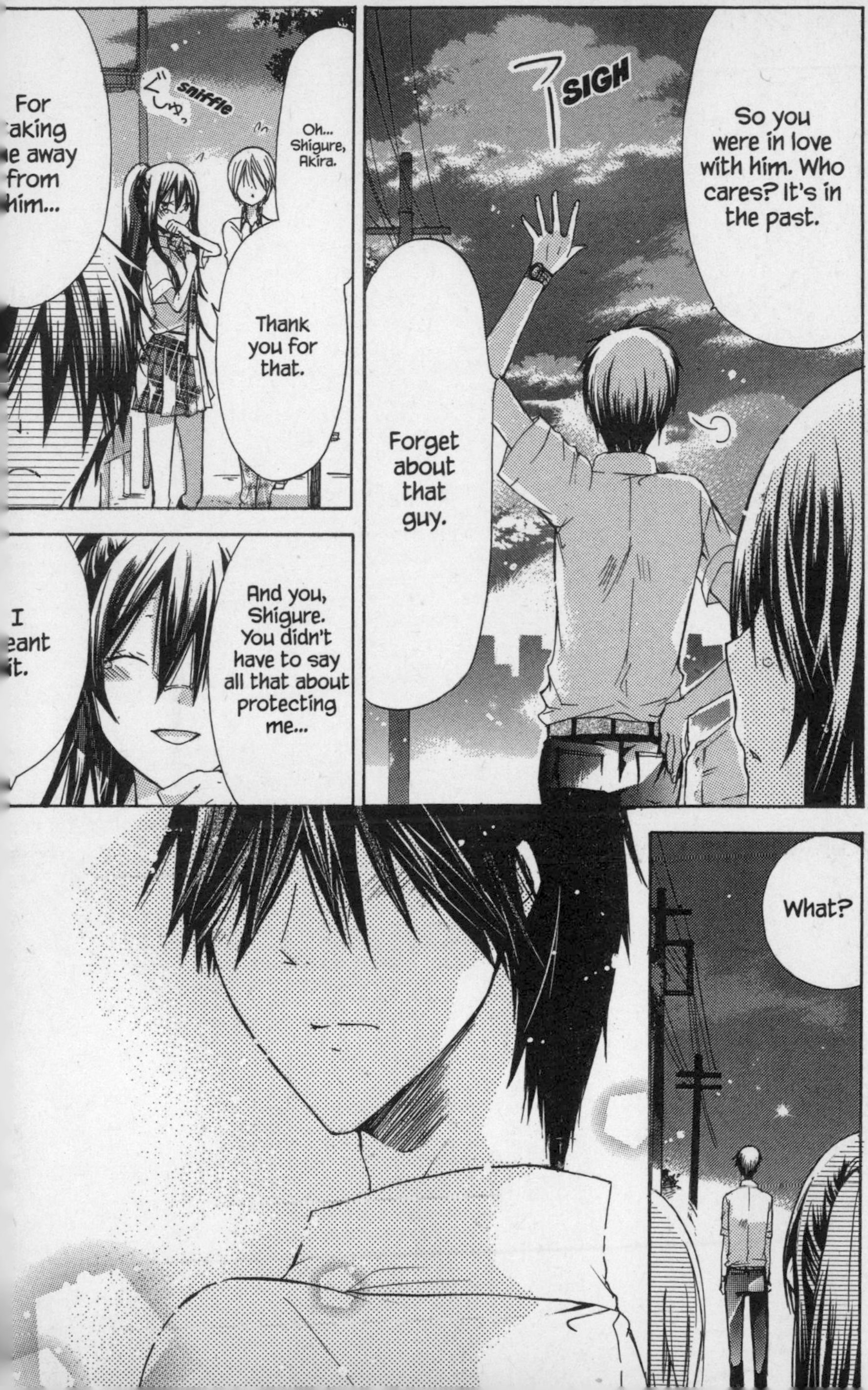
SIGH
So you were in love with him. Who cares? It's in the past.
Forget about that guy.
Oh... Shigure, Akira.
Thank you for that.
ぐしゅっ
sniffle
For aking e away from him...
And you, Shigure. You didn't have to say all that about protecting me...
I eant it.
What?

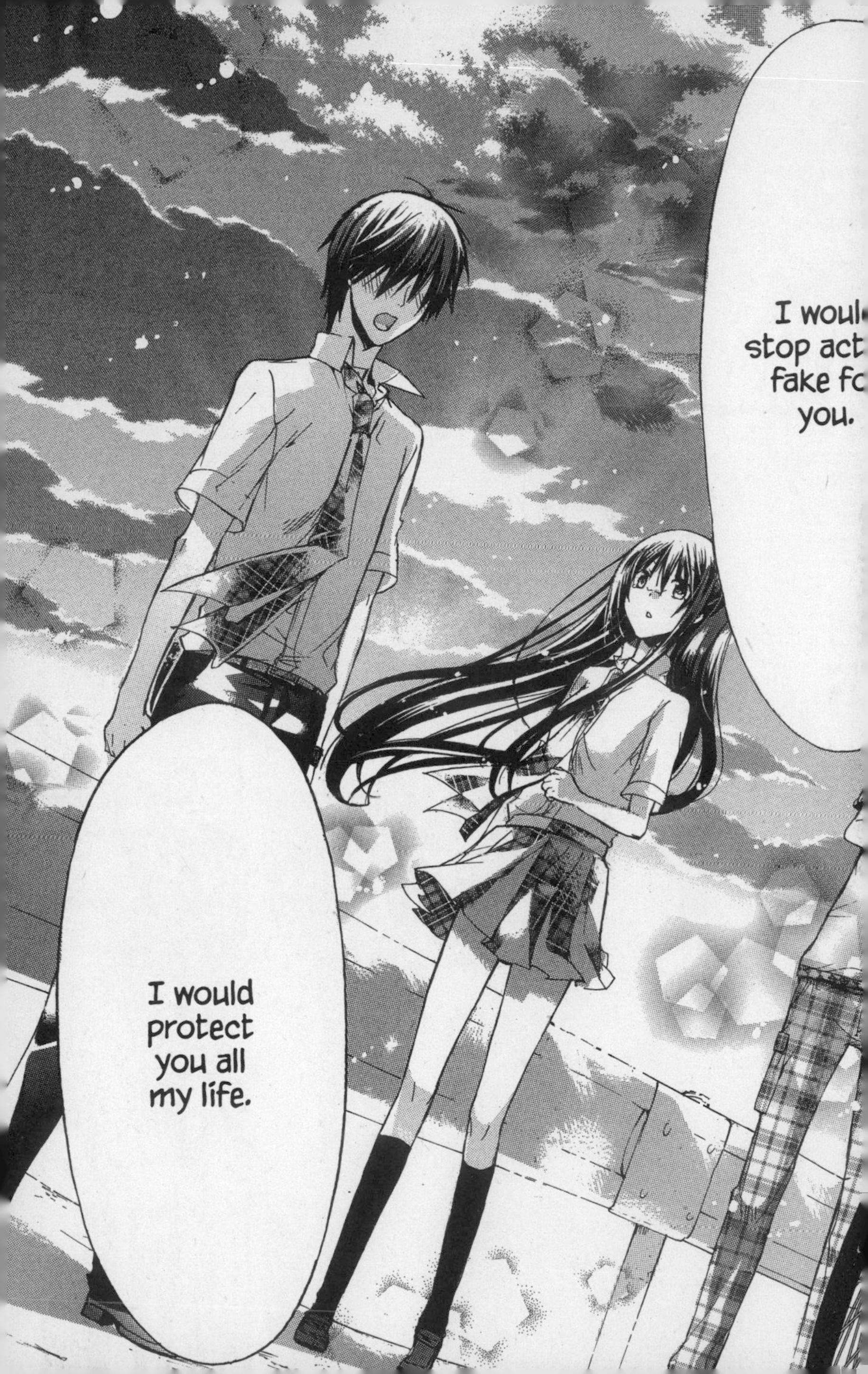
I woul stop act fake fo you.
I would protect you all my life.

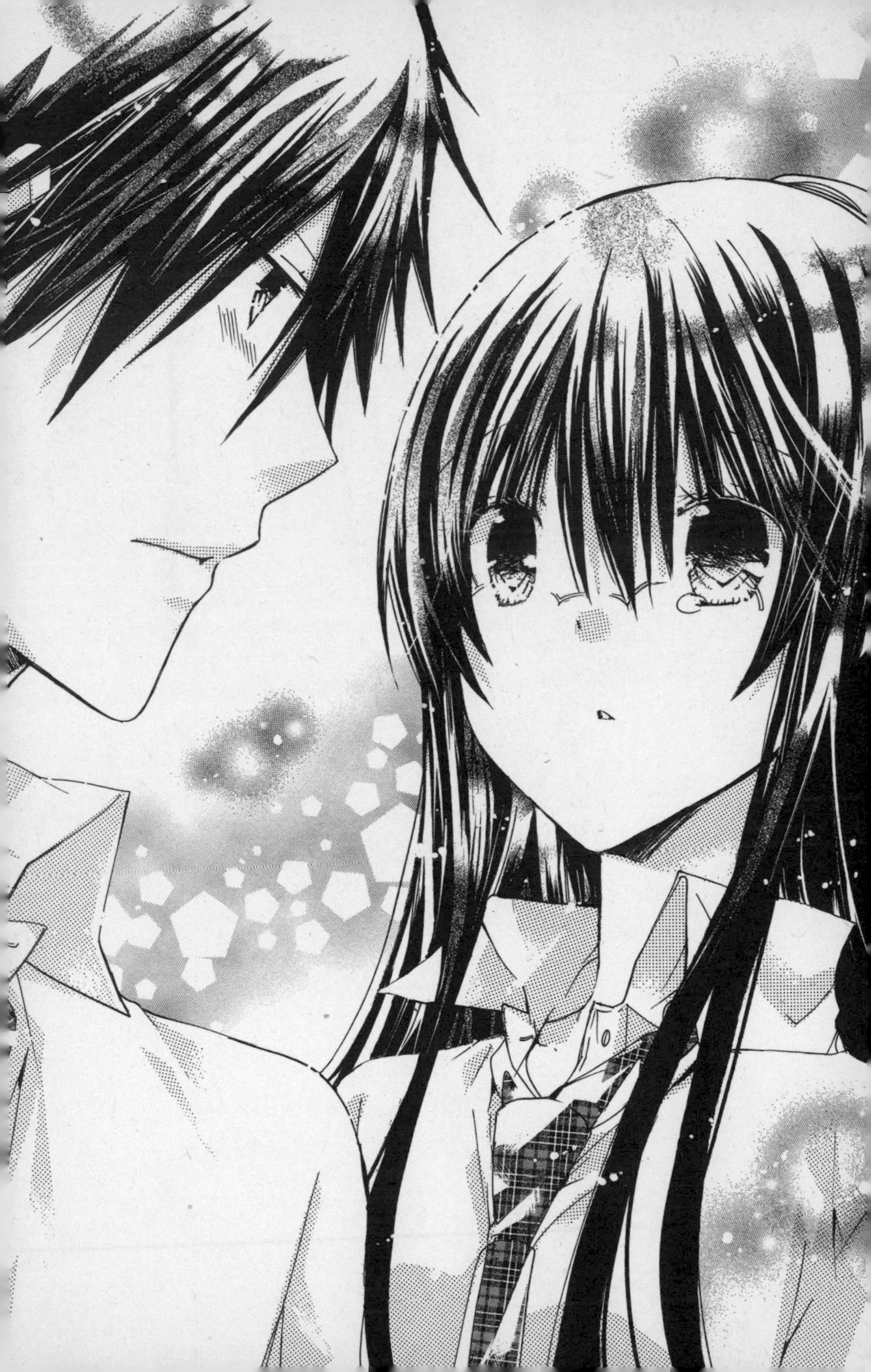

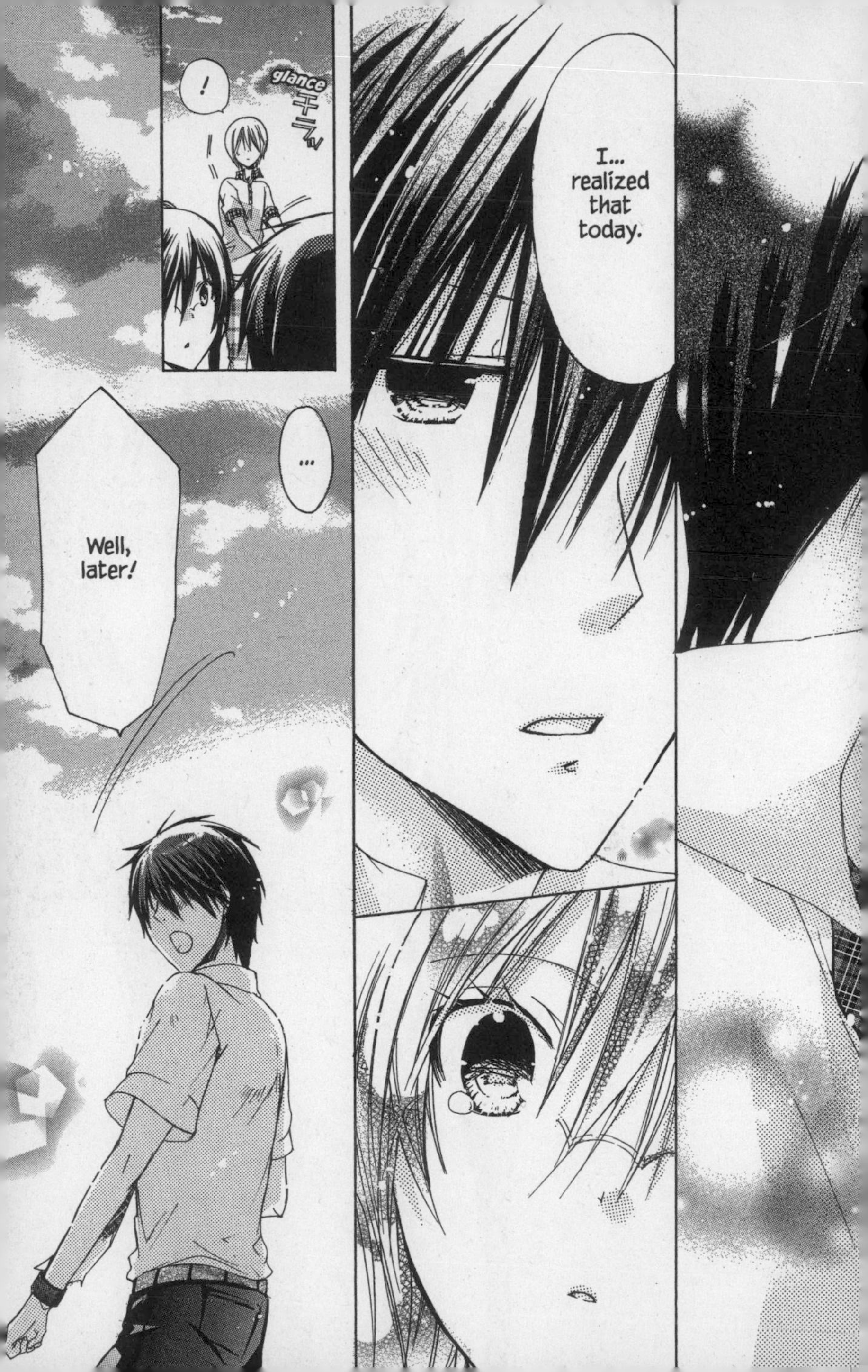
I... realized that today.
glance
!
...
Well, later!

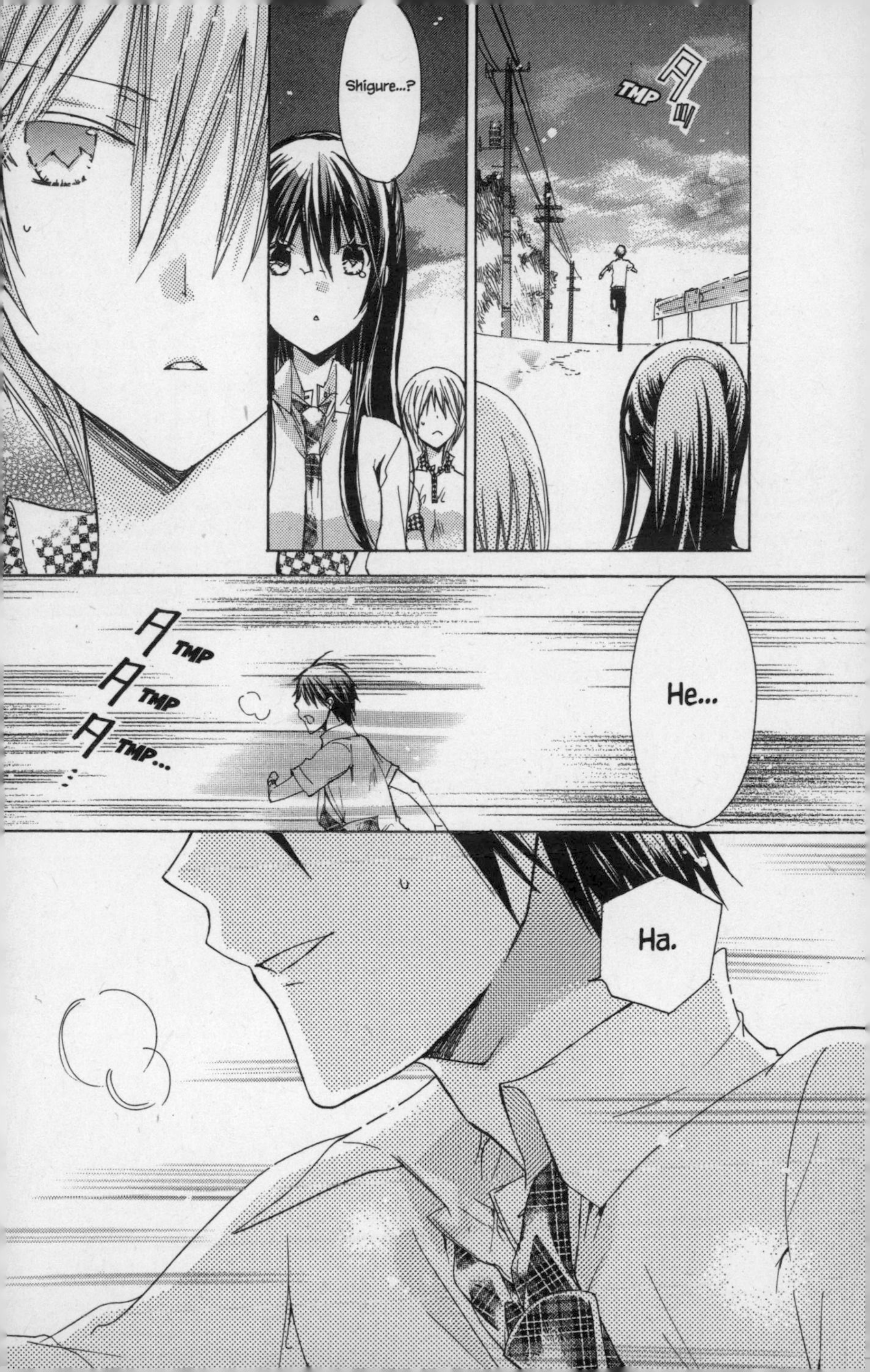
TMP
Shigure...?
He...
TMP
TMP
TMP...
Ha.

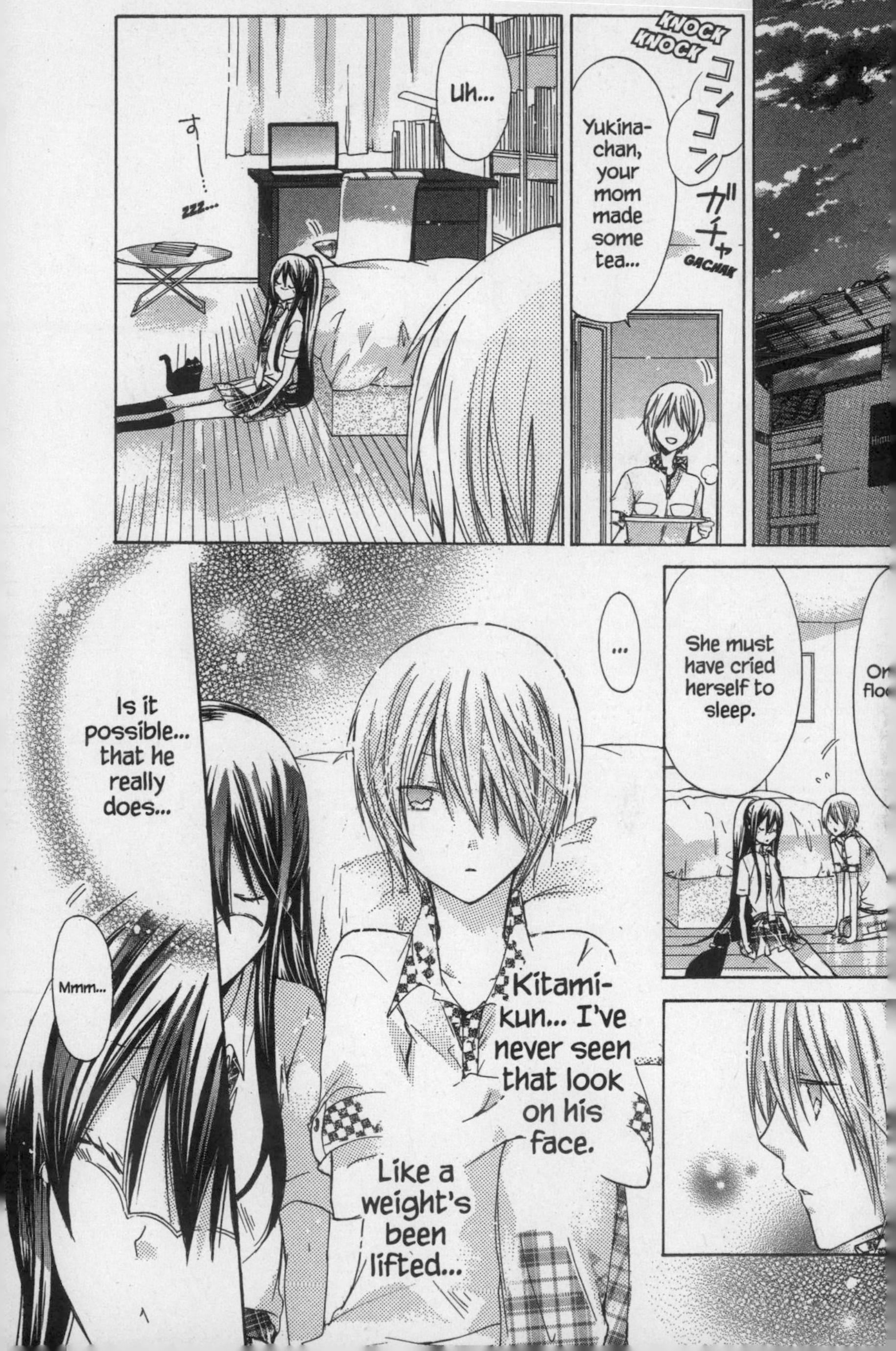
KNOCK KNOCK
コンコン
Yukina-chan, your mom made some tea...
ガチャ
GACHAK
Uh...
すー…
zzz...
She must have cried herself to sleep.
...
Kitami-kun... I've never seen that look on his face.
Like a weight's been lifted...
Is it possible... that he really does...
Mmm...

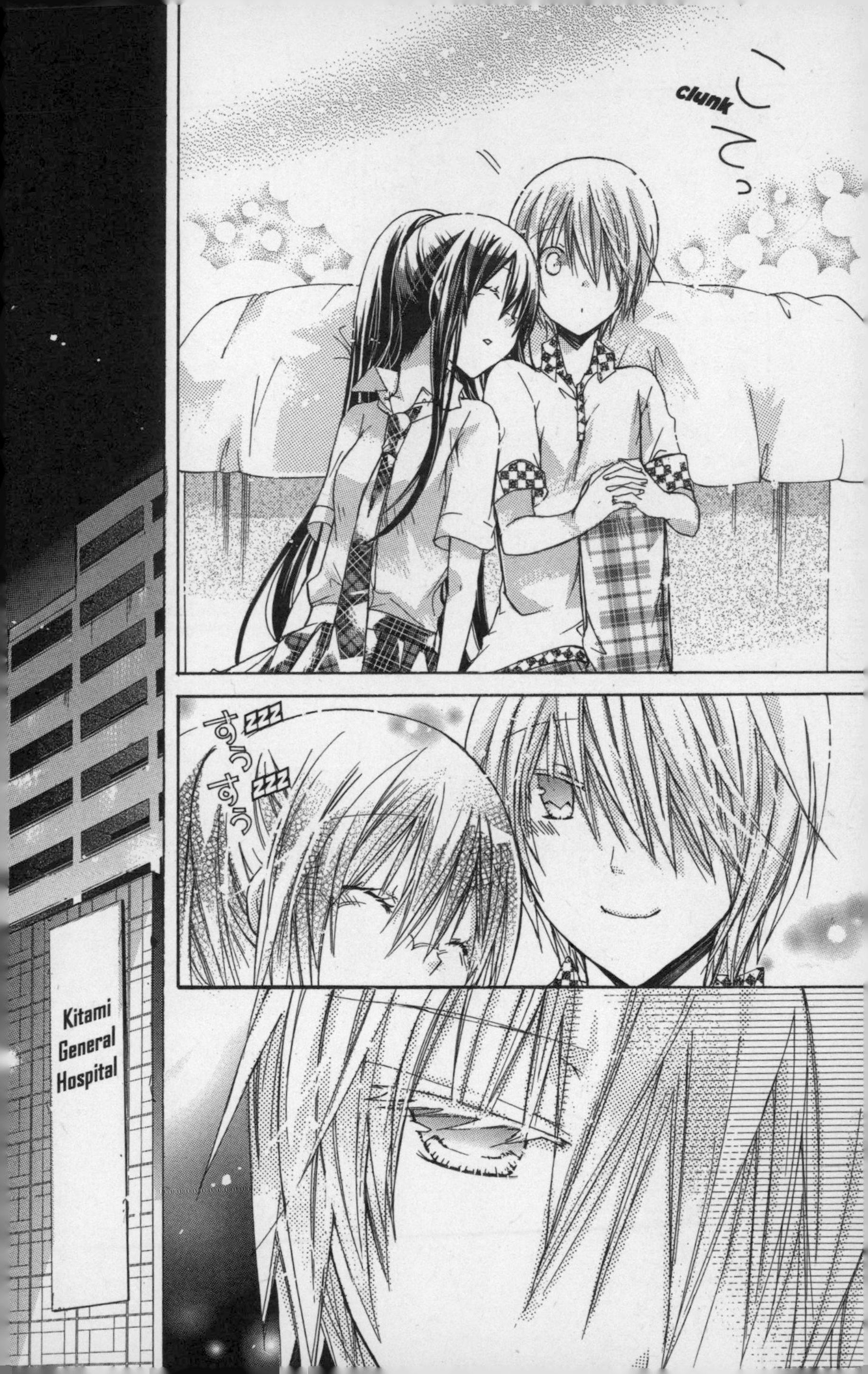
clunk
zzz
zzz
Kitami General Hospital

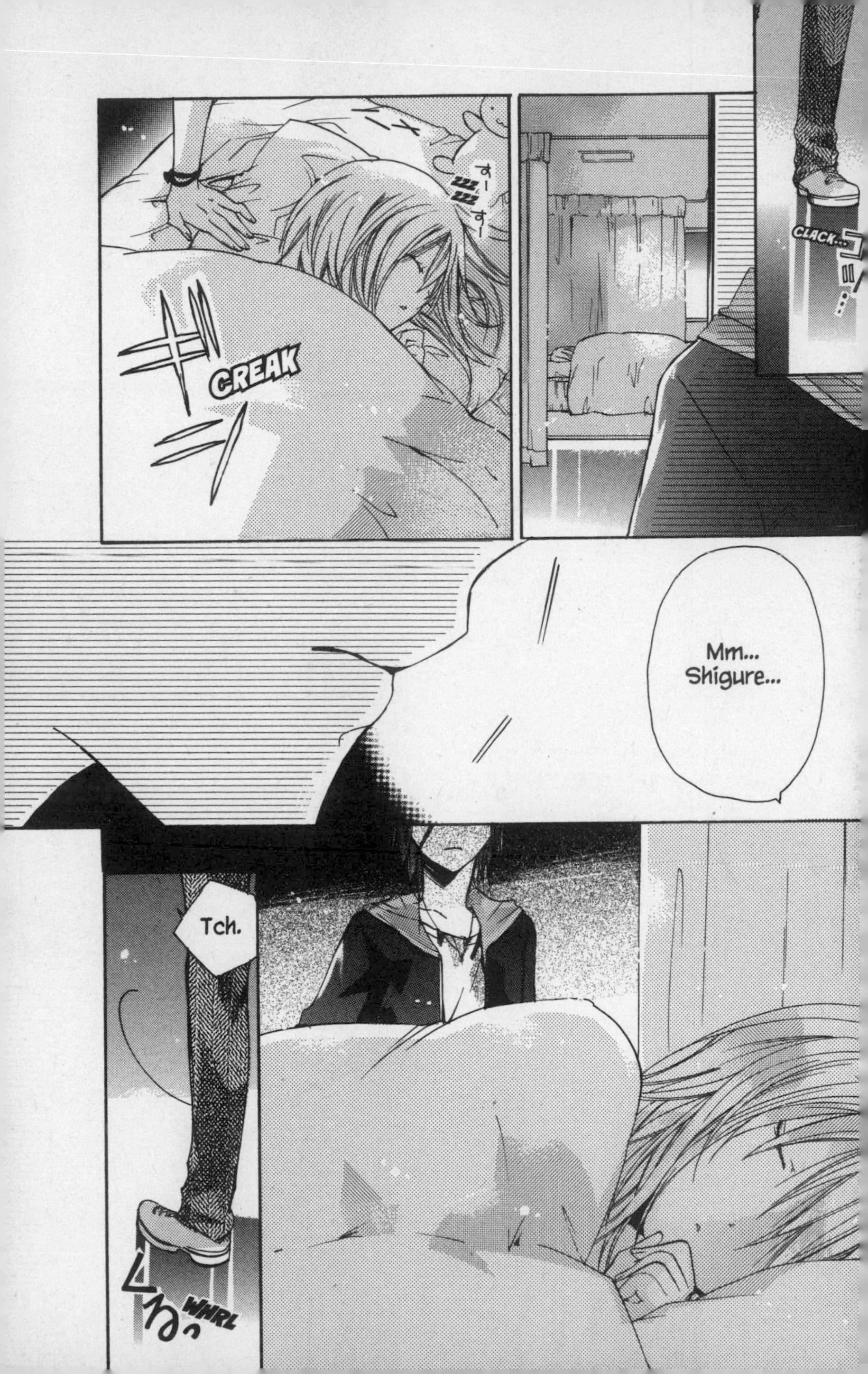
CLACK...
すー zzz zzz すー
CREAK
Mm... Shigure...
Tch.
WHRL

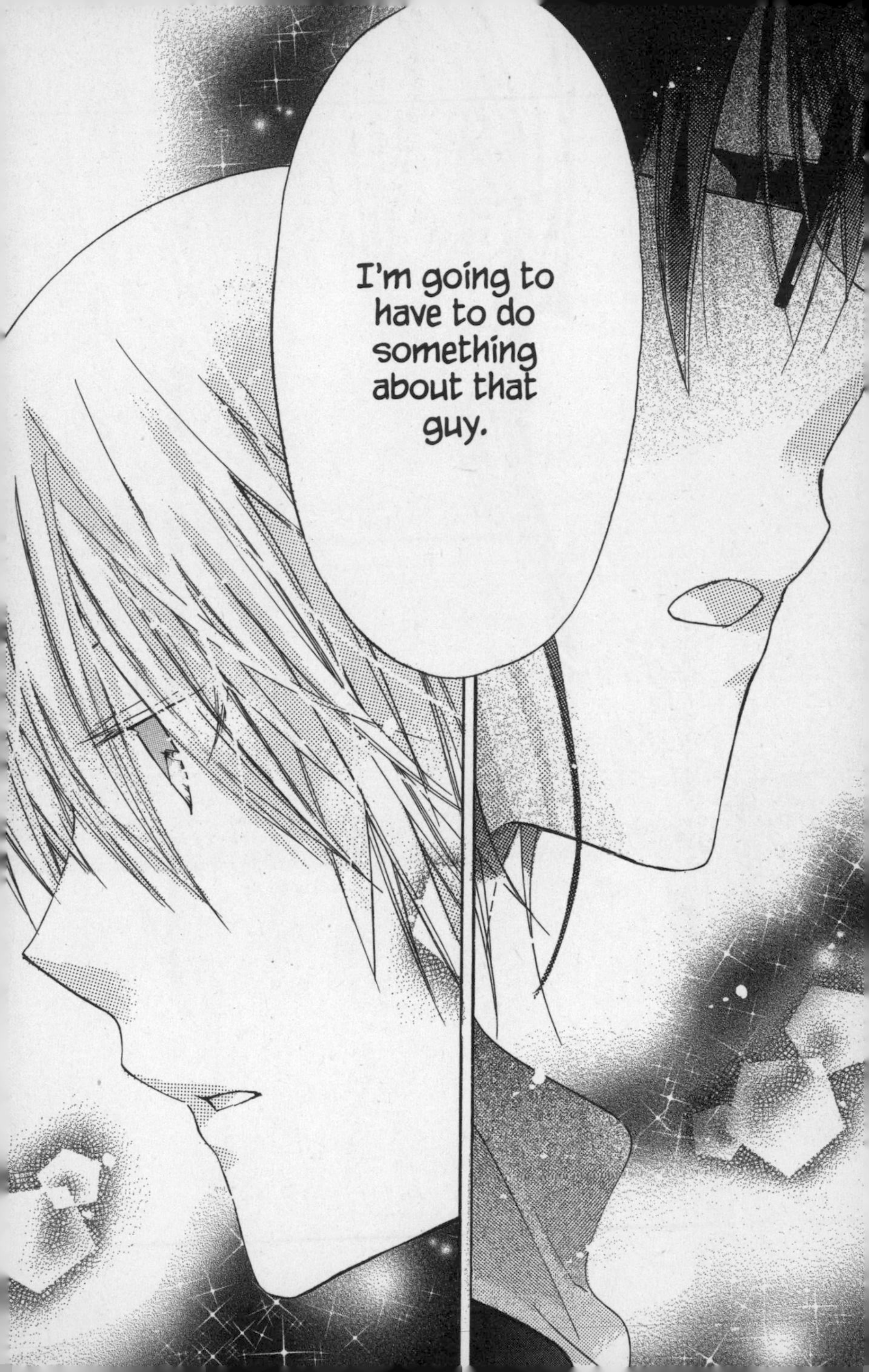
I'm going to have to do something about that guy.

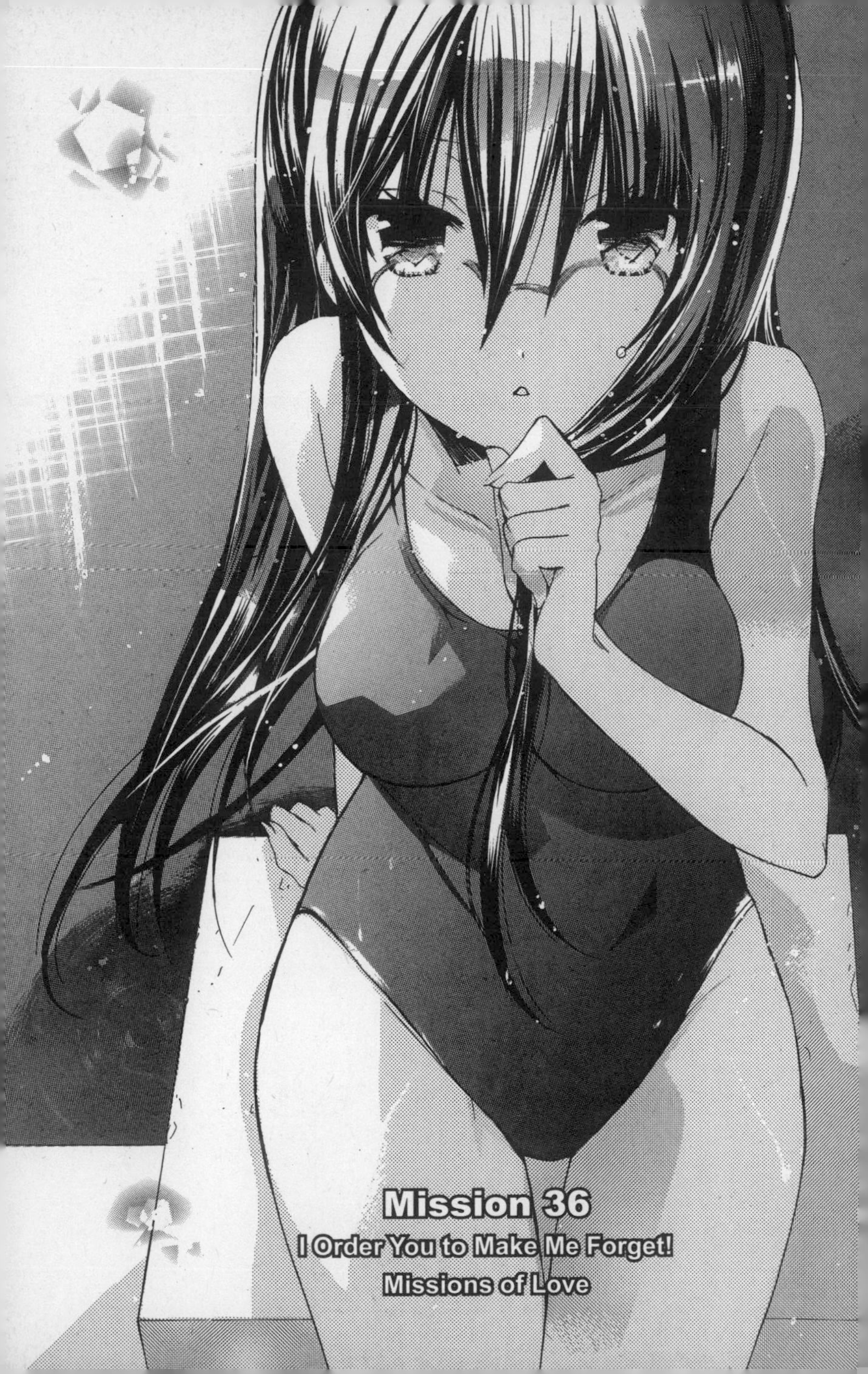
Mission 36
I Order You to Make Me Forget!
Missions of Love

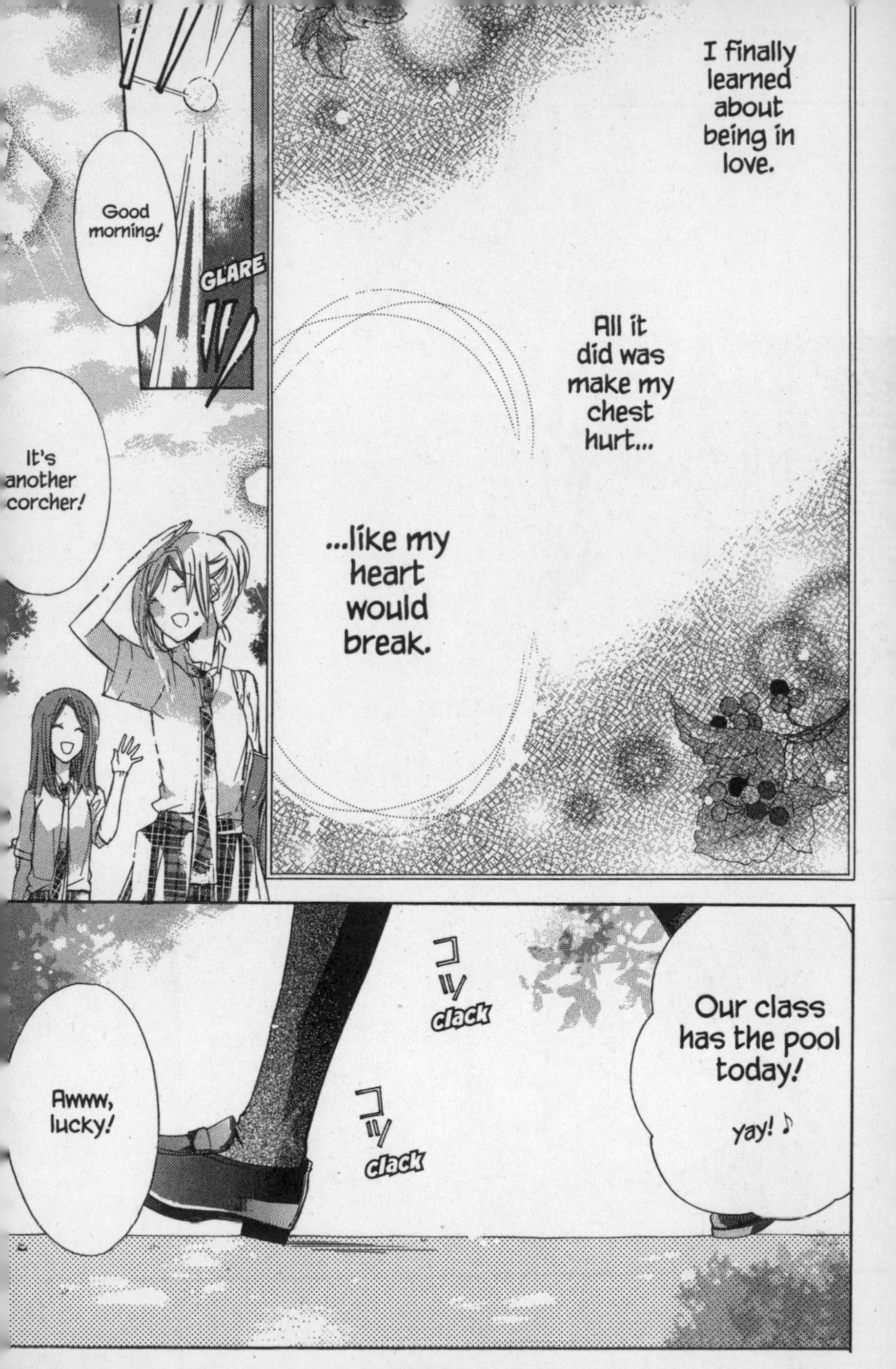
I finally learned about being in love.
All it did was make my chest hurt...
...like my heart would break.
Good morning!
GLARE
It's another corcher!
Our class has the pool today!
yay! ♪
コツ clack
コツ clack
Awww, lucky!

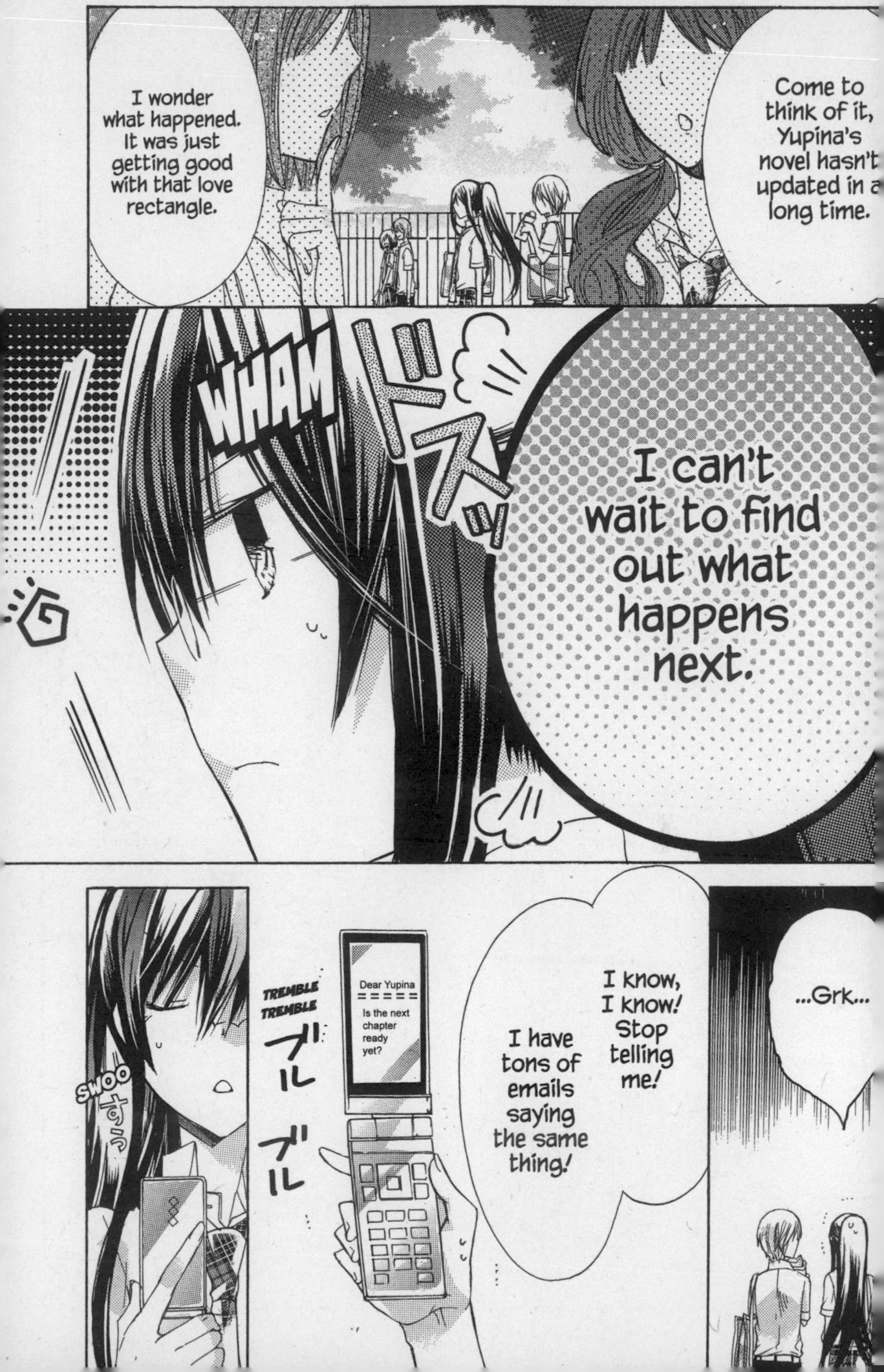
Come to think of it, Yupina's novel hasn't updated in a long time.
I wonder what happened. It was just getting good with that love rectangle.
WHAM
ドスッ
I can't wait to find out what happens next.
...Grk...
I know, I know! Stop telling me!
I have tons of emails saying the same thing!
Dear Yupina
=====
Is the next chapter ready yet?
TREMBLE TREMBLE
ブル
ブル
SWOO
すっ

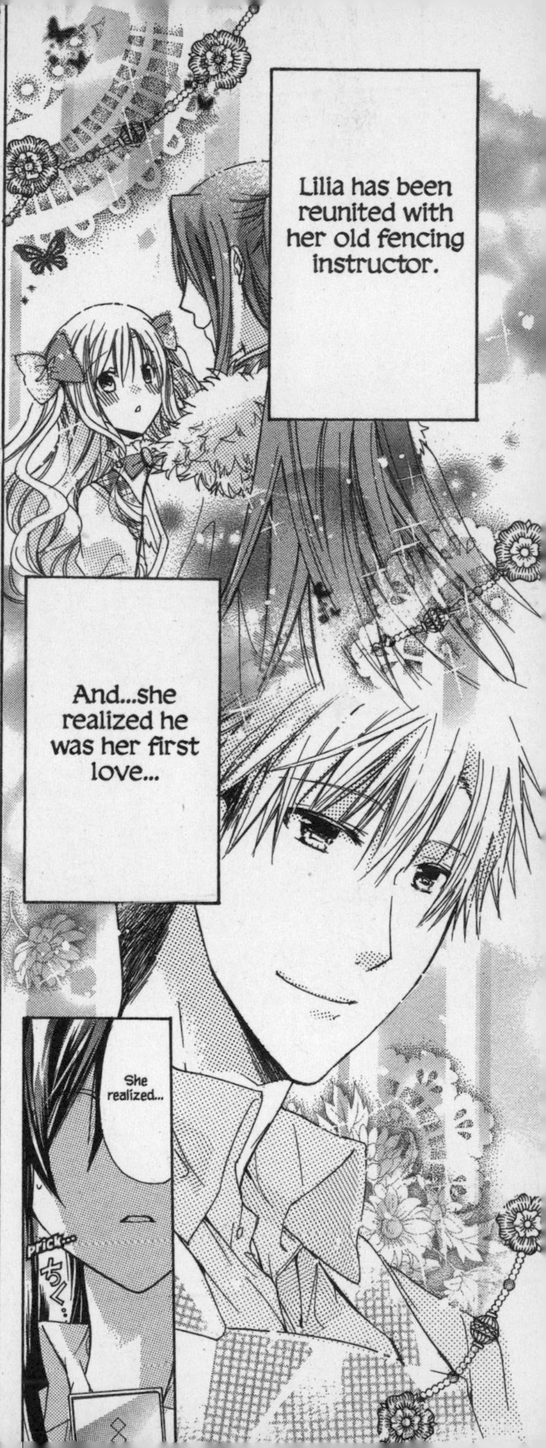
Lilia has been reunited with her old fencing instructor.
And...she realized he was her first love...
She realized...
prick...
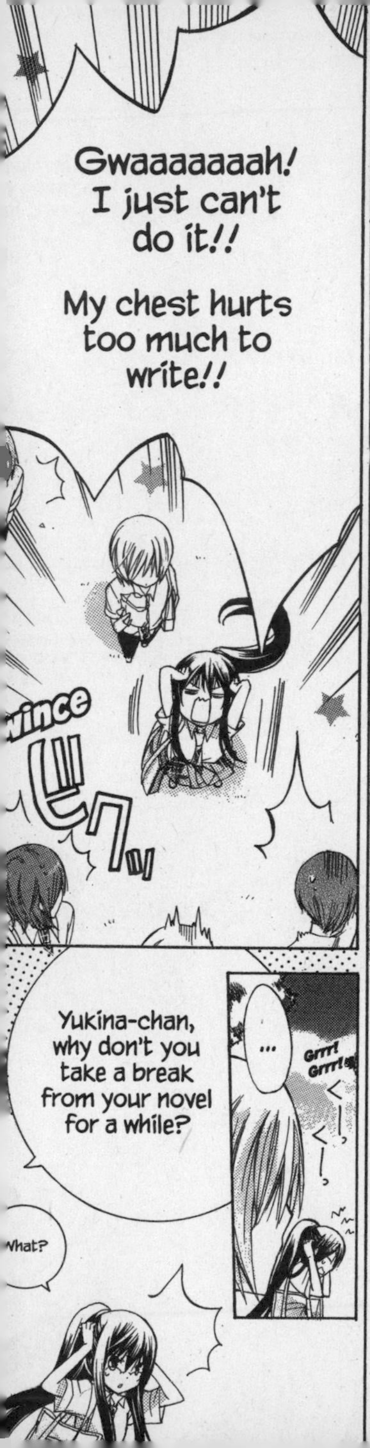
Gwaaaaaaah! I just can't do it!!
My chest hurts too much to write!!
wince
...
Grrr! Grrr!
Yukina-chan, why don't you take a break from your novel for a while?
What?

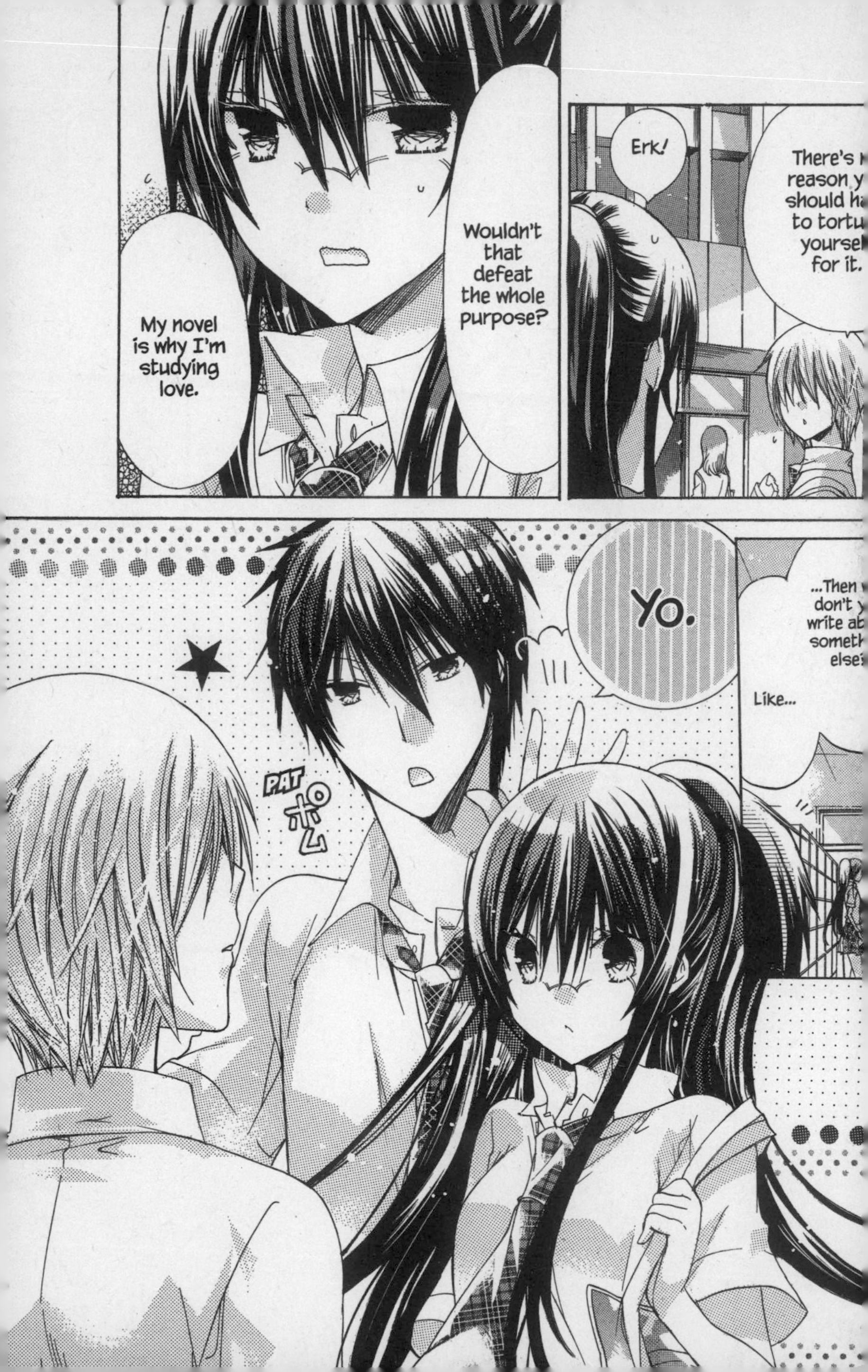
Erk!
There's reason y should ha to tortu yoursel for it.
Wouldn't that defeat the whole purpose?
My novel is why I'm studying love.
...Then don't y write ab someth else?
Like...
YO.
PAT
ポム

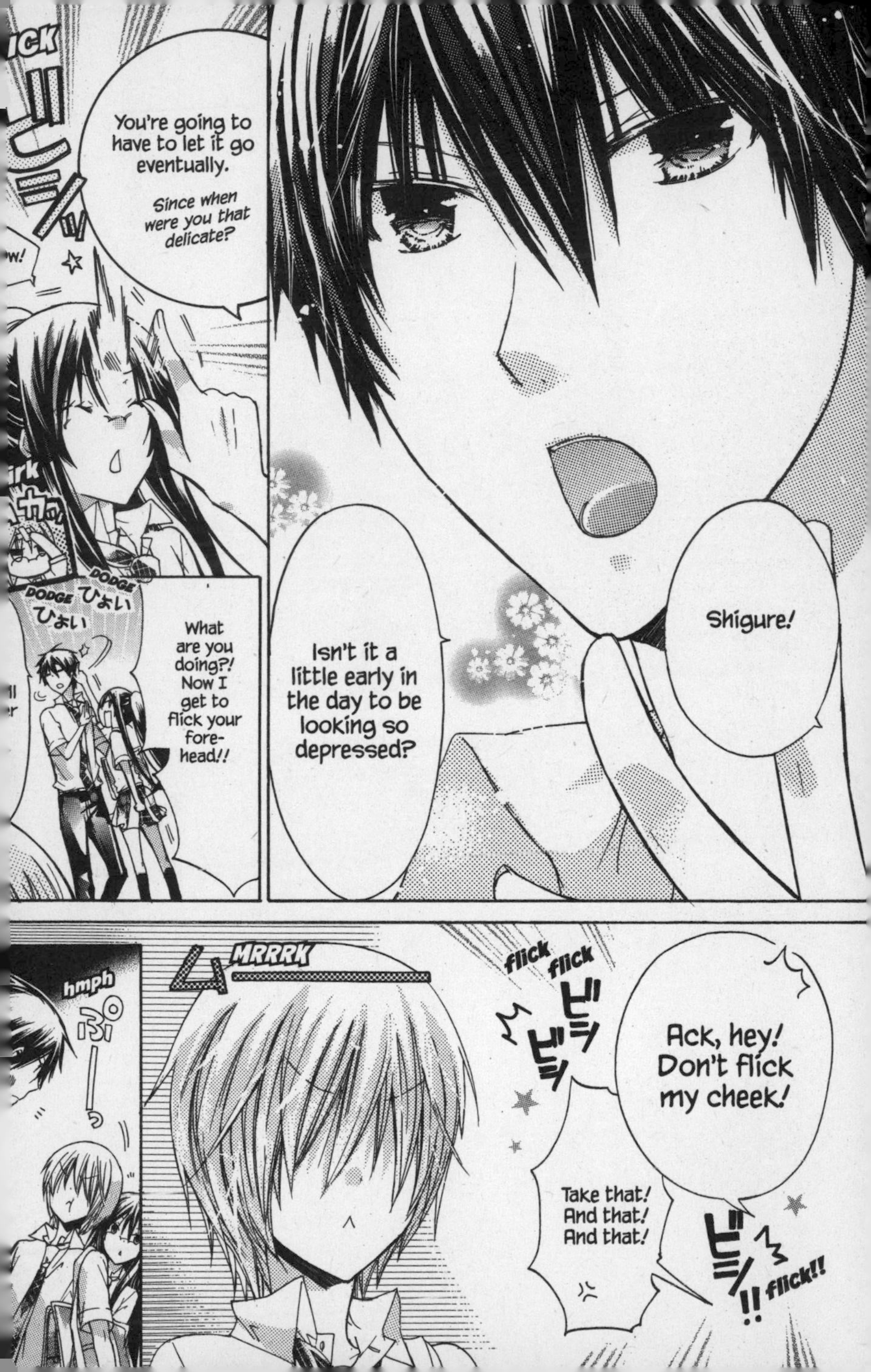
Shigure!
Isn't it a little early in the day to be looking so depressed?
FLICK
You're going to have to let it go eventually.
Since when were you that delicate?
DODGE ひょい
DODGE ひょい
What are you doing?! Now I get to flick your forehead!!
Ack, hey! Don't flick my cheek!
flick ビシ
flick ビシ
MRRRK ム
Take that! And that! And that!
ビシ!! flick!!
hmph ぷい

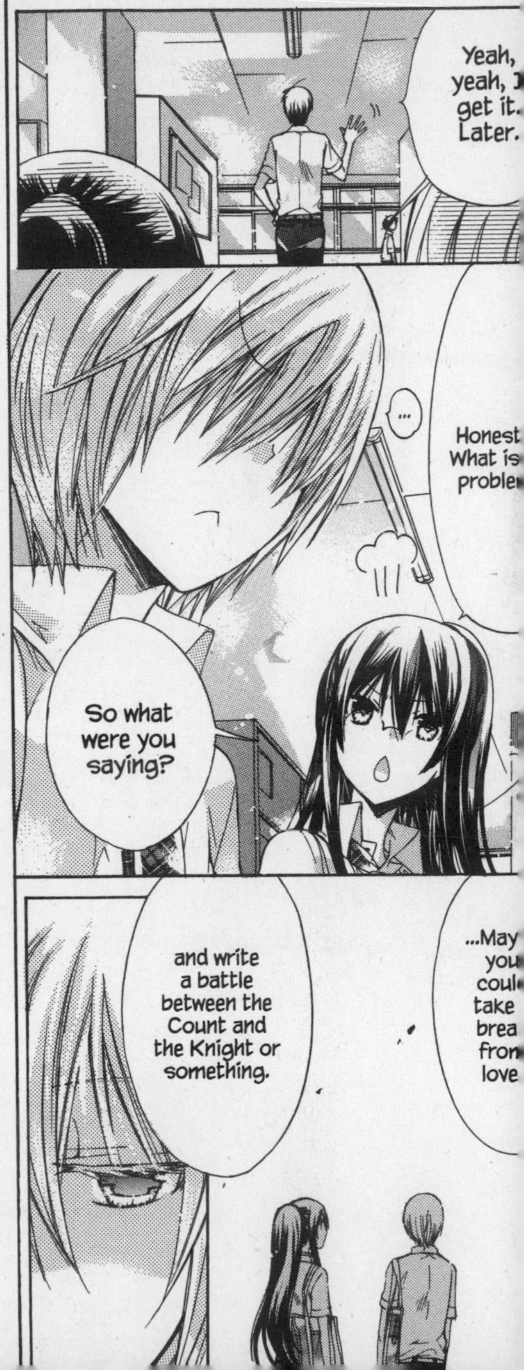
Yeah, yeah, I get it. Later.
Honest What is proble
...
So what were you saying?
...May you coul take brea fron love
and write a battle between the Count and the Knight or something.

The Freezing Bed 4

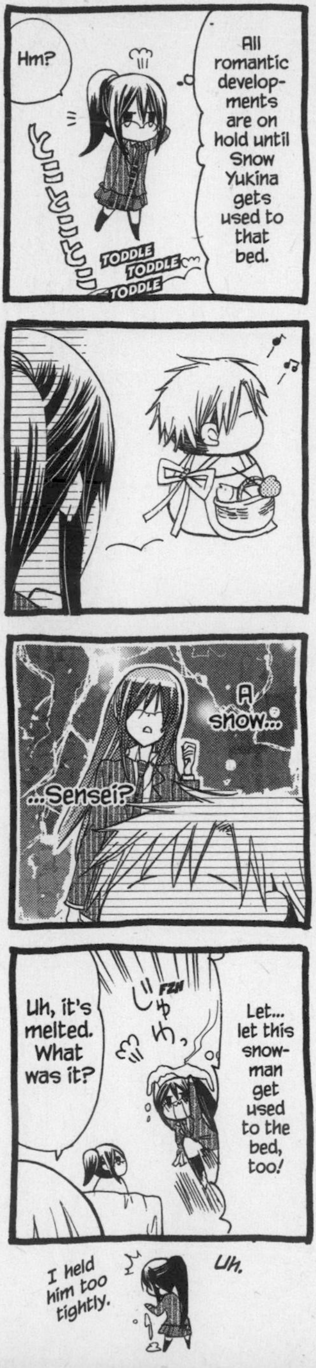
All romantic developments are on hold until Snow Yukina gets used to that bed.
Hm?
TODDLE TODDLE TODDLE
A snow...
...Sensei?
Let... let this snowman get used to the bed, too!
FZH
Uh, it's melted. What was it?
Uh.
I held him too tightly.

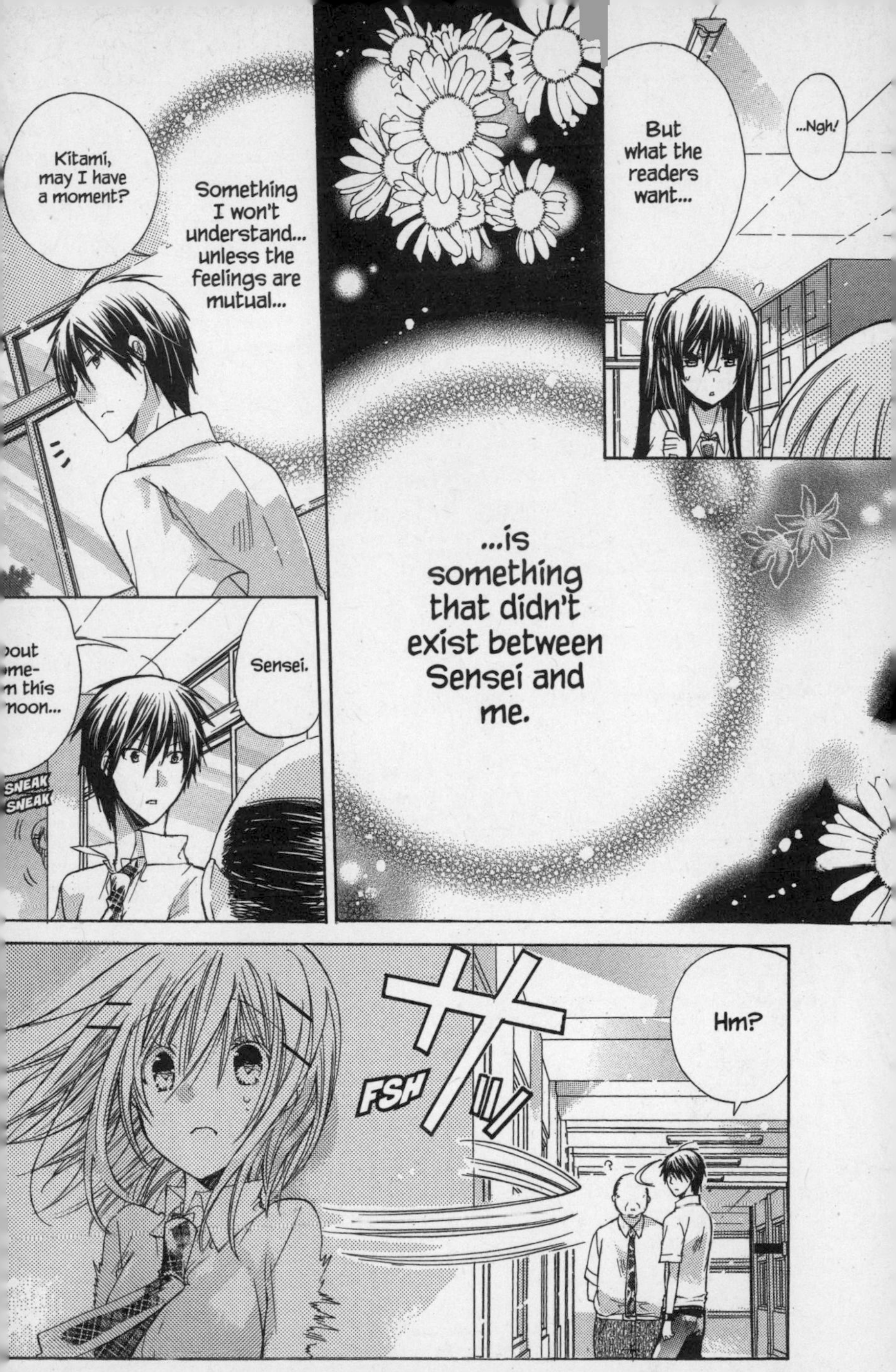

But what the readers want...
...Ngh!
...is something that didn't exist between Sensei and me.
Something I won't understand... unless the feelings are mutual...
Kitami, may I have a moment?
Sensei.
SNEAK SNEAK
Hm?
FSH

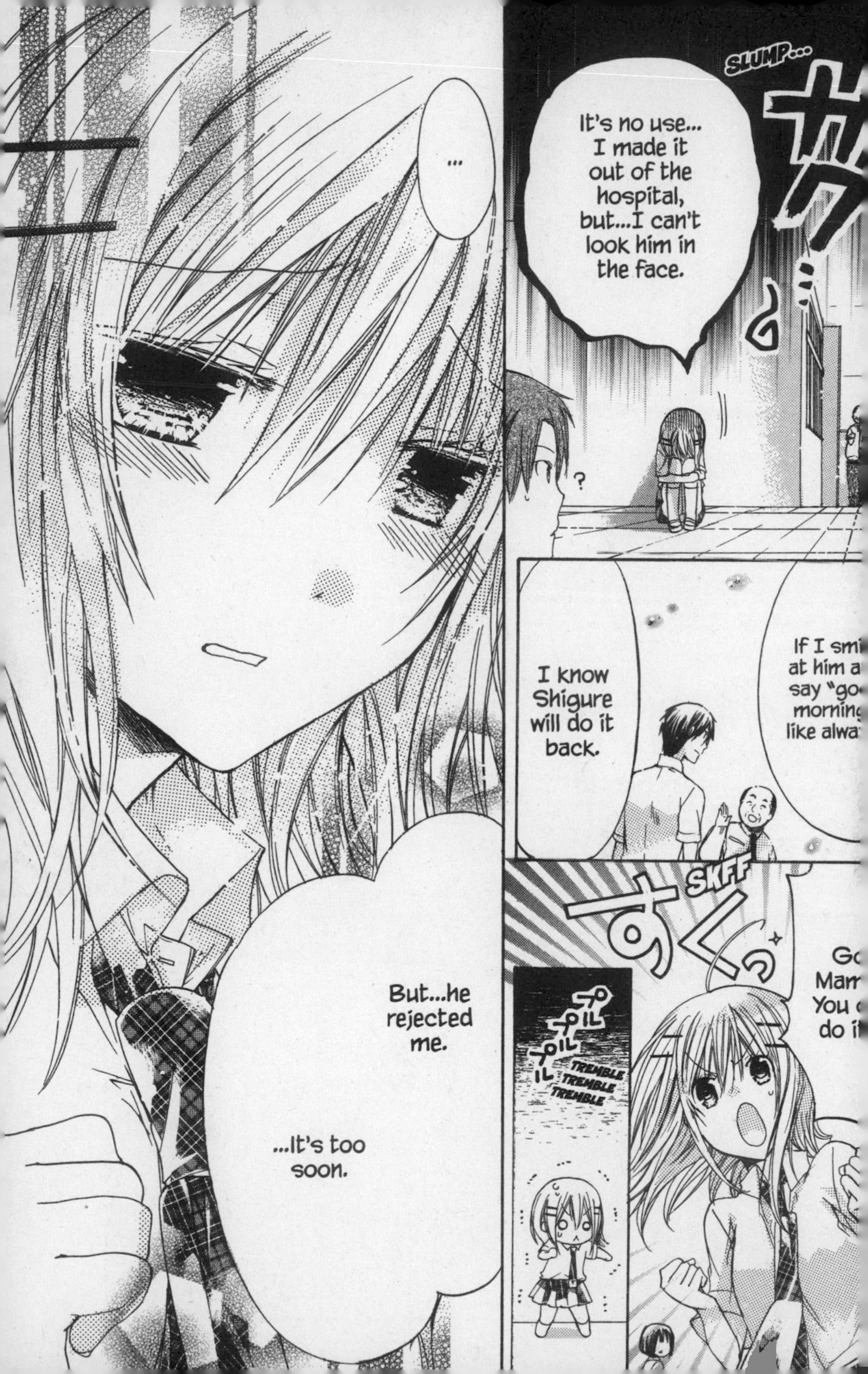
SLUMP...
It's no use... I made it out of the hospital, but...I can't look him in the face.
?
If I smi at him a say "go morning like alwa
I know Shigure will do it back.
SKFF
Go Mam You do it
TREMBLE TREMBLE TREMBLE
...
But...he rejected me.
...It's too soon.

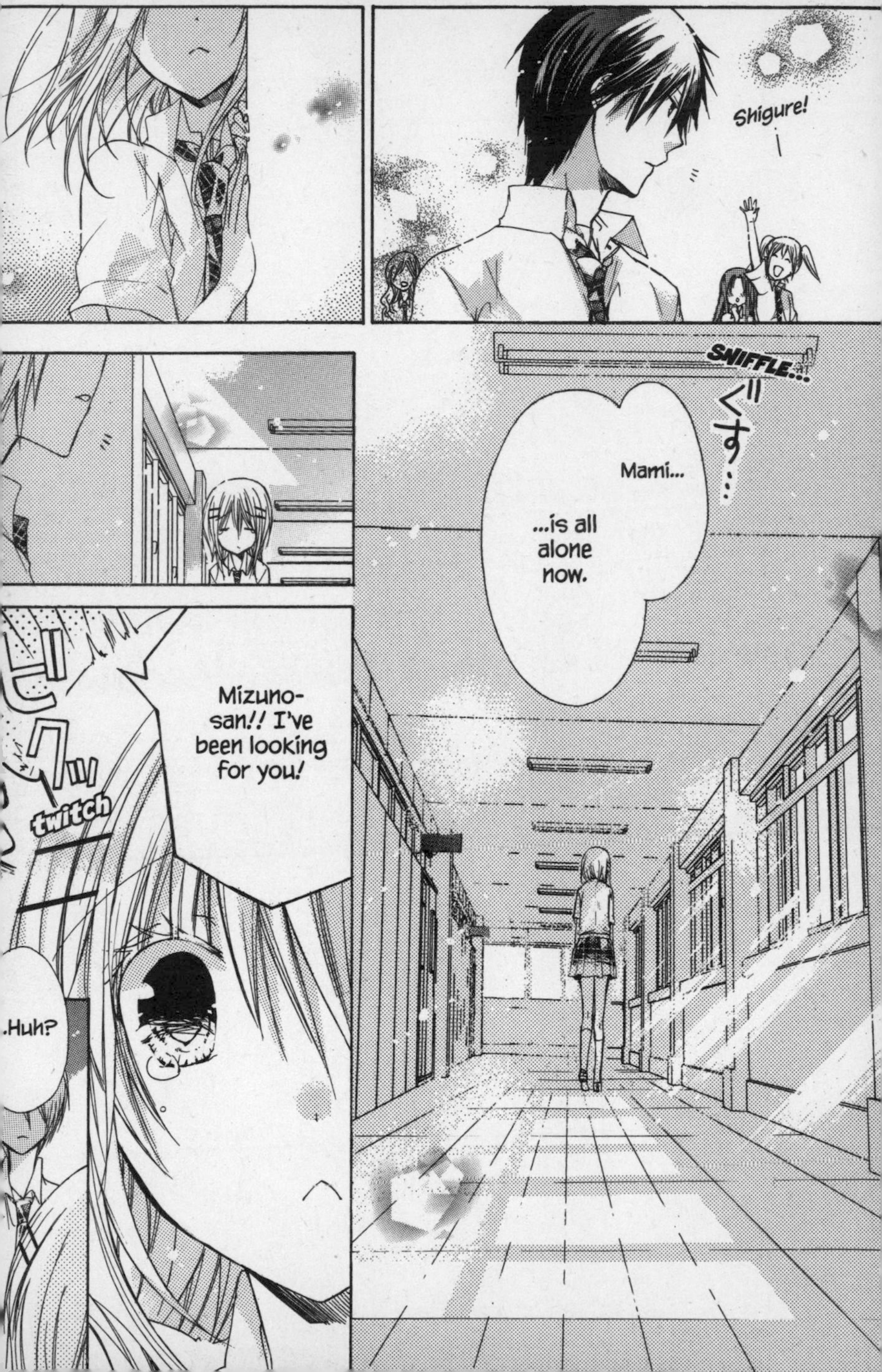
Shigure!
SNIFFLE...
ぐす‥
Mami...
...is all alone now.
Mizuno-san!! I've been looking for you!
twitch
.Huh?

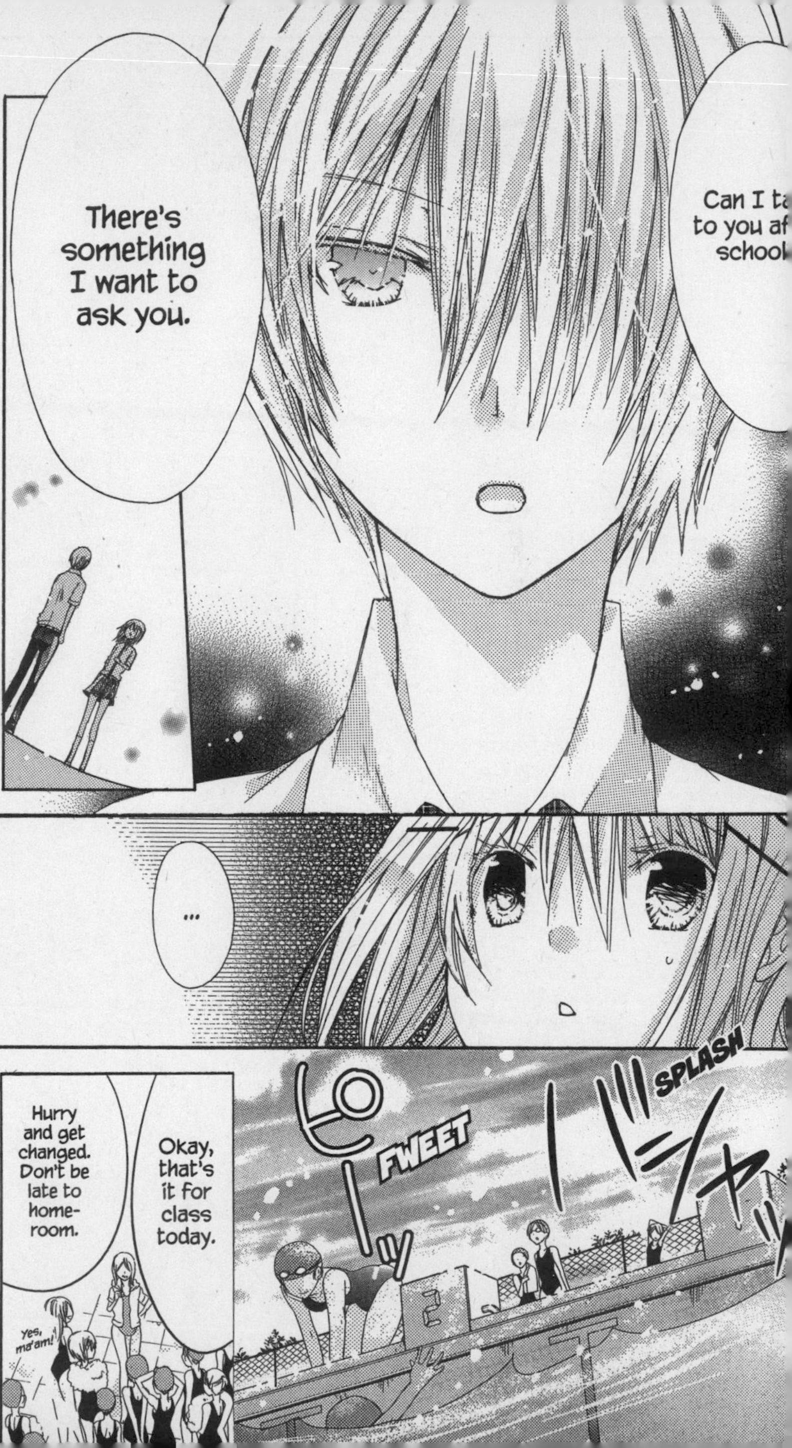
Can I ta to you af school
There's something I want to ask you.
...
SPLASH
FWEET
Okay, that's it for class today.
Hurry and get changed. Don't be late to homeroom.
Yes, ma'am!

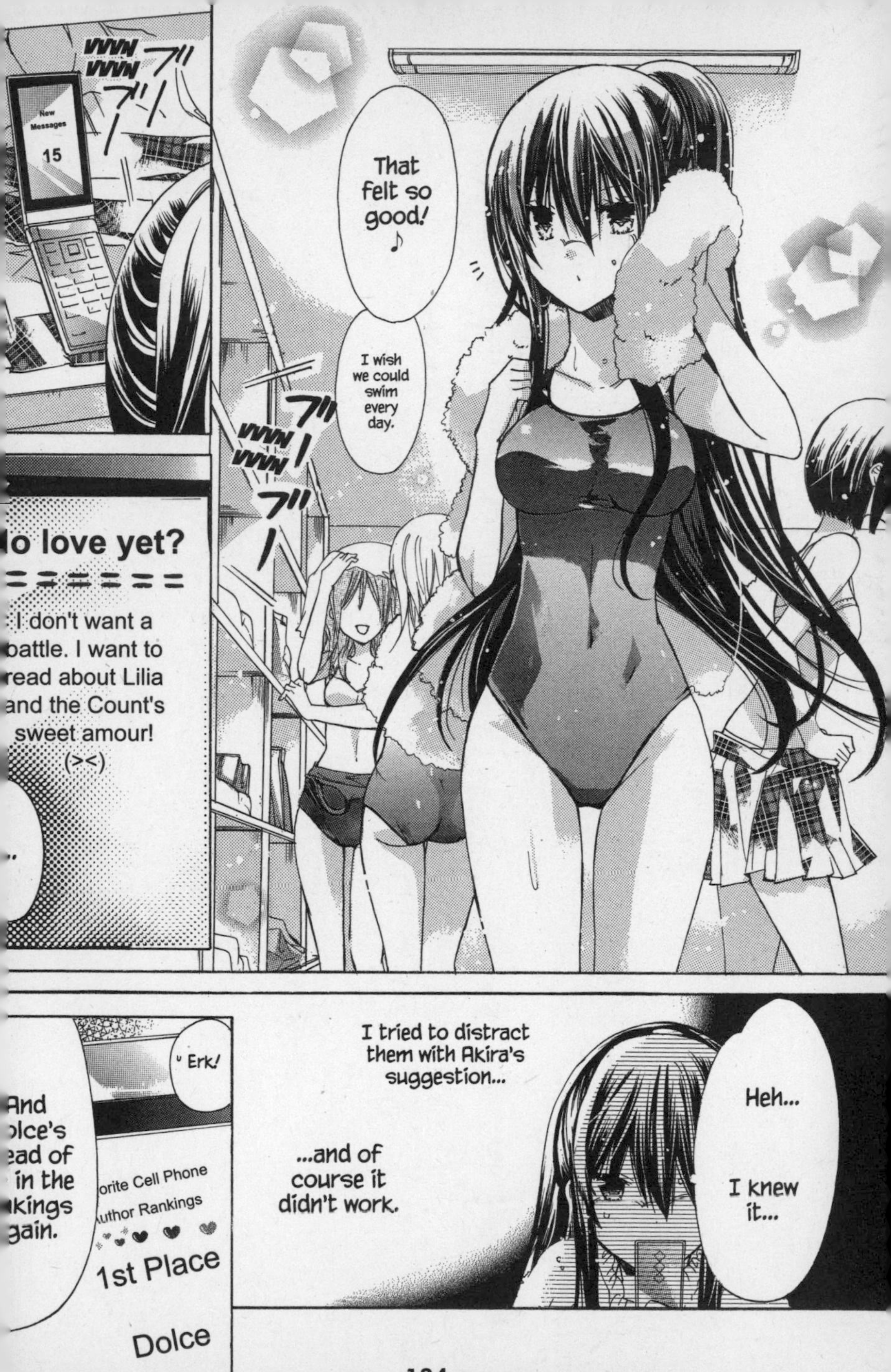
That felt so good! ♪
I wish we could swim every day.
VVVN VVVN
VVVN VVVN
New Messages 15
VVVN VVVN
lo love yet?
: I don't want a battle. I want to read about Lilia and the Count's sweet amour! (><)
Heh... I knew it...
I tried to distract them with Akira's suggestion...
...and of course it didn't work.
Erk!
And olce's ead of in the kings gain.
orite Cell Phone Author Rankings
1st Place
Dolce

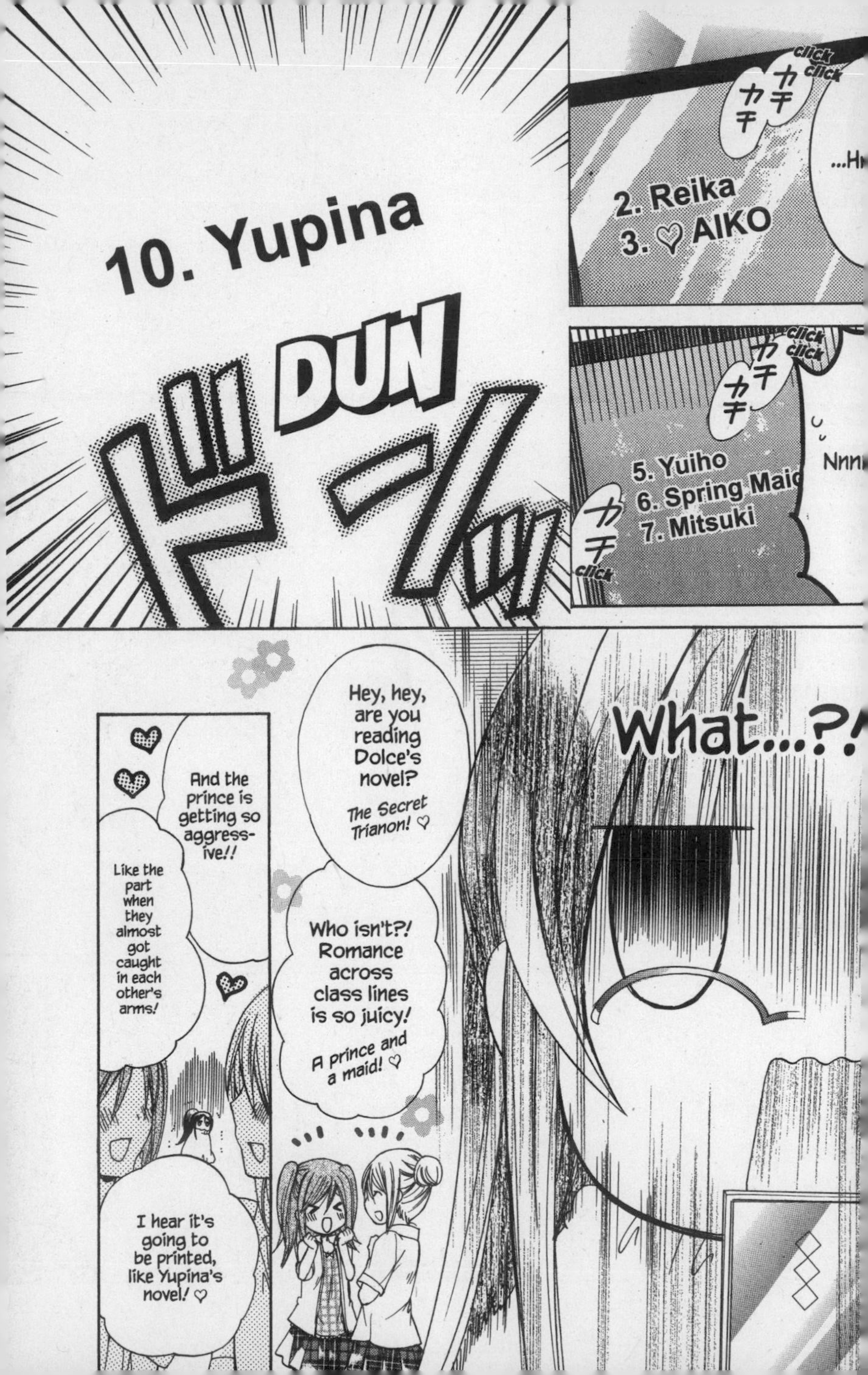

click click
カチ カチ
...Hr
2. Reika
3. ♡ AIKO
click click
カチ カチ
Nnn
5. Yuiho
6. Spring Mai
7. Mitsuki
カチ click
10. Yupina
ドーン DUN
What...?!
Hey, hey, are you reading Dolce's novel? The Secret Trianon! ♡
Who isn't?! Romance across class lines is so juicy! A prince and a maid! ♡
And the prince is getting so aggress-ive!!
Like the part when they almost got caught in each other's arms!
I hear it's going to be printed, like Yupina's novel! ♡

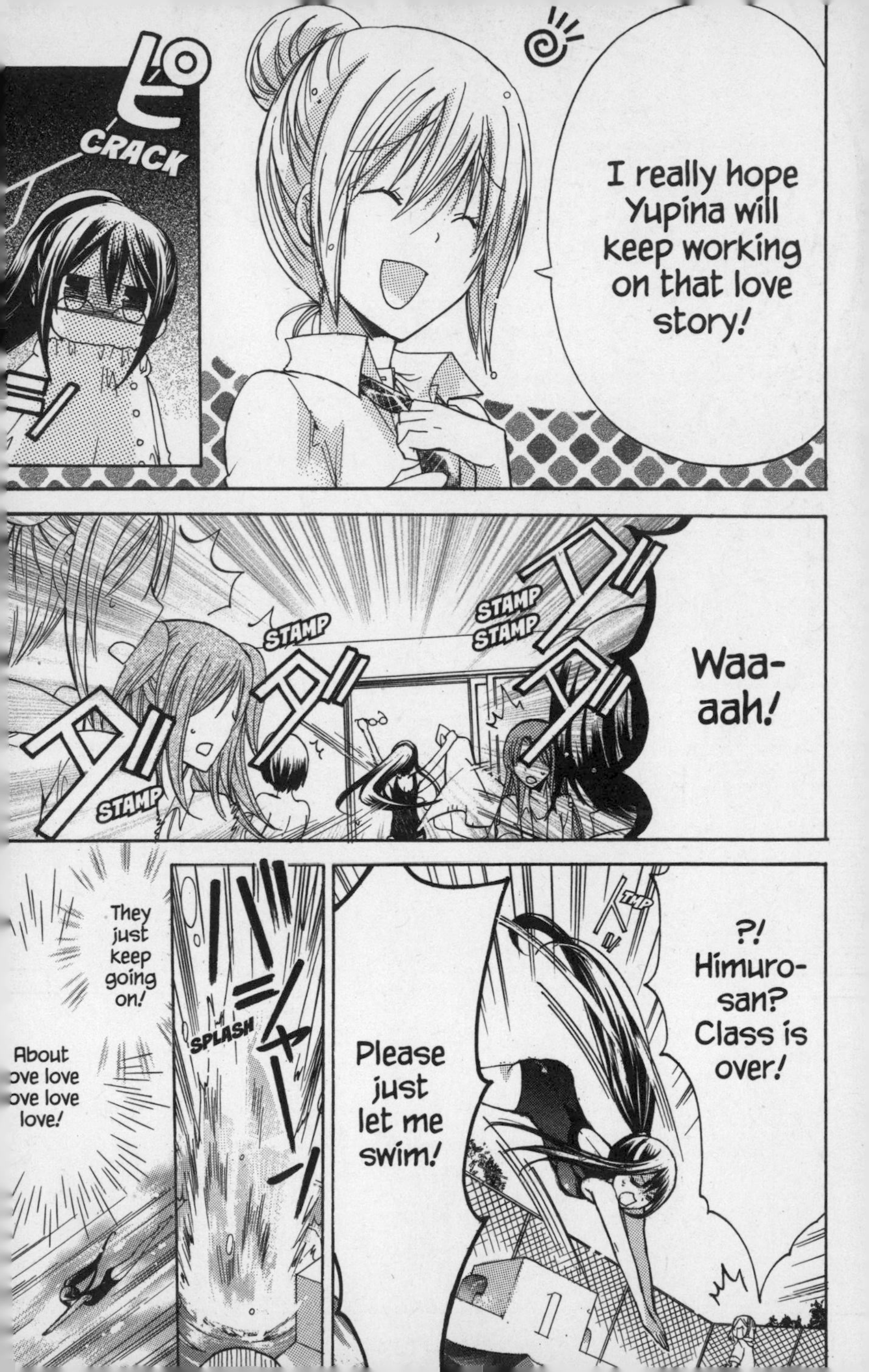
I really hope Yupina will keep working on that love story!
CRACK
Waa-aah!
STAMP STAMP
STAMP
STAMP
TMP
?! Himuro-san? Class is over!
Please just let me swim!
SPLASH
They just keep going on!
About ove love ove love love!

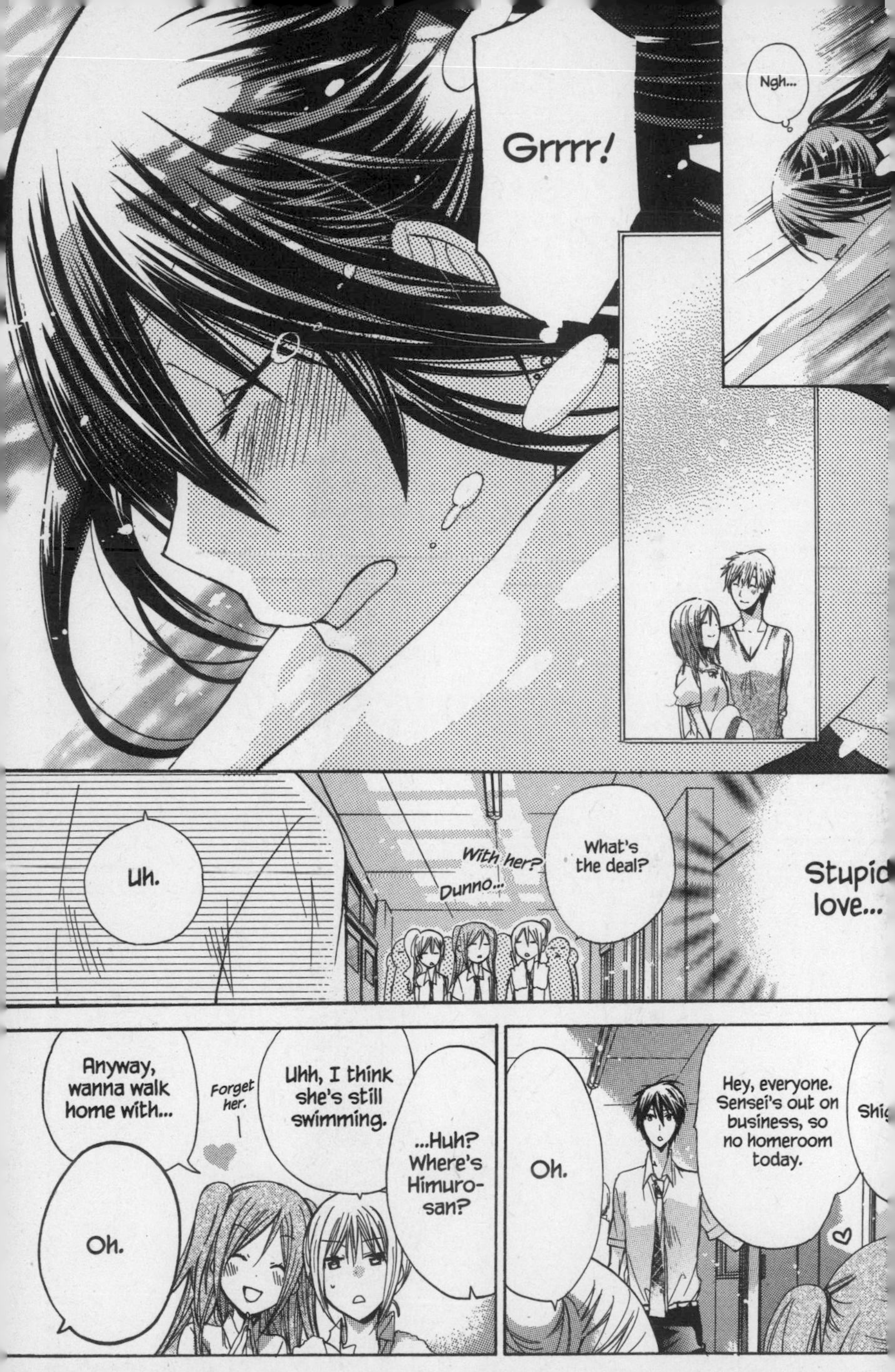
Ngh...
Grrrr!
Stupid love...
What's the deal?
With her?
Dunno...
Uh.
Hey, everyone. Sensei's out on business, so no homeroom today.
Oh.
...Huh? Where's Himuro-san?
Uhh, I think she's still swimming.
Forget her.
Anyway, wanna walk home with...
Oh.

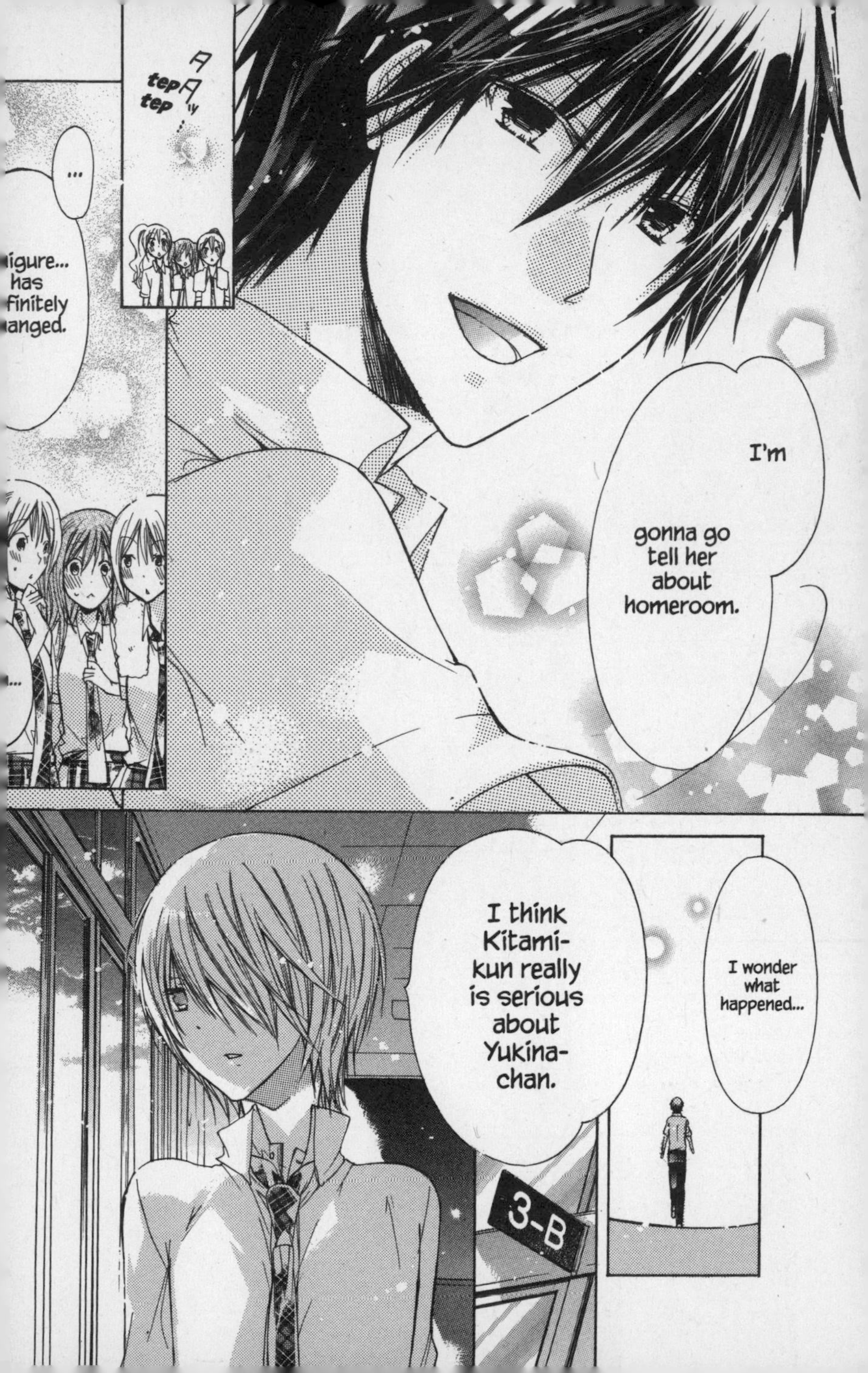
I'm gonna go tell her about homeroom.
tep tep
...
igure... has finitely anged.
...
I wonder what happened...
3-B
I think Kitami-kun really is serious about Yukina-chan.

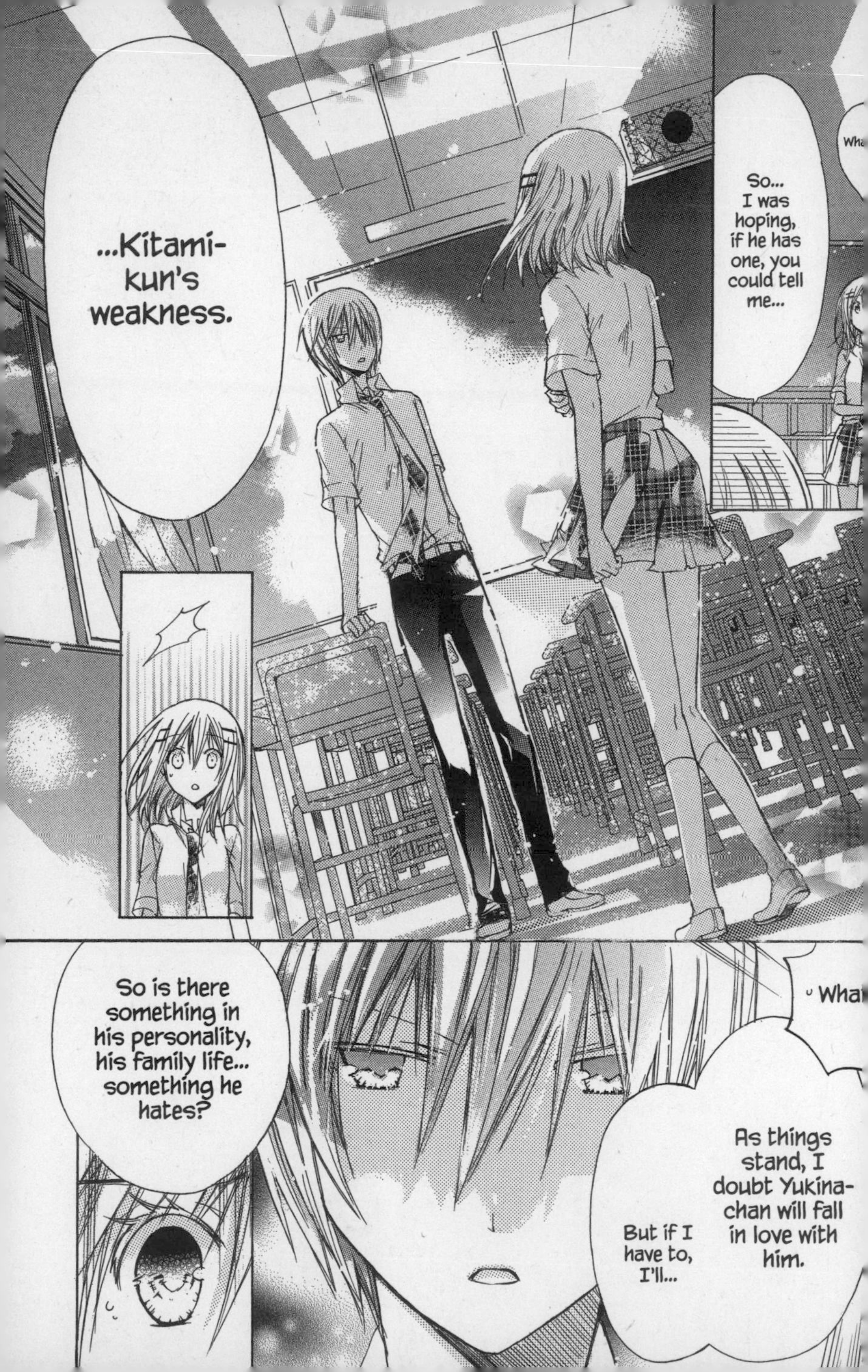

...Kitami-kun's weakness.
So... I was hoping, if he has one, you could tell me...
Wha
So is there something in his personality, his family life... something he hates?
What
As things stand, I doubt Yukina-chan will fall in love with him.
But if I have to, I'll...

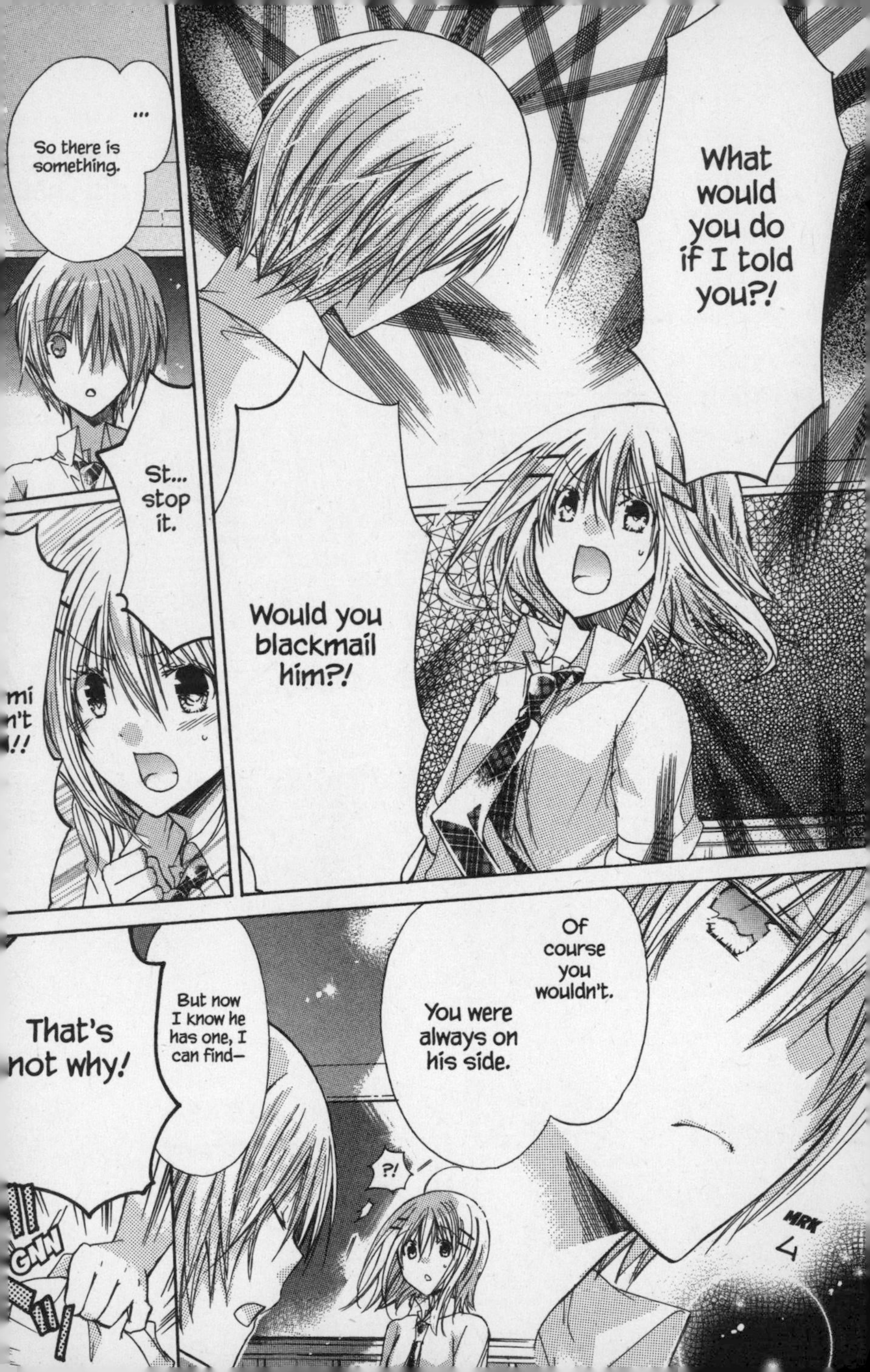
What would you do if I told you?!
Would you blackmail him?!
...
So there is something.
St... stop it.
Of course you wouldn't.
You were always on his side.
MRK
?!
But now I know he has one, I can find—
That's not why!
GNN

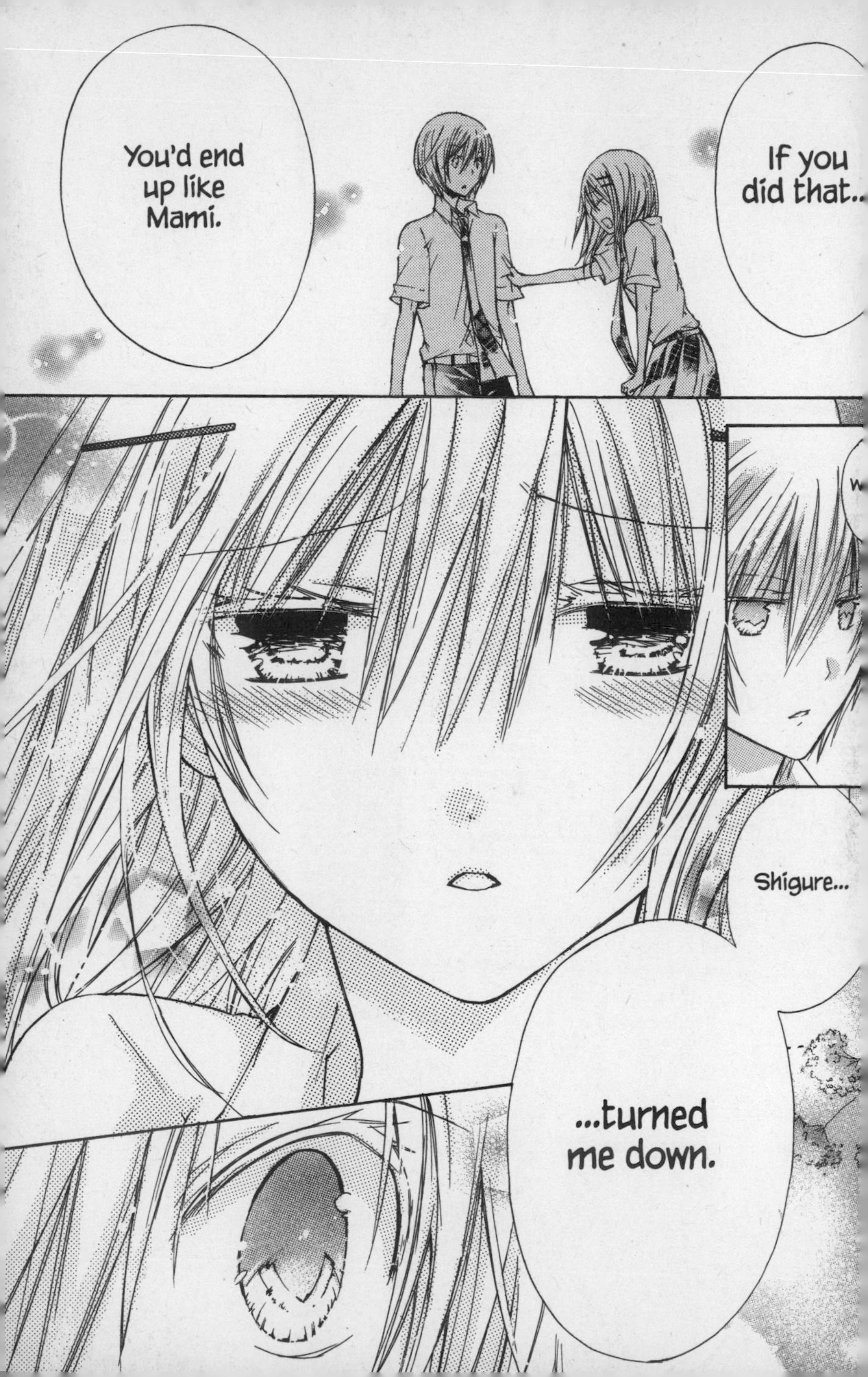
If you did that...
You'd end up like Mami.
Shigure...
...turned me down.

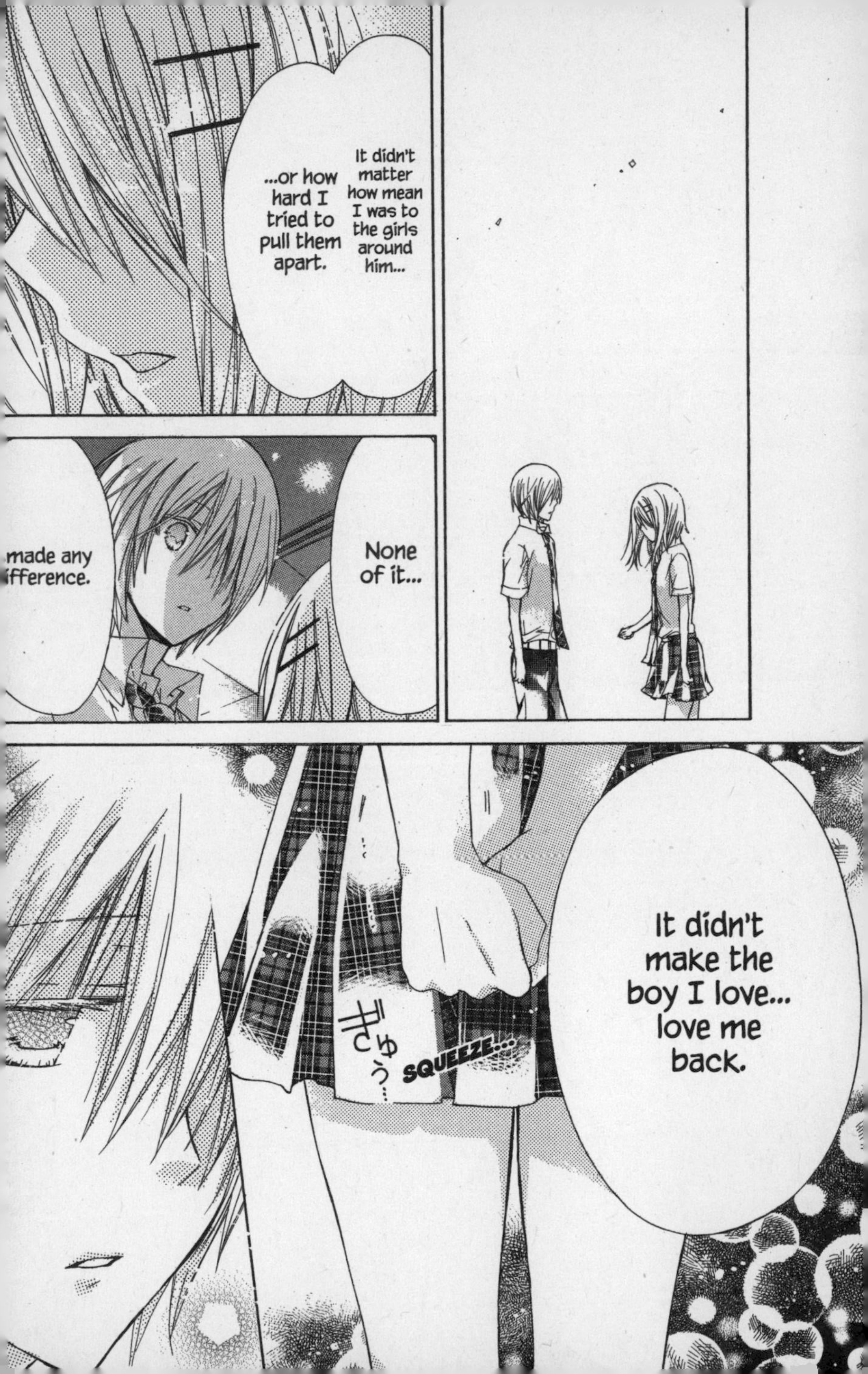
It didn't matter how mean I was to the girls around him...
...or how hard I tried to pull them apart.
None of it...
made any difference.
It didn't make the boy I love... love me back.
ぎゅう…
SQUEEZE...

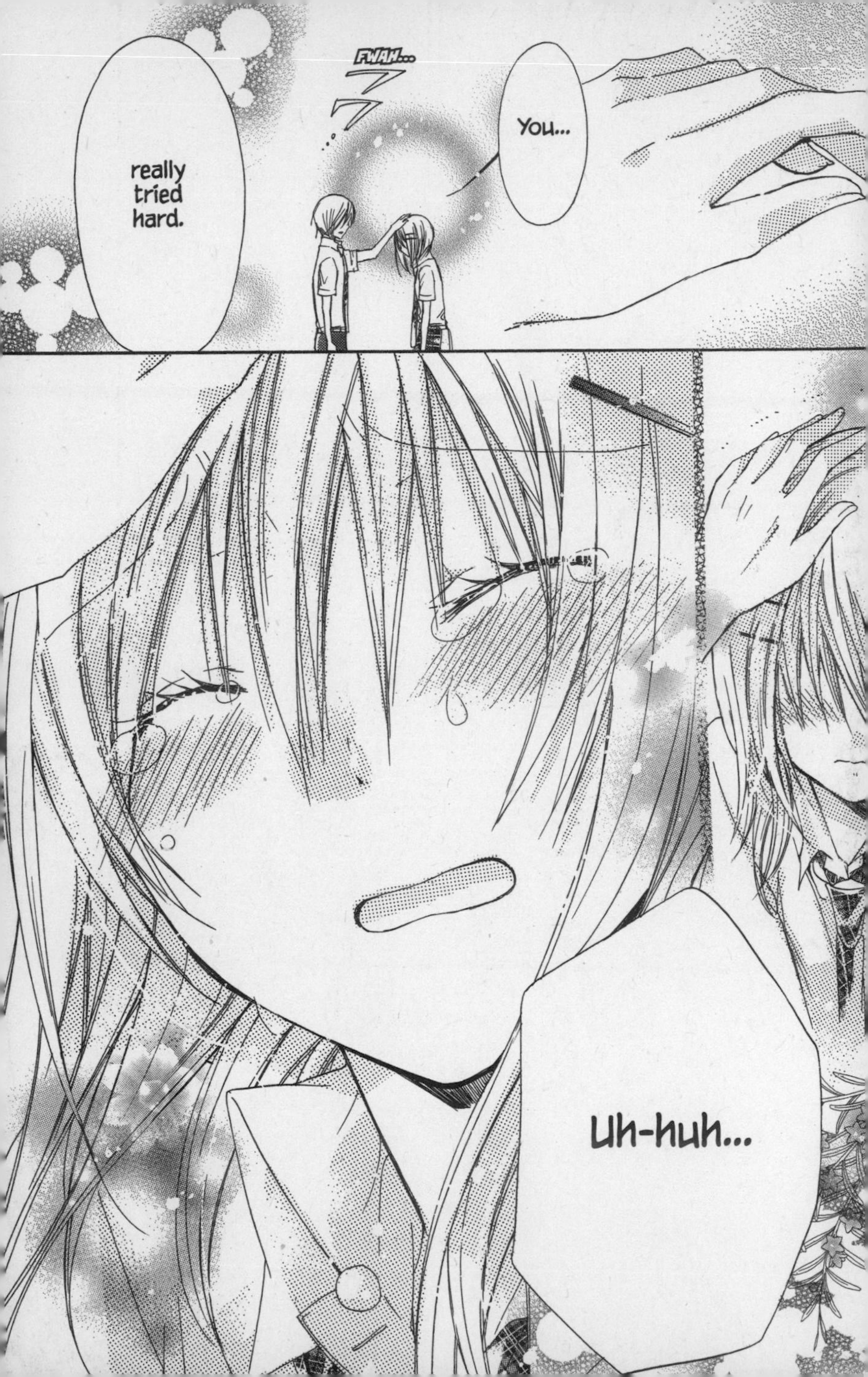
You...
FWAH...
really tried hard.
Uh-huh...

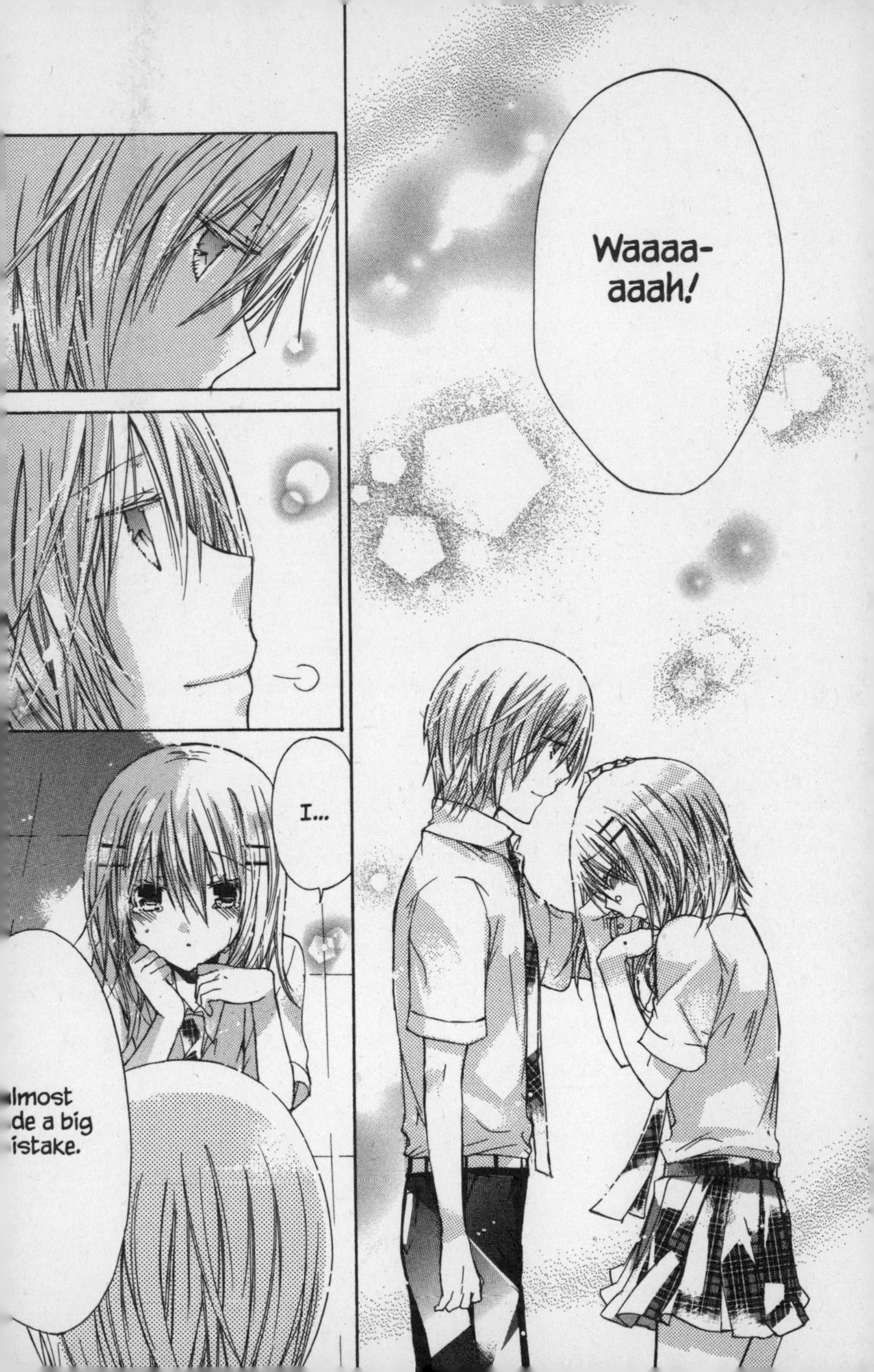
Waaaa-
aaah!
I...
lmost
de a big
istake.

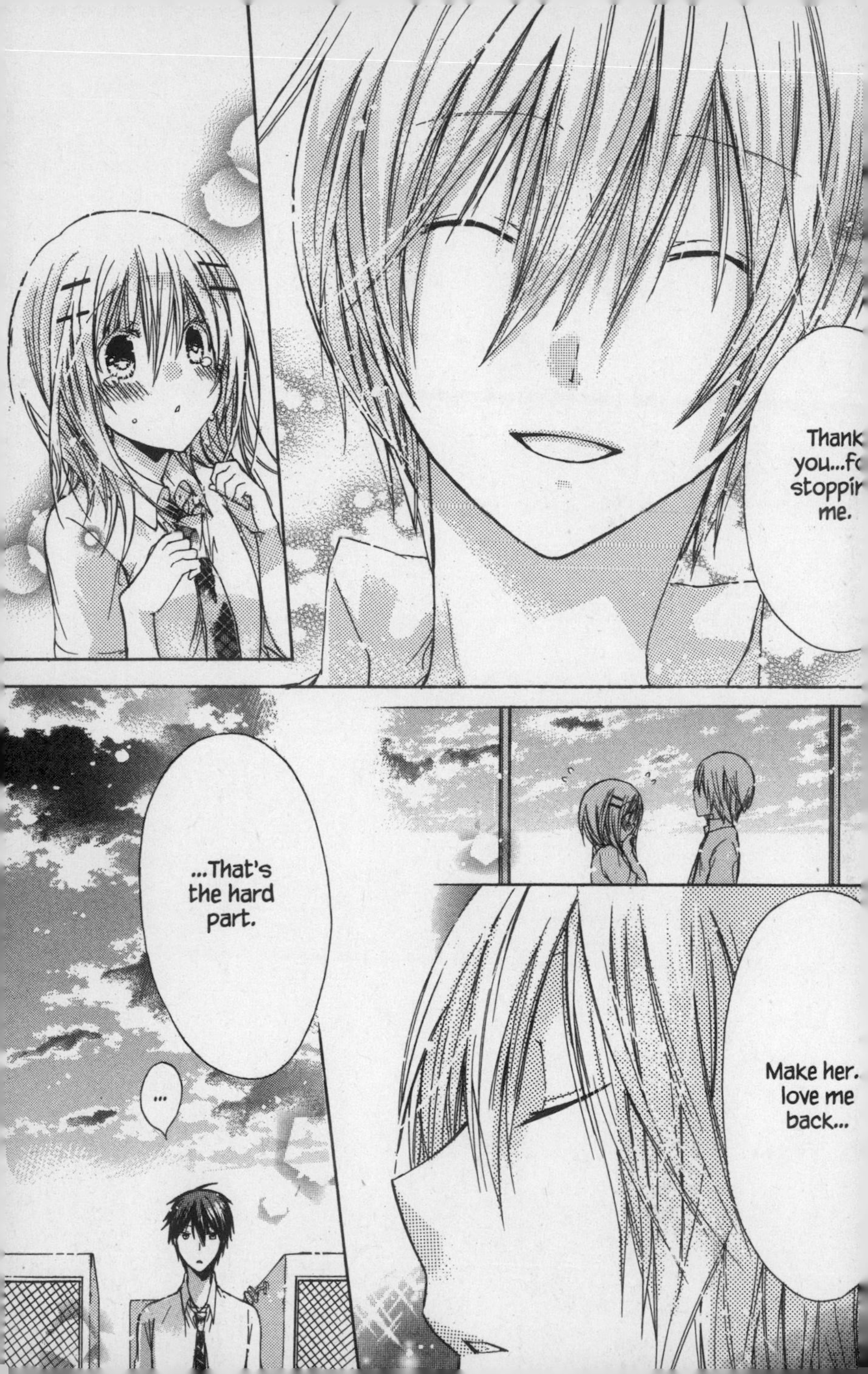

Thank you...fo stoppin me.
Make her. love me back...
...That's the hard part.
...

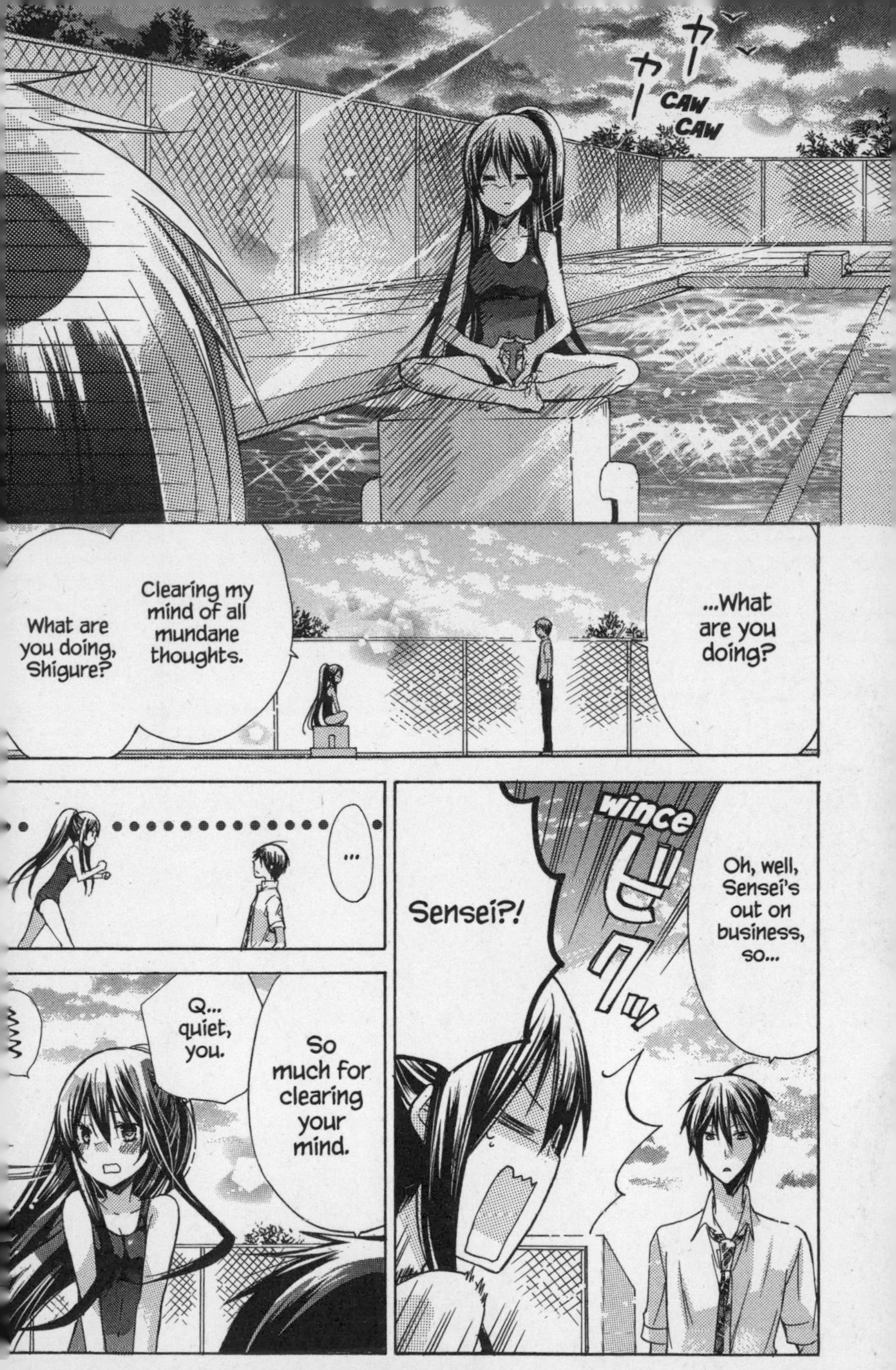
カー カー
CAW CAW
...What are you doing?
Clearing my mind of all mundane thoughts.
What are you doing, Shigure?
Oh, well, Sensei's out on business, so...
wince
ビクッ
Sensei?!
...
So much for clearing your mind.
Q... quiet, you.

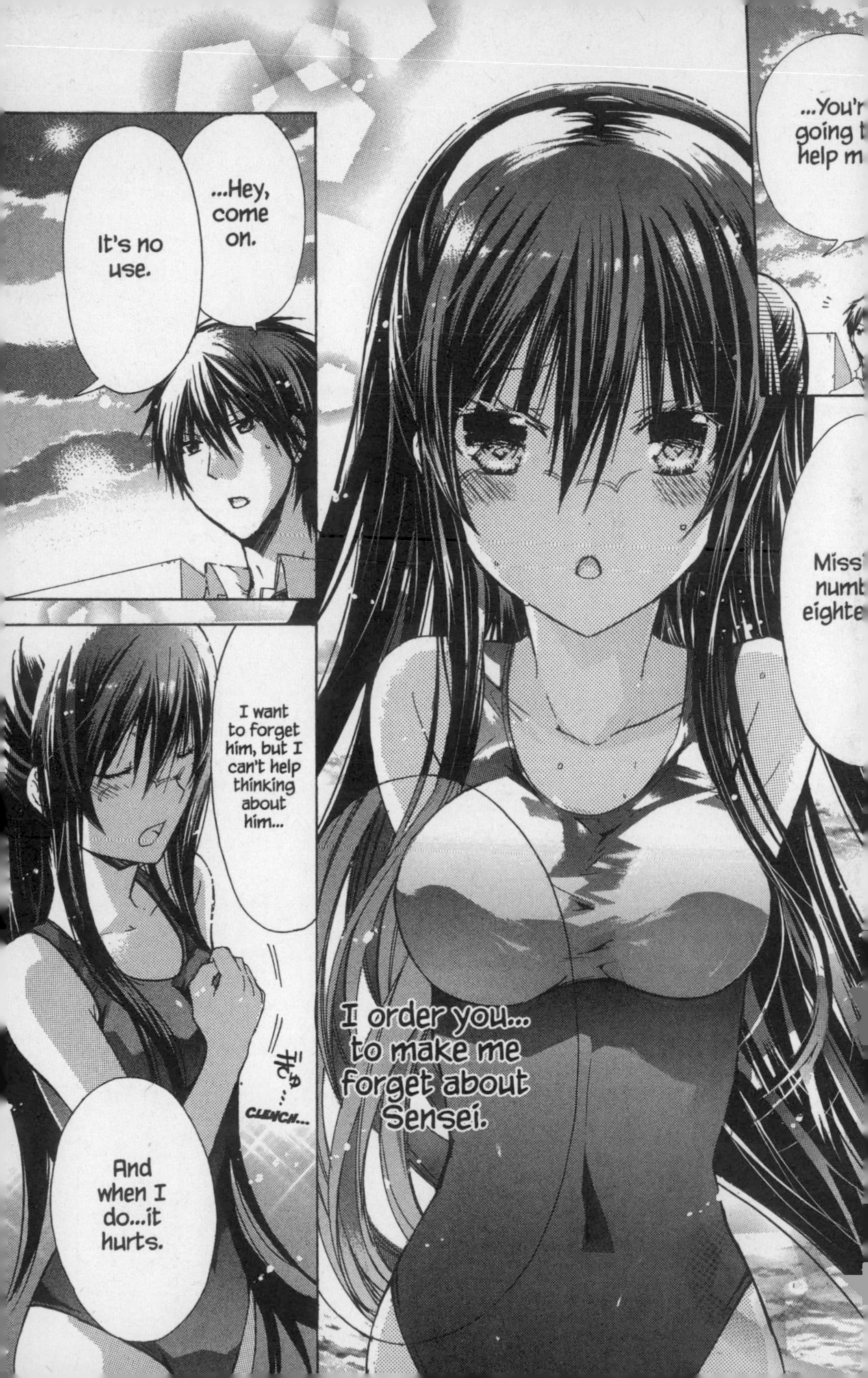
...You'r going t help m
Miss numb eighte
I order you... to make me forget about Sensei.
...Hey, come on.
It's no use.
I want to forget him, but I can't help thinking about him...
CLENCH...
And when I do...it hurts.

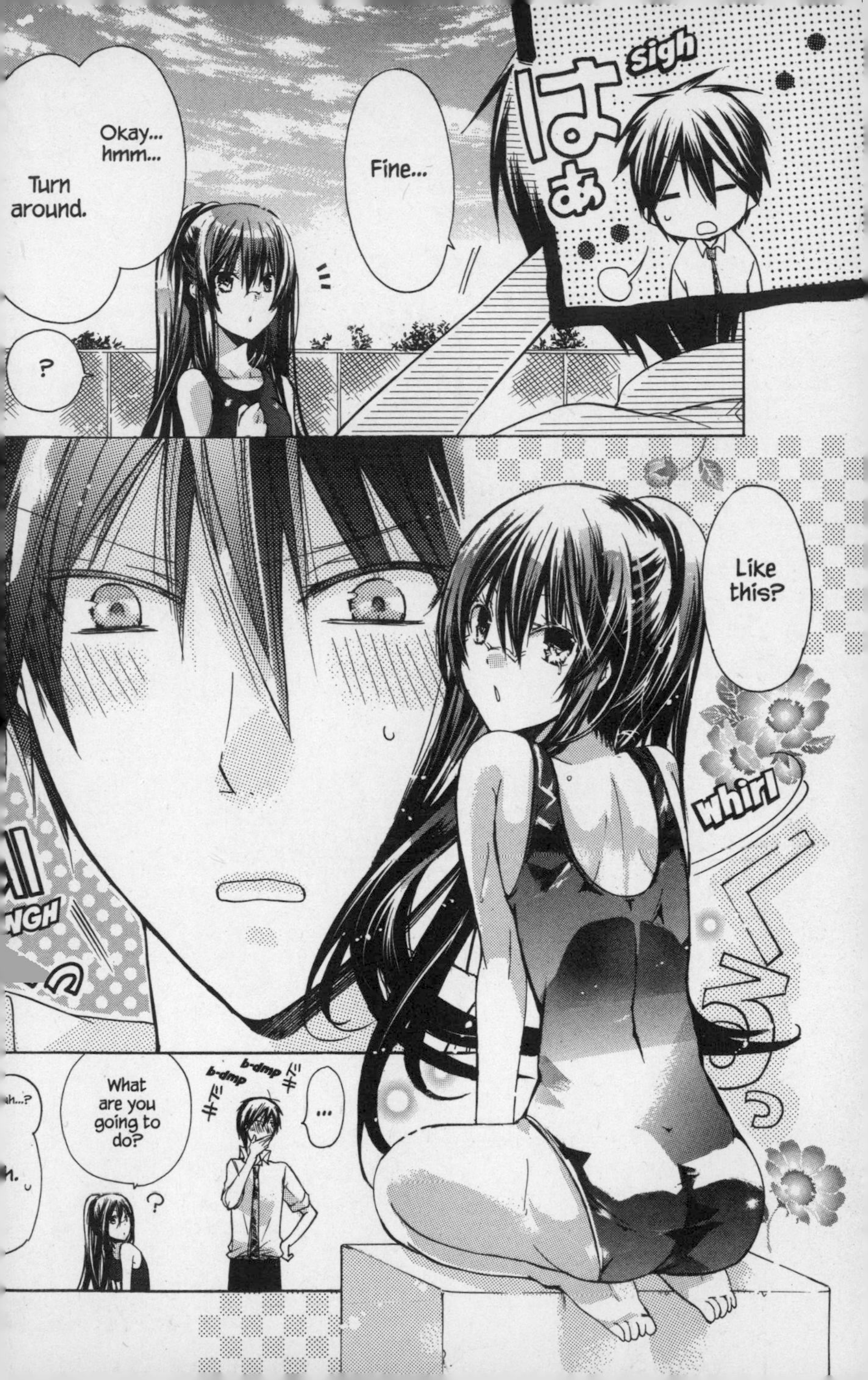

sigh
Fine...
Okay... hmm...
Turn around.
?
Like this?
whirl
NGH
...
b-dmp
b-dmp
What are you going to do?
?

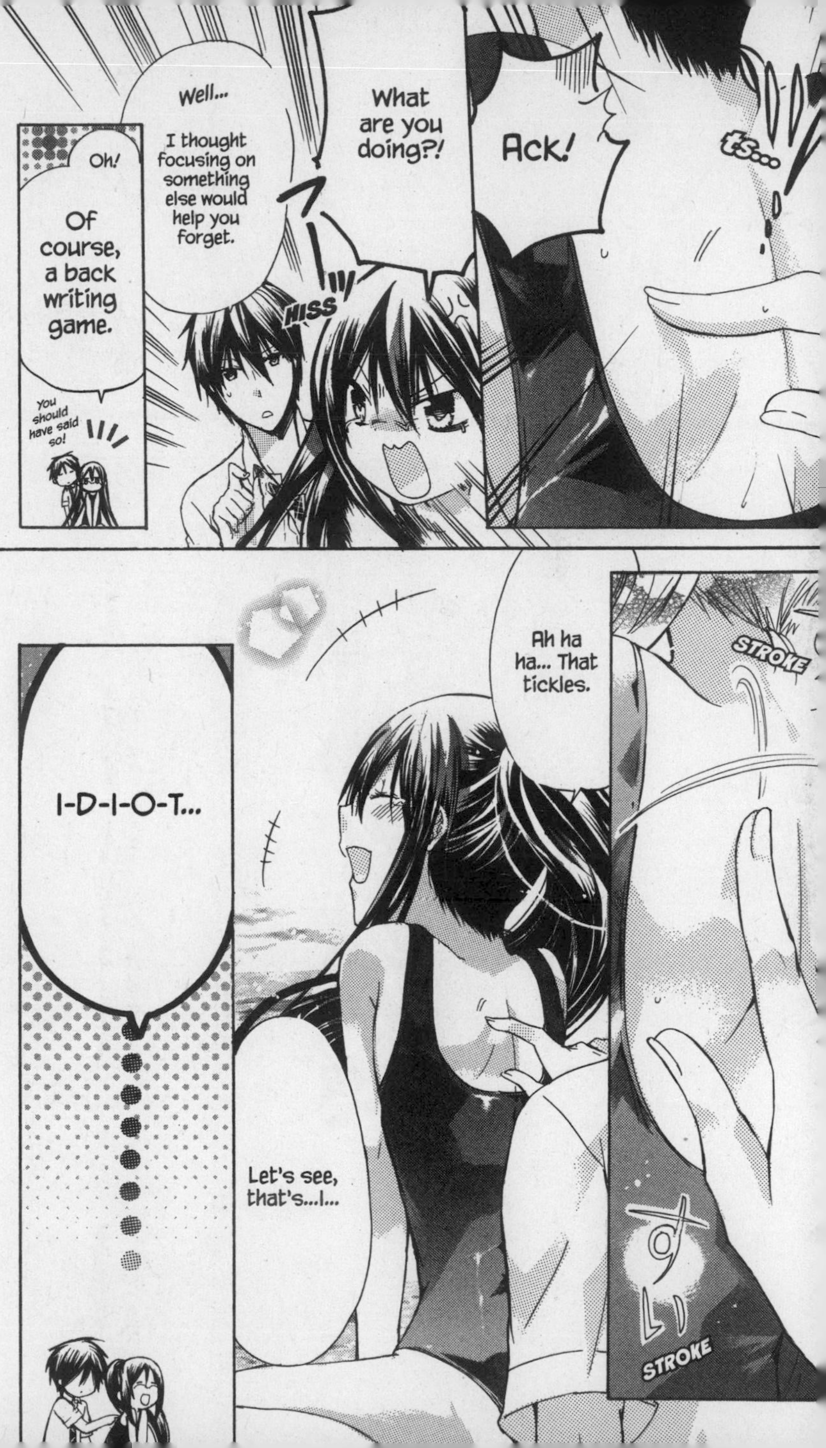
tS...
Ack!
What are you doing?!
Well...
I thought focusing on something else would help you forget.
HISS
Oh!
Of course, a back writing game.
You should have said so!
STROKE
STROKE
Ah ha ha... That tickles.
Let's see, that's...I...
I-D-I-O-T...

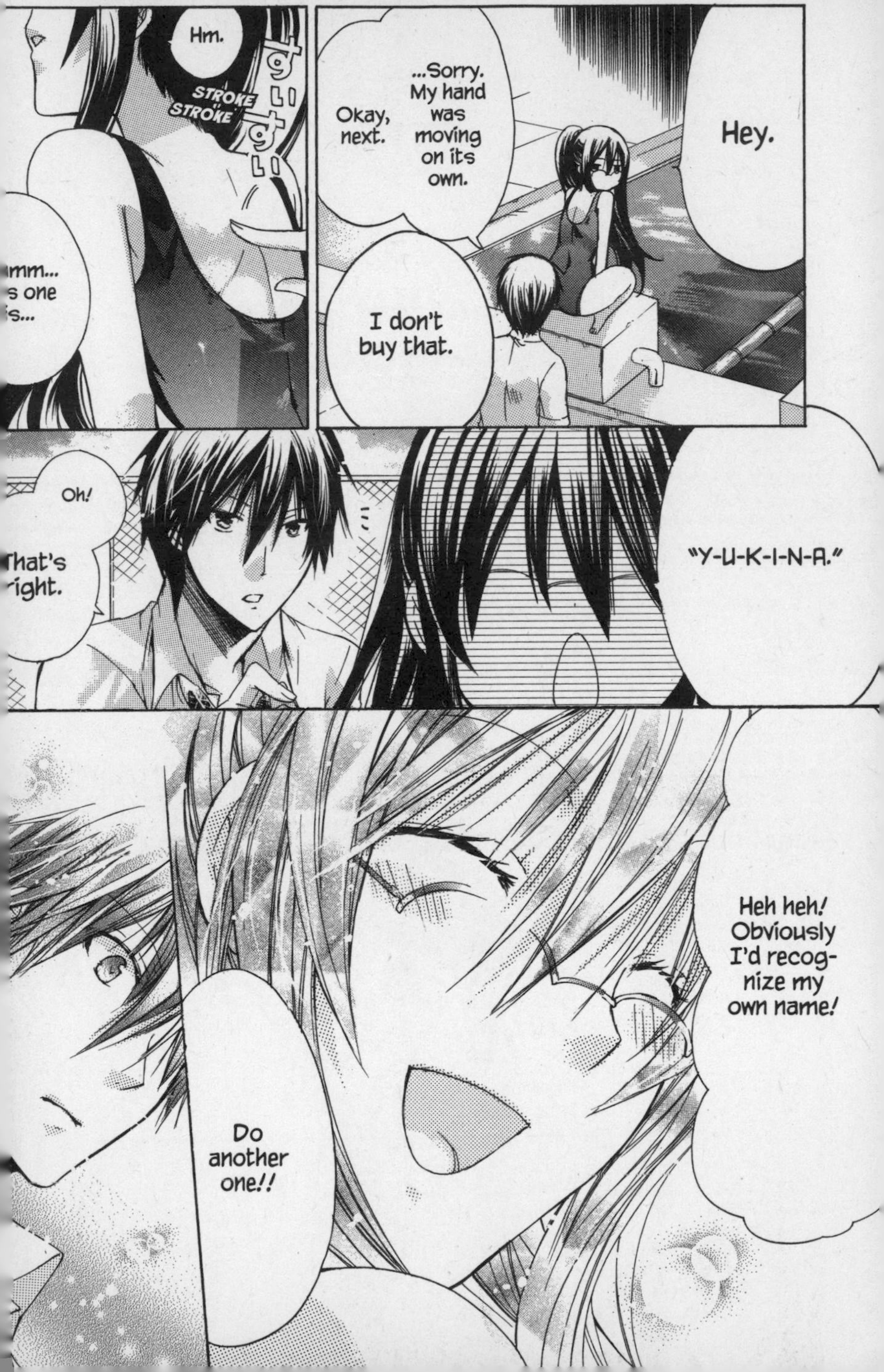
Hey.
...Sorry. My hand was moving on its own.
Okay, next.
I don't buy that.
Hm.
すり すり
STROKE STROKE
mm... s one s...
"Y-U-K-I-N-A."
Oh!
hat's ight.
Heh heh! Obviously I'd recognize my own name!
Do another one!!

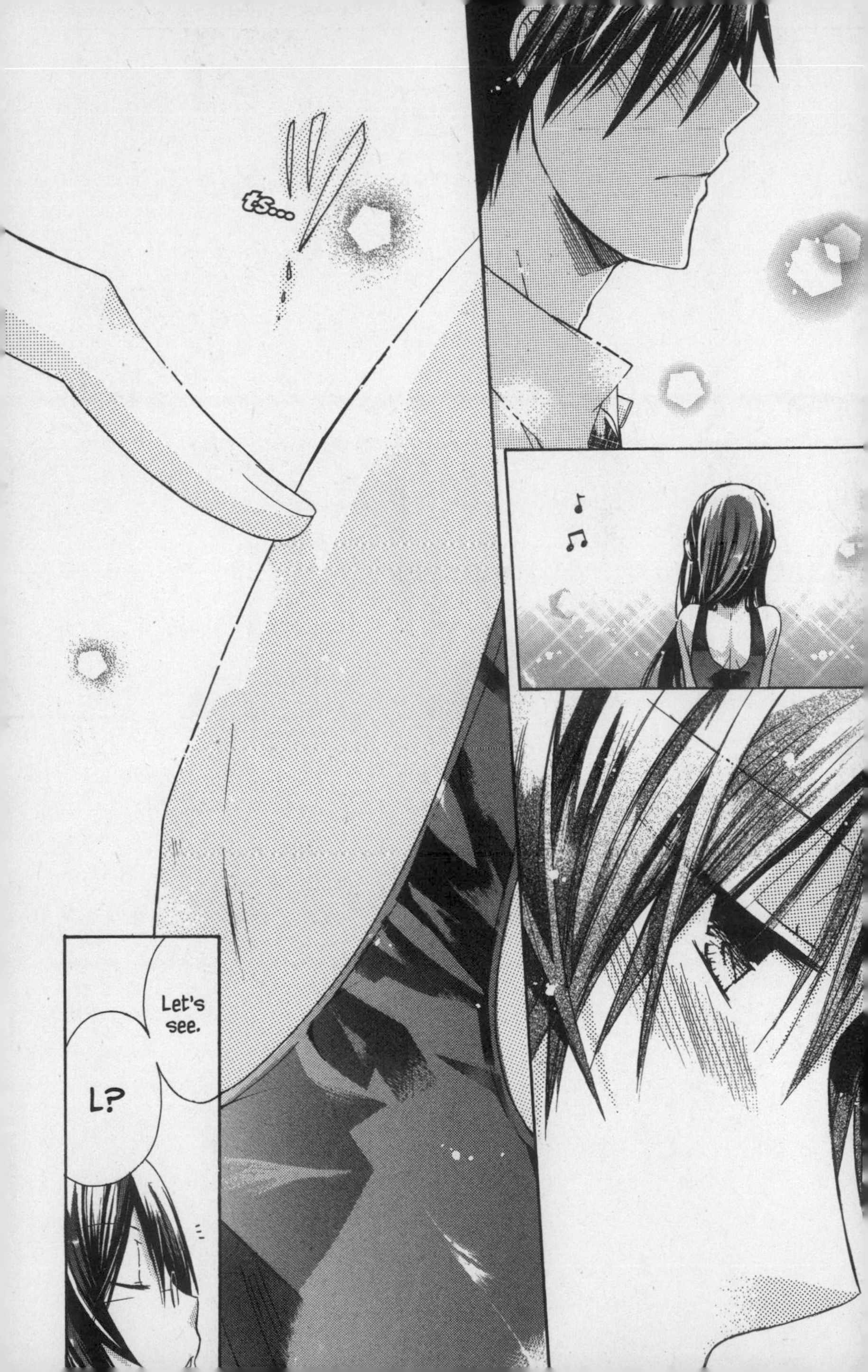
ts...
Let's see.
L?

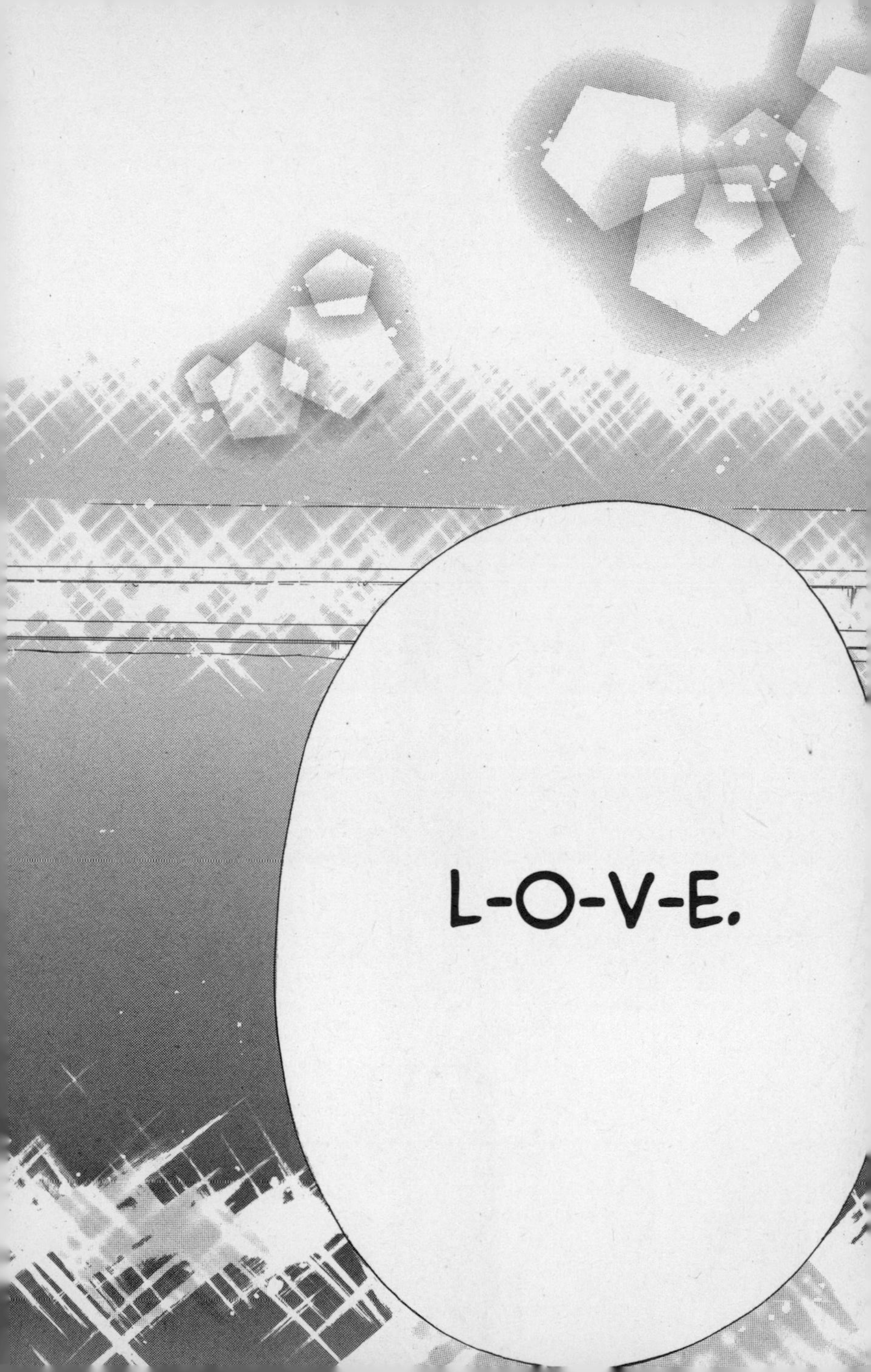
L-O-V-E.

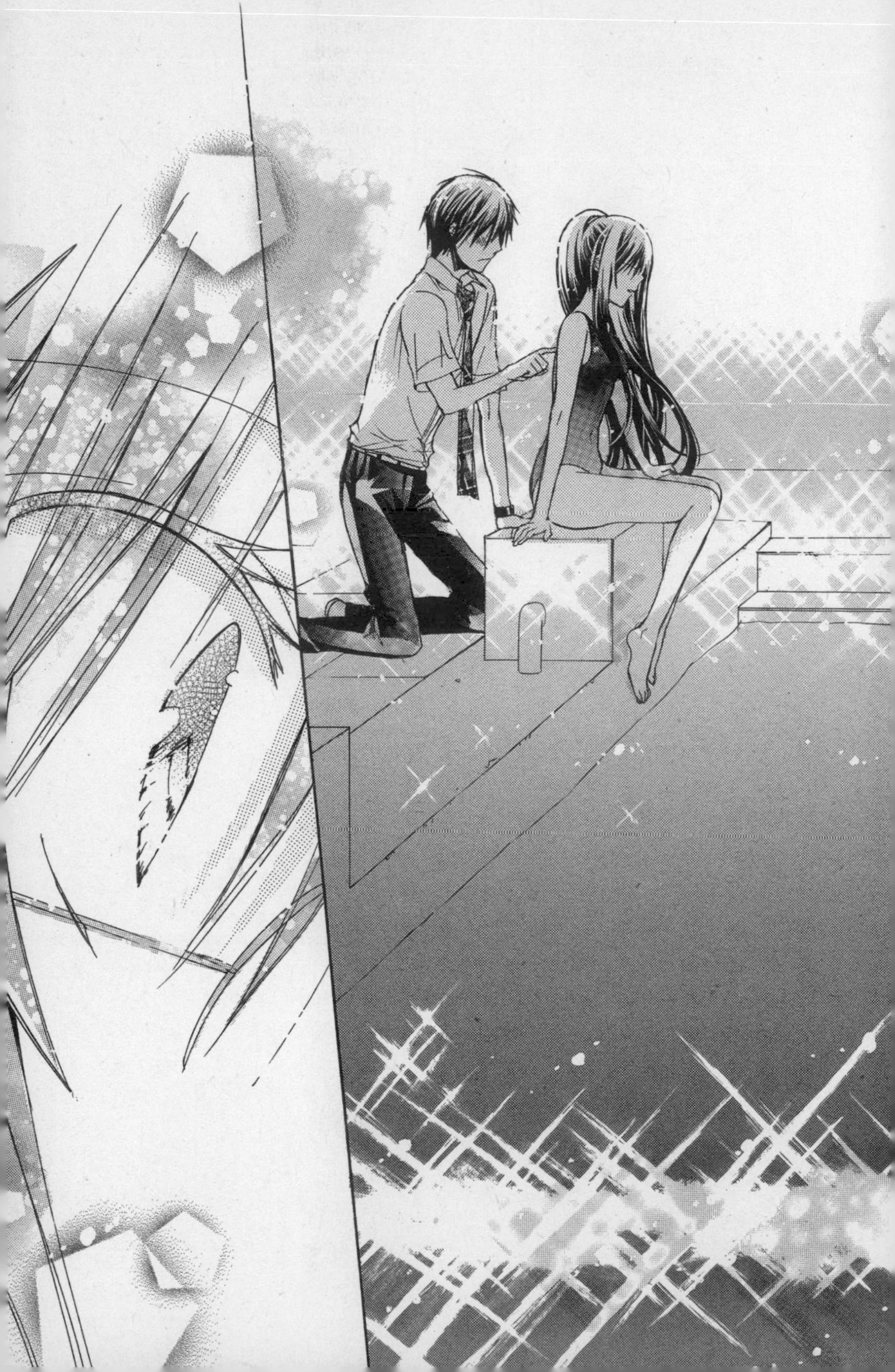

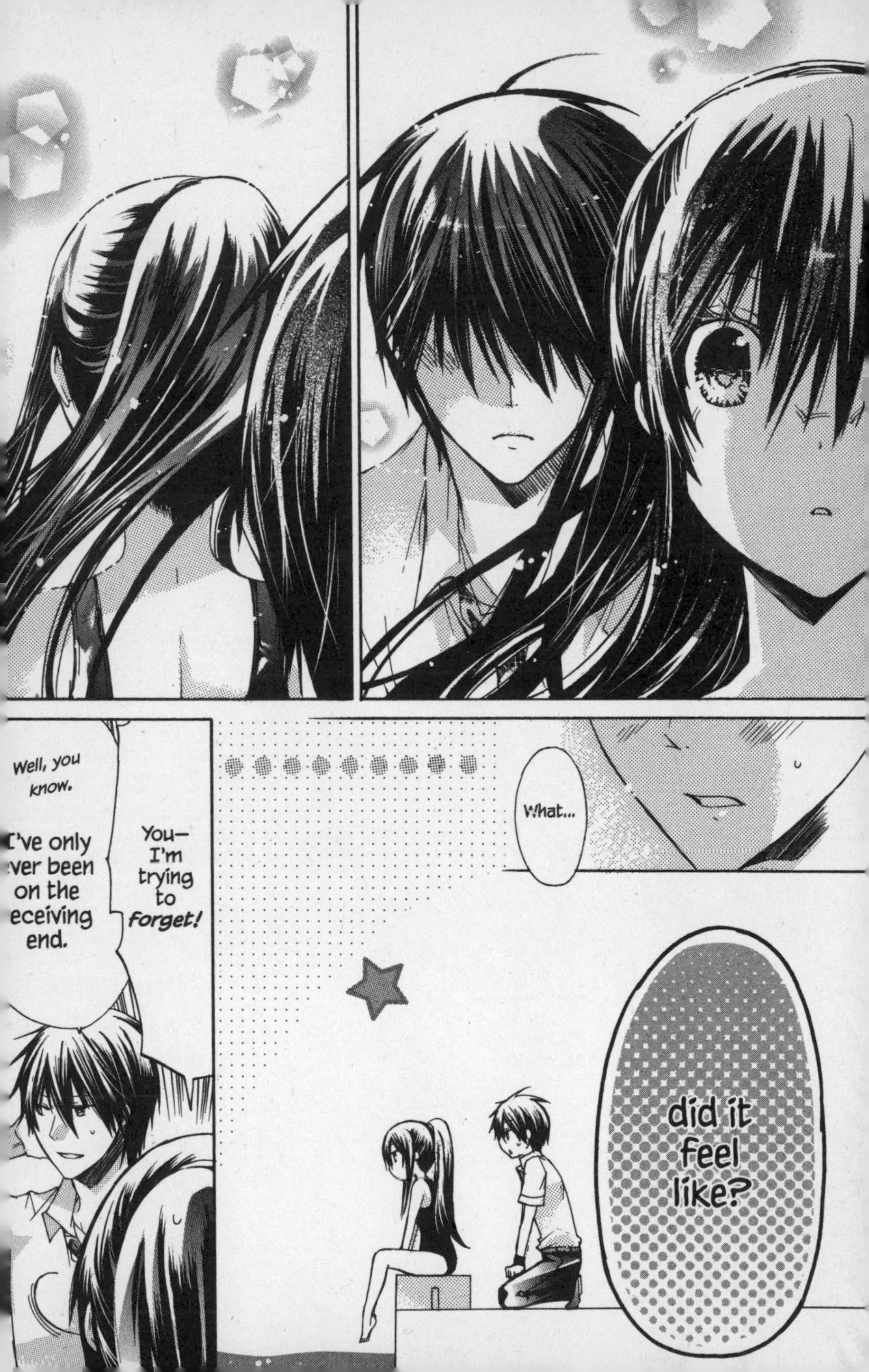
What...
did it feel like?
You— I'm trying to forget!
Well, you know.
I've only ver been on the eceiving end.

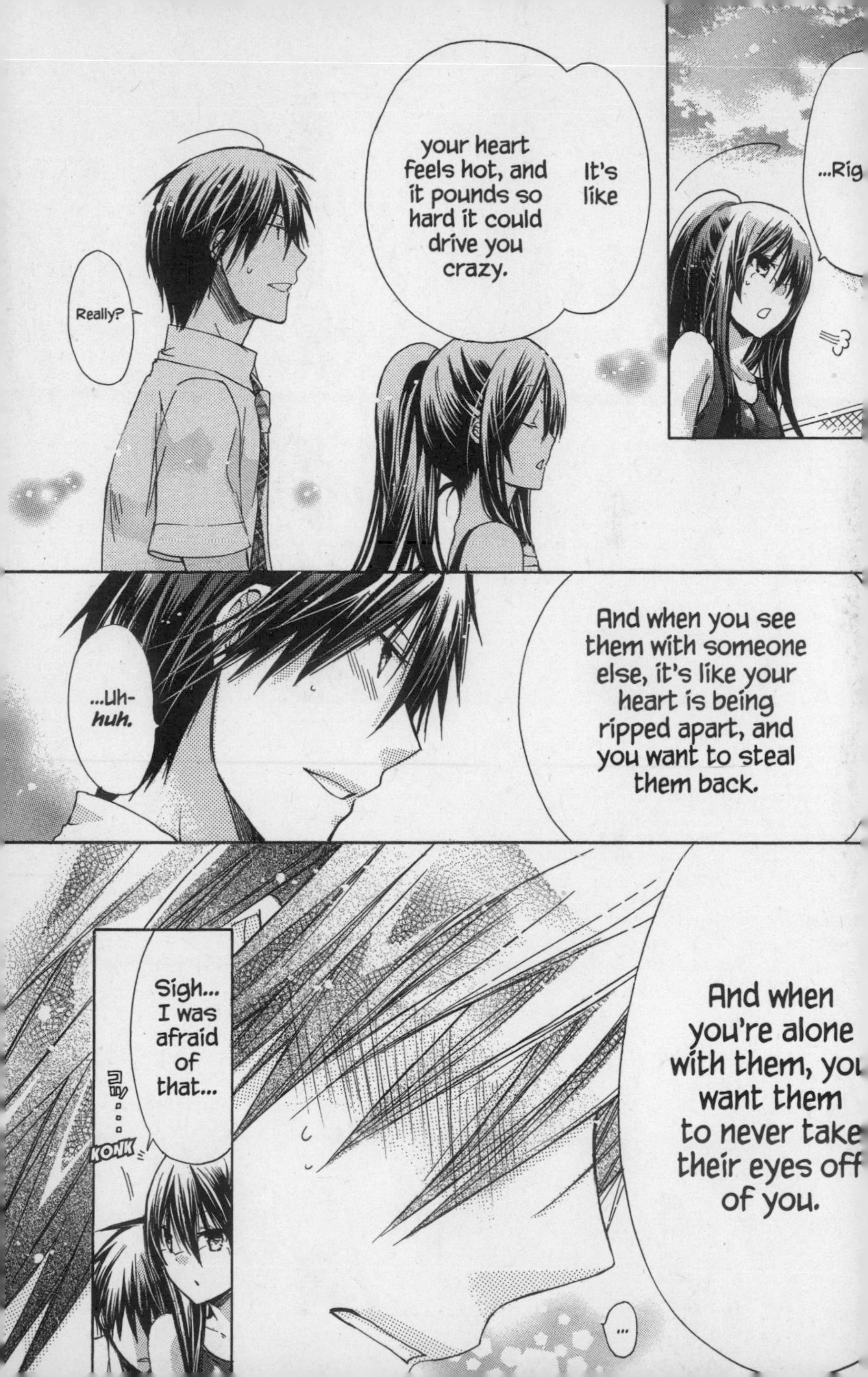

...Rig
It's like
your heart feels hot, and it pounds so hard it could drive you crazy.
Really?
And when you see them with someone else, it's like your heart is being ripped apart, and you want to steal them back.
...Uh-huh.
And when you're alone with them, yo want them to never take their eyes off of you.
...
Sigh... I was afraid of that...
KONK

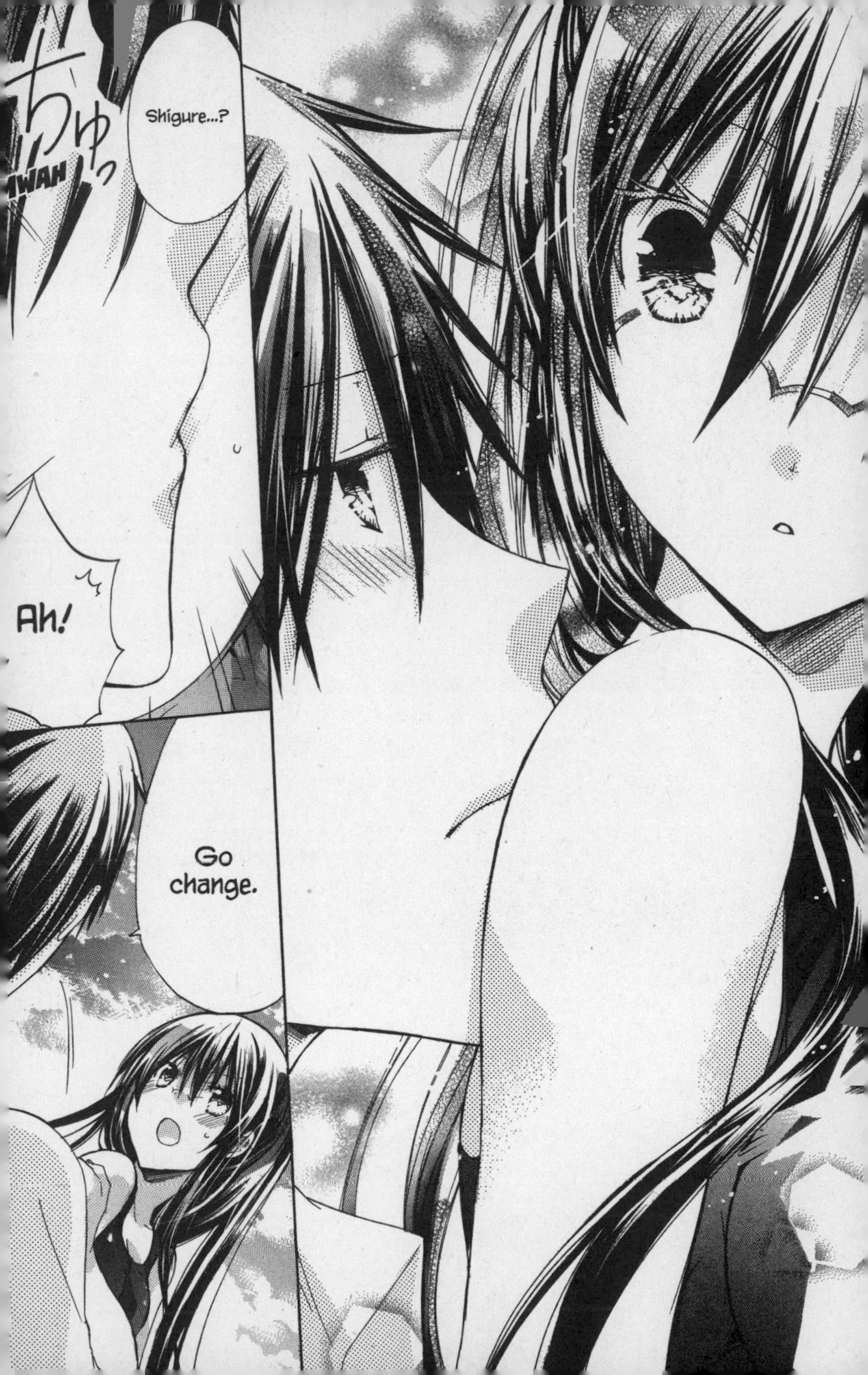
Shigure...?
ちゅっ
MWAH
Ah!
Go change.

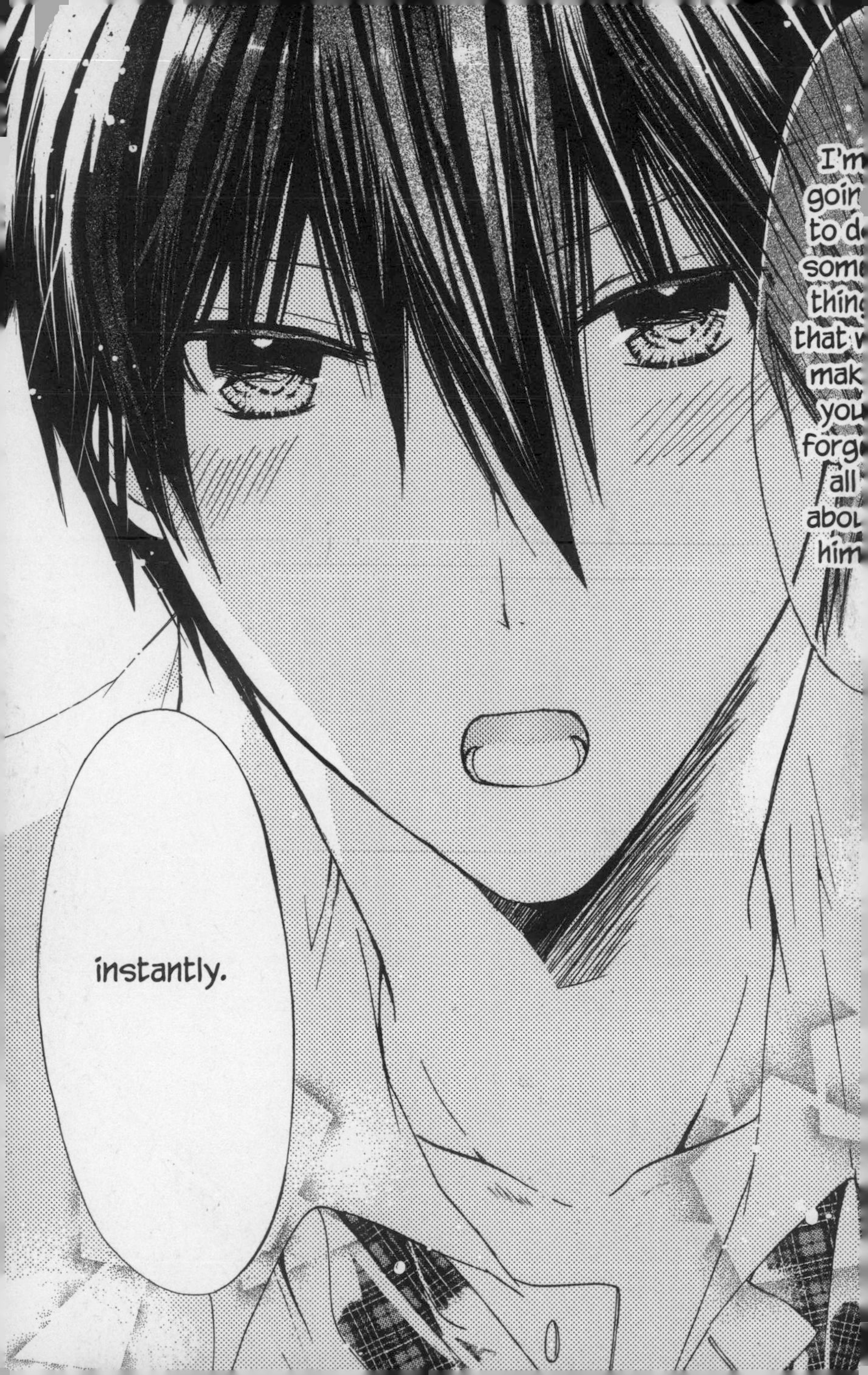
I'm goin to d some thing that mak you forg all abou him
instantly.

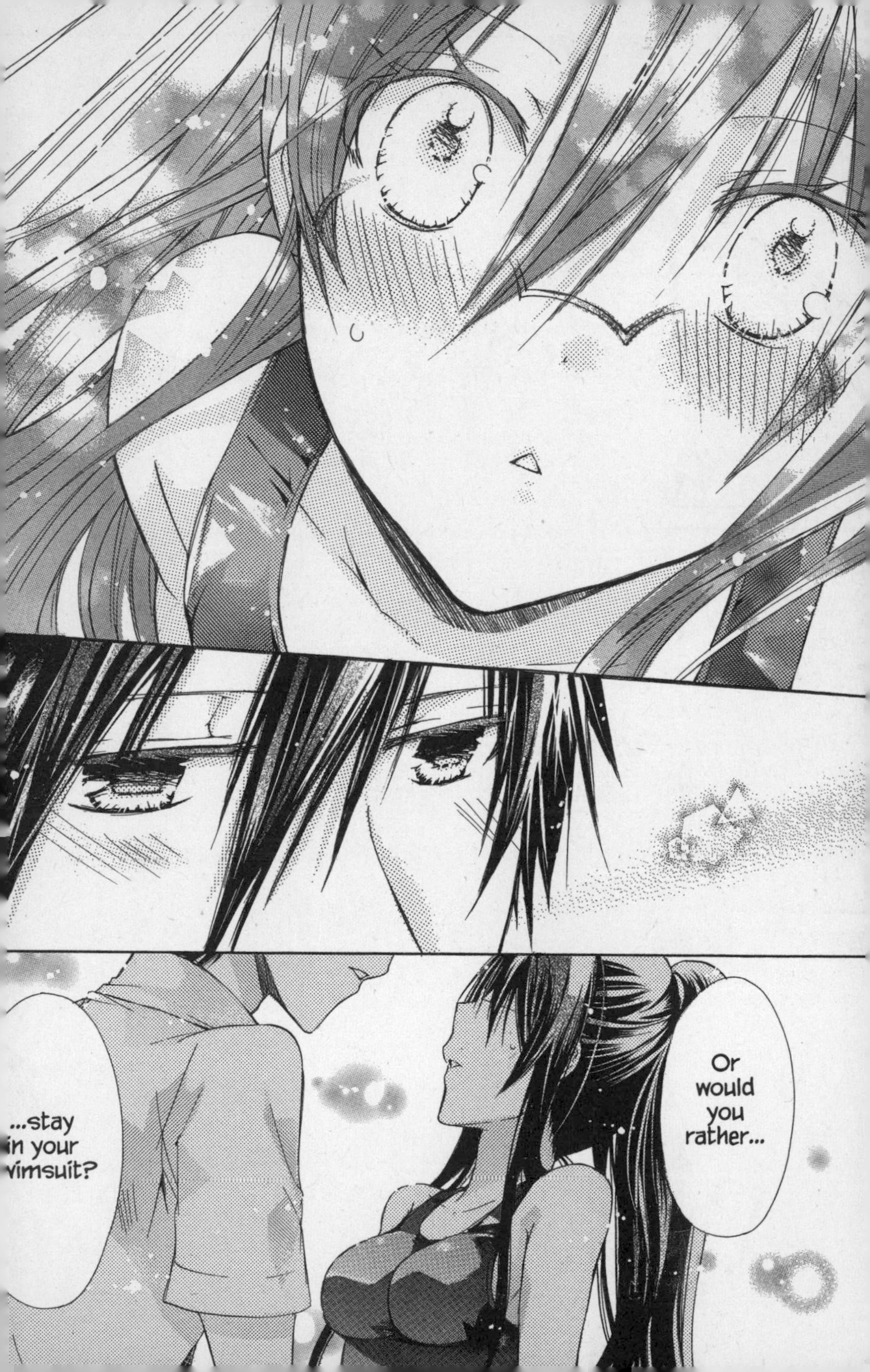
Or would you rather...
...stay in your vimsuit?

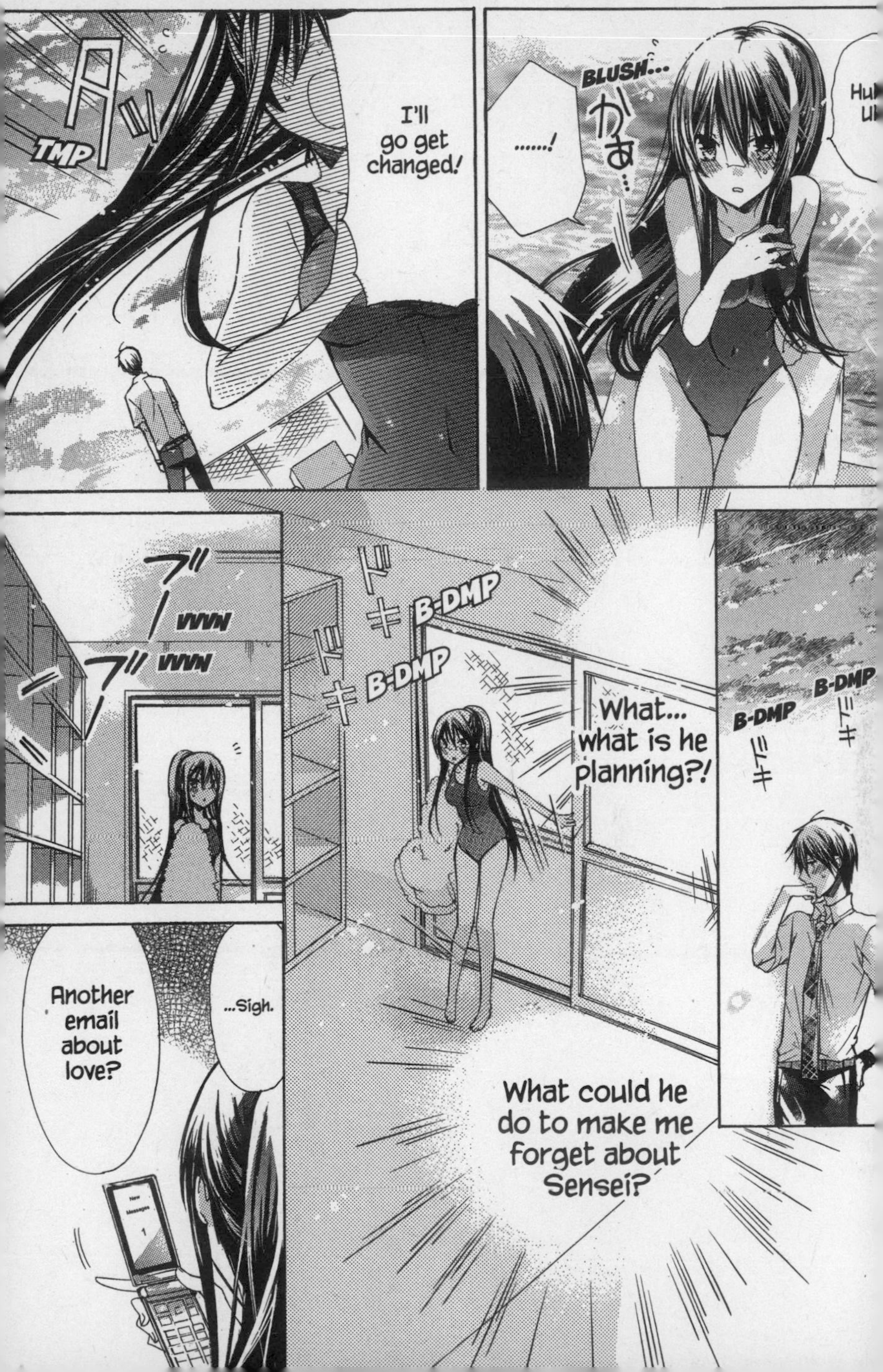

BLUSH...
かぁ…
......!
I'll go get changed!
TMP
B-DMP
ドキ
B-DMP
ドキ
ドキ B-DMP
ドキ B-DMP
What... what is he planning?!
What could he do to make me forget about Sensei?
VVVN
VVVN
...Sigh.
Another email about love?
New Messages
1

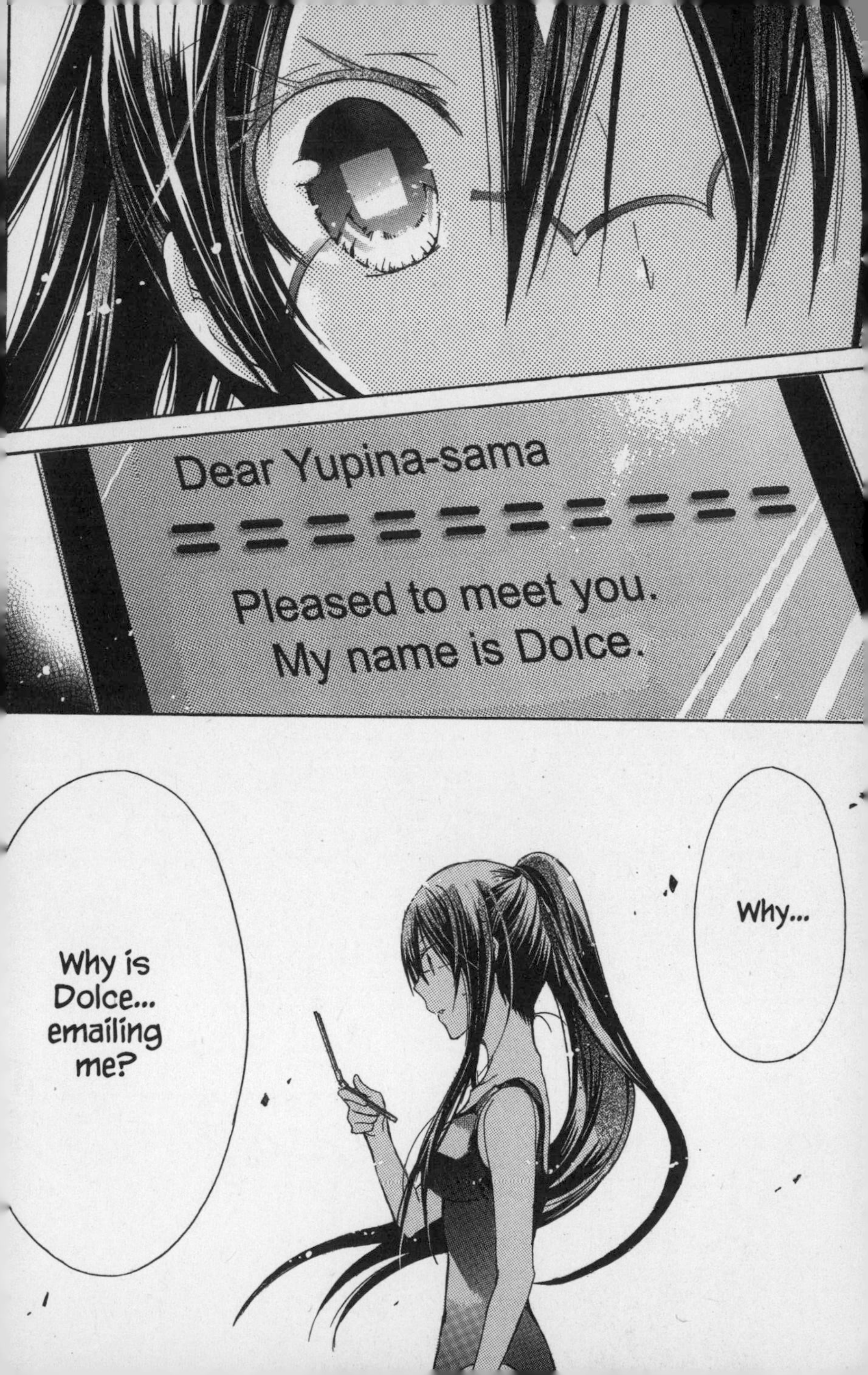
Dear Yupina-sama
Pleased to meet you. My name is Dolce.
Why...
Why is Dolce... emailing me?

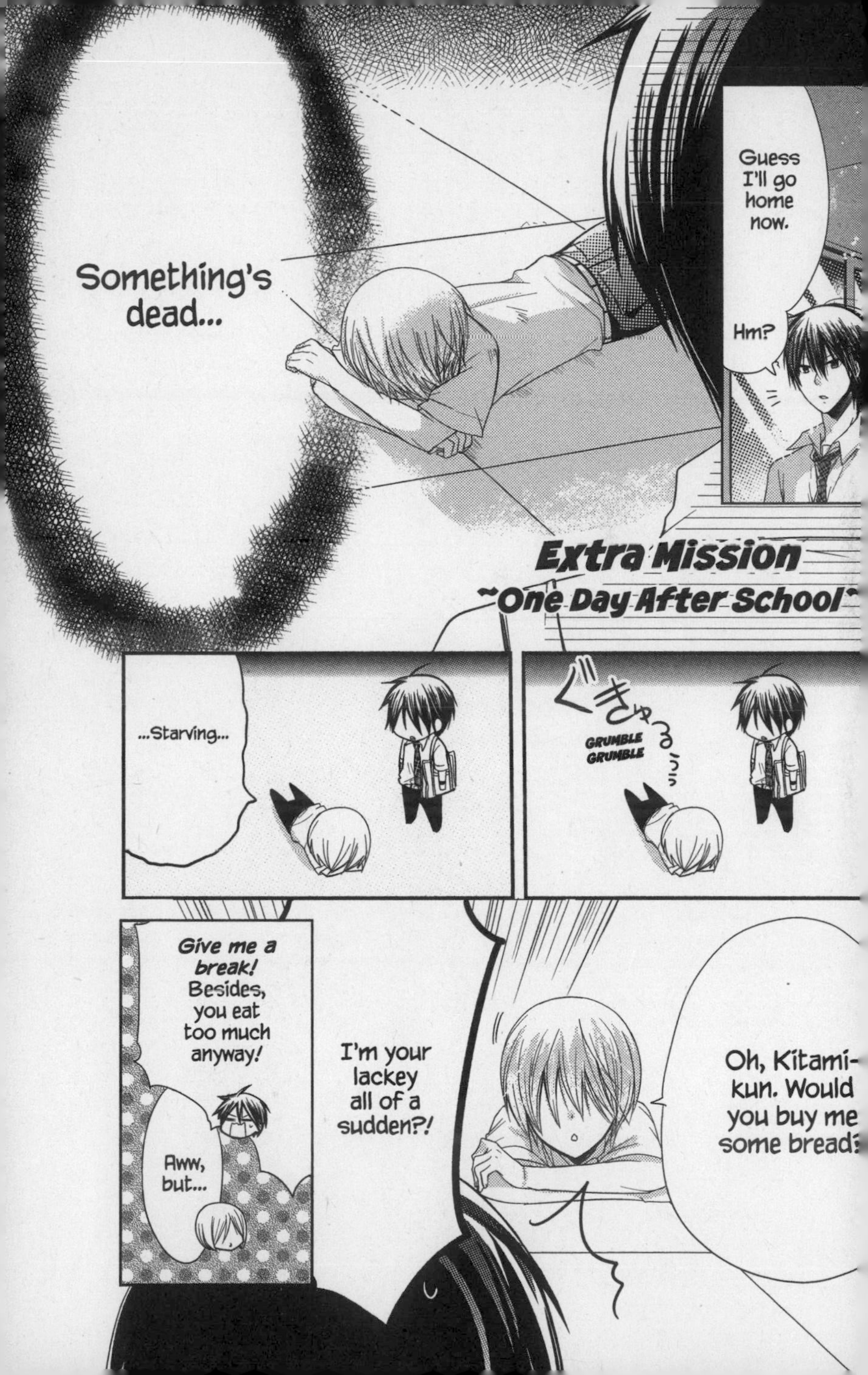
Guess I'll go home now.
Hm?
Something's dead...
Extra Mission
~One Day After School~
GRUMBLE GRUMBLE
...Starving...
Oh, Kitami-kun. Would you buy me some bread?
I'm your lackey all of a sudden?!
Give me a break! Besides, you eat too much anyway!
Aww, but...

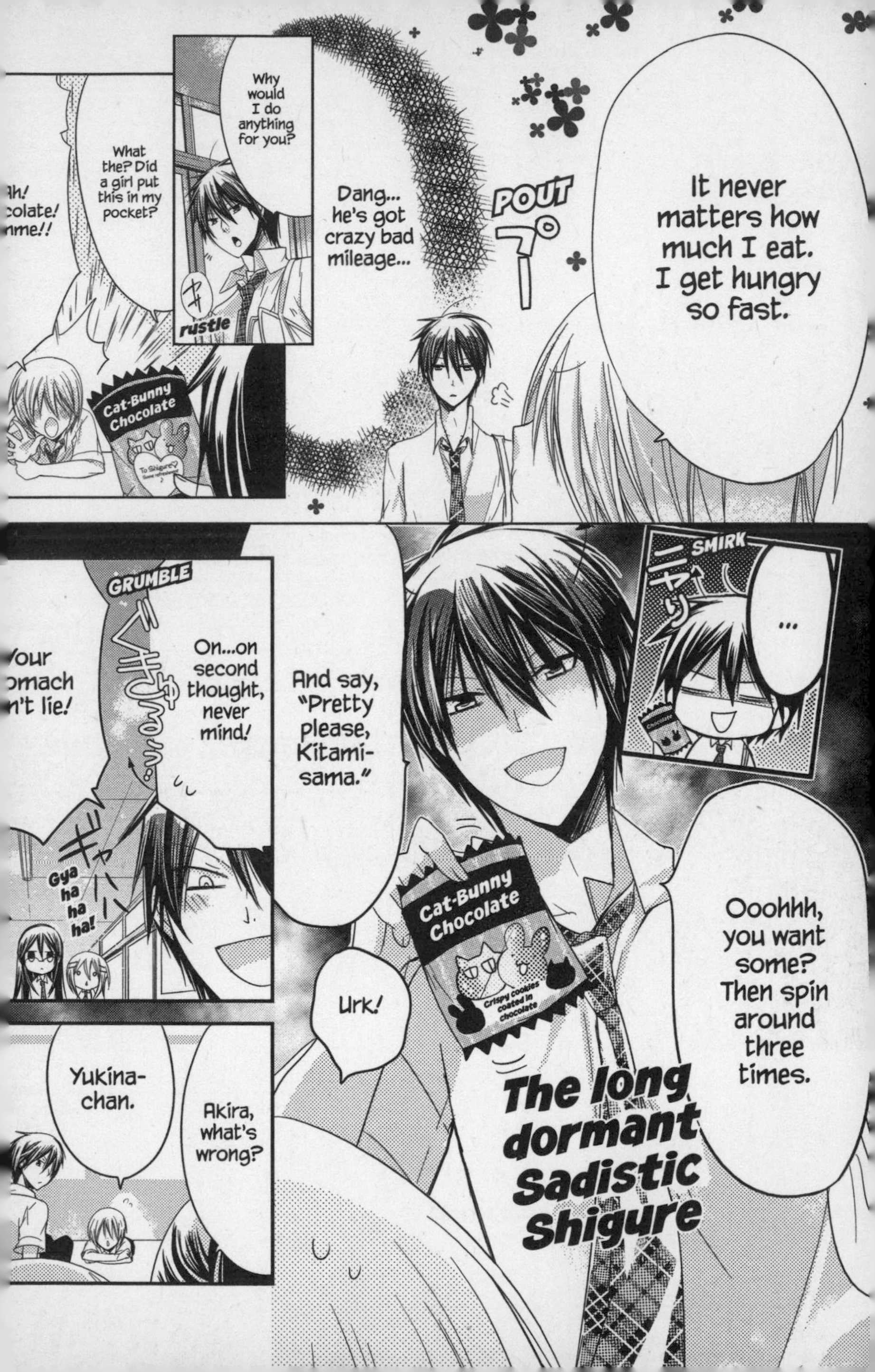
It never matters how much I eat. I get hungry so fast.
POUT
Dang... he's got crazy bad mileage...
Why would I do anything for you?
rustle
What the? Did a girl put this in my pocket?
Ah! colate! nme!!
Cat-Bunny Chocolate
SMIRK
...
Oooohhh, you want some? Then spin around three times.
And say, "Pretty please, Kitami-sama."
Cat-Bunny Chocolate
Crispy cookies coated in chocolate
Urk!
The long dormant Sadistic Shigure
GRUMBLE
On...on second thought, never mind!
Your omach n't lie!
Gya ha ha ha!
Akira, what's wrong?
Yukina-chan.

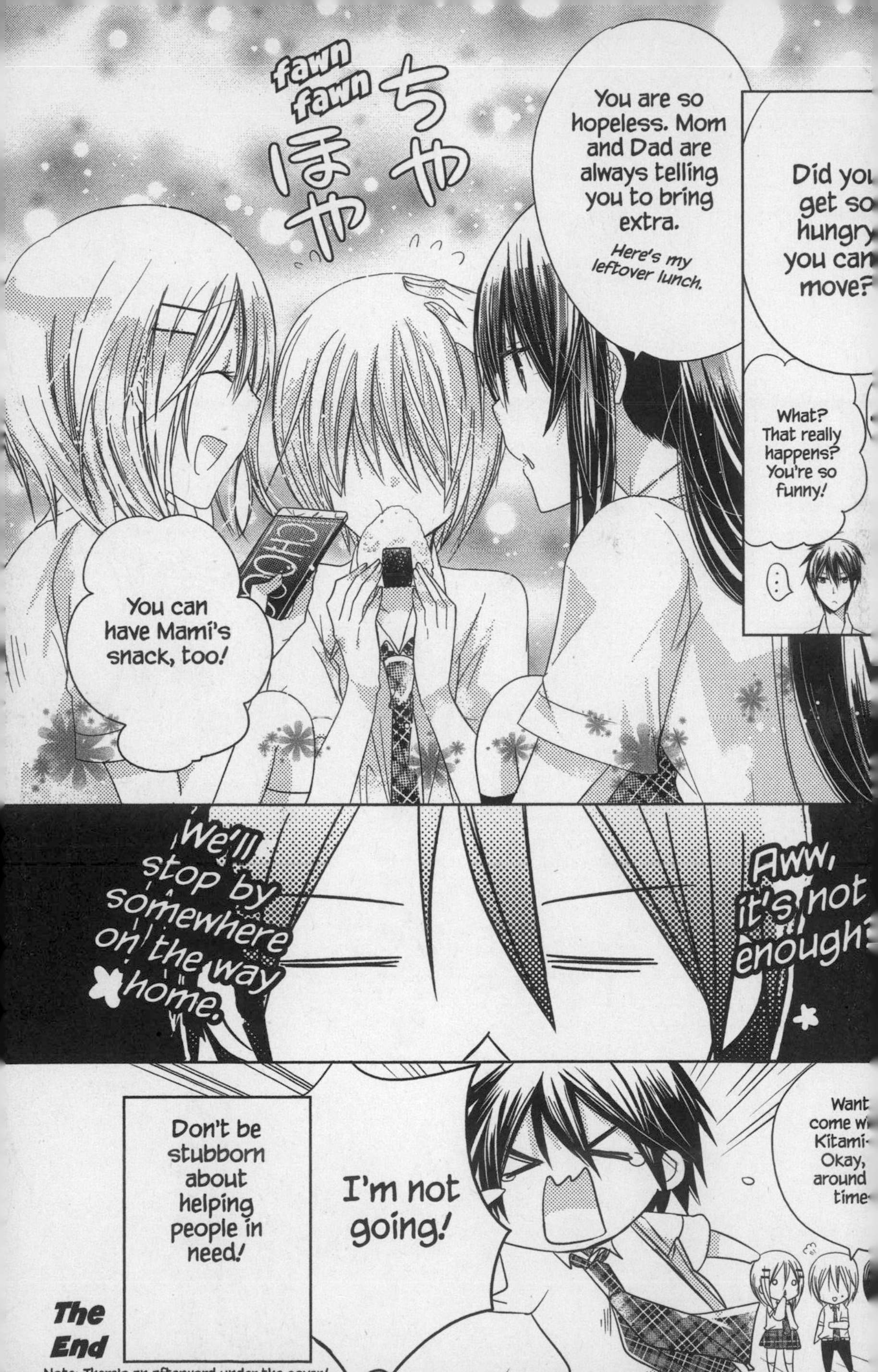
Did you get so hungry you can move?
What? That really happens? You're so funny!
...
You are so hopeless. Mom and Dad are always telling you to bring extra.
Here's my leftover lunch.
fawn fawn
ちやほや
You can have Mami's snack, too!
Aww, it's not enough
We'll stop by somewhere on the way home.
Want come w Kitami- Okay, around time
I'm not going!
Don't be stubborn about helping people in need!
The End

Note: There's an afterword under the cover!

Next Mission

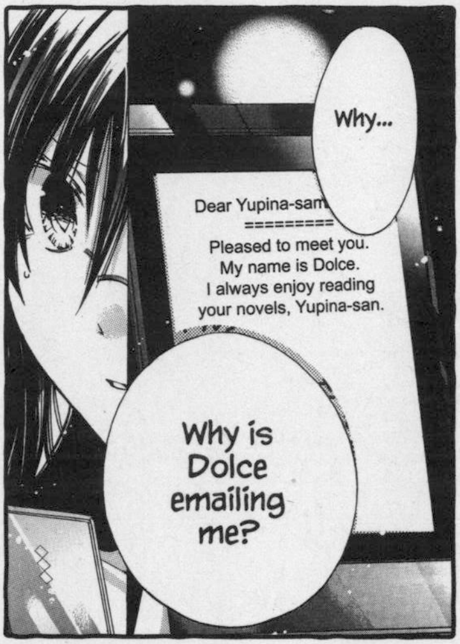
Why...
Dear Yupina-sam
==========
Pleased to meet you.
My name is Dolce.
I always enjoy reading
your novels, Yupina-san.
Why is Dolce emailing me?

It started with an email from the rival novelist Dolce.

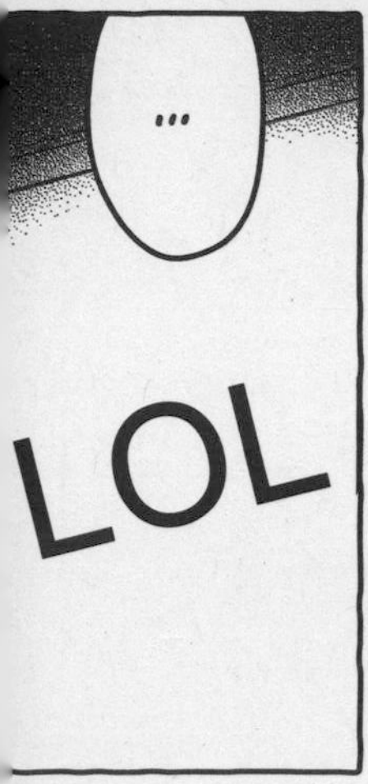
...
LOL

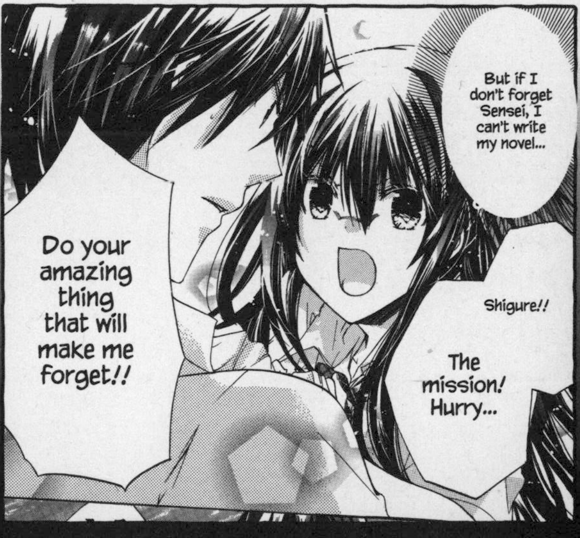
But if I don't forget Sensei, I can't write my novel...
Shigure!!
The mission! Hurry...
Do your amazing thing that will make me forget!!

The greatest love mission in history is about to begin!!

On sale soon!!

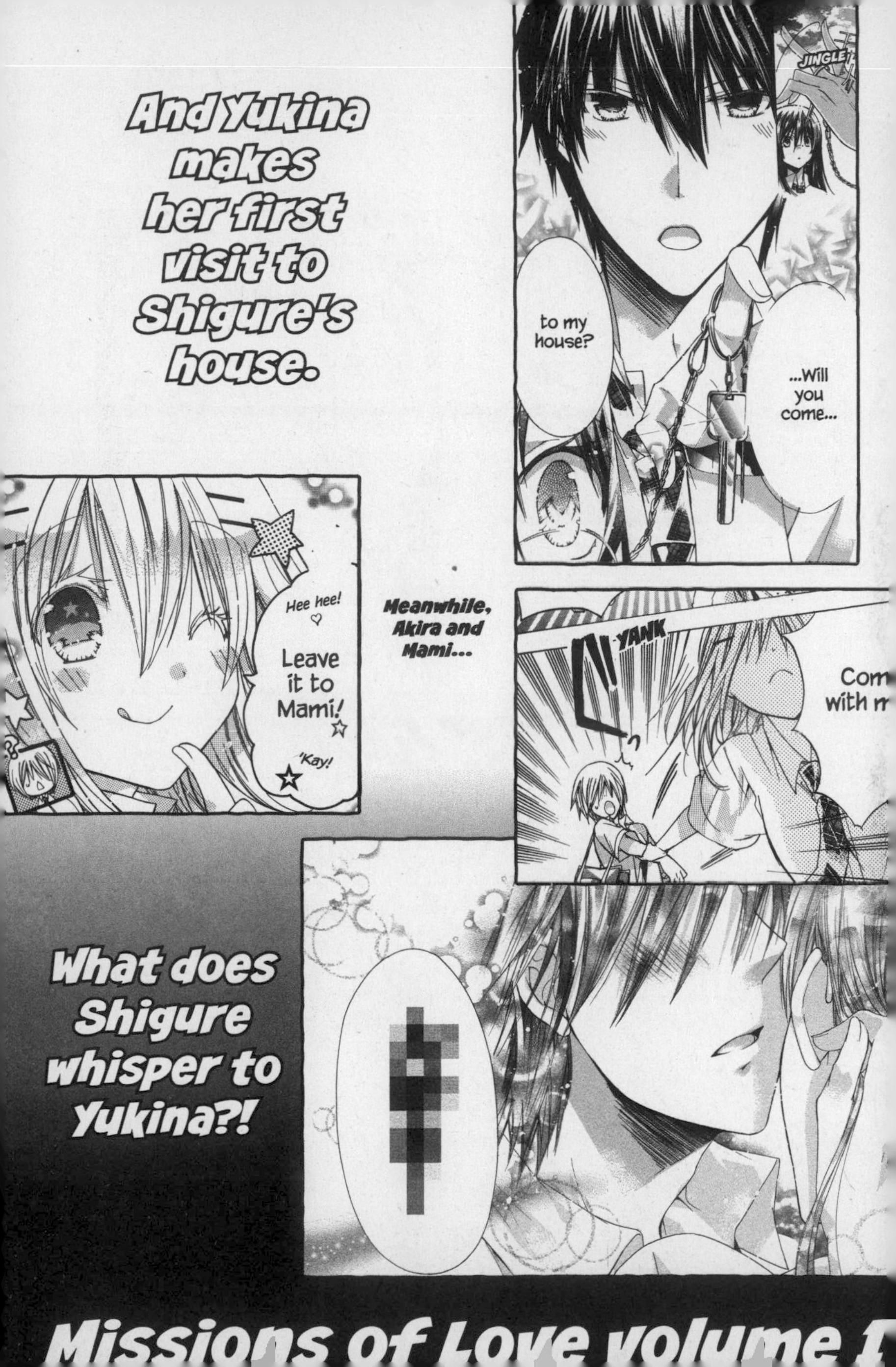
JINGLE
...Will you come...
to my house?
And Yukina makes her first visit to Shigure's house.
YANK
Com
with m
Meanwhile, Akira and Mami...
Hee hee! ♡
Leave it to Mami! ☆
'Kay!
What does Shigure whisper to Yukina?!
Missions of Love volume

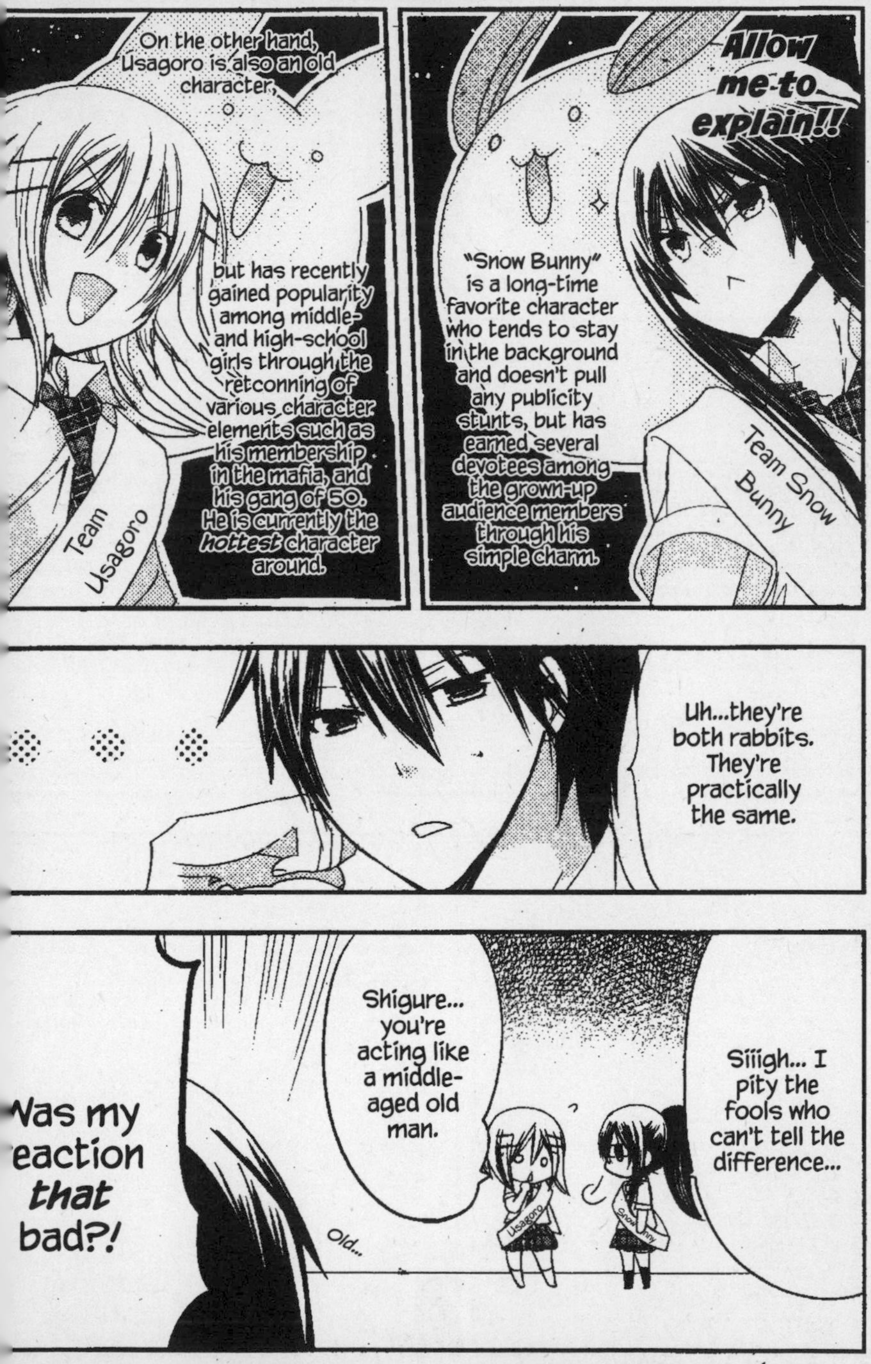
Allow me to explain!!
"Snow Bunny" is a long-time favorite character who tends to stay in the background and doesn't pull any publicity stunts, but has earned several devotees among the grown-up audience members through his simple charm.
Team Snow Bunny
On the other hand, Usagoro is also an old character,
but has recently gained popularity among middle- and high-school girls through the retconning of various character elements such as his membership in the mafia, and his gang of 50. He is currently the hottest character around.
Team Usagoro
Uh...they're both rabbits. They're practically the same.
Siiigh... I pity the fools who can't tell the difference...
Shigure... you're acting like a middle-aged old man.
Usagoro
Old...
Was my reaction that bad?!

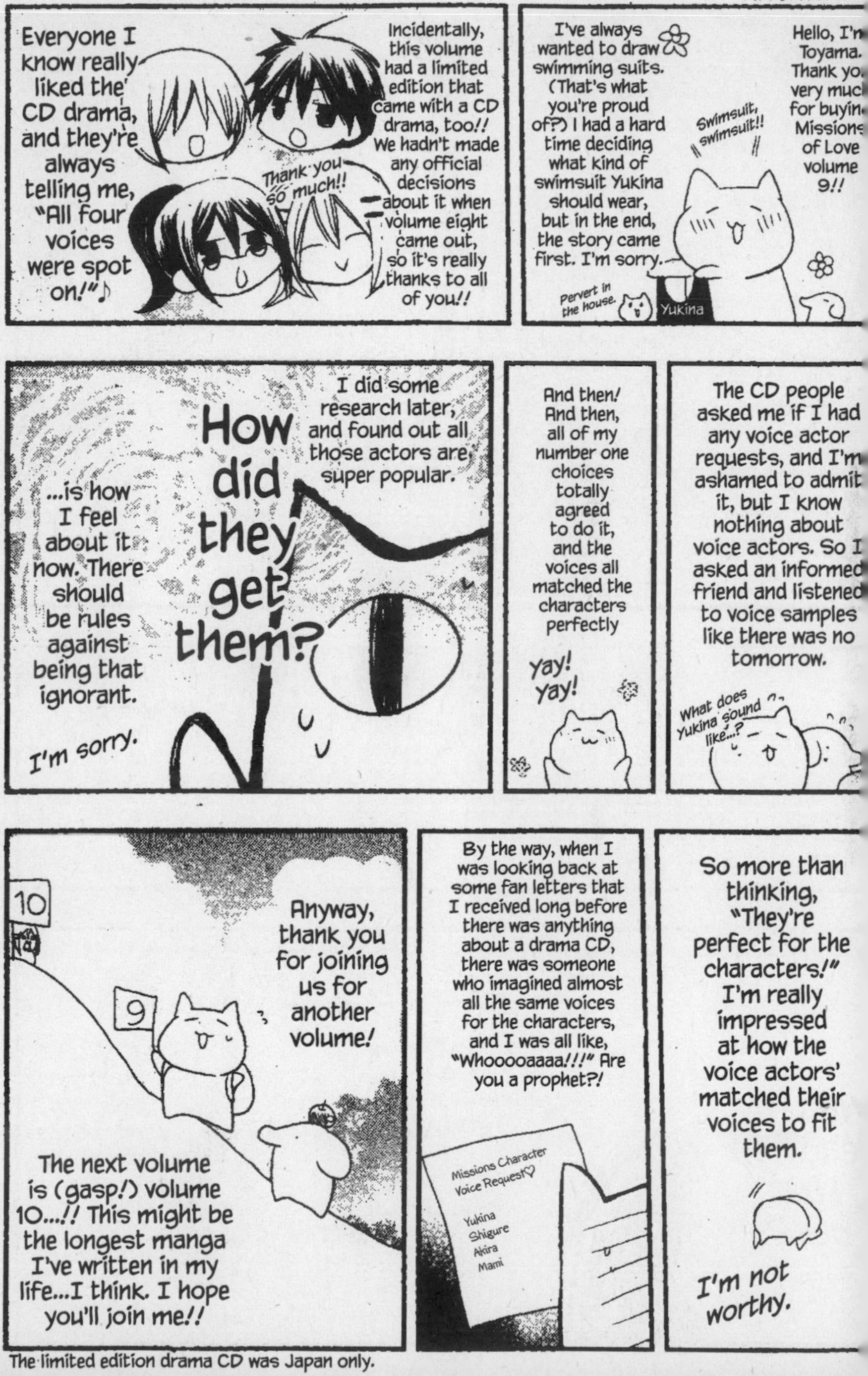
Hello, I'm Toyama. Thank you very much for buying Missions of Love volume 9!!
I've always wanted to draw swimming suits. (That's what you're proud of?) I had a hard time deciding what kind of swimsuit Yukina should wear, but in the end, the story came first. I'm sorry.
Swimsuit, swimsuit!!
Pervert in the house.
Yukina
Incidentally, this volume had a limited edition that came with a CD drama, too!! We hadn't made any official decisions about it when volume eight came out, so it's really thanks to all of you!!
Thank you so much!!
Everyone I know really liked the CD drama, and they're always telling me, "All four voices were spot on!"♪
The CD people asked me if I had any voice actor requests, and I'm ashamed to admit it, but I know nothing about voice actors. So I asked an informed friend and listened to voice samples like there was no tomorrow.
What does Yukina sound like...?
And then! And then, all of my number one choices totally agreed to do it, and the voices all matched the characters perfectly
Yay! yay!
I did some research later, and found out all those actors are super popular.
How did they get them?
...is how I feel about it now. There should be rules against being that ignorant.
I'm sorry.
So more than thinking, "They're perfect for the characters!" I'm really impressed at how the voice actors' matched their voices to fit them.
I'm not worthy.
By the way, when I was looking back at some fan letters that I received long before there was anything about a drama CD, there was someone who imagined almost all the same voices for the characters, and I was all like, "Whoooaaaa!!!" Are you a prophet?!
Missions Character Voice Request♡
Yukina
Shigure
Akira
Mami
Anyway, thank you for joining us for another volume!
10
9
The next volume is (gasp!) volume 10...!! This might be the longest manga I've written in my life...I think. I hope you'll join me!!

The limited edition drama CD was Japan only.

hor: Ema Toyama
ı May 23. Gemini. Blood
B
out work: *Tenshi no*
ago, winner of 36th Annual
ayoshi Newcomer Manga
rd, Special Award, and
ished in the September
3 issue of *Nakayoshi*.
resentative Works:
e Pop: Gokkun! Pūcho;
ıakore; *I Am Here!*
ama: We've made it to
me nine! It's a strange
ng, like I've been drawing
manga for a very long time,
ike it's been no time at all.
nt to grow up and mature
g with Yukina and the
rs, but it's hard when
e already a grown-up!

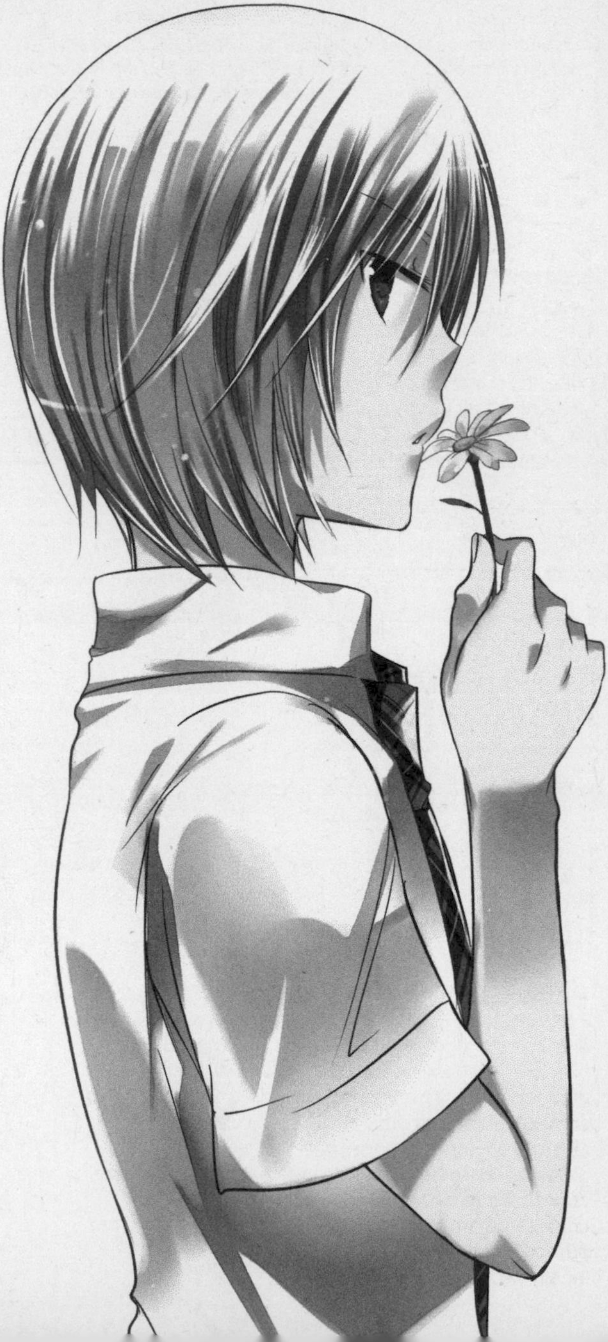

Translation Notes

Japanese is a tricky language for most Westerners, and translation is often more art than science. For your edification and reading pleasure, here are notes on some of the places where we could have gone in a different direction in our translation of the work, or where Japanese cultural reference is used.

Pretending to be good, page 28

There's a somewhat good reason that Mami wears a cat hat to indicate when she is pretending to be a good girl. In Japanese, the phrase Shigure and Mami use for "acting like a good kid" is neko-kaburi, which literally means "wearing a cat on one's head." Because the word for "cat" is the same as the word for a kind of mat. One theory is that the phrase originally came from "wearing a mat over your head and pretending you know nothing." Another theory is that cats are thought to be exceptionally good at adapting to their surroundings, and making things work to their advantage. Either way, Mami demonstrates her version of the abstract concept with a more literal example.

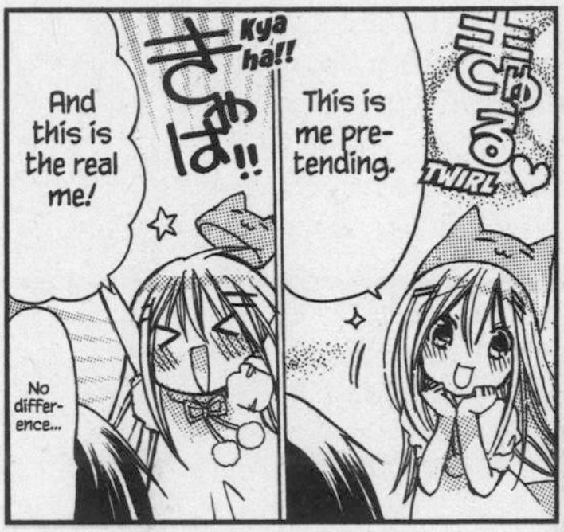
This is me pretending.
TWIRL
Kya ha!!
And this is the real me!
No difference...

Can I still be your friend?, page 32

A more literal translation of Mami's question is, "Can I still be by your side?" In other words, she's asking Shigure if it's okay for her to stay in his circle of friends, or if she should keep her distance.

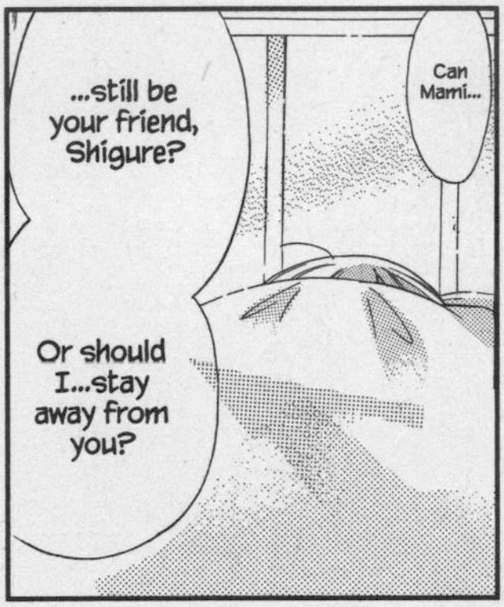
Can Mami...
...still be your friend, Shigure?
Or should I...stay away from you?

Yukina's graduation, page 53

For readers thinking, "Only one more year? But she's only in ninth grade!" you are correct: Yukina is only in her third year of middle school (ninth grade). However, in Japan, high school is not a compulsory part of education. So if Yukina decided she had something more important to do, she is perfectly within her rights to choose not to go to high school. On the other hand, since she would not be considered an adult until age 20, she would need her parents' permission to get married (which she can legally do at age 16).

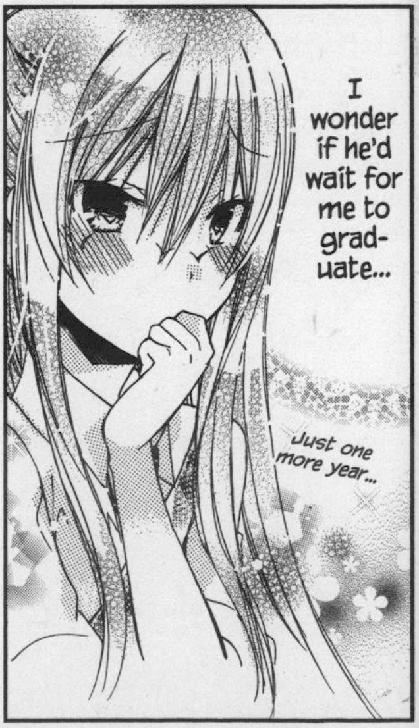
I wonder if he'd wait for me to graduate...
Just one more year...

The Pretty Guardians are back!

★

Kodansha Comics is proud to present *Sailor Moon* with all new translations.

For more information, go to **www.kodanshacomics.com**

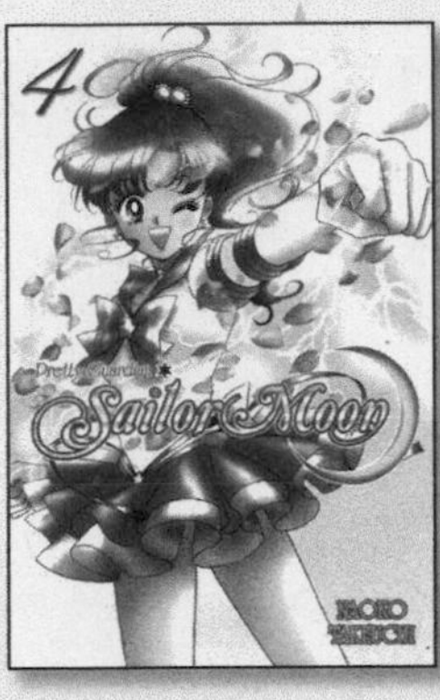
4
Pretty Guardian
Sailor Moon
NAOKO TAKEUCHI
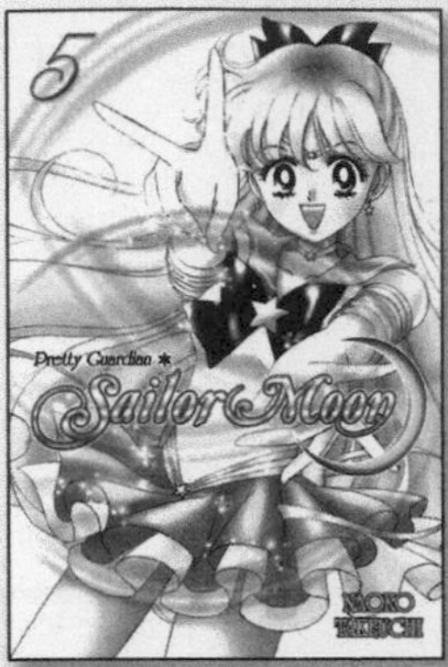
5
Pretty Guardian
Sailor Moon
NAOKO TAKEUCHI
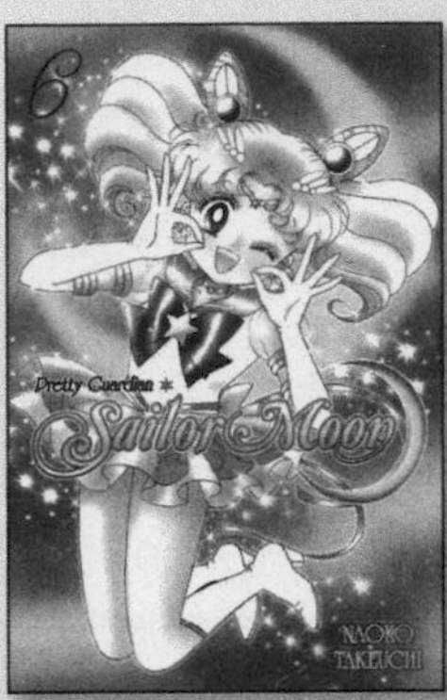
6
Pretty Guardian
Sailor Moon
NAOKO TAKEUCHI
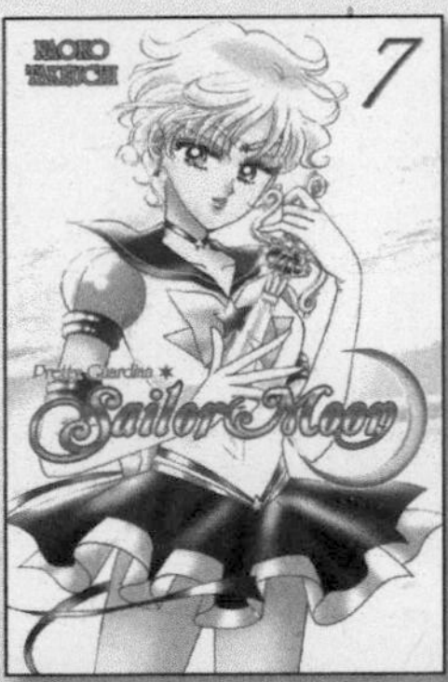
NAOKO TAKEUCHI
7
Pretty Guardian
Sailor Moon
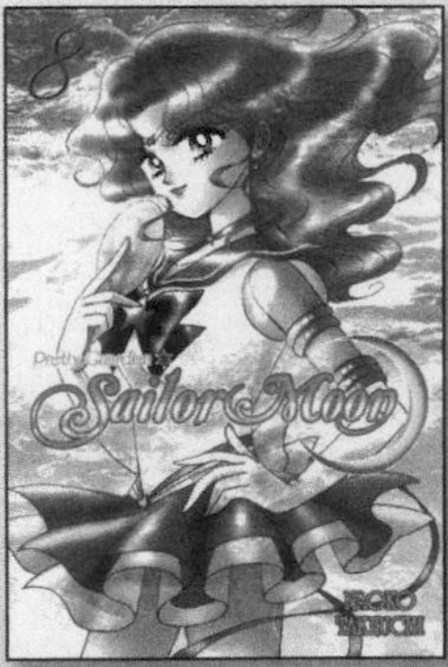
8
Sailor Moon
NAOKO TAKEUCHI
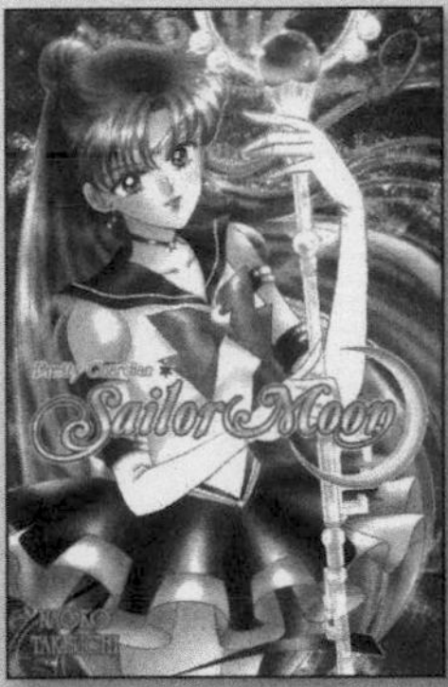
Pretty Guardian
Sailor Moon
NAOKO TAKEUCHI
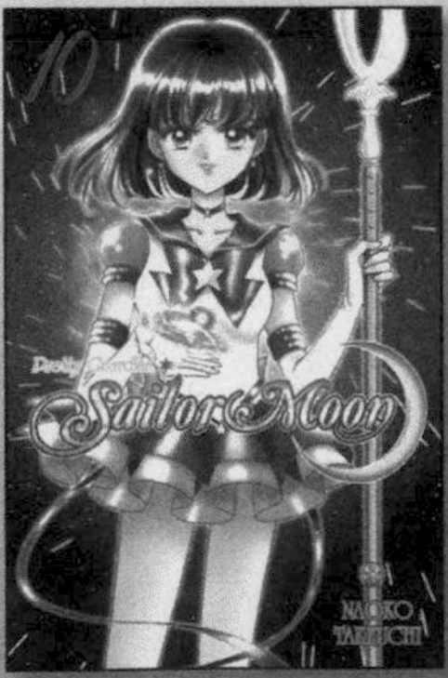
10
Sailor Moon
NAOKO TAKEUCHI
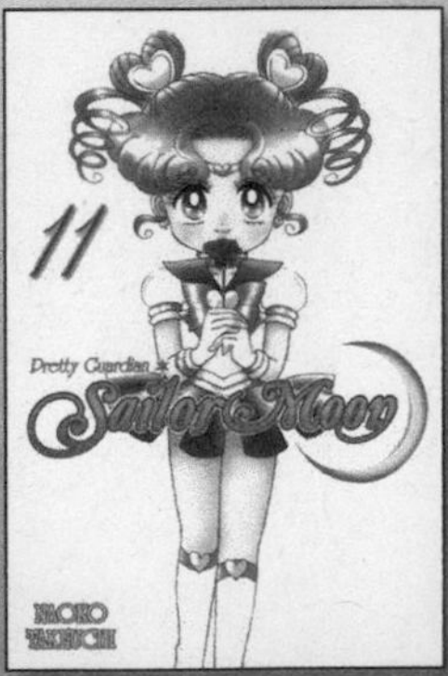
11
Pretty Guardian
Sailor Moon
NAOKO TAKEUCHI
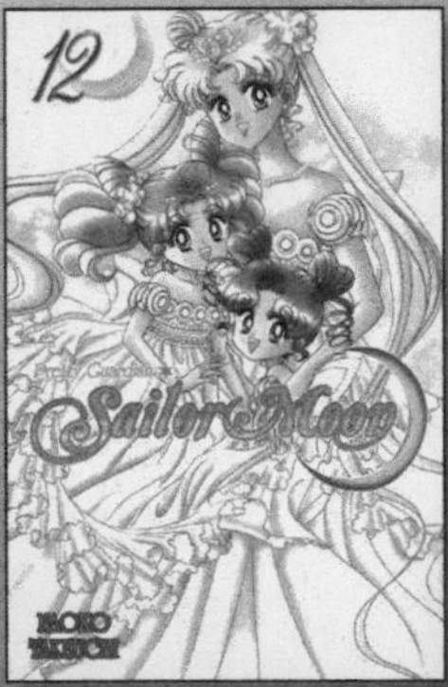
12
Sailor Moon
NAOKO TAKEUCHI

KC
KODANSHA COMICS

Praise for the anime:

"The show provides a pleasant window on the highs and lows of young love with two young people who are first timers at the real thing."

-The Fandom Post

"Always it is smarter, more poetic, more touching, just plain better than you think it is going to be."

-Anime News Network

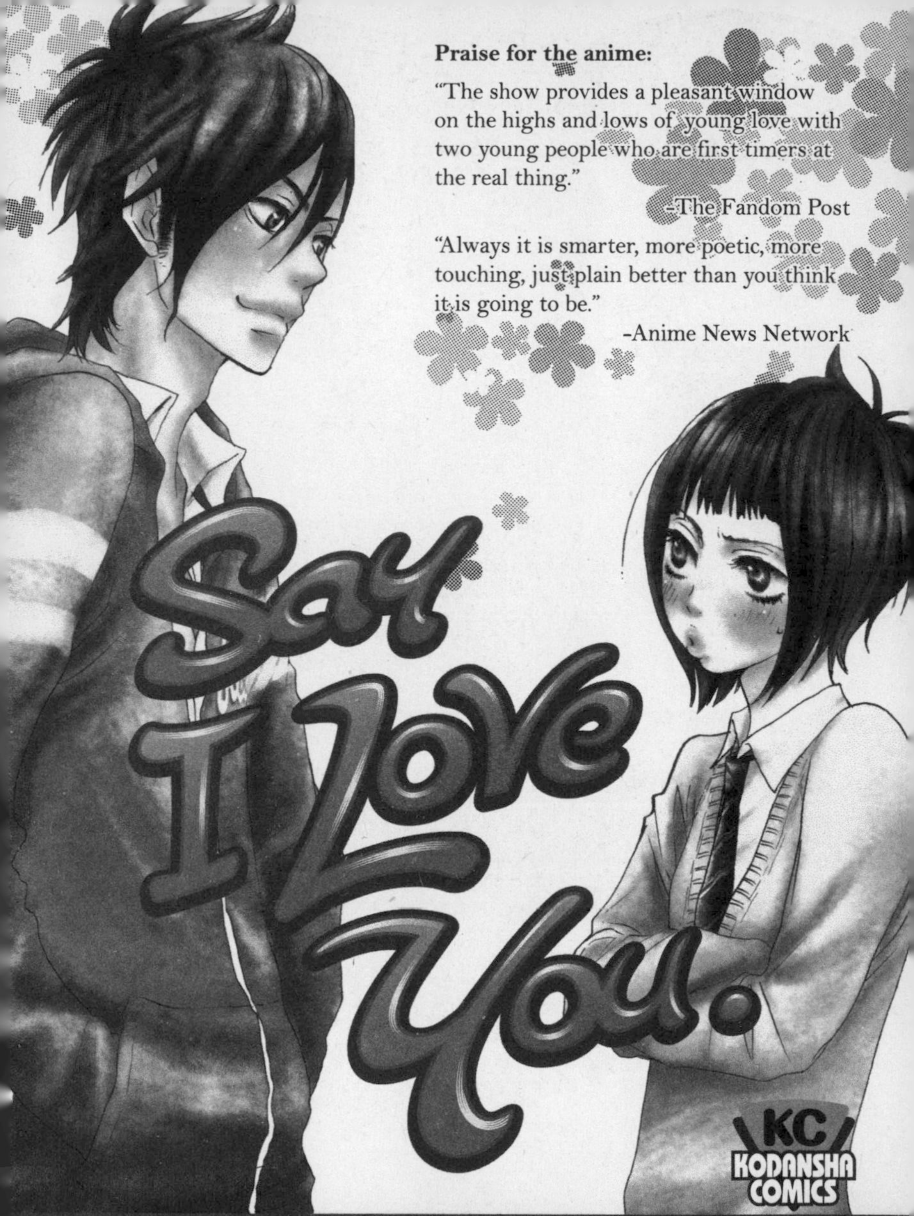
Say I Love You.
KC
KODANSHA COMICS

Mei Tachibana has no friends — and says she doesn't need them!

But everything changes when she accidentally roundhouse kicks the most popular boy in school! However, Yamato Kurosawa isn't angry in the slightest—in fact, he thinks his ordinary life could use an unusual girl like Mei. But winning Mei's trust will be a tough task. How long will she refuse to say, "I love you"?

My Little Monster

OPPOSITES ATTRACT...MAYBE?

Haru Yoshida is feared as an unstable and violent "monster." Mizutani Shizuku is a grade-obsessed student with no friends. Fate brings these two together to form the most unlikely pair. Haru firmly believes he's in love with Mizutani and she firmly believes he's insane.

KC
KODANSH
COMICS

SANKAREA

undying love

"I ONLY LIKE ZOMBIE GIRLS."

...hiro has an unusual connection to zombie movies. He doesn't feel bad for ...survivors – he wants to comfort the undead girls they slaughter! When ...pet passes away, he brews a resurrection potion. He's discovered by ...al heiress Sanka Rea, and she serves as his first test subject!

KC
KODANSHA
COMICS

A Kodansha Comics Trade Paperback Original.

Published in the United States by Kodansha Comics, an imprint of Kodansha USA Publishing, LLC, New York.

Publication rights for this English edition arranged through Kodansha Ltd., Tokyo.

First published in Japan in 2012 by Kodansha Ltd., Tokyo as *Watashi ni xx shinasai!*, volume 9.

ISBN 978-1-61262-577-5

Printed in the United States of America.

www.kodanshacomics.com

9 8 7 6 5 4 3 2 1

Translator: Alethea Nibley and Athena Nibley
Lettering: Paige Pumphrey

Mission 0: Go Right to Left.

'apanese manga is written and drawn from right to left, which is •pposite the way American graphic novels are :omposed. To preserve the original orienta- ion of the art, and maintain the proper torytelling flow, this book has retained he right to left structure. Please go to vhat would normally be the last page nd begin reading, right to left, op to bottom.

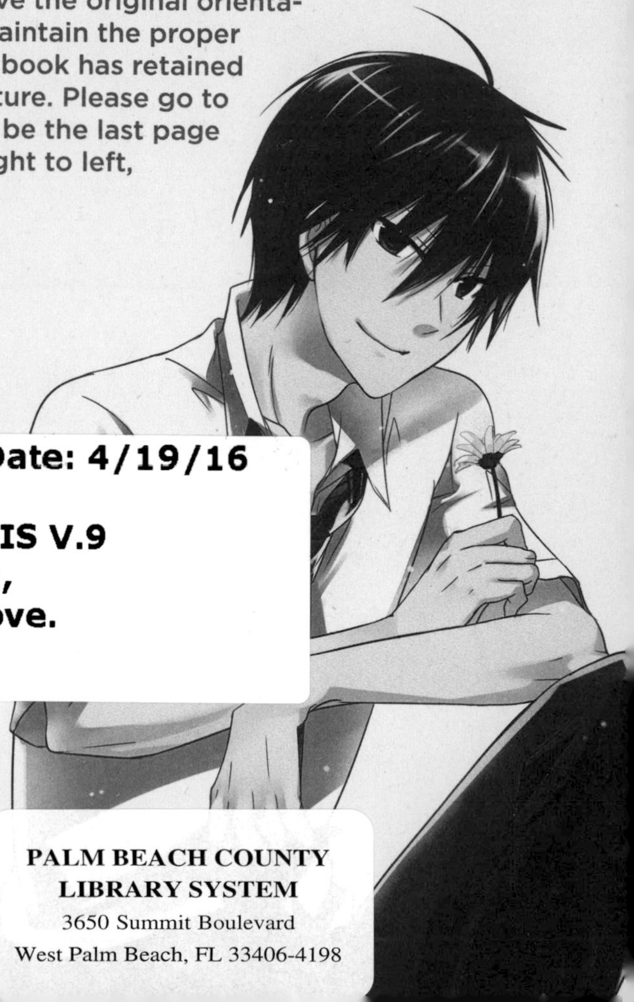